JUL 2005
2004 JUN
JUN 0 9 ANS'D
JUL X X 2015

A PANORAMA OF RUSSIAN LITERATURE

A Panorama
of Russian Literature

Janko Lavrin

University of London Press Ltd

84-145

ACKNOWLEDGEMENTS

The publisher wishes to thank the following copyright-owners
for permission to reproduce copyright material : Oxford University
Press (*Nikolai Gogol*, translated by George Reavey); Messrs Macmillan
London and Basingstoke (*A Book of Russian Verse*, edited by
C. M. Bowra); Messrs Routledge and Kegan Paul Ltd (*Boris Godunov* by
Alexander Pushkin, translated by A. Hayes); Messrs William
Heinemann Ltd and The Macmillan Company, N.Y. (*The Possessed, Notes from
the Underworld, Crime and Punishment*, and *The Brothers
Karamazov*, translated by Constance Garnett).

ISBN 0 340 07257 1

First published 1973
Copyright © 1973 J. Lavrin

University of London Press Ltd
St Paul's House, Warwick Lane, London EC4P 4AH

Printed and bound in Great Britain by
Hazell Watson & Viney Ltd, Aylesbury, Bucks

CONTENTS

The scope of this book is to give a concise survey of the growth and the character of Russian literature from its beginnings to the present day. The emphasis is, of course, on the nineteenth century, when Russian *belles lettres*, having assimilated Western influences, became one of the leading literatures of the world, in fact a great literary power. An earlier abbreviated edition of a number of chapters appeared in my book, *Russian Writers*, published in 1954 by Van Nostrand (U.S.A.), now out of print.

The passages quoted from Russian authors are taken from various English translations, with the names of publishers and translators mentioned in each particular case. English versions of a number of poems were made especially for this work by the late R. M. Hewitt, Walter Morison, and V. de Sola Pinto. To all translators and publishers my thanks and acknowledgements are due.

The names of the Russian authors are provided with the proper stress in the Index of Names at the back of the book. Those readers who are interested in the Russian titles of the works discussed will find most of them in brackets.

J. L.

CHAPTER ONE

The birth of a literature

I

Russian civilisation began towards the end of the tenth century when the Kievan ruler Prince Vladimir was baptised and imposed Christianity upon his subjects. Kiev, situated on the river Dnieper, was in those days a city guarding the trade route 'from the Varangians to the Greeks'. Hence it was natural that Christianity should have come to Kievan Russia not from Rome but from Constantinople. Yet this was one of the reasons for that breach between Russia and the West which was destined eventually to play a vital part in the political and cultural history of Europe.

At the time of Kiev's adoption of Christianity Byzantium was passing through its third period, the 'silver age', of its cultural and artistic revival, and the new Slav converts were by no means indifferent to it. Together with the Christian religion, Byzantine church architecture and painting were imported into Russia. It did not take long, though, before the Russians imbued both with a flavour and accent of their own. As a general commercial and feudal centre of the far-flung Russian tribes and principalities, Kiev itself had a fair chance of becoming a new and natural focus of culture.[1] The beauty of the city, too, was impressive enough to make a German traveller of that period (Adam of Bremen) compare it favourably even with Constantinople. Nor was there a lack of contact between Kiev and other parts of Europe. Prince Yaroslav the Wise, who was responsible for the building of the magnificent St Sophia church at Kiev (1037), married one of his daughters to the King of France, another to the King of Norway, and a third to the King of Hungary. He was, moreover, responsible for the important legal codex of old Russia, known as *The Russian law* (*Rússkaya právda*), written in the spoken Russian of that period. The same prince was also a great lover of books which he read—so the chronicle says—'continually day and night'. One of his successors, Prince Vsevolod, was even able to speak five languages, Latin and Greek included.

Since the Kievan Russians did not accept the Greek language for church usage, they borrowed their early liturgical and also some other writings from the Balkan Slavs who had adopted Christianity in the ninth century and whose language did not differ in those days very much from their own. This 'Church-Slavonic' language (based on a Macedonian dialect) was from then on used by

1. The Kiev state, ruled by the Rurik dynasty, included, up to the end of the eleventh century, a number of other extensive domains including Novgorod and Rostov.

the Russians for ecclesiastical purposes. In their secular writings too it persisted, though mixed with the spoken language, until as late as the second half of the seventeenth century when the spoken language gained the upper hand. The rich folklore of Russia, with its fairy-tales, legends, epic sagas, lyrical songs, proverbs and sayings, developed more or less independently and often preserved a fair amount of pagan elements intermingled with Christian motifs.

2

Written literature existed at that early date of Kievan Christianity both in translations and compilations from the Greek, and in material taken direct from the Balkan Slavs, in which case the language or even the contents were often somewhat adapted for Russian readers. This happened to the still preserved, highly artistic *Ostromir Gospel*, the Slav text of which had to be slightly modified when it was copied in 1056-57 for the Novgorod *posádnik* (burgomaster) Ostromir. Apart from such general medieval tales as those of Troy and Alexander, Kiev had an abundant crop of pious admonitions, legends, apocrypha, and lives of the saints. A number of these were collected in the *Prológue* dating from the twelfth century. Parts of the Bible were also accessible to the Kievans, above all the Psalms, Proverbs, and the Apocalypse. *The Kiev Patericon* (early thirteenth century), on the other hand, contained—in fine ornate language—original hagiographic tales about monks of the famous crypt monastery (Pecherskaya Lavra) at Kiev. Among other original products there were some beautiful sermons, especially those by the Kiev Metropolitan Hilarion, Cyril—the Bishop of Turov, the Novgorod Bishop Zhidyata and the Kiev Prior Feodosy. Another notable contribution was Prior Daniel's *Pilgrimage to the Holy Land* (*Khozhdénie igúmena Daniíla*, 1106-08)—a warmly written account, full of sincere piety and of equally sincere love for Russia and her people. Prior Daniel visited the places connected with Christ's life and was treated by King Baldwin of Jerusalem as a friend. There existed also a free, late eleventh-century version of Flavius's *Judaic War*. It is narrated with a dramatic verve and contains a few unique passages (not to be found in the Greek text), the questionable authenticity of which has recently aroused quite a lively controversy. As far as the various didactic Miscellanies (*Izbórniki*) are concerned, the one compiled in 1076 is particularly good.

Among widespread borrowed legends and apocrypha the tale *Barlaam and Josaphat* was popular in Kiev. Although of Indian origin, this would-be biography of Buddha was modified in such a way as to underline its Christian tendency and spirit. There was even a tale about the anchorite Zosima's journey to the land of the blessed Rakhmans who live without sin in the kingdom of India. A strongly moralising Christian tendency was also imparted to the romantic *Adventures of Devgény* (Digenis). Devgeny is described as a Saracen who was baptised and whose subsequent exploits raised him to the status of an ideal hero in the feudal-Christian sense. Purely secular however is *Alexandria*—a narrative about Alexander the Great, his victories over the Persian king Darius and the Indian king Porus. It includes Alexander's friendly conversation with the wise Indian Brahmans, as well as his imaginary exploits in the country of the Amazons, where he met such fantastic creatures as dog-headed men and speaking birds. A later version of *Alexándria* deals with the romance between Alexander and Roxana, and with Roxana's suicide after Alexander's death. Twelfth-century translations include *The Bee* (*Pchelá*, in Greek *Melissa*)—a popular miscellany of proverbs and sayings; *Hexameron* (*Shestodnéy*) which tells about the creation of the world in six days; and *The Physiologus* (*Fiziólog*) containing a number of tales about animals, both fabulous and real.

Among the original secular documents of the Kievan era the quaint *Supplication of Daniel the Exile* (*Molénie Daniíla Zatóchnika*) stands by itself. Who this Daniel was or by whom he had been offended is not known. Judging by his temperamental 'Supplication', he must have been a disgraced courtier or expelled servant of a prince by whom he wanted to be employed again. Dating probably from the early thirteenth century, the document itself is written in the spoken language, but in an ornate and bombastic style, sprinkled with flatteries, proverbs, copious sayings and quotations from the Bible—all of them calculated to impress the lofty addressee. While complaining of being deserted by his friends, parents, and persecuted by the boyars (powerful aristocrats possessing large estates and privileges), the petitioner stresses his particular dislike of monks and women, in fact of the whole world. But at the same time he takes good care to boast of his own uncommon intelligence, knowledge and wisdom. Altogether this petition reveals a curious character and at the same time gives one a clue to certain *mores* of the period concerned.

Quite a different portrait of a man is obtained, however, from another secular document of the Kiev period: *The Instruction* (*Pouchénie*) of Vladimir Monomakh to his sons. Written in the spoken language, it is often referred to as his *Testament*. Monomakh, who was married to an English princess, reigned as the Grand Prince of Kiev from 1113 until 1125, during which period he championed unity among the quarrelling princes in order to ward off the threat of Mongol raids and invasions. As he pointed out to his sons, he was merciless to the nomad Polovtsians with whom he had to wage continuous wars. On one occasion all the captured chieftains 'whom God delivered alive into my hands' were killed and cast into the river. The same fate befell about two hundred other prisoners. But this was Monomakh the warrior. Severe in this capacity, he was intrepid also as a hunter. Although tossed by two bisons, gored by a stag and an elk, and bitten by a bear, he came out of it all none the worse. Yet the same man was humane enough to demand of his sons that they should protect and help the poor, support the widows and orphans, and respect every human life without exception.

3

The manuscript of this intriguing document was found inserted in the so-called *Primary Chronicle* or *The Tale of Bygone Years* (*Póvest' vrémennykh let*) which is one of the principal works of Kievan literature. There were chronicles of several other towns and regions, but this one stands out for its matter and manner. It has come down to us in two forms—Laurentian and Hypatian, one of them bringing the history of early Russia up to 1110 and the other up to 1200. For a long time its authorship was ascribed to the Kievan monk Nestor, the author of the *Life (Zhítie) of Feodosy, the Abbot of the Cave Monastery*.[1] According to more recent research, *The Tale of Bygone Years* is not the work of Nestor. It is largely a compilation from several previous chronicles (now lost). Modelled on Byzantine chronicles, notably on the one by Hamartolas, it begins with Noah's sons, Shem, Ham and Japhet, who divided the earth after the flood. The land of the Russians and the Slavs in general, with a number of other countries big and small, fell to the lot of Japhet. In a simple style the narrative then passes to the early history of Slavs and Russians, and dwells in particular on their conversion to Christianity. As the authors and compilers of the chronicle were monks, conversion was bound to occupy much space. Yet surprisingly enough, as far as the two early Kievan rulers, Princess Olga and the Grand Prince Vladimir are concerned, the chronicler does not even try to conceal their 'horrid past' before their baptism.

Olga, the widow of the ruling Prince Igor, can certainly be singled out as the epitome of vengeful ferocity. It all began with her husband's visit to Prince Mal, the ruler of the tribe of the Drevlyans, from whom he wanted to collect the exorbitant tribute they were paying to Kiev. Hoping that if Igor were slain, his wife Olga might be inclined to marry their own Prince Mal and thus relieve them of the tribute, the Drevlyans killed Olga's husband. No sooner had this been done than they sent by boat a deputation of twenty of their best men to Kiev with the task of persuading Olga to come to their country and marry their own ruling prince.

> Olga made this reply, 'Your proposal is pleasing to me; indeed, my husband cannot rise again from the dead. But I desire to honour you to-morrow in the presence of my people. Return now to your boat, and remain there with an aspect of arrogance. I shall send for you on the morrow, and you shall say, "We will not ride on horses, nor go on foot; carry us in our boat." Thus she dismissed them to their vessel. Now Olga gave command that a large and deep ditch should be dug within the castle outside the city. Thus, on the morrow, Olga, as she sat in the hall, sent for the strangers, and her messengers approached them and said, 'Olga summons you to great honour'. But they replied, 'We will not ride on horseback nor in wagons, nor go on foot; carry us in our boat.' The people of Kiev then lamented, 'Slavery is our lot. Our prince is killed and our Princess intends to marry their prince'. So they carried the Drevlyans in their boat. The latter sat on the cross-benches in great robes, puffed up with pride. They thus were borne into the court before Olga, and when the men had

1. Nestor was also the author of a hagiographic account (*Chténie*) of the two young princes, Boris and Gleb, murdered by their own brother Svyatopolk in 1015 so that he should have no rival (after the death of Prince Vladimir) for the Kievan throne. Soon, however, Svyatopolk himself was defeated by Prince Yaroslav who replaced him as ruler.

brought the Drevlyans in, they dropped them into the trench along with the boat. Olga bent over and inquired whether they found the honour to their taste. They answered that it was worse than the death of Igor. She then commanded that they should be buried alive, and they were thus buried.[1]

But this was only a small part of her revenge. For Olga sent to the Drevlyans a message that she was willing to come to them and marry their prince, provided they would send to Kiev the best men of their land to accompany her. Ignorant of her action, the Drevlyans complied with her wish and sent their notables to escort her on the journey. But when the Drevlyans arrived, Olga commanded that a bath should be made ready, and invited them to appear before her after the bath. The bathhouse was then heated, and the Drevlyans entered it. Olga's men closed up the bathhouse behind them, and gave orders to set it on fire from behind the doors, so that the Drevlyans were all burned to death. Through further tricks she then managed to destroy the whole town in which her husband had been assassinated. Having killed or else enslaved all its inhabitants, she later left for Constantinople, where the Emperor Constantine Porphirogenitus and the Patriarch persuaded her to accept Christianity. They gave her the name of Helena—after the mother of Constantine the Great. As the chronicler piously concludes,

> Olga was the precursor of the Christian land, even as the day-spring precedes the sun and as the dawn precedes the day. For she shone like the moon by night, and she was radiant among the infidels like a pearl in the mire, since the people were soiled, and not yet purified of their sin by Holy Baptism (*The Russian Primary Chronicle*).

The people were 'purified', though, when Olga's grandson Vladimir, the ruling Prince of Kiev (972-1015), decided to be baptised and to impose Christianity upon his subjects no matter whether they were ready for it or not. Until then he had been leading a life which was the greatest contrast to everything Christian. To quote the chronicler again, he was 'overcome by lust for women. . . . He had three hundred concubines at Vyshgorod, three hundred at Belgorod, and two hundred at Berestovo. He was insatiable in vice'. And evidently in alcohol as well. When the Volga Bulgars, who were Mohammedans, sent emissaries to Prince Vladimir, they were doing their best to make him join their faith. But on hearing that wine was forbidden to all Moslems, he replied, 'Drinking is the joy of Russia (*Rúsi est' vesélie píti*)', and refused to have any further dealings with such a preposterous religion. Nor were the Catholics more lucky. Finally, he decided—for political reasons—to join the Greek Church on condition that he should marry the Byzantine Princess Anna (the Emperor's sister). As such a condition seemed plausible to Constantinople, Prince Vladimir was baptised and married at the town of Korsun (Kherson) in the year of grace 988. The first thing he did on his return to Kiev was to issue a command that all

1.   *The Russian Primary Chronicle*, translated by S. H. Cross and O. P. Sherbowitz-Wetzor (The Medieval Academy of America), Cambridge, Massachusetts.

Slav idols be smashed, cut to pieces, thrown into the river Dnieper or burned. At the same time he ordered that his subjects should from now on be Christians, and that was that. Both he and his grandmother Olga (alias Helena) were canonised.

4

The Tale of Bygone Years was compiled by pious Kievan monks in the ecclesiastic Church-Slavonic language. There were several regional Chronicles which narrated events of the past: the concise *Nóvgorod Chronicle*, for instance, or the *Galícian-Volhýnian Chronicle*. But whereas the latter are primarily historical, the Kievan one is, by nature of its artistic quality, an important literary document as well. Another literary masterpiece of the twelfth century, this time a purely secular one, was the short heroic epic, *The Lay of Igor's Campaign* (*Slóvo o polkú Ígoreve*), a portion of which is now known to the world through Borodin's famous opera, *Prince Igor*. Written largely in the spoken language and in a poetic rhythmical prose, *The Lay* reaches a high level of literary excellence. But it also has a documentary historical value, since it reflects the conditions of the country when Kiev was losing its control over the other principalities, whose rulers were constantly wrangling with each other as if unaware of the fact that the Mongol hordes were awaiting the chance for an all-out invasion.

There were, generally speaking, three successive waves of Asiatic invaders intent on plundering the Russian territory. The Pechenegs were the first to come. Then, in the middle of the eleventh century, there appeared the Polovtsians or the Koumans. They were driven by the Russians back beyond the Don region whence they continued to make frequent raids, especially in the second half of the twelfth century—the period of Igor's campaign. Finally, the Polovtsians were replaced by the Tartars who in 1238-40 invaded practically all the Russian lands and held them in subjection for some two hundred and forty years. The Polovtsians had failed to take Kiev, but they disturbed the commerce with Constantinople and succeeded in closing the trade route from Dvina to the sea of Azov. In this manner they cut off the Kiev Russians from their distant commercial city of Tmutarakan between the Sea of Azov and the Black Sea.

Harassed by such raids, the ruling Prince Svyatoslav of Kiev made a coalition with some other princes against the Polovtsians and was at first successful. But personal ambitions, feuds, and jealousies among the lesser rulers kept undermining that unity which was essential for warding off the nomadic hordes. In 1185 Svyatoslav prepared a joint expedition against the enemy who were restive at the time. Yet spurred on by a vision of personal glory, Prince Igor, son of Prince Svyatoslav of Novgorod-Seversk (in the Chernigov area), decided to make a raid on the Polovtsian territory on his own. With the help of his brother Vsevolod, his son Vladimir, and his nephew Svyatoslav Ol'govich, he turned it into a kind of family affair and even scored a victory at first. Later he was defeated and taken prisoner, while the victorious Polovtsians continued to ravage the land of Russia. In the autumn of the same year Igor escaped from his captors and arrived—via Chernigov—in Kiev where he was received with joy. The finale thus had a symbolic touch, since Svyatoslav of Kiev was a champion of unity and of common action against the Mongols. Such is the gist of this epic, which is supposed to have been written by a professional bard belonging to the Prince's retinue (*druzhína*). The poet does not unfold the account logically in all its phases but concentrates on a series of dramatic-lyrical episodes. These are preceded by an introduction in which he hints at the existence of other bards, naming a certain Boyan who must have been a singer of exceptional repute.

> Might it not befit us, brethren, to begin in ancient style the heroic tale of the raid of Igor son of Svyatoslav?
> Then let this song rather begin according to the events of our time, and not after Boyan's invention.
> For when Boyan the seer wished to make someone a song, he would fly in fancy over the trees, like a grey wolf across the land, like a blue-grey eagle beneath the clouds.
> For recalling, quoth he, the slights of olden times, it was his wont to loose ten falcons on a flock of swans; whichever swan was overtaken was the first to sing a song.
> But indeed Boyan did not loose ten falcons on a flock of swans, my brethren, but laid his own magic fingers upon the living strings, and they would of themselves sound forth the glory of the princes—
> Let us then, brethren, forego this tale from Vladimir of old to Igor of our days, who proved his mind with firmness and sharpened his heart with valour.
> Filled with martial spirit, he led his brave hosts against the Polovtsian land in defence of the land of Rus'.

This opening, redolent of folklore, introduces the actual account. There follows—after several ill omens—a condensed description of the march of the warriors who are inspired by the knightly ideal of honour for themselves and glory for their princes. The poem is pervaded by a Christian spirit, but with an admixture of pagan features as well. The names of the Slav pagan gods are not yet forgotten. Still, the initial victory of the Russians is regarded as a gift of God, whereas their subsequent defeat is looked upon as a punishment for their sins. The defeat itself is rendered with an imagery full of poetic parallelisms, nature-symbols, effective refrains, and repetitions.

> Already ahead of his misfortune the birds hide in the oaks; wolves in the ravine howl in the storm; eagles with their cries summon beasts to the bones; foxes bark at the scarlet shields.
> One day they fought, they fought another, and on the third, towards midday, the banners of Igor fell!
> Then the two brothers parted on the banks of the river Kayali.
> Then the bloody wine ran dry.

Then the bold sons of Rus' finished the feast; they gave the wedding guests to drink, and themselves they lay down for the Russian land.

The grass bends in sorrow, and the tree is bowed down to earth by woe.

In spite of Igor's defeat, after which 'anguish flooded the Russian land', the princes continued their mutual feuds. But they are severely rebuked and condemned by the bard. And so the poem turned from the battlefield to Svyatoslav—the champion of unity. Svyatoslav in Kiev has a dream full of evil forebodings. The dream is followed by an outburst against his two nephews Igor and Vsevolod, and by a patriotic harangue against the princes on account of their quarrels and egoism. Each of the ruling princes is given a brief but trenchant characterisation. Then the scene suddenly shifts to Putivl' where on the city ramparts Yaroslavna—the wife of Igor—bewails her fate 'like a cuckoo singing without tidings at morn' in the manner of the old Russian laments and folksongs.

Yaroslavna weeps at morn at Putivl' on the city wall, wailing:

'Wind, O Wind! Wherefore, Lord, blowest thou so fiercely?

'Wherefore carriest thou the Huns' arrows upon thy carefree wings against the warriors of my beloved?

'Is it not enough for thee to blow on high, beneath the clouds, rocking ships upon the blue sea?

'Wherefore, Lord, hast thou scattered my joy over the grass of the plains?'

Yaroslavna weeps at morn in Putivl' upon the city wall, wailing:

'O bright and thrice-bright Sun! Towards all art thou warm and fair.

'Wherefore, Lord, hast thou shed thy scorching rays on the warriors of my beloved and wherefore in the waterless plain hast thou parched their bows with thirst, locked their quivers with weariness?'

After Yaroslavna's complaint there follows the escape of Igor who, with the help of God, speeds towards the bank of the Donetz. He is pursued by two Polovtsian chiefs, but Nature herself is on Igor's side. Along the whole of his road birds are either silent so as not to give him away, or else they indicate to him the direction which he ought to take.

Then crows croaked not, daws grew silent, magpies did not chatter.

Woodpeckers climbed upon the willows: with their knocking they show the way to the river; and lo! nightingales announce the dawn by gay songs.

Finally, all ends well, and there is jubilation in Kiev.

The sun shines in Heaven: Igor the Prince is in the Russian land! . . . The countries are glad, the cities rejoice.

Hail Princes and retinue, fighting for Christendom against the infidel hosts!

Glory unto the Princes and to their retinue honour![1]

---

1. Translated by S. H. Cross in *La Geste du Prince Igor* (École Libre des Hautes Études, N.Y., and Université Libre, Bruxelles, 1948).

5

Like *La Chanson de Roland*, or the Serbian cycle of the Kosovo ballads, *The Lay of Igor's Campaign* sings of a defeat. It was written soon after the event by a man who evidently had taken part in it. The epic, which must have been finished not later than in the Spring of 1187, i.e., some two years after the campaign, bears witness not only to the author's poetic gift but to his familiarity with Byzantine and Russian writings, as well as with the folk-songs. Its style is similar to the rhythmical prose of another original product of Kiev literature, *The Lay (Slóvo) of Adam to Lazarus*. And the bond between man and nature in a true animistic spirit is always there. So, surprisingly enough, is the poet's ardent advocacy of national unity as the only hope of a successful resistance to the Asiatics. Strong national consciousness at the end of the twelfth century is surely an interesting phenomenon. The reproaches hurled at the quarrelling princes who have destroyed the unity that prevailed under former rulers, shows the poet's rare political and civic sense.

> Victory over the infidels is gone, for now brother said to brother :
> 'This is mine, and that is mine also', and the princes began to say of little things, 'Lo! This is a great matter', and to forge discord against themselves.
> And on all sides the infidels were victoriously invading the Russian land.

At the time this poem was written the edifice of Kievan Rus' was already cracking. The Polovtsians were followed by the mightier and better organised Tartar hordes who sacked Kiev in 1238 and soon became masters of Russia—just as the bard of this epic predicted. An 'iron curtain' fell between Russia and the West, cutting off practically all cultural contacts between the two. And when at the end of the fifteenth century the 'curtain' was lifted, the gap was already too great to be bridged on terms of parity.

The only manuscript of *The Lay of Igor's Campaign* (an early sixteenth-century copy) was discovered by Count A. I. Musin-Pushkin in a monastery-the conflagration of Moscow during Napoleon's invasion in 1812 the original manuscript perished. What survived, though, was a copy which had been made library at Yaroslavl' in 1795. Its first printed edition appeared in 1800, but in for Catherine II, but with some words and passages badly transcribed. The discovery of this masterpiece caused a sensation in Russia and later also abroad. Remembering McPherson's *Ossian* as well as the poems fabricated by Chatterton (purported to be the work of an imaginary fifteenth-century monk, Thomas Rowley) some scholars began to question its authenticity. In 1832 Professor Kachenovsky held at Moscow University an open dispute with the poet Alexander Pushkin, trying to prove that the epic was a literary fake. But Pushkin's opinion won the day.[1] The studies and explorations written about this work

1. It may be of some interest that the Czech romantic poet and philologist Vaclav Hanka (1781–1861) 'discovered' manuscripts of 'old Czech' poems faked largely in order to rival the fame of *The Lay of Igor's Campaign*.

during the last hundred and fifty years would fill a library. Recently (1940) Professor André Mazon made in his *Le Slovo d'Igor* a new onslaught on it. The cudgels were again taken up by a number of scholars, and the results were not in favour of Professor Mazon's theory. An adequate answer came from Professor Roman Jakobson and Professor George Vernadsky in *La Geste du Prince Igor*. Among the more recent works on the subject those by V. N. Perets, S. K. Shambinago, A. S. Orlov, and N. Gudziy may be mentioned. Authoritative opinion has vindicated beyond any doubt the authenticity of this masterpiece of old Russian literature.

CHAPTER TWO

The Tartar yoke and its aftermath

I

The worst of the calamities the Russians had to face in the course of their early history was the Tartar conquest of their country, between about 1238 and 1241. The plight of the people was the more precarious because, while the Mongol hordes were still active, the Germans and Swedes were anxious to benefit from the situation by trying to occupy the Neva area and lake Ladoga. They were, however, stopped by the Novgorod Prince Alexander, a great-grandson of Vladimir Monomakh. He was barely twenty when, on 15 July 1240, he beat the Swedes on the Neva. Hence his name—Alexander Nevsky. In the following year he drove the Germans out of Pskov, and on 5 April 1242 he smashed the entire army of the Knights of the German Order on lake Peipus. Later, under the Tartars, he became the ruling Prince of Vladimir and proved to be not only an able diplomat in his dealings with the Golden Horde at Kazan', but also a staunch defender of the rights of the Russian people in general. After his death he was canonised by the Russian Church and his deeds were recorded in the account *About the Life and Bravery of the Orthodox*[1] *Grand Prince Alexander Nevsky*, as part of the Pskov Chronicle.

However terrible the destruction wrought by the new rulers of Russia, the Tartars were mainly concerned with tribute, the collection of which was left to the hereditary Russian princes. Russia actually saved Western Europe from a major Tartar invasion, since her Mongol masters did not dare go further West, thus leaving the entire Russian population behind their backs. Outwardly the Russian princes had to be on good terms with their conquerors. They even vied with each other in currying favour with them. And since the Moscow princes proved to be by far the shrewdest, they soon gained ascendancy over their rivals. In 1328 one of them, Ivan Kalita or the 'Moneybag', became the ruler of Moscow and Grand Prince of all Russia. Moscow was thus turned into a new political and religious centre for the entire Russian people.[2]

Protected by forests and rivers, this city was a much safer capital than Kiev (situated in the steppe) had ever been. Hence it was easier for her to devise such measures as were likely to lead to subsequent liberation. The most important of these measures was unity through a policy of ruthless centralisation.

1. *Blagovérny*, i.e. professing the true faith.
2. The Head of The Russian Church had moved from Kiev first to Vladimir in Suzdal' in 1300, and twenty-five years later to Moscow.

Religious unity of the Russian people was strengthened by the Tartar invasion which was generally interpreted as God's punishment for their godless ways. Even in *The Tale of Bygone Years* it was stated clearly enough that 'God in his wrath causes foreigners to attack a nation, and then, when its inhabitants are thus crushed by the invaders, they remember God'. And in the five sermons by Serapion, the Bishop of Vladimir (he died in 1275) it is particularly stressed that the Tartar invasion was a punishment inflicted by God. During the Tartar period literature was not abundant, but church architecture and religious church painting reached a level of perfection. Frescoes and icons flourished above all in the rich commercial city of Novgorod which continued its trade—Tartars or no Tartars—with the Hanseatic League. Politically, Moscow knew how to play her part dexterously, however trying the conditions. It was the Moscow Prince Dmitry Donskoy who, in 1380, dealt the first smashing blow to the Tartars on the Kulikovo field (the Don region). This was, however, only a prelude to the complete liberation brought about by the Grand Prince Ivan III exactly one hundred years later.

2

As long as the Tartar rule lasted, literary activities were bound to be hampered. While western and southern Europe were progressing towards the height of the Renaissance movement in making culture secular and independent of theology, Russia under the Tartars was separated from that process. In addition to hagiographic works, pious sermons (especially those by Serapion of Vladimir) and some less important chronicles, several descriptions of the invasion of the land of Russia were written. The best of these was probably the lost *Lay about the Ruin of the Russian Land* (*Slóvo o pogíbeli rússkiya zemlí*) which has been preserved only in a fragment of forty-five lines. *The Tale about the Destruction of Ryazán'* is an accumulation of horrors inseparable from such invasions. The Russian victory in the field of Kulikovo, on the other hand, is recorded in *The Story of the Rout of Mamai* (*Póvest' o Mamáyevom pobóishche*), and particularly in *Trans-Doniad* (*Zadónshchina*) whose author, the Ryazan' priest Sophonia, must have been acquainted with *The Lay of Igor's Campaign*, the poetic élan of which he tried to emulate. As for narratives with altogether different subject-matter, *The Story about Peter and Fevronya* (*Póvest' o Petré i Fevrónii*) must have been very popular, since it has been preserved in some hundred and fifty written copies. Reflecting the regional Murom background, the story, which also recalls borrowed (Scandinavian) motifs, is an apotheosis of ideal love between husband and wife both of whom died on the same day and were buried in the same grave.

Conspicuous among the religious activities in the latter part of the Tartar rule was the polemic between the two currents of monastic life. Nil Sorsky (1433–1508), a mystical writer and the leader of the pious elders from beyond the Volga, voiced the idea that monasteries should not possess any property, the latter being contrary to true Christian life. He found a vigorous polemical supporter in his disciple, Prince Vassian Patrikeyev, who also became a monk. Nil Sorsky's opponent, Joseph Volotsky (1439–1515), on the other hand, was a defender of monastic property, and in the Church Assembly of 1503 won a victory over Nil. He also advocated a revision of Church-Slavonic liturgical texts. It was mainly for this reason that the learned monk Maxim Grek (Maxim the Greek) was summoned in 1518 from Mount Athos to Moscow. But he was soon involved in numerous misunderstandings not only because of the revision but also on account of his outbursts against the evil aspects of life he had found in Russian monasteries. Eventually he was flung into a monastery-prison, after which he was dragged for years from one penitentiary to the other until his death in 1556.

Before passing to the Moscow period after the liberation in 1480, one ought to mention at least in passing some regional literatures as well, those of Novgorod and Tver', for example. Novgorod preserved a variety of stories, pious and otherwise. One of these bears the title, *The Story (Póvest') about the Journey of the Novgorod Abbot Ioann on a Demon to Jerusalem*. The pious Abbot had imprisoned a demon in a jug of water and promised to release him only on condition that the demon should take him to Jerusalem and back during one single night. Having assumed the shape of a horse, the demon flew the Abbot to the Lord's tomb at Jerusalem and brought him back as stipulated. The devil's tricks did not cease thereby; still, the tale had a happy ending for the Abbot.

Quite a different voyage is recorded in the rather quaint *Journey beyond Three Seas (Khozhdénie za tri mórya)*. Its author Afanasy Nikitin was an ordinary merchant from Tver' who in 1466 made a journey via Baku and Persia to India and stayed there until 1472. While travelling far and wide over the country, he wrote down—in the vernacular—his impressions which are naïve and not always reliable. He even believed that in India monkeys were able to be organised into an army and fight their human opponents. His account of the magnificence indulged in by Indian nobles and rulers may also be exaggerated. This is what he says about a place called Beder, for example.

> The land is overstocked with people; but those in the country are very miserable, whilst the nobles are extremely opulent and delight in luxury. They are wont to be carried on their silver beds, preceded by some twenty chargers caparisoned in gold, and followed by three hundred men on horseback and five hundred on foot, and by horn-men, ten torch-bearers and ten musicians. The sultan goes out hunting with his mother and his lady, and a train of ten thousand men on horseback and fifty thousand on foot; two hundred elephants adorned in gilded armour, and in front one hundred horn-men, one hundred dancers and three hundred common horses in golden clothing, one hundred monkeys, and one hundred concubines, all foreign.[1]

1. Translated by Count Wielhorsky in *India in the Fifteenth Century*, (Hakluyt Society, 1857).

3

The fifteenth century was responsible for important changes in Muscovy. The Grand Prince of Moscow Ivan III, who liberated Russia, was married to Sophia Paleologue, the niece of the last Byzantine emperor. As Sophia had been educated in Rome and had a Western orientation, she summoned several Italian architects to Moscow. It was they who built the walls and a large portion of the present-day Kremlin. The beginning of contacts with the West was thus established, although Russia could not help looking upon the latter with suspicion. Moreover, after the fall of Constantinople to the Turks in 1453 Russia began to regard herself as the rightful heir of Byzantium and the only centre of true Christianity.[1] This was why under the next ruler, Vasily III, Moscow was actually raised (by the Pskovan monk Filofey) to the status of the 'Third Rome' as something final. Polemical works proving the supremacy of Moscow and her princes (formerly princes of Vladimir) became conspicuous, although both Novgorod and Tver', the two rivals of Moscow, insisted on their own rights. The Novgorod *Tale of the White Mitre* (*Póvest' o bélom klobuké*) is about the mysterious wanderings of the Emperor Constantine's mitre which eventually reached not Moscow but Novgorod and was in the possession of the Novgorod Archbishop as its rightful owner. Tver', on the other hand, produced (about 1453) the tendentious *Lay* (*Slóvo*) *of Praise to Boris Alexandrovich* by the monk Fomo. This was nothing less than a panegyric proclaiming the Grand Prince Boris of Tver' the paragon of all ruling princes.

In spite of this, Tver' was annexed by Moscow in 1485, while the annexation of Novgorod had taken place seven years earlier. The conquest of other towns and regions too was only a matter of time. This process of centralisation had to be justified by the requisite writings, and so it was. *The Tale* (*Skazánie*) *of the Princes of Vladimir* even claimed that the rulers of Moscow were descendants of the Emperor Augustus. Similar claims can be found in *The Book of Generations* (*Stepénnaya kníga*) whose compiler was the Moscow Metropolitan Makary. Tales of military prowess on the part of Moscow, beginning with the defeat of the Tartars on the Kulikovo field, were also important. Due record was made of the conquest of Pskov (1510), Smolensk (1514) and Ryazan' (1517) by the Moscow ruler Vasily III whose son Ivan IV, better known as Ivan the Terrible (he ruled from 1547 to 1584), enlarged his empire by adding to it not only Kazan' and Astrakhan' but also a large portion of Siberia. He proclaimed himself *Tsar'*, i.e., autocrat, of all the Russias.

In order to preserve his autocratic and centralising rule he had to contend not only with external but also with internal enemies—the boyars. These proud aristocrats with large possessions he tried to weaken by ruthless persecutions (as well as executions) on the one hand, and by fostering the rise of the military and serving nobility on the other. He found a ready defender of his autocratic rights in the versatile Ivan Peresvetov whose pamphleteering tales were written in a spoken matter-of-fact language. The tsar's own pamphleteer-

1. Russia took part at the Council of Florence (1439) where union of the churches was discussed, but she categorically refused union with Rome.

ing talent came out in his venomous correspondence with the escaped boyar Prince Andrey Kurbsky (1528–83). During the war between Moscow and Lithuania (in 1564) for the possession of the Baltic coast, Kurbsky was the commander of the Russian army. After suffering a reverse, he fled to Lithuania where he was endowed by the Polish-Lithuanian king, Sigismund August, with vast estates. It was from there that he wrote to the tsar several condemnatory letters, which were promptly answered by his enraged addressee. The correspondence between the two occupies quite a distinct place in Russian pamphleteering literature. Whereas Kurbsky, the boyar opponent of the tsar's tyrannical methods, is cultured and more or less politely logical even in his indictments, the tsar's cruel temperament comes out in his caustic and savage irony interspersed with swear-words hardly befitting a sovereign.[1] For the benefit of his Polish-Lithuanian hosts Kurbsky composed also a scathing *History of the Grand Prince of Moscow* (he refused to call him tsar).

Ivan the Terrible established a printing-press in Moscow, and the first book that came out of it was *The Acts of the Apostles*. The complete *Bible* to be printed in Moscow did not appear until 1663, although one had appeared earlier (1581) in Ostrog. Of the works issued in Moscow the *Stóglav* (*Book of a Hundred Chapters*) stipulated obedience to the rules prescribed by the Church. The notorious *Domostróy* (*House Builder*) however provided a catalogue of 'patriarchal' measures—whipping and beating included—to be applied by the head of a family to those under his control. Conspicuous on the religious side was the Saints Calendar or *Chétyi Minéi* (*The Reading Minea*) in twelve volumes. Compiled with more good-will than good method by the Metropolitan Makary, it contains lives of the saints for every day of the year.

4

Ivan's tyranny kept the vast territory of Russia compact and fairly quiet as long as he was alive. Yet only a few years after his death in 1584 the so-called 'troubled period' ran its course. It began after the mysterious assassination of Ivan's infant-son Dmitry (Demetrius) in 1591, when Dmitry's feeble-minded elder brother Fyodor was the ruling sovereign. In 1598 the childless Tsar Fyodor suddenly died, and the National Assembly (*zémsky sobór*) elected his crafty brother-in-law, Boris Godunov, to the throne. Godunov proved to be in some respects an able and wise ruler, but he was under the suspicion of having murdered Dmitry. Moreover, in 1603 there appeared an impostor who pretended to be Dmitry miraculously saved from the murderers' plot. This 'false Dmitry' fled to Poland where, for political reasons, he was sponsored and helped by some magnates. With an army composed of Poles, Ukrainian Cossacks and volunteers, he eventually moved against Moscow where Godunov's timely death made it easier for him to impose himself upon the people as the rightful ruler of Russia. In spite of the intelligence and even relative mildness he showed

---

1. Typical also was the letter he sent to the abbot of the Kirillo-Belozersky monastery, blaming him for not being more severe with the boyars imprisoned in it.

during his reign, he was soon murdered. And so were the two other impostors or false Dmitries who came, one after the other, out of the blue once the first one had been 'liquidated'. The country was in a state of utter chaos. But in the end the Poles were driven out, and in 1613 the National Assembly elected Mikhail Romanov to the throne.

This opened up a new era in the political, literary and cultural history of Russia. Contacts with the West (which had been encouraged by Godunov) now began to develop on quite a large scale until they culminated in the activities of Peter the Great. As regards independent literary creations, the three chroniclers of the 'troubled period', Avraamy Palitsyn, Ivan Katyryov, and the scribe Ivan Timofeyev, deserve a mention. Of the three Palitsyn has the best account— imbued with a keen dramatic sense. Timofeyev may be affected and full of rhetorical tricks, but he seems reliable with regard to the facts recorded. Among the best literary writings of the era are two such different works as *The Life of St Juliána Lazarévskaya* (1604) whose author was her son, and *The Story of the Defence of Ázov against the Turks* (1641). The first is an account of the deeds of a simple woman whose life was one long example of charity and goodness. The second is a spirited document of military prowess, written specially for the tsar, but in a vein which would naturally have a wider appeal as well.

A significant factor in the seventeenth century was the gradual secularisation of Russian literature under the impact of western influence. This increased after the rebellious Ukrainian Cossacks had joined Russia (in 1654), adding the fairly westernised city of Kiev to her domains. The motifs of *Gesta Romanorum*, *Speculum Magnum*, even of *Decameron* and the *Fabliaux* were belatedly transmitted—via Poland and the Ukraine—to Russia where they now found a soil ready to absorb them. Some of these, such as *Bová Korolévich* (*Bovo d'Antona*) and *Eruslán Lázarevich*, became Russian fairy-tales and were spread in chapbooks far and wide. In the *Story of Sávva Grútsyn* there even emerged a Russian version of the Faust motif, but with a happy ending: having pawned his soul to the devil, Savva tricks the devil by escaping to a monastery where he finds salvation. A *fabliaux* motif forms the intensely realistic story of *Frol Skobéyev*. Its hero is a shameless opportunist of low birth who succeeds in marrying a nobleman's daughter, whereby he raises his social status in life and gets away with it. *The Story of Woe Ill-Luck* (*Póvest' o Góre- zloschástii*), on the other hand, is about a young man of good family who leaves his parental home and is doomed to proceed in his sinful life from bad to worse, until he too finds refuge in a monastery. Among the many satirical tales in the second half of the seventeenth century, the one called *Yorsh Schetínnikov* is a fine skit on legal proceedings in Old Muscovy.

5

The penetration into Muscovy of the Jesuit school drama also helped the spread of Western influences. But since this belongs to the development of the theatre and drama in Russia, it is briefly dealt with in another chapter. In a discussion of seventeenth-century literature, especially of that under Tsar Alexey Mikhailovich, one cannot bypass two such authors as Kotoshikhin and Kriz-hanich, both of whom remained practically unknown until the second half of the nineteenth century. Grigory Kotoshikhin (1630–67) escaped in 1663 from Muscovy to Sweden where he obtained a post in the Swedish civil service. It was in order to enlighten his adopted country that he wrote a highly un-complimentary account of the Russian system, life and manners under the title *About Russia during the Reign of Alexey Mikhailovich*.[1] Incidentally, Koto-shikhin was eventually executed by his Swedish hosts for manslaughter.

A different though more curious personality was Yury Krizhanich (1617 or 1618–83). He was a Croat priest who, under Alexey Mikhailovich, came to Moscow in 1658 in order to preach Catholicism and pan-Slavism. For some obscure reason he was exiled to Tobol'sk in Siberia where he spent about fifteen years and wrote (in a quaint mixture of Croat, Russian and Church-Slavonic) a number of works. The bulkiest of these bears the title, *Politica or Discourse about Ruling*. It must have been written between 1661 and 1666, but was first published in 1859 as *The Russian State in the Middle of the Seventeenth Century*. This is not only a kind of encyclopaedia about the Muscovite State in those days, but also a miscellany of politics, history, sociology, theology, and even of the Slav problem as this earliest champion of pan-Slavism conceived it at the time. It is interesting that more than three hundred years ago Krizhanich was anxious to bridge the gap between East and West, between Russia and Europe. This he thought to achieve by two means. The first was to turn Russia into a Catholic country (of the Uniat persuasion[2]); and the second was a union of all the Slavs with Russia whose combined task should be to expel the Turks from Europe. For this purpose Russia should direct her policy towards the Black Sea and the Aegean—a policy which began to materialise under Peter the Great and reached its first climax under Catherine II. All this is, however, a matter of politics rather than literature. If we are to come nearer to the literary achievements of seventeenth-century Muscovy, we must turn first of all to the striking per-sonality of the Archpriest Avvakum.

1. The manuscript of Kotoshikhin's work was discovered in Swedish archives by Russian historians in the first half of the nineteenth century.
2. The Uniats among the Ukrainians and some Yugoslavs are former Greek-Orthodox Christians who have accepted the supremacy of the pope, while yet retaining their Ortho-dox Church-Slavonic rites and liturgy.

CHAPTER THREE

Avvakum

1

While in the seventeenth century Western influences were growing quite conspicuous in Russia, the tendency to keep her own traditions intact was yet far from being silenced. It asserted itself with considerable force in the second half of the century, when the question of revising the Church-Slavonic liturgical books (a question previously raised by Nil Sorsky and Maxim Grek) was raised again under the Patriarch Nikon (1652–58). Although of humble birth, Nikon was exceptionally conceited. One of his ambitions seems to have been the supremacy of the Russian Church over the Russian State. As an overbearing head of the Church he not only wanted to correct the Church-Slavonic liturgical texts by going back to the Greek originals, but he demanded that some of the minor age-old Russian habits, such as crossing oneself with two fingers, should be given up in favour of the Greek way of crossing oneself with three fingers. His 'reforms' were accepted and confirmed by the Church Assembly in 1656. Yet a large portion of priests and believers, in whose opinion Russian Orthodoxy was final and sacrosanct, looked upon any changes, however small, as a heretical innovation which ought to be resisted at all costs.

These opponents soon became known as Old Believers or *raskól'niki* [1] and were responsible for the most important schism in the Russian Orthodox Church. The schism itself gave rise to quite a remarkable Russian prose-work whose author was no less a person than the stubborn and dynamic leader of the dissidents—the Archpriest Avvakum. It was under the rule of Alexey Mikhailovich, the gentlest and spiritually most accomplished of the Russian tsars, that this archpriest was doomed to pass through such ordeals and trials as few human beings would have been able to endure. He not only bore them bravely but even recorded them in *The Life of the Archpriest Avvakum Written by Himself* (*Zhítie protopópa Avvakúma, im samím napísannoe*), a book which, in spite of its small size, is something of a landmark in the evolution of Russian literature.

2

Avvakum Petrovich was born into a priest's family in 1620 or 1621 in Grigorova, a village in the Nizhni Novgorod (now Gorky) district. He himself became a

1. Schismatics, from the Russian word *raskól* (split).

village priest at the age of twenty-two and was raised, some eight years later, to the rank of a protopop or archpriest. During that time he made a name for himself by his independence, his oratorical talent, blunt honesty, and also by a kind of ruthless puritanism which made him as severe to others as he was to himself. This brief but telling extract from his autobiography shows what his morality must have cost him at times, since he too was a man of flesh and blood.

> And in these days of my ministry a young woman came to confess to me, burdened with many sins, guilty of fornication and of all the sins of the flesh, and, weeping she began to acquaint me with them all, leaving nothing out, standing before the Gospels. And I, thrice accursed, though a leech, fell sick myself. I inwardly burned with a lecherous fire, and that hour was bitter to me. I lit three candles, and fixed them on the lectern and placed my right hand in the flame, and held it there till the evil passion was burned out and, when I had dismissed the young woman and laid away my vestments, I prayed and went to my house, grievously troubled in spirit.[1]

No less typical is the incident which occurred when he found his wife and her maid-servant in so violent a quarrel that, in a fit of anger, he beat them both. But no sooner had the beating been administered than he began to repent of his un-Christian action. In order to atone for it he lay down and ordered that all those who were in the parlour should beat him forthwith (with a scourge) upon his back.

> There were twenty people. And my wife and my children and all of them, weeping, did beat me. And I spake and said, 'If there be any man that doth not beat me, let him have no part with me in the kingdom of heaven.' And they beat me, against their will, and weeping; and I, at every blow, said a prayer. And when they had all beaten me and I was stood up, I pronounced forgiveness before them all.

Such was the man who was destined to lead that community which broke off from the official Orthodox church and has remained in opposition to it until the present day.

He certainly had the virtues marking him out as a leader: integrity, ruthless courage, the gift of words, and even a literary talent. His numerous polemics, epistles, admonitions, and above all his *Life* are all written in the racy spoken language, sprinkled with Biblical and Church-Slavonic phrases. Avvakum's autobiography was the first Russian masterpiece in prose written mainly in the people's tongue in order to be accessible to the people. But it had a strong personal flavour as well—the flavour of a narrow-minded, fanatically convinced and heroic demagogue. The author not only showered it with homely idioms and similies, but made effective use of his sardonic wit, his sense of realism and even humour. Infinitely tender towards his friends, he could be savage indeed towards his opponents for whom no epithet was vile enough.

1. All quotations in this chapter are taken from *The Life of the Archpriest Avvakum by Himself*, translated by Jane Harrison and Hope Mirrless (L. and V. Woolf, 1924).

He presented things very simply, because he himself saw them only in terms of black and white. For him a thing was either true or false, so there was no quibbling, no compromise, between the two. According to him the Patriarch Nikon and the Nikonites were on the side of error; hence they were the instruments of the devil and deserved to be punished accordingly. 'We would begin by quartering the devil Nikon and afterwards all the Nikonites', he wrote to the tsar. And he meant it.

The only trouble was that the Nikonites, being in power, were able to use, and eventually did use, the same charitable ways and means towards Avvakum himself. They remained in power even after 1658, when Nikon—defeated and curbed in his ambitions—had to give up his high office. Having sized up the vigour of their opponent, they tried again and again to win Avvakum to their own side, or at least to make him silent, but all in vain. The formidable archpriest would make no concessions. In one of his epistles he actually urged his followers to suffer death at the stake rather than think of compromise. 'Your burning will not last long—only a moment —and then your soul will be free.' A kind of spiritual masochism, with a lust for martyrdom, or even for self-immolation, spread among those 'Old Believers' who took his injunctions literally. The first collective self-immolation of a religious community, which refused to submit to the official Church, took place in 1675.[1] But Avvakum was not spared either. Nor did he want to be spared. He not only underwent all sorts of trials and tortures for the sake of his faith, but actually revelled in them, as we can gather from his *Life* which was above all a confession written at the request of his spiritual father, the Elder Epiphany, so that the 'word of God should not be given to forgetfulness.' Such was the origin of this strange, inhumanly human, historical document of the Moscow period.

3

Avvakum's trials and wanderings are of such a fantastically cruel kind as to be almost incredible. They take us first to his Siberian exile (1653) in one of the then unexplored Trans-Baikal regions where scores of early settlers, wandering together with him and dying of cold and hunger, were at the mercy of the sadistic Cossack commander Pashkov.

> And in winter we would live on fir-cones, and sometimes we found the bones of stinking carcasses of wild beasts left by the wolves, and what had not been eaten up by the wolves that did we eat; and some would eat frozen wolves and foxes—in truth, any filth that they could lay their hands on. A mare foaled, and, in secret the starving folk devoured the foal together with the caul. And Pashkov got wind of it, and he flogged them with his knout to the point of death. And another mare died, and desperation seized them all, inasmuch as they had pulled the foal out of her stealing a

---

1. The last act of Musorgsky's opera *Khovánshchina* gives an example of such a voluntary collective *auto-da-fé*.

march on nature. When naught but the head had as yet emerged from the womb, they tore it out, yea, and then began to eat the blood that came away with it. Ah, me! What a time! And two of my little sons died from these sore straits, and roaming the hills and the sharp rocks with my children that survived, naked and barefoot, living on grass and roots, what did I not endure?

The Cossack brute was particularly merciless towards the condemned religious dissenter Avvakum, as can be seen in the following passage:

Then he roared like wild beast and struck a great blow first on one cheek and then on the other, and then again on the head, and knocked me off my feet; and seizing his leather sword-strap struck me, where I lay, thrice on my back, and then, tearing off my shirt, gave me seventy-two strokes on my naked back with the knout . . . and after that they brought me to the fortress Bratsky, and flung me into a dungeon, and gave me straw to lie upon. And there I lay till Advent in a freezing tower.

The most surprising thing, however, was the stoicism with which Avvakum's wife and children shared with him all those hardships for the sake of a truth or ideal in which they firmly believed. They were the first to encourage him in his intransigence. When Avvakum himself had a moment of doubt as to whether on account of his family he should not be silent and cease to preach, he revealed his thoughts to his wife. And this was her answer:

'I and the children give you our blessing, continue the preaching of the word of God as heretofore, and take no thought for us until such time as shall seem good to God; when that time comes, remember us in your prayers; Christ is strong and He will not abandon us. Get thee gone, get thee gone to Church, Petrovich! Unmask the whore of heresy!' and I bowed myself to the earth before her and shook myself free from the blindness of a troubled mind and began once more to preach and teach God's Word in the towns and in all places until such time as I could boldly tear the mask from the heresy of Nikon.

4

After the greatest trials and humiliations undergone in those wastes Avvakum was suddenly recalled to Moscow in 1662. Here he was received by the tsar, the boyars and the official clergy, all of whom were hoping to find the great preacher more amenable after his lesson in Siberia. Honours and riches were showered upon him, but he remained as unflinching as ever and continued to preach what he himself regarded as just and right.

And so he was exiled, together with his family, once again—this time to Mezen' in the cold and inhospitable Archangel region. In 1667 the dissenters were condemned by the Church Assembly in Moscow. This meant that from now on the schism between the Orthodox and the 'Old Believers' or raskól'niki was complete. Avvakum was unfrocked and then imprisoned in a dismal place called Pustozersk within the Arctic circle. It was from here that he persisted in sending to his followers all sorts of polemics, comments, letters, petitions, homilies and exhortations. It was here, too, that he wrote (between 1672 and 1675) his autobiography, the straightforward realism of which can best be illustrated by some further quotations.

> And I, too, while I was celebrating vespers, was arrested by Boris Nele-dinsky and his musketeers, and together with me they arrested nigh on sixty souls and took them off to prison, and me they fastened with a chain for the night in the Patriarch's court. And when the Sabbath dawned they placed me in a cart and stretched out my arms and drove me from the Patriarch's court to the monastery of Andronicus, and there they put chains on me and flung me into a black dungeon, dug into the earth, and there I lay for three days, and I had nothing to eat or drink in the darkness, as I sat there bowing myself to the earth against my chains, though I knew not, as I made my obeisances, which was east and which was west. No one came to me but mice and black beetles, and the crickets chirped, and of fleas there was abundance.

So much for the man's undaunted courage and spiritual pride which pervades the whole of this book. It was not only the piety of the old Russia but also her intolerant dogmatism that flared up in Avvakum at a time when unavoidable contact with the West could not but foster certain innovations in all fields, Church and religion included. The patriarchal Muscovite mentality—unfamiliar with scepticism—found in Avvakum its most inflexible champion. And however Christian he may have been at heart, there was no Christian charity in him towards those with whom he disagreed. 'Filthy dogs', 'fat-bellies', 'fornicators'—such were some of the milder epithets with which he branded the adherents of Nikon.

Avvakum and two other priests were burned at the stake on April 14, 1682 (under the new Tsar Fyodor), but this martyrdom was by no means a final victory for such diehards. The western spirit was slowly but surely groping towards the East. Moscow herself had developed by then a foreign or 'German' suburb (*nemétskaya slobodá*) whose style of life was European. Also a Slavo-Graeco-Latin School of higher theological learning had been founded in the Russian capital, to which some of the monks from the westernised Theological College of Kiev were invited. It is clear that the secularisation of culture, which in the West had been accomplished by the Renaissance movement, was filtering into Moscow even before the reforms of Peter the Great. Western literary influences, too, were on the increase. In fact one can say that the second half of the seventeenth century was the turning point marking the end of old-Russian literature. Yet the traditionalist spirit continued to crop up and assert itself in all sorts of ways, until the problem of Russia and Europe, of East and West, assumed quite unexpected dimensions. The problem is not only one of mere politics and culture—it is above all one of psychology. Avvakum's *Zhítie* has the merit of providing at least some clues to that Russian mentality which so often puzzles the more sober and sceptically attuned western minds.

CHAPTER FOUR

Lomonosov, Derzhavin, Karamzin

I

The foundation of St Petersburg in 1703 by Peter I marked the beginning of a new period in Russian history and culture—the 'Petersburg period', which lasted until the revolution in 1917. To describe Petersburg as a 'window on Europe' is an understatement. The new Russian capital was more than that. Whereas Moscow still remained the capital of the Russian people with all its traditions more or less intact, Petersburg became the capital of the Russian empire and at the same time the gateway through which Europeanisation surged in on a grand scale, often accompanied by methods which had little to do with Europe. The course was neither simple nor easy, yet the very conflicts between the old and the new proved stimulating. The process, with all its ups and downs, was destined to help the Russian consciousness undergo in some two hundred years an evolution which normally would have taken three times longer. Needless to say, certain features of the imported European civilisation were bound to remain superficial. Others took deeper root. Thus what is known to the outside world as Russian literature was largely an outcome of this process, and its phenomenal growth coincided with the second half of the Petersburg period.

Early efforts at Europeanisation were confined to members of the aristocracy and landed gentry without really touching the peasants. When Peter I made it compulsory for the Russian nobility, whether high or low, to 'grow European', he had also to build schools to provide them with the necessary qualifications. Yet millions of illiterate serfs still remained tied to their masters' lands as firmly as ever and continued in slavery until the reform in 1861. The gap between the classes became even greater, since to the social and economic gap a wide cultural gap was now added. The latent or overt hostility on the part of the masses, who continued to cling to their old ignorance and superstitions, was certainly not decreased.

As far as literature was concerned, the final adoption of spoken Russian, sanctioned also by Peter I, was an important step forward. Once the influence of the dead Church-Slavonic language was removed, a closer contact between literature and folklore, or folk literature, with its magnificent *byliny* [1] and other genres, became possible. The gateway for literary activities of all kinds in the

1. Some of these—on historical themes—were first gathered and written down (in Moscow) by an Englishman, Richard James, in 1619.

spoken language was thus opened, and the man who made the first attempt to standardise colloquial Russian was Mikhail Lomonosov (1711-1765), who was also a successful poet and prose-writer in this living medium. To quote the words of the critic Belinsky, Russian literature 'begins with Lomonosov; he was its father and nurse; he was its Peter the Great.'

2

Lomonosov's personality is all the more striking because of his humble origin. He was a fisherman's son in the semi-arctic district of Archangel. Having availed himself of every opportunity to learn what he could, at the age of nineteen he went to Moscow where he continued his studies under great privations. Six years later he was already abroad—at the university of Marburg in Germany. Here he was soon enrolled by force into a Prussian regiment from which he escaped and eventually returned to Russia. Once back in his native country, he became (in 1745) professor of chemistry. As a member of the recently-founded Russian Academy in Petersburg, he was an enthusiastic pioneer and promoter of science; but at the same time he was active as a poet, grammarian and reformer of the language. Having systematised (in 1757) the spoken language for literary purposes, Lomonosov divided its application into three 'styles'. In the rhetorical 'grand style' used for odes, epics and tragedies a certain amount of the old Church-Slavonic words and expressions was still permissible. For other less solemn genres, however, the colloquial 'middle', or even 'low style' (for comedies and fables), was established. His own contribution to Russian poetry was not negligible, but in order to appreciate it, the poetic work of his highly cultured contemporary, Prince Antiokh Kantemir (1709-1744), should also be considered.

Kantemir was the first poet of the post-Petrine era to write in the colloquial language. In contrast to Lomonosov he still adhered to the archaic syllabic verse, which had been used before him by Simeon Polotsky and Feofan Prokopovich. He made some translations from Anacreon and Horace; he also wrote love-verses (now lost), odes and fables, but his reputation rests entirely on his satires which are filled with a genuine civic and humanitarian spirit. His voice and manner were those of a didactic satirist defending Peter's reforms and attacking anyone who dared to deny the benefit derived from them. His very first longish satire is directed against scorners of learning. This is how he ridicules their objections.

> Now Silvan sees this danger in the nation :
> Learning, he says, will lead us to starvation,
> We lived ere learning Latin, runs his lay,
> In far more plenty than we live today.
> In ignorance we reaped more grain, instead
> Now learning foreign tongues, we lose our bread.

The man is mad who would investigate
The confines of the soul, who sweats till late
To learn the order of the world, the cause
And change—a futile march for Nature's laws!
Will I live longer, or my chest become
A penny richer? Can I learn therefrom
What stewards steal per year? How to add more
Rain to my pond, or bottles to my store?[1]

The very frankness of Kantemir's lively didactic carping was enough to turn against him both a number of officials and also the clergy. So much so that a collection of his satires had been published in London (in a French translation) thirteen years before it was allowed to be printed in Russia in 1762, that is eighteen years after his death.

Yet the fact that Kantemir had used the syllabic verse, which had been taken over from Poland, was enough to make his poetry sound old-fashioned after Lomonosov and Vasily Trediakovsky. It was Trediakovsky who had first pointed out, in his treatise *A New and Brief Manner of Making Russian Verses* (1735), that the syllabic metre, based on an equal number of stressed syllables only (usually eleven or thirteen in each line) with a caesura in the middle and the use of feminine rhymed couplets, should be replaced by the tonic metre, that is by a regular sequence of stressed and unstressed syllables as being more suitable for the Russian language. Trediakovsky himself was also a prolific poet, but without much taste or talent. By the sweat of his brow he even manufactured a version in hexametres of Fénélon's *Les Aventures de Télémaque*—he gave it the title of *Telemakhída*. His verse reform was important, though, especially after it had been endorsed in practice by Lomonosov.

3

Lomonosov the poet abandoned his early Anacreontic lyrics for sonorous odes. He wrote twenty-four of them, most of which were intended to stimulate the reader's civic, patriotic and religious spirit. He even left an unfinished epic about Peter the Great. As a scientist again—and a scientist of above average ability—he could not help making occasional use of scientific imagination or even writing poems on scientific subjects: his *Letter about the Use of Glass*, for example. In addition he wrote on biblical motifs and made some poetic paraphrases of psalms. He also concocted the 'naughty' satirical parody—*A Hymn to the Beard*, which enraged the bearded higher clergy. His two tragedies, *Tamira and Selim*, and *Demofont*, were, however, inferior to his odes, an idea of which may perhaps be given by the first three stanzas of his *Evening Meditation on Seeing the Aurora Borealis*.

The day retires, the mists of night are spread
Slowly o'er nature, darkening as they rise;

1. Translated by Jeanette Eyre in *The Slavonic and East European Review XXI*.

The gloomy clouds are gathering round our head,
And twilight's latest glimmering gently dies :
The stars awake in heaven's abyss of blue;
Say, who can count them?—who can sound it—who?

Even as a sand in the majestic sea,
A diamond atom on a hill of snow,
A spark amidst a Hecla's majesty,
An unseen note where maddened whirlwinds blow,
Am I 'midst scenes like these—the mighty thought
O'erwhelms me—I am nought, or less than nought.

And science tells me that each twinkling star,
That smiles above us, is a peopled sphere,
Or central sun, diffusing light afar;
A link of nature's chain;—and there, even there
The Godhead shines display'd—in love and light,
Creating wisdom—all-directing might.[1]

The principal literary influences came, in those days, mainly from France whose pseudo-classical rules concerning poetry and tragedy were adopted by the Russians. There were also attempts to create a heroic Russian epic in that style: Mikhail Kheraskov's rather pompous *Russiáda* (1779), for example. It celebrates the conquest of Kazan' by Ivan the Terrible. He dedicated it to Catherine II who, although of German birth, wrote some mediocre Russian comedies of manners and regarded herself as a patroness of Russian letters on condition that the authors should not indulge in dangerous thoughts and utterances. It was in her reign that pseudo-classical Russian tragedy in the works of Sumarokov, Ozerov, and Knyazhnin flourished. And so did the poetry of Gavriil Derzhavin. The works of the three tragedians have now mainly an historical value. Derzhavin, on the other hand, is still considered to be the greatest Russian poet before Pushkin.

But before dealing with him some reference ought to be made to Russian prose before and during the reign of Catherine II which lasted from the 'liquidation' of her husband Peter III in 1762 until her own death in 1796.

Lomonosov himself was a pioneer of the new Russian prose which he handled with dexterity in his scientific essays. But significant writers of fiction were still scarce. Translations from other languages, notably from French, were plentiful, and there seemed to be a ready market for them. Thus the Russian version of Lesage's *Gil Blas* came out in 1754 and passed through eight editions before the end of the century. Among the poorer country gentry translations of Marivaux and Abbé Prévost were popular. Aristocrats, however, preferred to read the fashionable authors in French, since even in their families this language was often spoken in preference to Russian. The lower middle-class readers enjoyed all sorts of adventure stories and sentimental or crudely realistic narra-

1. John Bowring, *Specimens of the Russian Poets* (1823).

tives. The now forgotten works by Matvey Komarov and Matvey Chulkov were of the kind to satisfy their tastes. Chulkov's realistic novel of adventure, *The Comely Cook* (*Prigózhaya Povaríkha*, 1770) even gave the portrait of a Russian Moll Flanders of the Catherine period. The first truly polished prose writer was Nikolai Karamzin (1766-1826). He started his literary career under Catherine II, when Derzhavin's fame was at its height. But the period to which he belonged already pointed to currents which came after Derzhavin.

4

Gavriil Romanovich Derzhavin (1743–1816) could not boast of either wealthy or famous ancestors. As a member of an unprosperous upper-class family he had quite early to put up a hard fight in order to earn his living. In 1773 he took part in the campaign against Pugachov and his rebellious peasant army, after which he was employed as a civil servant in St Petersburg. This gave him enough leisure for writing poetry in which he soon distinguished himself. With his poetry the age of the Russian classical period was practically coming to a close. He himself superseded it not so much by any formal innovations as by his incredible, almost barbaric vitality, for whatever theme he took up, he filled it with the full-blooded power of his 'Tartar genius' (Pushkin's phrase) and with a broadness which found an outlet in the diversity of his poetry : from majestic odes at their best to Epicurean verses celebrating the simple pleasures of the manor and the countryside.

The bulk of Derzhavin's poetry is still in the baroque tradition with its grand and sonorous features. His odes, in particular, abound in a variety of rhythmical and majestic images, in colourful passages and a range of thought which is quite astonishing at times. The beginning of his long *Waterfall* can give one at least an approximate idea, however old the translation :[1]

Lo! like a glorious pile of diamonds bright,
Built on the steadfast cliffs, the waterfall
Pours forth its gems of pearl and silver light :
They sink, they rise, and sparkling cover all
With infinite refulgence; while its song,
Sublime as thunder, rolls the woods along—

Rolls through the woods—they send its accents back,
Whose last vibration in the desert dies :
Its radiance glances o'er the watery track,
Till the soft wave, as wrapt in slumber, lies
Beneath the forest shade; then sweetly flows
A milky stream, all silent as it goes.

Catherine II appreciated Derzhavin's poetry, especially his patriotic odes, to the extent of showering rewards upon him. Derzhavin, on the other hand,

1. All quotations of Derzhavin's poems are taken from John Bowring's *Specimens of the Russian Poets* (1823).

was never a time-server and did not mind being gruff with the Empress herself. Even when addressing her in his good-humoured ode *Felítsa*, he made several 'digs' at her parasitic court-circle. He is at his strongest, though, in some of his meditative and philosophic odes. His dirge on the death of Prince Meshchersky, for example, vibrates with true accents touching upon the mystery of death.

> Oh, that funeral toll! loud tongue of time!
> What woes are centred in that frightful sound!
> It calls! It calls me with a voice sublime,
> To the lone chambers of the burial ground.
>
> My life's first footsteps are 'midst yawning graves;
> A pale, teeth-chattering spectre passes nigh;
> A scythe of lightning that pale spectre waves,
> Mows down man's days like grass, and hurries by.

After this introduction there follows an entire verbal symphony with a wealth of meditative and emotional passages which cannot but affect even a sophisticated modern reader. More on the rhetorical side is his famous ode *God* which was translated into a number of languages, including Chinese and Japanese, while its author was still alive. But parallel with this one can enjoy Derzhavin's verses also in a lighter Anacreontic vein. As he puts it in his poem *To a Neighbour*:

> While all seems fair and bright,
> O do not dream of sorrow's night!
> Feast, neighbour, feast—and dance and sing—
> Life's sun has but a summer's glow,
> And joy is innocent—but know,
> 'Tis but that joy which bears no sting.

In order to flatter the poet the Empress presented him with the estate of Zvanka near Novgorod; and his stay at Zvanka inspired him with several bucolic poems which he wrote in his old age. He also made some attempts at tragedies, but these are of no interest nowadays. His Memoirs, however, are good reading, since his prose shows something of the same robust and virile power which was typical of his poetic work.

5

Derzhavin may have been a belated follower of pseudo-classical poetry, but by the mere force of his personality he created works which outstripped the fashion of the day. Something similar can be said of the late Russian poet of fables—Ivan Krylov (1768-1844). He was at first connected with the satirical journals edited and published by Nikolai Novikov; then he translated La Fontaine's fables (1805), wrote some plays, two of which, *The Fashion Shop* (1806) and *A Lesson for Daughters* (1807), had some success on the stage. Finally he achieved real fame with his own fables which justifiably earned him a permanent place in Russian literature.

There were several Russian authors of fables before him, from Kantemir to Khemnitser, Izmailov and Ivan Dmitriev, but Krylov's contribution in this respect is unique. For he knew how to combine the freshness and inflection of the peasant language with the shrewd common-sense and humour of the Russian people at their most typical. He preserved the pseudo-classical form of the fable, yet his uneven lines, his idiomatic raciness and peculiar articulation are so strong at times as to defy any translator.

Krylov, who was born in the eighteenth century, lived long enough to witness the Pushkin period. But between Derzhavin and the Pushkin era there was a sentimental current whose principal Russian representative in verse and prose, towards the end of the eighteenth century, was Nikolai Karamzin (1766–1826). Mikhail Kheraskov in some of his poems illustrated the transition from classicism to sentimentalism, while Ippolit Bogdanovich (1743-1803) gave in his *Psyche* (*Dúshenka*, 1775) a polished rococo paraphrase of La Fontaine's *Psyché et Cupidon*, tinged with a sentimental flavour. Ivan Dmitriev, too, belonged to the sentimental school, although he had several odes and over sixty fables to his credit. Alexey Merzlyakov wrote some good sentimental lyrics in the style of Russian folk-songs—a genre which became quite popular in those days and was further enhanced by Nikolai Tsyganov. As for Karamzin, he was an admirer of Rousseau and a free-mason, but his sentimental inclinations were fostered by *Ossian* and Lawrence Sterne. He thus introduced English influence into Russian literature and even translated Shakespeare's *Julius Caesar*. His first important feat was, however, his own variety of a 'sentimental journey'. As it happened, he travelled in Germany, Switzerland, France and England, and recorded his impressions in his voluminous *Letters of a Russian Traveller* (1790, 1801). Written in the polished upper-class language (which he championed in literature), with plenty of incident and thought, this work took the readers by storm. And so did his sentimental, philanthropic story *Poor Liza* (*Bédnaya Líza*, 1792) the tragedy of a common girl jilted by a nobleman.

In his poetry Karamzin still kept to the classical tradition, while filling it with sentimental contents. His contemporary, Konstantin Batyushkov (1787-1855), excelled, however, like Bogdanovich, in lightness of touch and simple language, in which qualities he was an important forerunner of Pushkin. He did not depart from classical prosody, but imbued it with quite unexpected euphony and music. Vasily Zhukovsky (1783-1852) applied the same kind of musical harmony to his own poems which form a transition from the sentimental to the romantic trend.

Like Karamzin, Zhukovsky was under the spell of English literature, although German writers influenced him as well. He made his debut in 1802 with a splendid translation of Gray's *Elegy*. His was a tender, contemplative soul suffering from frustrated love and inclined to quasi-mystical moods which came out in some of his mellifluous personal lyrics. Yet he was to assert his talent even more through his remarkable translations, which included Goethe, Schiller, Uhland, and Byron whose *Prisoner of Chillon* he rendered in a matchless Russian version (with masculine rhymes from the first to the last line). He also wrote ballads and narrative poems with motifs from folklore. Towards the end of his life he translated the whole of Homer's *Odyssey*, a magnificent version of the *Iliad*—in the grand style—having been made in 1809 by Nikolai Gnedich. It was above all Zhukovsky who, together with Batyushkov, heralded the rise of that 'golden age' of Russian poetry which received its mightiest impetus as well as its climax in the genius of Pushkin. But before passing to the Pushkin era a brief survey of the Russian dramatic literature of the period might be helpful.

CHAPTER FIVE

Fonvizin and Griboyedov

I

A tradition of drama and theatre as is known in the West did not exist in old Russia for the simple reason that both were an abomination in the eyes of the ecclesiastical authorities. This does not mean that Russian life and folklore were entirely devoid of theatrical elements. Itinerant groups of *skomorókhi* (mummers) were popular as far back as the eleventh century. They used to take part in folk-gatherings, fairs and festivities, where they performed all sorts of comic or satirical scenes mixed up with music, dancing and juggling. Puppets, also, with Petrúshka—the Russian equivalent of the English Punch or the Italian Pulcinello—were among favourite entertainments of the Russian masses. Later on the so-called *balagán* (extemporised people's show) made its appearance, and its repertory included genuine folk-pieces, such as the *Comedy about Tsar Maximilian and his Disobedient Son Adolph*. The Russian Church had to make some concessions to the people's dramatic instinct by introducing into her rituals the so-called *Furnace Action* (*Peshchnóe déystvo*): the miracle of the three youths who, by order of Nebuchadnezzar, were thrown into a burning furnace but remained unscathed. A theatre in the Western sense made however its first groping attempts in Russia in the seventeenth century, and the man responsible for it was a German.

It was under the reign of Alexey Mikhailovich (1645–76 that Johann Gottfried Gregori, a Pastor from the German suburb in Moscow, staged in the specially erected wooden building at Preobrazhenskoe—the tsar's summer residence—the biblical play *Ester or the Action of Arthaxerxes*. The play was performed in German by sixty-four German actors and lasted some ten hours. The tsar, who was able to follow it because he had a Russian translation, was so pleased that Gregori had to train a group of Russian actors who performed plays on biblical subjects, but only for the tsar and his Court. This venture proved however a temporary affair, since Gregori died in 1675 and the tsar himself only a year later.

It was about the same period that the first equivalents of the Jesuit school drama (under the influence of Poland) were written by the orthodox monk and poet Simeon Polotsky (1629–80)—a former student of the Theological College or *búrsa* at Kiev and later a teacher at the same kind of institution in Moscow. He wrote two plays, both on biblical subjects: *A Comedy of the Parable of the Prodigal Son* and *On Nebuchadnezzar, the Golden Calf and the Three Children*

Unburned in the Furnace. Written in rhymed syllabic verse, they were performed by students at the college, and during the intervals between the acts comic intermezzi on secular and often topical themes would be interpolated. Even that zealous supporter of Peter's reforms, the Archbishop Feofan Prokopovich, wrote *St Vladímir* (1705)—a play more in the style of a Renaissance drama, recording Russia's conversion to Christianity. A good *Nativity Play* was written by the pious (in fact saintly) Metropolitan of Rostov—Dimitry Rostovsky (1651-1709) who was also responsible for the shorter and well-composed *Saints Calendar* or *Chétyi-Minéi*, based partly on Makary's work and partly on some Western sources. Secular prose drama had, however, a slow and difficult development, beginning with some bad translations from the German. A keen interest in theatrical performances of a worldly kind was shown by Peter the Great's sister Natalia. Such performances were frequently given in the Cadet school by the students themselves. A permanent professional theatre was established at St Petersburg only as late as 1756, with its first director the author of classical tragedies Alexander Sumarokov (1718-1777).

Sumarokov made his literary debut as a poet of satirical fables and of lyrics imitating the Russian folk-song manner. But from 1747 he concentrated on tragedies, beginning with his *Khorév*, after the pattern of Racine and Voltaire. His compatriots labelled him—somewhat hastily—'our Russian Racine'. He wrote nine stilted tragedies (in six-footed rhymed iambics) mostly on themes taken from the Russian past. One of these, *Dmitry the Usurper*, dealing with the 'troubled period' at the beginning of the seventeenth century, became rather popular. He also took over, from a French adaptation, the subject of Shakespeare's *Hamlet*, but with a happy ending. For Hamlet triumphs over his enemies and marries Ophelia who admonishes him at the close of the play :

> Go, my prince, into the temple,
> Show thyself to the people.
> And I will go and pay
> My last duty to the dead.

Sumarokov wrote some not very original comedies (fourteen of them) as well as librettos for operas.[1] An active tragedian was Yakov Knyazhnin (1742-1791) who scored a considerable success with his *Dido* (1769). He also wrote several amusing comedies and was an enthusiast for progressive ideas which he voiced in his tragedies, especially in *Vadím of Nóvgorod* (1795) glorifying old Novgorod freedom. So much so that this tragedy, printed after the author's death, was publicly burnt. Another, younger, dramatist, Vladislav Ozerov (1769-1816), already mixed his classicist tragedies with elements of sentimentalism of the Karamzin school and even of the Ossianic variety—one of his plays was actually called *Fingal*. His most popular tragedies were *Oedipus in Athens*, the ultra-patriotic *Dmitry Donskóy*, and *Polixéna*. All three were produced during the first decade of the nineteenth century. With Ozerov classi-

---

1. The comic opera was a great favourite with the Russians. Alexander Ablesimov's *Miller, Wizard, Quack and Matchmaker* (1770) in particular was an enormous success on account of its unpretentious fun and gaiety.

cal (or rather classicist) tragedy came to an end, even though it survived for a while in one of Pushkin's talented contemporaries—Pavel Katenin (1792-1853). To acquaint ourselves with plays which proved to be enduring on the stage, we must turn to such authors as Fonvizin and Griboyedov.

2

Denis Fonvizin (1745-92) was born into a fairly well-to-do upper-class family. For a while he studied at the newly-established (1755) University of Moscow, but for some reason he left it without taking a degree and entered the army. Later he joined the cabinet of the minister I. P. Elagin and finally that of the progressive-minded Count Nikita Panin. His literary activities started modestly in 1761—with a translation (from the German) of the didactic fables whose author was the Danish playwright Ludvig Holberg. Fonvizin himself wrote at the time fables of his own, in some of which he ridiculed both church and state. In the early 1770s he was connected with the satirical journals edited and published by the enterprising freemason Nikolai Novikov, and in 1777-78 he accompanied his chief on a journey abroad. Judging by the letters he sent home, the *après nous le déluge* atmosphere he found in France was not to his liking. In fact he found it so distasteful that he felt proud of being a Russian. 'In nothing in this world,' he wrote, 'have I been so mistaken as in my opinion about France. I am heartily glad to have seen her personally, and that no one can any more delude me with tales about her.' Liberal-minded as he was, he yet stood nearer to the Russian freemasons of the Novikov type than to the French encyclopaedists who kept flattering Catherine II and praising the 'enlightened' façade of her rule. The reality behind that façade was, of course, a different matter.

The early and the middle years of Catherine's reign were full of plausible liberal slogans, with a promise of measures she was careful to see did not encroach upon the privileges of the serf-owning nobility who, from 1762 on, were free from the obligatory state service introduced by Peter I. In 1766-68 a commission designed to regulate relations between the landed nobility and the serfs was set up and the Novikov circle favoured the rights of the serfs. They had little success, however, and the serfs were left in much the same plight as before. In order to diminish the influence of Novikov's periodicals the Empress founded her own mildly liberal and satirical journal *Pell Mell* in which she herself concocted articles implying that everything was perfect under her wise rule. The peasant rising led by Pugachov in 1773-75 told a rather different story; but Pugachov was defeated, and this was a further triumph for the advocates of serfdom. Landowners insisted on their rights by reason of their aristocratic blood, which made them regard their superiority over the villeins as a law of nature. Shocked by all this, Fonvizin decided to debunk such would-be superiority as mercilessly as he could. This he did in his two satirical comedies of manners *The Brigadier* (*Brigadír*) and *The Minor* (*Nédorosl'*).

Fonvizin's turn of mind was particularly suited to satire, whether in the form of fables, epistles or imaginary letters, but it was in drama that his talent really culminated. His early version of Voltaire's *Zaïre* and his adaptation of Gresset's *Sidney* (Fonvizin gave it the title of *Korión*) were only exercises for his own plays to come. The first of these was *The Brigadier*, written probably in 1768-69, but published in 1786.

As the literary historian Alexey Veselovsky pointed out, in writing this work Fonvizin must have taken a great deal from the eighteenth-century comedy *Jean de France* by the 'Danish Molière' Ludvig Holberg. Since Holberg himself had written it under the partial influence of Wycherley's *The Gentleman Dancing Master*, this first Russian comedy of manners forms an indirect link with English Drama. But whatever Fonvizin's sources and influences, he assimilated them to perfection and made them typical of the manners and conditions he found among the Russian provincial gentry at the time of Catherine II. He did this so well that his play deserved the success it earned. Moreover, each of his dramatis personae is endowed with the lively individual language of which Fonvizin proved to be a master.

The Brigadier is not rich in action. The stress is on the characters and the general picture of manners in a remote corner of Russia. His method is still that of Molière, or, in this case, of Holberg's classical tradition, with the three unities of time, place and action preserved; yet the realistic sense which pervades the plot and the dialogue is entirely Fonvizin's. The Brigadier and his wife pay a visit to a wealthy landowner and councillor in order to woo his pretty daughter Sophia for their son Ivanushka (Johnny), who has come with them. Like the hero of Holberg's *Jean de France*, Ivanushka is infected with the Franco-mania fashionable among young fops and snobs of that period. He is as silly, vulgar, and depraved as are his parents or, for that matter, the parents of Sophia. Sophia's father—the councillor—begins to run after the Brigadier's wife, while both the Brigadier and his son compete for the councillor's wife's favours. There is an irresponsible erotic mix-up after the manner of the eighteenth century, but with a strong provincial flavour. Sophia and her secret sweetheart—the only decent (but conventional) characters in the comedy—thus have their own way, while the scheming vulgarity of the others is shown up during the dénouement. Fonvizin's satire was effective enough to castigate the age and its manners as they deserved; and he gave another indictment of this sort in *The Minor* or *The Young Hopeful*.

3

Fonvizin worked at this second comedy for a number of years and finished it in 1781-82. Published in 1783, it showed even better characterisation and a greater variety of motifs than *The Brigadier*, and is still being performed on the Russian stage. It contains at least three converging motifs, the bestiality of the primitive rustic gentry being one of them. Then there is the humanitarian motif: the demoralising influence of serfdom upon the serf-owners. And finally, interwoven with the two is the motif of a Russian 'gentleman's' education in those days—presented in all its appalling grotesqueness.

Once again the action takes place in the provinces, on the estate of the Prostakovs (Mr and Mrs Simpleton). The character of the tyrannical, stupid and greedy Mme Prostakova is highly convincing in its realism. No less vivid is the portrait of her worthy brother Skotinin (Mr Beastley) who, needless to say, does full justice to his name. Mme Prostakova's sixteen-year-old son, the 'young hopeful' Mitrofan (a kind of Russian Tony Lumpkin), is an eloquent product of the atmosphere in which he has been brought up. As class snobbery demanded that at least one teacher in a squire's household should be either French or German, the 'young hopeful's' education had conformed to this rule. But towards the end it transpires that his German mentor is an ex-coachman who has found the post of tutor in a Russian nobleman's family more profitable than a cabby's profession. Lastly, there is the conventional secret love between Sophia and Milon, while the 'young hopeful' and his Uncle Skotinin compete for Sophia, or rather for her sudden fortune. On hearing of Sophia's big financial prospects, Mme Prostakova does all she can to secure her hand for Mitrofan, until her intrigues too are foiled. The comedy has a happy ending for the two secret lovers, but a much less happy one for Mme Prostakova and her beloved offspring.

Such is the framework of the play which serves as a pretext for invective and indictment. The very first scenes illustrate (through Mme Prostakova's behaviour) the sub-human treatment meted out to serfs. Her brother Skotinin is no better in this respect; nor is the 'young hopeful'. As a contrast Fonvizin puts forward two positive types—two noblemen whom he wants to show as being really noble. Unfortunately, his Pravdin (Mr True) and Starodum (Mr Oldsense) are both abstract *raisonneurs* as well as the author's mouthpieces. Starodum's didactic tirades have been made even heavier by the subsequent addition of sententious passages found among the author's papers. On the other hand, it was through these two characters, or rather types, that Fonvizin vented his contempt for Catherine II and her collection of richly rewarded gigolos— each more despicable than the last. Starodum, who had to leave the court because he was both unwilling and unable to adapt himself to it, mentions this fact to his friend Pravdin who reacts as follows:

> *Pravdin*   Men with a moral code like yours should not be dismissed from the court, rather they should be asked to enter that career.
> *Starodum*   To enter it? And what for?
> *Pravdin*   What for? Why is a physician necessary for a sick man?
> *Starodum*   My friend, you are mistaken! It is no use to call in a doctor to an incurable patient. In this case a physician can do no good—he may even contract the disease himself.[1]

4

It required a fair amount of courage to be so outspoken about the Russian court. Fonvizin knew, of course, what he was doing even before his association with

1. Translated by George Y. Patrick and George Rapall Noyes, in *Masterpieces of Russian Drama* (Appleton. 1933).

Novikov enabled him to exercise his satirical gift to the full. Yet the Empress was not inactive, and in 1783, together with Princess Dashkova, she began to edit a periodical called *The Interlocutor (Sobesédnik)*[1] in order to influence public opinion as a 'teacher' in her own right. Her object was to group around it the best Russian authors of the period, Fonvizin included, but he was not so easy to win over. In 1788 he launched a liberal journal of his own under the title of *An Honest People's Friend or Starodúm;* but because of his attacks on Catherine II and her favourites the periodical was clamped down by the censor. The panic which seized the Empress after the French Revolution made things worse. Banking on her 'enlightenment', one of the remarkable men of that generation, A. V. Radishchev (1749–1802), dared to publish in 1790 his *Journey from Petersburg to Moscow* containing virulent attacks on serfdom and autocracy. The author's political radicalism can best be gathered from his *Ode to Liberty* (printed in the same book) which contains the following lines addressed to Cromwell:

> 'Aye, you were cruel and perfidious, a bigot and a hypocrite; you have profaned things sacred; you were the greatest villain in the world; for, possessed by the plenitude of power, you have abolished every manifestation of freedom in your people. And yet you are a great man, because you have been the first to dare show a beneficent example to the people by executing, in accordance with the people's judgement, your King Charles; you have taught mankind how to avenge itself on its oppressors.'

The book was banned and burned, while its author was sentenced to death. The death sentence was commuted to exile in Siberia from whence he returned only after Catherine's death in 1796. Radischev's case is an illustration of what was likely to happen once the Empress had shed her so-called liberalism. Novikov, too, was imprisoned. As for Fonvizin, he remained silent. Fear even drove him to a kind of avowal expressed in his unfinished *Open-hearted Confession of my Deeds and Thoughts.* During his last years he had a stroke and became an invalid, with fits of religious delusions, until his death in 1792.

Fonvizin was not a prolific playwright. Apart from the two comedies mentioned, he wrote only one other, *The Choice of a Tutor,* which was never completed. Yet of all the Russian eighteenth-century dramatists he is the only one who is still performed in his country. Of his two comedies the first was written in an exclusively critical spirit, whereas the second—however critical—was constructive as well, although the didactic element (expressed by Pravdin and Starodum) is not truly integrated with the rest of the play. Even so, both plays gave a good start to the realistic comedy of manners in Russia. They led up to Vasily Kapnist with his cruel dramatic satire in verse, *Chicane (Yabedá,* 1798), to be followed in the first half of the nineteenth century by Griboyedov and Gogol. The early years of the nineteenth century were marked by a change of taste in the direction of sentimental melodrama and romantic plays, alongside which there was a strong demand for light comedies and vaudevilles. The most prolific supplier of these was Prince Alexander A. Shakhovskoy (1777–

---

1.   Actually *The Interlocutor of the Lovers of the Russian Word.*

1846) at a time when French, German and Italian companies were welcomed and applauded by the theatre audiences of St Petersburg.

Shakhovskoy himself, though versatile and prolific, was not a great dramatist, but he did have a success with such comedies as *The New Sterne* (1805) and *The Spa of Lípetsk* (1818), both of them ridiculing the fashion of the lachrimose melodramas of Kotzebue. During the romantic period proper he dramatised Scott's *Ivanhoe* and *The Fortunes of Nigel*. He also adapted from Shakespeare *The Tempest* (his own translation, 1821) and *Falstaff* (1825). His most fruitful work was, however, a ceaseless endeavour to raise the standard of Russian acting. For some sixteen years (1802–1818) he was director of repertory in the Imperial theatres at St Petersburg, and after that remained to the end an indefatigable instructor and adviser of the younger generation of actors. Under his guidance Russian theatre reached a high level. This in itself may have been enough to foster the dramatic aspirations of the playwright Griboyedov, although his famous play *The Mischief of Being Clever* was of a nature that would hardly be allowed to appear on the stage.

5

Alexander Griboyedov (1795–1829) is one of those authors whose fame rests upon one single work, *The Mischief of Being Clever*, or *Woe from Wit* (*Góre ot umá*), a comedy great enough to stand on its own merits through all the changes of literary fashions. Formally the play adheres to the tradition of classical comedies, but it is written in rhymed verse of uneven length like Krylov's *Fables*. Highly disciplined and economic in language, it is rich in wit as well as sarcastic sallies. Griboyedov must have struggled hard at times with his verbal material, but his terse and lively dialogue is a proof that he mastered it in the end. Stress is laid not so much upon an involved plot as upon characters and conversation. His dramatic contrast rests above all upon the conflict between two generations of the same social stratum. On the one hand we have Famusov, the conservative head of a government department and a representative of that ossified bureaucracy for which title, rank, wealth and decorations are the alpha and omega of all things. His secretary Molchalin is a social outsider, but he has succeeded in adapting himself to that circle so completely that for purely opportunistic reasons he pretends to be in love with Famusov's daughter Sophia, while at the same time making secret advances to her maid Liza. The other characters, whether military or civil, fit perfectly into this atmosphere of snobbery, slander and stagnation.

On the other hand we have Chatsky, an impetuous young man who, after three years abroad, has just returned to Moscow and is in a hurry to get to Famusov's in order to greet his former sweetheart Sophia. But Sophia, a stubborn, coldly witty and reserved character, has changed in the meantime and has more or less conformed to her father's circle of bureaucratic time-servers. She approves even of Molchalin's 'love' and does not reject his dishonourable advances. Chatsky, having sized up the entire collection, condemns Famusov and his like and comes to the conclusion that he has made a mistake in coming back to Russia and to Moscow at all. He not only feels alienated from every-body, including Sophia, but is even proclaimed a madman during a ball at Famusov's house. A final confrontation with Molchalin, Sophia and her father (after the ball) only makes him confirm his decision that Sophia, whatever his one-time love for her, can never be his.

> Don't fear I threaten you with my solicitations!
> You'll find another, quite a catch,
> Who'll make his way and scrape and court,
> A perfect paragon, in short,
> For dear papa-in-law a match!
> So! My delirium is past!

And then, after a final confrontation with Famusov, Chatsky does not spare anyone he has seen during that fateful day.

> Whom have I been with? What has brought me to this town?
> All curse and drive me out,—a mob that hounds you down,
> Of friends in friendship false, unflagging in their hatred,
>   Tale-mongers not to be placated;
> The silly would-be wit, the crooked simpleton,
>   Old maids, malicious everyone,
> And old men babbling out some folly or some fad—
> No wonder, all the gang proclaimed that I was mad.
> You're very right! That man could pass through fire unscathed,
> Who had spent a live-long day with you
> And in the self-same air had bathed
> And yet had kept his reason too.
> I'll out of Moscow straight! I'll journey here no more!
> I'll fly and not look back! Where no ill tongues disparage,
> I'll seek me out a nook for heart that's tried too sore.
>   My carriage here! My carriage! (*He drives off*) [1]

Griboyedov's other works include poems and some comedies which are not on a level with his satirical masterpiece. His official duties and his short life hardly left him enough time for a prolific literary output. As one of the brilliant young men of his generation, he spent a great deal of his brief life in the diplomatic service, particularly in Persia. After the unsuccessful December rising in 1825 he was arrested on suspicion of having been implicated with the rebels, some of whom were his friends, but he defended himself so well that he was freed and reinstated in the service. Eventually he was appointed Russian Minister to Persia, and was given the task of negotiating the Peace of Turkman-chai in February, 1828. When he brought the Treaty to Tabriz and Teheran some of its clauses were so much resented by the Persians (especially the demand that all Christian women should be removed from Persian harems) that the in-furiated mob attacked the Russian Legation at Teheran and Griboyedov fell fighting on 30 January, 1829.

1. Translated by Sir Bernard Pares (School of Slavonic Studies).

CHAPTER SIX

Pushkin and his era

I

Apart from being the central figure in Russian literature, Alexander Sergeyevich Pushkin (1799–1837) can be regarded as a unique phenomenon. Under one of the most tyrannical regimes in Europe, he knew how to preserve his artistic freedom and, in the teeth of all obstacles, to crystallise the irrepressible vitality and *joie de vivre* of his belated Renaissance spirit into works of perfect harmony and beauty. A Russian to the very core, he yet absorbed organically the literary and cultural heritage—in fact, the entire humanistic tradition—of the West and made it part and parcel of his own creative life and mind. The greatest national poet of Russia thus became the principal link between the literature of his own country and the literature of Europe, notably of England. He not only brought one literary period to a brilliant conclusion, but indicated, in and through his own work, that kind of cultural synthesis between Russia and Europe which could serve as a pointer to the future. In spite of this, Pushkin is probably the only genius whose reputation outside Russia rests on trust rather than on actual knowledge of his work. A foreigner, ignorant of the Russian language, may of course take his greatness for granted: nevertheless he can hardly understand what the name of Pushkin means to a Russian and what it stands for.

This drawback is further increased by a lack of adequate translations. And Pushkin still remains one of the most difficult poets to translate—difficult mainly on account of his uncanny ease, obviousness (he is perhaps the greatest genius of the obvious) and simplicity. Equally uncanny is his flair for the *mot juste*, for the right inflection, as well as for the orchestration of sounds, rhymes and rhythms which he always worked out with matchless clarity and precision. Few poets indeed have been able to extract the full value from words with that Hellenic instinct for art that conceals art, which is one of Pushkin's primary qualities. In his poems each word, each image, seems to be born out of another with that inevitability which excludes anything artificial, forced and laboured. And the more perfect and disciplined the result, the stronger is the impression of spontaneity. The texture of his verse, too, is so individual that it is impossible to confuse it with that of anyone else. The economy and lucidity which as a boy Pushkin had learned from the French (including Voltaire and Parny), he later combined with his own realistic sense, and with that broad perception of life which in one of his lyrics made him compare his poetic work to the echoes which, reproducing all the sounds and vibrations around, themselves remain unanswered.

> When cries of beasts the forest fill,
> The thunder rolls, the trumpets shrill,
> A maiden sings behind the hill.
>   To every sound
> Responsive, sudden echoes thrill
>   The air around.
>
> They hear the thunder's roaring glee,
> The stormy sobbing of the sea,
> The shouts of shepherds on the lea,
>   And answers find,
> Themselves unanswered.—How like thee,
>   Poetic mind.[1]

Intensely human and very much of this world, Pushkin 'echoed' everything he observed and experienced in terms of visual images and symbols, that is, of concrete reality. However intimate his personal experiences, he knew how to sublimate them, especially in his matchless love-lyrics, by means of 'shorthand' realism into things of beauty the significance of which is above the merely personal. It becomes universal, applicable to all whose imagination can respond to such experiences. This avowal of love may be quoted as a proof:

> I loved you. Even now I may confess
> Some embers of my love their fire retain.
> But do not let it bring you more distress—
> I do not want to sadden you again.
> Hopeless and tongue-tied, yet I loved you dearly,
> With pangs the jealous and the timid know.
> So tenderly I loved you, so sincerely,
> I pray God grant another love you so.[2]

One of Pushkin's most haunting lyrics, *Remembrance*, may serve as another example.

> When trade and traffic and all the noise of town
> Is dimmed, and on the streets and squares
> The filmy curtain of the night sinks down
> With sleep, the recompense of cares,
> To me the darkness brings not sleep nor rest.
>
> A pageant of the torturing hours
> Drags its slow course, and writhing in my breast,

1. Translated by Walter Morison. The theme of this lyric is a paraphrase of an English poem, *The Sea-Shore Echo*, by Barry Cornwall.
2. This and the next poem were translated by R. M. Hewitt.

A fanged snake my heart devours.
My fears take form, and on the wearied brain
Grief comes in waves that overflow,
And memory turns a scroll to tell again
A legend that too well I know.
Reading the past with horror, shame, and dread,
I tremble and I curse,
But the repentant tears, the bitter tears I shed,
Will not wash out a single verse.

Poems like the ones just quoted speak for themselves. Far from being a 'mere classic', dutifully read in schools and then forgotten, Pushkin is a permanent companion to every educated Russian. One turns to him again and again not only because of his all-embracing comprehension, but also on account of his balance between the physical, the mental, and the spiritual planes. In him there is no hostility, no gap, between 'soul' and 'body': they are complementary. No matter how impulsive, passionate, even turbulently passionate, he may have been as a man, as a poet he remained to the end one of the most balanced creative personalities in world literature. His was not a static, but a dynamic balance which made him experience life as *élan* and perpetual movement. Feeling at home in this world in spite of all, he adopted that affirmative attitude which accepts all life—whether 'happy' or 'unhappy'—provided it is really intense. What he hated was sham-life, anti-life, camouflaged by all sorts of respectable labels. For this reason he welcomed human existence with all its joys and sorrows, even the most tragic sorrows. Such acceptance is perhaps best expressed in his *Elegy*, which is full of a readiness to face any adversities without saying *no* to life.

The frenzied merriment of misspent years
Like wakening from wine my spirit sears:
Like wine, the poignant imprints of past pain
Grow stronger in me as in years they gain.
My path is sombre; fraught with toil and sorrow
The storm-encompassed ocean of tomorrow.

And yet, my friends, I do not ask for death;
Life I desire, for pain and contemplation.
I know I shall be stirred by pleasure's breath
'Mid all my grief, and care, and agitation.
Again at times with melody I'll throb,
My fancy's fruit again will make me sob;
And maybe, as my last sad days decline,
Love with a farewell smile on me will shine.[1]

1. This lyric and the verses quoted in sections 2 and 3 have been translated by the late Walter Morison partially for this essay.

2

Pushkin's appetite for life was so strong that on a purely human plane and amidst ordinary circumstances he was, despite his poetic discipline and sense of measure, often swayed by excesses—the causes of which may, perhaps, be traced to his exotic ancestry. Whereas on his father's side he came of aristocratic Russian stock six hundred years old, his maternal great-grandfather had been an Abyssinian princeling, bought in the slave market at Constantinople and sent as a present to Peter the Great who took good care of his education and his subsequent career. Pushkin's own parents were rather commonplace, without any particular talents or distinctions, but he saw little of them. The only person for whom he felt geniune attachment in his childhood, boyhood and early manhood was his old nurse Arina. This lovable peasant-woman was destined to form something of a bridge between the poet and the people. At the age of twelve he was sent to the newly opened *lycée* or privileged boarding school at Tsarkoye Selo (now called Pushkin), where the atmosphere was so much to his liking that, years afterwards, he always commemorated in verse the opening day—19 October. One of these poems, *19 October, 1825*, ranks among his finest and best-known creations. Its first two stanzas may serve as an example of what the whole of it (written in exile) is like :

> The autumn wood casts off its crimson gown,
> The faded field is silvered o'er with frost,
> The sun peers forth, a sad, reluctant ghost,
> And hurriedly behind the hill goes down.
> Burn brightly, pine-logs, in my lonely cell;
> And thou, O wine-cup, that in autumn rains
> Dost comfort so, in my sad heart instil
> A brief oblivion of bitter pains.
>
> How sad I am, no friend to comfort me,
> With whom my sorrows I might solve in drink,
> Whose trusty hand in my hand I might link
> And wish him all his days felicity.
> I drink alone; in vain my fancy calls
> To visit me the friends of former years;
> No pleasure I await; no footstep falls
> With sweet familiar ring upon my ears.

The five or six years of Pushkin's schooling at the *Lycée* were responsible for the enduring friendships to which he alludes in the two verses quoted. But these years also coincided with one of the most eventful and promising eras in modern Russian history. The younger generation, which had witnessed Russia's victory over Napoleon in 1812, could not but expect a better future for their country. The young Pushkin was in the avant-garde both politically and as a poet. In 1817 he became a member of the exclusive 'Arzamas' society where he was welcomed by such poets as Zhukovsky and Batyushkov. The aim of this society was to fight and parody the conservatives or reactionaries in literary matters, led by Admiral Shishkov, who advocated ample use of Church-Slavonic, despite the reforms from Lomonosov to Karamzin. Among the 'Arzamas' members Pushkin met several young liberals who cherished the idea of making Russia a free and democratic country. Such basic evils of Russia as serfdom and autocracy weighed heavily on all those who hoped for eventual changes for the better; but as the years passed things only became worse under the jackboot of reaction. Still, the ideas bequeathed by the French Revolution could not be entirely suppressed even in Russia, where a considerable portion of the young aristocrats aimed at reforms corresponding to the more liberal spirit of the age. Disappointed in their hopes, these liberals found an outlet in secret societies. Finally, on 14 December, 1825 (old style) an open revolt broke out against the new Tsar Nicholas I, the brother of the deceased Alexander I. It was engineered chiefly by officers of the Guards, but their venture ended in a *débâcle*: the more so because they had neglected to win the support of the masses. Five of the most prominent 'Decembrists' (as they were called henceforth) were hanged. The rest were sent to Siberia. Yet in spite of its failure, this revolt from above became a landmark in the social history of Russia and a source of inspiration for all subsequent fighters for freedom.

Pushkin, who belonged to the same class of landed gentry, had a number of friends among the 'Decembrists' and was in fact their favourite poet. Quite a few of his earlier poems were permeated with the spirit of rebellion. One of these, *The Dagger* (*Kinzhal*), he dedicated to the German student Sand, who in 1819 stabbed to death the notorious reactionary and spy (in the Russian service) Kotzebue, otherwise known as one of the most popular German playwrights of that period. Sand's instrument of revenge, the dagger—a 'secret punisher of Freedom's rape'—is addressed by Pushkin in terms outspoken enough:

Like dart from Hell, or bolt by gods released,
The silent blade gleams in the tyrant's eyes;
   He trembles, as around he spies
   For death amidst the feast.

Where'er he be, thy point seeks out his sin:
On land, on sea, in temple, in the field,
   On passion's couch, among his kin,
   By secret locks concealed.

After the total defeat of the rebels, Pushkin's revolutionary zeal was temporarily cooled, yet his allegiance to the cause of freedom never faltered. In the very heyday of Nicholas's 'leaden regime' he wrote his Message to Siberia (addressed to his 'Decembrist' friends), which ends with the promise that eventually:

Will the heavy fetters fall,
The prison crumble; freedom's words
Will greet you by the dungeon wall.

3

The frustration among the younger intellectuals of the upper classes, who were still the guardians of Russian culture, can be imagined. Yet by some paradox of history it was in these years of reaction and oppression that Russia passed through her 'golden age' of poetry. The starting point was the publication of Pushkin's *Ruslán and Ludmíla* (1820), which brought him national fame. Here a fantastically romantic theme is treated with the classical discipline, detachment, and sparkling wit typical of the previous century. Pushkin's gaily sensuous acceptance of life is equally reminiscent of that easy-going age. But by the time this sprightly epic appeared its author had already been banished from Petersburg, because of some biting epigrams. He was exiled to the South of Russia from where he made a journey to the Caucasus and the Crimea. He was then transferred to Kishinyov in Bessarabia (where he lived much as he pleased). From there he went to the more civilised Odessa, and finally, in the summer of 1824, he was ordered to his mother's estate, Mikhailovskoe, in the North—not very far from Pskov.

This compulsory absence from Petersburg, apart from having prevented Pushkin from joining the December revolt, gave him enough leisure to deepen his literary interests and to bring his genius to maturity. The products of his exile were amazingly good and varied, however painful his loneliness must have been at times. But in the autumn of 1826 the poet was summoned by the Tsar's special courier to Moscow, where the coronation festivities were in full swing. Nicholas I received Pushkin amiably, pardoned his past 'transgressions', and cunningly offered to be the only censor of his future writings.

The Tsar's intention may have been to turn the foremost Russian poet into a glorifier of the reactionary regime. In this he failed, although, beguiled at first by his assumed friendliness, Pushkin became for a while quite well-disposed towards him personally. Entanglements with the Tsar and the Court, however involuntary on his part, assumed only a few years later a character which led to his tragic and premature death. It all started after his marriage (in 1831) to the beautiful but not over-intelligent Natalia Goncharova. Natalia was graciously (too graciously) noticed by the Tsar himself. In order to enable her to attend the exclusive court balls Nicholas in 1834 made her husband a 'gentleman of the chamber'—an office suitable for a youth of eighteen, but hardly for a man of thirty-five and a leading national poet into the bargain. It was obviously an affront, which Pushkin resented but could do nothing about.

Meanwhile, the queue of Natalia's admirers was on the increase, the Tsar himself being at the head of it. The most persistent was a certain d'Anthès —a French refugee with a commission in the Russian Guards, who, having been 'adopted' by the Dutch Ambassador, Baron Heeckeren (notorious as a sexual pervert and intriguer), was able to cut a fine figure in society. For some obscure reason Heeckeren did all he could to bring about a liaison between Natalia and his smart 'son'. Gossip and slander took their usual course. Disgusted with the 'gilded rabble', Pushkin thought of escaping to Mikhailovskoe, where he hoped to live in his own way—

> ... called to render
> Account to no one; free to serve and suit
> Oneself alone; not forced to bend one's neck,
> One's conscience, thoughts to livery and power,
> At liberty to wander here and there
> And savour all the beauty of creation.

But Natalia would have none of it. She was much too fascinated by the empty glitter of society, and it was made clear to the poet that the Tsar would be displeased by such an 'ungrateful' move. So Pushkin stayed on—he had to. Intrigue, with all its attendant scandal and gossip, gradually reached such proportions that he found it necessary to defend his wife's honour as well as his own. On 27 January, 1837, a duel between him and d'Anthès took place. Pushkin was mortally wounded and died, two days later, in his thirty-eighth year.

4

Despite such a short life, Pushkin left a great literary heritage in verse and prose. In both he showed a rare capacity for adapting himself to others in order to adapt them to himself. He came under a number of literary influences, without however succumbing to any of them. Having absorbed and digested them, he thereby increased the wide range and peculiar originality of his own genius. The strongest influences came from England and were connected with the names of Byron, Shakespeare and Sir Walter Scott. Yet all of them, while acting as stimuli, were remodelled by Pushkin in his own image.

Pushkin's Byronic period came after an earlier spell of French influences and was responsible for his four Byronic tales in verse, all written between 1821 and 1824: The Prisoner of the Caucasus (Kavkásskiy plénnik), The Fountain of Bakhchisaray (Bakhchisaráiskiy fontán), The Robber Brothers (Brátya razbóiniki), and The Gypsies (Tsygány). Of these only the second is entirely romantic. The other three, for all their romantic motifs, abound in that terse classical realism which was one of Pushkin's secrets. True enough, The Prisoner of the Caucasus introduced to Russia the uprooted Childe Harold type, but even this essentially romantic hero is shown in a realistic Caucasian setting. Later, in The Gypsies, he debunked the Rousseauesque gospel of an escape 'back to nature', or to a more primitive state of consciousness which has already been left behind by history and civilisation. Finally, Pushkin debunked also the romantically attired Byronic poseur—fashionable in those days even on the banks of the Neva—in his famous Evgény Onégin (1823–31).

This 'novel in verse', as Pushkin calls it, is his central and in several respects most typical creation. It was here that he overcame Byron on Byron's own ground. His first intention seems to have been to write a satirical equivalent of Byron's Don Juan. But having realised that the Russian censorship would never allow such a satire to appear in print, he wrote a less aggressive masterpiece instead. This is how he introduces its hero in the first chapter :

When Uncle, in good earnest, sickened
(His principles were always high),
My own respect for him was quickened;
'This was his happiest thought,' said I.
He was a pattern edifying;
Yet, heavens! how boring and how trying,
To tend a patient night and day
And never move a step away!
And then—how low the craft and gross is!—
I must amuse a man half-dead,
Arrange the pillows for his head,
And bring, with a long face, the doses
And sigh, and wonder inwardly,
'When will the Devil come for thee?'

Such were a young scamp's meditations,
Posting through dusty roads; for he
Was left sole heir to his relations
By Jupiter's supreme decree.
Without more words—my tale this minute
Begins, and has a hero in it.

The hero, who has thus inherited his rich uncle's estate, is Evgeny Onegin —a spoilt and blasé child of Petersburg society of the early 1820s, when romantic pose and priggishness were fashionable in the Russian capital. But Evgeny, a typical product of that atmosphere, remained the same cold prig in his provincial manor and appeared even more so among the unsophisticated landowning neighbours. It was here that he met Tatyana—a shy, inexperienced product of the country-house. She fell in love with Onegin, and it was she who first confessed (in a touching letter) how much she loved him. But a *faux pas* of this kind was enough to make the professional dandy wince. With a few commonplaces to the effect that he was so disappointed with life as to be unable to love anyone, he returned her the letter she had, with such trepidation, addressed to him. After months of boredom and ennui, during which Onegin in a silly duel kills his only friend, he—like Byron's Childe Harold—spends a few years travelling. Finally he returns to his former 'high life' in Petersburg. There he meets Tatyana once again: now a mature beauty married to an elderly dignitary and admired by all as one of the most charming members of that exclusive circle. This time it is Onegin who falls in love with her and, in his turn, keeps sending her letters which remain unanswered. When, in a fit of despair, he contrives to tell her personally about his feelings, she acknowledges with candour that she still loves him but intends to remain faithful to her husband, and she means it.

I entreat you, go:
You must; I know you animated,
At heart by honour; and your pride,

Integrity, will be your guide.
I love you (why sophisticate it?),
But am another's pledged, and I
To him stay constant, till I die.[1]

Thus frustration creeps into Onegin's fate which makes him feel out of place and superfluous in life. But as it happened this 'Muscovite in Childe Harold's cloak' started a whole series of 'superfluous men' in Russian fiction. However slender the plot of this 'novel in verse,' its art remains supreme from the first to the last line. The background of the 1820s is depicted so realistically that Pushkin's critic, Belinsky, saw in it 'a poetic picture of the whole of Russian society in one of the most interesting phases of its development. *Onégin* may be called an encyclopaedia of Russian life, and a national work in the highest degree.' The special 'Onegin' stanzas in which it is written (consisting of four-footed iambics and fourteen lines), lend themselves to a wide range of moods and states of mind.

Some of Pushkin's other narrative poems, such as the humorous *Count Núlin* (its theme is in the style of the eighteenth century *contes*) and *The Little House in Kolomna* (*Dómik v Kolómne*), are entirely realistic. The latter is even confined to a portrayal of lower middle-class characters, which was something of an innovation at the time. Different in plane and treatment however, are *Poltáva* and *The Bronze Horseman* (*Médny vsádnik*). Both of these deal with the larger destinies of Russia, while dwelling on the 'super-human' aspects of Peter the Great. *Poltava* combines two themes: the conflict between Russia and Sweden—in those days the most powerful maritime state in the North; and the tragedy of Maria Kochubey who had fallen in love with the aged Mazepa, a secret ally of the Swedish King Charles XII. Enticed far into Southern Russia, the Swedes and the treacherous Mazepa were beaten at Poltava (1709)—a victory which made Russia an indisputable European power. The appearance of Peter I among his soldiers during the battle of Poltava is described in a passage illustrating the condensed and dynamic matter-of-factness of Pushkin's poetry:

His eyes
Dart fire, his face commands surrender,
His steps are swift. The tempest's splendour
Alone with Peter's splendour vies.
He goes. They bring his charger, panting,
High-strung, yet ready to obey,
He scents the fire of the fray
And quivers. The blazing heat bores deeper,
the battle rests—a tired reaper.
The Cossack steeds, paraded, shine.
The regiments fall into line.
No martial music is redounding,

1. Translated by Oliver Elton (The Pushkin Press). Tchaikovsky's Opera, *Evgeny Onegin*, has made the contents of Pushkin's masterpiece known all over the world.

And from the hills the hungry roar
Of the calmed cannons breaks no more.
And lo! across the plain resounding,
A deep 'Hurrah!' roars from afar:
The regiments have seen the Tsar.[1]

The Bronze Horseman, commonly regarded as the greatest poem ever written in Russian, marks the height of Pushkin's poetic realism passing into the symbolic. The climax of the poem is a matchless picture of the flooding of Petersburg in 1824. During one of the severest gales the Neva—dammed and driven by the winds back up the gulf—suddenly began to flood the Petersburg streets and islands around the capital bringing panic and havoc in its trail. But instead of subsiding the storm only grew worse, while the swelling and roaring river

... like a maddened beast was hurled
Swift in the city. All things routed
Fled from its path, and about it
A sudden space was cleared; the flow
Dashed in the cellars down below;
Canals above their border spouted.
Behold Petropol floating lie
Like Triton in the deep waist-high!
A siege! The wicked waves attacking
Climb thief-like through the windows; backing
The boats stern-foremost, smite the glass,
Trays with their soaking wrappage pass.
And timbers, roofs, and huts all shattered,
The wares of thrifty traders scattered,
And the pale beggar's chattels small,
Bridges swept beneath the squall,
Coffins from sodden graveyards—all
Swim in the street![2]

The capital is at the mercy of the elements which have no regard for the works of man or for man himself. The number of victims grows. Yet Evgeny, an insignificant young *déclassé*, saves his life by clinging to one of the lions on the porch of the Senate House not far from the bronze monument of Peter the Great, the founder of the imperial city. Later he finds out that his sweetheart has perished in the disaster. He is so crushed by it that he loses his reason. A deranged vagrant, he wanders in the streets for weeks. One night he stops in the Square before Peter's statue and vaguely recollects all that has happened in the city whose founder now surges up like an evil demon on horseback. The mad-

1. Translated by Babette Deutsch in *The Works of Alexander Pushkin*, edited by Avrahm Yarmolinsky (Random House, N.Y.; Nonsuch Press, London).
2. Translated by Oliver Elton in *Verses by Pushkin and Others* (Arnold).

man flings curses at him and raises his fists. But here, in his dim mind, the bronze statue seems to have reared as though to attack and punish him. Frightened, Evgeny begins to run through the cobbled streets, all the time hearing the clatter of bronze hoofs behind him. It is not his business to question whether Peter, in his designs for Russia's destiny, had any moral right to disregard the happiness of the individual. Or, perhaps, it is! Pushkin only asks the question; but he does so with all the artistic power at his disposal.

5

While retaining the pattern of the Byronic tale in verse, Pushkin transcended Byron and took from him only what he needed for his own creative purposes. In a similar manner he absorbed the influence of Shakespeare, the principal result of which was his drama *Borís Godunóv*—now known all the world over because of Musorgsky's opera of the same title. Written at Mikhailovskoe in 1825, Boris Godunov was the first successful 'Shakespearian' play in Russian literature. It was not allowed to be printed until 1831, and even then it appeared in an expurgated form. Its first performance took place only in 1870. Pushkin took the subject matter from the 'troubled period' as presented in Karamzin's *History of the Russian Empire*. It is the story of the pretender False Dmitry (or Dimitry) who rose (with the help of the Poles) against the ruler Godunov—the supposed murderer of the Tsarevich Dmitry, heir to Ivan the Terrible. He modelled this work, written in five-footed iambics and blank verse, on 'our Father Shakespeare' largely in order to counteract the pseudo-classical plays which still lingered on the Russian stage. The result was an ably dramatised chronicle, in which (despite its title) the Pretender rather than Boris Godunov is the actual hero. While paying much attention to the 'convincingness of situations and naturalness of the dialogue', Pushkin also displayed here a surprising sense of history. Equally surprising was his understanding and treatment of the human characters. There is a great variety of dramatic scenes, twenty-four of them in all, and the dramatis personae represent all social layers: from the ruler Boris and the intriguing boyars to the comic monks in the tavern on the Lithuanian border; and from the venerable old chronicler in the Chudov monastery to the crowds of bemused ordinary citizens. In Poland again the Pretender Dmitry, who is being made use of by the Polish aristocrats for a war against Russia, falls so deeply in love with the beautiful Marina Mniszek (Mnishek) that he decides to reveal to her his actual identity (in the scene by the fountain in the garden):

> . . . carried away by pride
> I have deceived God and the kings—have lied
> To the world; but it is not for thee, Marina,
> To judge me; I am guiltless before thee.
> No, I could not deceive thee. Thou to me
> Wast the one sacred being, before thee

I dared not dissemble; love alone,
Love, jealous, blind, constrained me to tell all.

And when the ambitious Marina, full of disgust, turns proudly away from him, his tone too becomes equally proud, love or no love:

The phantom of the Terrible hath made me
Dimitry, hath stirred up the people round me,
And has consigned Boris to be my victim.
I am tsarevich.   Enough!   'Twere shame for me
To stoop before a haughty Polish dame.
Farewell for ever; the game of bloody war,
The wide cares of my destiny, will smother,
I hope, the pangs of love. O when the heat
Of shameful passion is o'erspent, how then
Shall I detest thee! Now I leave thee—ruin,
Or else a crown, awaits my head in Russia;
Whether I meet with death as fits a soldier
In honourable fight, or as a miscreant
Upon the public scaffold, thou shalt not
Be my companion, nor shalt share with me
My fate; but it may be thou shalt regret
The destiny thou hast refused.

Marina.   But what
If I expose beforehand thy bold fraud
To all men?

Pretender.   Dost thou think I fear thee? Think'st thou
They will believe a Polish maiden more
Than Russia's own tsarevich? Know, proud lady,
That neither king, nor pope, nor nobles trouble
Whether my words be true, whether I be
Dimitry or another. What care they?
But I provide a pretext for revolt
And war; and this is all they need; and thee,
Rebellious one, believe me, they will force
To hold thy peace. Farewell.

Marina.   Tsarevich, stay!
At last I hear the speech not of a boy,
But of a man.[1]

Without quoting any further passages, one can say that, although *Borís Godunóv* was based on the pattern of Shakespeare's History Plays, its condensed 'natural dialogue' was Pushkin's. This play was not his only contribution to the Russian drama. The four miniature plays, which he finished in the autumn of 1830, are small in size but not in artistic value. Here again English stimuli were

1. Translated by A. Hayes (Kegan Paul, Dutton).

at work. It was Barry Cornwall's now almost forgotten *Dramatic Scenes* that suggested to Pushkin the idea of writing his own series of 'little tragedies'. One of these, *The Feast at the Time of the Plague* (*Pir vo vrémya chumý*), was taken from John Wilson's *The City of the Plague* (1816) and paraphrased into a Russian masterpiece in blank verse. Pushkin intended to write at least ten miniature plays of this kind, but finished only four. Each of them deals with one of the cardinal human passions. *In Mozart and Salieri* it is envy; in *The Miser Knight* (*Skupóy rýtsar'*)—avarice and will to power; in *The Stone Guest* (*Kámenny gost'*) it is carnal lust; while the scene taken from *The Feast at the Time of the Plague* is worked out to stress man's defiance of fate in the very teeth of death.

Knowing full well that these themes had been widely used in European literature before him, Pushkin decided not to repeat what had been said already, but to show them in a new light and from a new angle, which he succeeded in doing. In these short plays he created (again under the influence of Shakespeare) such complex characters as the Hamlet-like Salieri (the supposed poisoner of Mozart in the first of the four 'little tragedies'), and the hero of *The Miser Knight*, so different from Molière's Harpagon and interesting enough to have inspired, later on, one of the 'ideas' in Dostoevsky's novel *A Raw Youth*. He is like a Rothschild in a beggar's garb, which makes him all the more aware of his paradoxical power, as one can judge by the end of his famous monologue in the cellar, amidst coffers stuffed with ducats:

What does not own my sway? I, like some demon,
From here can dominate the universe.
I have but to wish. Palaces rise straightway,
And through the thickets of my glorious gardens
Fair nymphs go running in a merry crowd.
The Muses bring their tribute to my feet.
Free Genius is my slave and works for me.
Virtue and Toil, labouring sleeplessly,
Will humbly wait on me for recompense.
I shall but whistle and submissively
Will bloodstained Crime come crawling to my feet,
Timidly lick my hand, look in my eyes,
And read in them the signal of my will.
All shall be subject to me, I to nothing.
Out-stripping all desires I shall know peace.
I understand my power; this knowledge
Will be enough for me.[1]

Pushkin's beautiful but not entirely finished poetic play *The Water Fairy* (*Rusálka*) can only be mentioned in passing. Here the central idea of retribution is intertwined with Russian folklore, the spirit and the flavour of which he had splendidly rendered in his *Fairy-Tales* (*Skázki*) in verse.

1. Translated by V. de Sola Pinto and W. Marshall.

6

In addition to his poetic activities Pushkin was a pioneer of modern Russian prose. Here too, as in poetry and drama, he acted as a creative intermediary between English and Russian literatures. This time it was Sir Walter Scott who served as a stimulus for Pushkin's narratives: *The Negro of Peter the Great* (*Aráp Petrá Velíkogo*—unfinished, 1828), *Dubróvsky* (1833, first published in 1841) and *A Captain's Daughter* (*Kapitánskaya dóchka*, 1836).

The first of these dealt with Pushkin's Abyssinian maternal great-grand-father, Hannibal. Pushkin never went beyond the initial five chapters, but even within so small a compass he gave a fine picture of early eighteenth-century manners, as well as a portrait of Peter the Great in his homelier and more human moods. *Dubróvsky* (not quite completed either) is based on a romantic plot; its central figure is a polished young gentleman who has turned brigand in order to avenge the wrongs done to his father by an unscrupulous feudal neighbour. The dramatic incidents, slightly reminiscent at times of *The Bride of Lammer-moor*, are set against the background of the uncouth provincial gentry in the reign of Catherine II. Pushkin's principal work in prose, *A Captain's Daughter* depicts the same period but on a larger scale. Its subject matter is the rising of the Ural Cossacks against Catherine II under the leadership of the illiterate peasant Pugachov, who gave himself out to be the supposedly escaped Tsar Peter III (Catherine's 'liquidated' husband), and for a while threatened a con-siderable portion of the central and lower Volga region. The narrative is much shorter than any of the Waverley Novels, and its style, modelled on clear eighteenth-century prose, is enlivened by Pushkin's inimitable touch and inflec-tion. A similar result might have been expected if one of Scott's novels had been written or rewritten, say, by Jane Austen. The whole of it has the character of a 'family chronicle' narrated in the first person by a young nobleman whose fate became strangely entangled with that of Pugachov and of his semi-Asiatic *Jácquerie*. Pushkin's research into the events described in this novel is recorded in his *History of Pugachóv*, which he began with his studies in the State archives and completed on a journey to the regions concerned. *A Captain's Daughter* was, of course, not the first historical novel in Scott's manner in Russia. Mikhail Zagoskin's would-be historical *Yury Miloslávsky* or *The Russians in 1612* (1829) —a readable novel about the 'troubled period'—enjoyed quite a vogue; so did Ivan Lazhechnikov's *The Last Nóvik* (1831-33) about the time of Peter the Great, and *The Ice Hut* (*Ledyanóy dómik*, 1835) set in the period of the Empress Anna. The pseudo-historical romances by Alexander Bestuzhev-Marlinsky (1797-1837), a former 'Decembrist' exiled in the Caucasus and writing in a rather flowery language, were much relished by the average reader.

Among Pushkin's other prose writings *The Tales of Belkin* (*Póvesti Bélkina*, 1830) and *The Queen of Spades* (*Píkovaya dáma*, 1833) enjoy a deservedly high reputation. The five tales, supposed to have been told by the 'late Ivan Petrovich Belkin'—a simple, pathetic, yet appealingly comic figure, are reduced to their 'naked' essentials, while yet skilfully preserving the narrator's tone and manner. One of these tales, *The Posting-Station Master* (*Stantsiónny smotrítel'*) was not without influence upon subsequent Russian narratives in so far as it introduced the insignificant 'little man' into Russian fiction. The would-be narrator Belkin himself is such a 'little man', and his touching comicality becomes even more pronounced when we meet him, once again, as the compiler of Pushkin's post-humous unfinished satire on the serfdom system in A History of the Village Goryukhino (Istóriya selá Goryúkhina).

An amazing example of Pushkin's prose is The Queen of Spades, in which his art of the naked word is displayed to even better advantage than in his other prose works. A fantastic Hoffmannesque anecdote about a gambler, who in a mysterious way obtains the secret of winning at cards a large sum of money but loses the whole of it at his last stake and goes mad, is here worked out with incredible economy and detachment. Last but not least, Pushkin's prose style scintillates in his letters—the finest in Russian literature.

7

When all is said and done, Pushkin seems to refute our current ideas about a 'Russian' genius. It would be futile to look in him for any morbid introspection, or for the passionate questing typical of Dostoevsky and Tolstoy. In his artistic detachment, at any rate, he was so balanced that he is frequently referred to as a Hellene of the North. It was the broadness as well as the sanity of his genius that made him so universal. This enabled him to graft his own late humanist universality upon the belles lettres of Russia which he turned into a significant and highly creative part of European literature as a whole. Having made use of the previous literary achievements of his country, he opened up new possibili-ties, the consequences of which were far-reaching. There is not a single impor-tant genre in which he did not excel or produce something memorable, and the number of new themes which he introduced helped to enlarge the area of Rus-sian literature beyond all recognition. It was he, too, who directed it towards that simple yet monumental realism which became one of its most prominent characteristics in the second half of the nineteenth century.

Finally, in spite of being a supreme example of upper-class culture in Russia, Pushkin helped to impart to the literary creations of his country a decidedly democratic and, in his early period, even revolutionary trend. He was the first Russian poet to be read by all social classes. And when Russian litera-ture, in the course of its growth, diversified into a number of trends and cur-rents, Pushkin was accepted as the standard of aesthetic values and also as a symbol of cultural continuity up to our own day.

'Pushkin is our all,' said Apollon Grigoryev—one of the eminent Russian critics and poets in the middle of the last century. And Pushkin's work, far from having aged since then, is still as vital as ever. He is the most widely read classic in Russia and because of the intrinsic value of his work, he deserves to be more widely known and read outside his own country.

8

Pushkin was the apex of the 'golden age' of Russian poetry. But when he died, the Russian Parnassus was not devoid of poets trying to keep up the high standard set by him. Among the older poets Krylov was still alive and active. The spirited warrior poet Denis Davydov (1784-1839), the religious bard Fyodor Glinka (1786-1880), the polished and cultured defender of romanticism Prince Peter Vyazemsky (1792-1878), not to mention Zhukovsky, were all making valuable contributions to Russian poetry in its 'golden age'. Konstantin N. Batyushkov wrote some important poetry but lost his reason in 1821, after which he remained silent. Ivan I. Kozlov (1779-1840) began to write rather late —after having gone blind. He achieved considerable success with his Byronic narrative poem *The Monk* (*Chernéts*) in 1825, but his subsequent *Natálya Dolgorúkaya* and *The Mad Girl* (*Sumasshédshaya*) found less favour with the readers. He is still remembered for his beautiful version of Thomas Moore's *The Evening Bells*.

As for Pushkin's actual *pléiade*, Baron A. A. Delvig's (1798–1831) poetic output was small but technically perfect. He excelled in sonnets, idyllic verse, and in 'Russian songs', i.e., literary stylisations in the manner of folksongs (fashionable already towards the end of the eighteenth century). He died nearly six years before Pushkin. William Kuechelbecker (1797–1846) who, like Delvig, had been Pushkin's school-friend at Tsarskoye Selo, was a fine critic and wrote philosophic as well as civic verses. Together with that other civic poet, Kondraty Ryleyev (executed in 1826), he too had belonged to the 'Decembrists' and ended his days in Siberia. As far as sheer quality is concerned, Evgeny Baratynsky often came near to Pushkin in perfection. His lyrics are charged with intensified thought, and his innate realistic sense is at its best in such narrative poems as *Eda* and *The Ball*. He spent five years as a soldier in Finland (his *Eda* is based upon a Finnish motif) whose sombre beauty he much admired. His most typical collection of poems has the title of *Twilight* (*Súmerki*). It reflects his pessimistic view of life and was published only two years before his sudden death at Naples in 1844 at the age of forty-four. A more cheerful and exuberant poet was Nikolai M. Yazykov (1803-46)—a lover of wine and women, and full of a boisterous *joie de vivre*. His rhythmical and verbal wealth threatened to overwhelm him at times, but in the end he always mastered it 'as an Arab masters his fiery steed' (to use Gogol's phrase). He joined the Slavophil party, but his Slavophil and nationalist verses are less impressive than his personal lyrics.

An interesting phenomenon among the poets of this generation was Alexey V. Kol'tsov (1809–42). He was the son of a cattle-dealer at Voronezh and never had any formal education, but his natural gift for poetry led him to write from a surprisingly early age. His verses in the manner of folk-songs were novel in that they portrayed everyday life—peasant work, ploughing and mowing, harvests, village life and the broad expanse of the steppe—in forms derived from the rich, melodious rhythms of the songs of the Russian people. Another talented, though very different young poet who left a mark on Russian literature, in spite of dying at the age of twenty-two, was Dmitry V. Venevitinov

(1805-27)—a member of the Moscow 'wisdom lovers' (*lyubomúdry*) who were strongly influenced by German idealism, especially by the philosopher Schelling. He, like Pushkin, was in sympathy with the 'Decembrists', but wrote mainly philosophical and metaphysical verses.

Among the less known poets, such as A. Polezhayev and Prince A. Odoyevsky (both of whom were exiled to the Caucasus, where they died young), one ought to mention Carolina Pavlova née Jänisch (1807–93), who was German by birth but became a Russian poetess with an intimate and contemplative style. She was also a good translator from Russian into German, and vice versa. But on the whole, after Pushkin's death the taste and the high quality typical of the 'golden age' began to decline. An example of this decline was the immense popularity of the 'drawing-room' poet Vladimir Benediktov whose facile and fluent verses were relished by the average bourgeois reader. Still, at the time when general interest was shifting from poetry to prose, there remained two names to be reckoned with: Lermontov and Tyutchev. Both are great enough to deserve special treatment.

CHAPTER SEVEN

Nikolai Gogol

I

When Pushkin died, Russian literature rested on firm foundations of its own. Yet the interest in poetry and the high standard of craftsmanship which typified the Pushkin era were, from the 1840s onward, less conspicuous. As compensation a mighty wave of prose set in, and the leadership in Russian letters now fell upon the shoulders of the great prose-writer of that period, Nikolai Vasilyevich Gogol (1809-1852) who in almost every way was a strange contrast to Pushkin. Whereas Pushkin marked the apex of the upper-class period in Russian culture, Gogol's creative activities coincided with the formation of the intelligentsia, led by the critic Belinsky (1811-48). Pushkin, who was a classical realist even in his romantic works, had felt at home in the world, however much he may have disliked some of its aspects. Gogol, on the other hand, was so maladjusted and frightened of what he saw that he was never in harmony with surrounding reality. This attitude is conspicuous in his works. Primitive, archaically primitive at times, but never simple, he became the first enigmatic figure in modern Russian literature—a puzzled questioner for whom creative writing was a process of self-examination, self-defence, and catharsis all in one, and which presented the artist in him with two alternatives: one romantically escapist, the other searchingly and aggressively realistic. He started his literary career with the former approach, but finished it with the latter. This was logical, since the two attitudes are often complementary.

A disappointed and maladjusted idealist of Gogol's stamp, who is haunted by life to such an extent as to be unable to find a shelter even in romanticism, may in the end turn art itself into a 'realistic' weapon for self-defence. And the greater his romantic rancour against the reality he is unable to accept or to alter, the stronger will be his realism of indictment. His bitter laughter will be a revenge upon reality which—in the end—he will try to show up as something ridiculously vulgar and unworthy of acceptance.

Such an attitude is typical of Gogol's later writings and in fact of his whole style. For in contrast to Pushkin's disciplined calm, the style of Gogol is agitated, emphatic, full of superlatives, and always ready to pass from solemn and at times almost hypnotic exuberance, to a realistic accumulation of details, especially if these can be twisted and distorted into something grotesquely comic. His ornate, lyrical passages verge on rhetoric, the pitfalls of which he avoids thanks to his uncanny sense of verbal rhythm and music. At the same time the realism of his description of the *petits faits* and deformities of life is unforgettable, precisely on account of his comic exaggeration. All this makes Gogol one of the most puzzling figures between the romantic and the realistic periods in literature —puzzling both as man and writer since, in his case, it would be impossible to separate one from the other. A few biographical data may be helpful in our approach.

2

He was born at Sorochintsy in 1809 into an impoverished Ukrainian land-owning family of Cossack stock, and spent his childhood in the idyllic countryside near Poltava. From 1821 until 1828 he was educated at the *lycée* in Nezhin. Then he lived for some eight years in Petersburg, which represented the greatest possible contrast to his warm and sunny Ukraine. The years between 1836 and 1848 he spent chiefly in Rome—always dear to his romantic temperament. In 1849 he returned to Russia and stayed for the most part in Moscow, where he died in February, 1852.

Small and unimpressive in appearance, Gogol was of a nervous disposition. As though under the weight of a social and moral 'inferiority complex', he became morbidly touchy and always ready to attack in others the defects from which he himself suffered or thought he suffered. This fostered not only his gift of observation (confined mainly to negative features), but also that intensely satirical and ridiculing vein which became so conspicuous in his writings. At the same time he was anxious to counter, even as a schoolboy, the feeling of inferiority by compensatory day-dreams of future greatness. While still at Nezhim, he indulged in visions of a brilliant career waiting for him round the corner. It may have been with such high hopes that, at the age of nineteen, Gogol went to Petersburg. It did not take long, though, for a naïve provincial youth of his type to discover that without money and connections he was less than a nobody in that cold and inhospitable city. Having tried his luck repeatedly without success, he decided to flee to America. He took a boat to Luebeck, but as the money at his disposal was soon exhausted, he had to return to the Russian capital and make new efforts to find a living. This time he obtained a humble underpaid post in one of the Government offices.

A victim of circumstances and disillusionment, Gogol—like so many other sons of the impoverished landed gentry—was in danger of becoming a failure, a social *déclassé*. But chance intervened. He used to write in the school magazines while still at the *lycée*, and now he renewed his literary efforts chiefly as a means of escape from the dreary reality preying upon him. The tales he had once heard from his Cossack grandfather, the picturesque life and folklore of the Ukrainian people, the sun-drenched landscape of the south, the banks of the Dnieper, the expanse of the steppe—all this came back to his memory with an alluring halo and shaped itself into a number of stories which he wrote down on the spur of the moment. Published (1831-32) in two volumes under the general title, *Evenings on a Farm near Dikanka* (*Vecherá na khútore bliz*

Dikánki), they were an immediate success. Their appeal was enhanced by their ethnographic and folkloristic flavour, which happened to be the fashion of the day. In spite of certain touches of Tieck and of Hoffmann, Gogol's romanticism, as exemplified here, had all the colourfulness of the Ukrainian countryside. The same holds good of his boisterous humour. The compositors setting the text were so amused by some of the passages that their laughter is supposed to have interfered with their work. Furthermore, the rhythm, the tone and the texture of Gogol's prose brought a new note into Russian fiction, which the readers were by no means slow to appreciate. While dexterously blending romantic themes with the spirit of folklore, Gogol created an ornate style of his own. His pages were full of verbal embroideries as though he wanted to lull himself into a trance by the pattern and music of his own language. The first story, *The Fair of Sorochintsy* (*Soróchinskaya yármarka*)[1] opens with a description of a Ukrainian summer day, abounding in so many superlatives and metaphors that, but for its musical quality, it would resemble a rhetorical improvisation. The moods and the motifs of this collection vary, and after situations full of boisterous fun and gaiety, one comes across such a story as *A Cruel Vengeance* (*Stráshnaya mest'*), which is more gruesome than any of the tales of Edgar Allan Poe. Constructed in the form of a folk-ballad and told in a language redolent of poetry, it is full of a magic of its own, emanating from Gogol's own sense of verbal rhythm. It also points to some rather disturbing 'complexes' in the writer himself, who thus found at least a temporary relief in his art.

In the whole volume there is only one story, *Ivan Shponka and his Aunty* (*Iván Fyódorovich Shpón'ka i egó tyótushka*), in which realistic details prevail. But, significantly enough, Gogol left it unfinished, although here already he showed that Hogarth-like quality which, in some of his works, he developed to perfection. The humour and the buffoonery of *Evenings* often abound in an over-loud gaiety which he probably wanted to be both a refuge and a tonic. He himself said a few years later: 'The cause of that gaiety which has been noticed in my first works was an inner need. I became a prey to fits of melancholy which were beyond my comprehension. . . . In order to get rid of them I invented funny characters in the funniest situations imaginable.'

But the word 'invented' is perhaps not quite right, since Gogol's capacity for invention was much weaker than his imagination. Instead of inventing complicated themes or plots of his own, he usually organised and intensified those he had heard from other people. And as for realism, his propensity for grotesque and satirical distortion is not yet imbued with that rancour which became so conspicuous in his works soon after *Evenings*. Externally, Gogol's 'realistic' manner has quite a few aspects reminiscent of Dickens; yet it would be wrong to compare the two in the way that is often done. For one thing, Dickens is devoid of Gogol's incurable rancour with regard to life; hence he can be affirmative even when he ridicules. The 'realism' of Gogol, on the other hand, is that of a wounded and frustrated romantic. Its inner motivation has certain affinities with the negative realism of Gustave Flaubert or of Thomas Hardy, however different his reactions otherwise may have been. His next

1. It was turned by Borodin into an opera.

collection of four narratives published under the title *Mírgorod* (1835) deserve further inquiry.

3

These stories, which at first look like a continuation of *Evenings*, mark the dividing line between the romantic and the realistic manner in Gogol's art. Two of them, *Tarás Búl'ba* and *Viy*, are romantic in the extreme, while the other two, *The Old-World Landowners* (*Starosvétskie poméshchiki*) and *The Story about the Quarrel between Ivan Ivanovich and Ivan Nikiforovich* (*Póvest' o tom, kak possórilsya Iván Ivánovich s Ivánom Nikíforovichem*) are—technically at least—realistic.

Taras Bul'ba is above all a splendidly romantic record of the Cossack past. Although inspired by the *Waverley Novels*, it is spun out in Gogol's ornate and agitated manner at its best. As in *A Cruel Vengeance*, the Cossack lore is turned into a narrative reminiscent of balladic poetry. The old Cossack leader Taras, the executioner of his own son, who (prompted by his love for a beautiful Polish girl) had gone over to the enemy, might have been taken straight from an Ukrainian or Cossack *dúma* (folk-ballad). Some other figures—the comic Jew Yankel and the swaggering Poles—have much in common with the traditional Ukrainian puppet show for the people. The whole of it is told with unflagging verve, and some descriptive passages—the night in the steppe, for example, the riotous Cossack life in Syetch, the scenes of starvation in the beleaguered Polish fortress, the battle episodes—are unforgettable. This work is often referred to, and perhaps rightly so, as the Cossack *Iliad*.

A romantic flavour of the same macabre variety as in *A Cruel Vengeance* emanates from the story *Viy*. According to Gogol's (not quite reliable) statement, Viy is the name of a symbolic monster taken from Ukrainian folklore. But the nightmarish monster, as represented here, is the projection of certain fears and phobias stored up in Gogol's own subconscious. The story is as complex as the two realistic narratives included in the volume are simple in their subject-matter. In *The Old-World Landowners* there is hardly a plot at all. It is a genre picture (in the Dutch manner) depicting the Ukrainian equivalent of Darby and Joan, whose thoughts never go beyond the fence of their orchard. The principal function of their idyllic life is eating and sleeping, yet both of them are contented and so touchingly attached to each other that when the old Pulkheria suddenly dies, her husband is past consolation and follows her soon after. It seems as though Gogol had put into this story his own romantic nostalgia for a haven of peace, even a vegetative peace, as a contrast to the turmoil of the metropolitan existence he had to endure in St Petersburg.

The same kind of vegetative atmosphere permeates the opening chapter of the quarrel between the two Ivans, but this time from a different angle. Nostalgia is here replaced by invective. The plot is again slender and, such as it is, borrowed from the older Ukrainian writer, Narezhny. The story depicts two bosom friends who for some idiotic reason quarrel and start a series of law suits against each other, dragging on and on until both are ruined. Here, for the first time, Gogol's comic laughter turned into that proverbial 'laughter through tears' which, from now on, clung to him with an increasingly sinister ring. His Hogarthian realism made him depict the negative features of his characters, as well as of life in general, with all the indignation of a wounded romantic idealist. The gloom and sadness which lurk behind this otherwise comic story protrude plainly enough towards the end, the author's departure from Mirgorod providing a final touch.

> The lean nags famous in Mirgorod as post-horses began to stamp their hoofs, which were buried in a grey mass of mud, with a sound displeasing to the ear. The rain poured in torrents upon the Jew seated on the box, covered with a rug. The dampness penetrated to my very bones. The dreary barrier with the sentry, an old soldier repairing his weapons, was passed slowly by. Once again the same fields, black in the places where they had been dug up, and of a greenish hue in others; wet daws and crows; monotonous rain, a tearful sky, without one gleam of light! . . . A gloomy place —this world, gentlemen!

4

'A gloomy place—this world, gentlemen,' became from now on Gogol's motto as well as his basic disposition. But he countered it by the laughter in which he sought both an escape from life and a revenge upon it. Unable to escape from reality, he tried to fight it by ridiculing its ugliness and drabness, which he did with all the vindictiveness at his disposal. From his Petersburg stories onwards Gogol's romantic temperament often took on a realistic garb. Three of these stories, A Portrait, The Nevsky Prospect and The Diary of a Madman (Zapíski sumasshédshego) appeared in his miscellany, Arabesques (1835). The Nose (Nos) was written about the same period, and his famous Greatcoat (Shinél') some four or five years later.

The least satisfactory from an artistic standpoint is A Portrait. Its romanticism may remind one of E. T. A. Hoffmann's Die Elexiere des Teufels, or of Maturin's Melmoth the Wanderer (which Gogol had read in a Russian translation). On the other hand, the story contains some of Gogol's own dilemmas and inhibitions, one of them being his belief in the demoniacal forces of evil inherent in life as a whole. We find in it also the elements of his subsequent conception of art as a promoter of moral good. Similarly revealing is The Nevsky Prospect, which expresses Gogol's frustrated idealism perhaps more directly than any other narrative. The very antithesis between the two main characters—one of them an incurable gay vulgarian and the other an incurable dreamer—only serves to point out the incompatibility of beauty and of life as it is.

Apart from his 'romantic irony', Gogol introduces here the background of Petersburg in its negative and de-humanising aspects. These come out even more potently in *The Diary of a Madman* and *The Greatcoat*, depicting the two varieties of the same 'little man': the humble office drudge, victimised by the big city—a predicament that (but for a lucky chance) Gogol might well have been in himself. While working in the Government office he was able to study this type from personal observation. Hence the detailed concreteness of his portrayal.

However insignificant in life, Poprishchin— the hero of *The Diary of a Madman*—does not surrender to his fate. He entrenches himself behind all sorts of wishful thinking and day-dreams, the object of which is the daughter of his omnipotent chief. He is deeply in love with her, although the pretty girl does not even condescend to notice his existence. This plunges him all the more into his compensatory dream-world, duly recorded in his diary. The heavier the blows he has to endure, the stronger his self-concocted antidote becomes. And when hearing at last that his idol has become betrothed to one of those 'social betters' whose hollow glitter is despised—in his opinion—even by dogs, his imaginary grandeur takes on the size of his defeat: he is no longer an underpaid scribe, but His Majesty Ferdinand VIII, the fugitive King of Spain. His manners assume at once a style worthy of such an exalted status. Even when he is taken to the lunatic asylum, he sees and interprets everything only in this light. During the painful manipulations he is compelled to undergo there, the truth as to his real condition flashes through his mind, but only for a moment. The world of madness closes upon him once again, and this time for good.

Akaky, the hero of *The Greatcoat*, is another Poprishchin, but he has been battered enough by life to accept his own humble status without grumbling. The only ambition which remains to him is to scrape enough money together to buy a fashionable greatcoat—with marten collar and all. With difficulty he makes his dream come true. One morning he enters the office in a smart greatcoat—like a real somebody. General surprise at this is crowned by his being invited to an evening party. At the party he drinks much more than is good for him and leaves the company rather late at night. While crossing a lonely square, he is suddenly knocked unconscious by two individuals. Coming to his senses he sees no trace either of the thieves or of his greatcoat. Full of despair Akaky falls ill and dies of grief. Such is the gist of this masterpiece of *Kleinmalerei*, which had quite a strong influence on the development of Russian realism.

Gogol's last Petersburg story, *The Nose*, can best be described as a satirical fantasy constructed on the pattern of a dream—something like Alice in Wonderland, but probably suggested by the 'nosological' passages in *Tristram Shandy* (he knew it from a Russian version). Devoid of any surface logic, it is yet—like *A Cruel Vengeance* and *Viy*—of great value to anyone interested in the working of the subconscious mind, and especially in the meeting point between psychoanalysis and literature. Its amusingly grotesque jumble hides what has been called Gogol's castration complex, as well as a few other peculiarities of his slightly irregular sex life. In this respect it is connected with certain passages of Poprishchin's gibberish in *The Diary of a Madman*, notably with those describing the earth falling upon the moon.

5

Further aspects of Gogol's art can be gleaned from his comedy, *The Government Inspector* (*Revizór*, 1836), and his novel *Dead Souls*, (*Myórtvye dúshi*, 1842), both of which occupy a very high place in Russian literature. The plots for these two works were not invented by Gogol—they were suggested to him by Pushkin; yet Gogol turned them into masterpieces in which, among other things, he gave full scope to his 'laughter through tears'. In *The Government Inspector*, his laughter assumed, moreover, a deliberately castigating role. He himself acknowledged in his *An Author's Confession*:

> I saw that in my former works I laughed in vain, uselessly, without know-ing why. But if we must laugh, why not laugh at what really deserves to be laughed at by us all. In my *Government Inspector* I decided to bring together and to deride all that is bad in Russia, all the evils which are being perpetrated in those places where utmost rectitude is required from man.

Here Gogol's attention was focused on the corrupt bureaucracy, and with so much malice that this comedy rightly belongs to the most biting specimens of its kind. The plot is simple: an irresponsible windbag, Khlestakov by name, who, together with his servant, travels from St Petersburg to his father's country estate, loses all his money at cards in a provincial hole and is in danger of being put into jail for his inability to pay the hotel bill. At that very time the *gorodníchy* (police governor) of the town awaits (by virtue of some secret infor-mation) the incognito arrival of the Government Inspector, the very thought of whom makes him shudder. And he knows why. Nor are the other officials in an elated state of mind, and they also know why. Two of the local worthies, who have just seen the starving Khlestakov in the restaurant wistfully inspecting other people's meals, come upon the idea that the inquisitive, smartly dressed stranger must be the dreaded Inspector. Unanimously, the officials decide to bribe him, and the *gorodníchy*—an expert in these matters—goes personally to the hotel in order to perform the time-honoured ritual. Frightened at first by the visit and then puzzled by it, Khlestakov soon regains his aplomb and enters into his new role with relish. He is feted, bribed, shown the specially dolled-up institutions of the town, and finally even becomes betrothed to the *gorodníchy's* daughter. Khlestakóv's sagacious servant guesses, however, that the worthy citizens must have mistaken his master for someone of consequence, and urges him to leave the hospitable town before it is too late. So the would-be inspector departs—his head full of pleasant memories and his pockets bulging with money. He promises, of course, to be back in time for the wedding. The *gorod-níchy's* arrogance is now unbounded. Puffed up by dreams of his future great-ness under the wing of such a mighty son-in-law, he now bullies the towns-people more than ever. All the 'notables' are so anxious to ingratiate them-selves that they hurry, together with their spouses, to congratulate the great man. It is a crowded gathering. But suddenly, like a bolt from the blue, the truth leaks out that the Inspector is a nobody. The local postmaster, always willing to enlighten himself by opening and reading other people's letters, could not resist opening the one Khlestakov had written (to a friend in Petersburg) boasting in the frankest terms of all the good things that had befallen him in that blessed town. As the intercepted letter (full of zoological references to the 'revizor's' benefactors) has been brought and read by the postmaster to the gathering, its effect can be imagined. But when the general consternation is at its height, a gendarme enters with the announcement that the real Government Inspector has just arrived and demands an immediate interview with the *gorod-nichy*. Here the curtain slowly falls.

The Government Inspector is a condensed picture of all the rottenness, corruption, and stupidity of that bureaucratic Russia which Gogol could not endure. The portraiture is, once more, thoroughly Hogarthian. As a satirical comedy of manners, the play continued the tradition which had started with Fonvizin and reached something of a climax in Griboyedov's *Woe from Wit*. It was bound to be an event in the 'leaden' atmosphere of the Nicholas regime. The first performance, on 19 March, 1836, took place by special command of the Tsar himself who, by a sudden caprice, came personally to see what it was like. 'Everyone has received his due, and I most of all,' Nicholas I is reported to have said after the performance. But the gall contained in the comedy was too much for those concerned. A hue and cry was raised against Gogol and before long assumed such proportions that he preferred to leave Russia alto-gether. He settled down in Rome, where he remained, with various inter-ruptions, until 1842. There he finished two more plays, *Marriage* (*Zhenít'ba*) and *Gamblers* (*Igrokí*). The first is a farcical comedy set against the background of the old-world merchants whose rich daughters were a bait for government officials and especially for noblemen, financially—and otherwise—gone to seed. The second is based on the cleverly constructed theme of cheating the cheat, with an impressive dénouement. It was in Rome, too, that Gogol completed the first volume of his *Dead Souls*.

6

This novel, which at once gained its rightful place in the world of letters, is difficult to classify. Gogol himself called it an epic (*poéma*). Like some of his other works, it is devoid of an involved plot and even the love motif, usually essential in a novel, is absent. The chapters follow one another like those of a picaresque narrative, the episodes of which are connected by the central charac-ter—a rogue, a travelling adventurer, or both. The book should really be called *Dead Serfs*; but as serfs were called 'souls' in Russia, its title has both a business-like and a symbolic meaning. Chichikov, the hero of the novel, is a travelling businessman and swindler, but with the bearing of an immaculate gentleman. The aim of his journey is to buy up a number of those serfs who have died so recently that they have not yet been struck off the register and are therefore officially recorded as being still alive. 'Now is the time,' he reasons, 'there has just been an epidemic, peasants have died, thank goodness, in great numbers.' Chichikov's intention is to mortgage such fictitious serfs in a bank for a substantial sum of money, after which he would disappear and start a respectable and comfortable existence in some province sufficiently remote to hide his past. This would hardly be too difficult, since his manners and appearance are so winning that everybody is charmed by him at first. In the provincial town chosen by him as the starting point for his enterprise, he is simply worshipped during his initial stay. But he has no time for adulation. He means business, and so a visiting tour to those landowners in the district who might be of use to him is a matter of urgency.

His interviews are achieved in Gogol's style at its best. The squires visited by Chichikov—the sentimental fool Manilov; the subhuman Sobakevich;[1] the miser Plyushkin; the batty widow Korobochka; the professional cheat and scandalmonger Nozdryov—they all parade in front of us like so many caricatures of humanity, seen with the eyes of a Hogarth or a Breughel. What increases the comicality of Chichikov himself is the contrast between the gentlemanliness of his appearance on the one hand, and the criminal nature of his errand on the other. Realising the delicate task he is engaged in, he broaches the subject with due circumspection, but his manoeuvres invariably lead up to the question whether and how many dead 'souls' are available—the kind of groping which, apart from its comic touches, is bound to give away the moral level of both the visitor and his host. In the end Chichikov's eagerness to get rich quick outstrips even his caution : he blurts out a word too much where silence would have been best. As a result the news about his strange purchases leaks out; and the same town which at first welcomed him as a paragon of charm, is all at once astir with the wildest rumours about his doings and even his identity. Sensible enough to clear out while the going is good, Chichikov makes a hasty departure in his *tróika* (a carriage drawn by three horses) at the end of the first volume—the only one that Gogol finished. Quite unexpectedly, the concluding note is a personal and lyrical digression on the part of Gogol himself. In contrast to the general mood of the work the conclusion strikes (in a major key and a manner which can serve as an example of Gogol's emotional style) a paean to the *tróika* and the wide open spaces of Russia. In the same passage, Gogol addresses Russia with a question which all her great authors have been asking since—asking in vain. But here is the passage itself :

'Chichikov was fond of fast driving, and as he rocked on the leather cushion he only smiled at the bumps. And what Russian does not love fast driving? And how should his soul not love it? For is he not prone to surrender to the sudden whirl of a spree? Is he not liable to cast discretion to the winds, saying 'the devil take it all' ? And therefore is not fast driving his delight? How can he not love its magic and incantation? And is not a galloping troika like a mysterious force that has swept you away on its wings, so that you find yourself flying along, and everything else is flying with you?

1.   From the word *sobáka*, the dog. Like Dickens, Gogol was a master at inventing suggestive names, most of which are untranslatable.

The milestones fly past to meet you, the merchants in their carts are flying by, on each side of you forests of dark fir and pine-trees are flying past to the thump of axes and the croaking of crows, the whole of the highway is flying on, no one knows where, into the receding distance; and there is a lurking terror in that glimpse of objects that keep flashing by rapidly and are gone before they can be identified; and only the sky overhead, the nimble clouds, and the emergent moon, appear motionless. Ah, you tróika! Bird-like tróika, who invented you? Surely you could only have been born among a spirited people—in a land which does not stop at jokes but has taken half the world in the embrace of its smooth plains so that one can go and count the milestones till one's head turns dizzy! Nor does it seem that much cunning was required to fabricate a sledge or carriage drawn by those three horses; it was improvised with the help of an axe and a drill by some handy Yaroslavl' peasant. Your driver wears no great top boots of foreign make: he is all beard and mittens, and sits perched on his seat the devil knows how; but when he stands up, cracks his whip and starts up a song, then the horses rush like a hurricane, the spokes of the wheels spin in one smooth disk, and only the road shudders beneath them while some passer-by cries out as he stops in alarm! And the tróika is off and away, away! . . . And very soon there is only a swirl of dust on the horizon.

'Russia, are you not speeding along like a fiery and matchless tróika? Beneath you the road is smoke, the bridges thunder, and everything is left far behind. At your passage the onlooker stops amazed as by a miracle divine. 'Was that not a flash of lightning?' he asks. What is this surge so full of terror? And what is this force unknown impelling these horses never seen before? . . . Russia, where are you flying? Answer me. There was no answer. The bells are tinkling and filling the air with their wonderful pealing; the air is rent and thundering as it turns to wind; everything on earth comes flying past and, looking askance at her, other people and States move aside and make way.' [1]

7

The meaning of these rhetorical passages, obviously added as an appendix, is clear enough. But the finale of the novel, even such a finale, does not distract the reader's mind from the weird pictures which occur throughout the rest of the book. The portraits of the land-owners remain in one's mind for good. The novel may not contain any direct propaganda against the serfdom system as such, yet indirectly it did draw attention to the anomaly of its existence. If in *The Government Inspector* Gogol dealt a blow at the bureaucratic regime of Nicholas I, in *Dead Souls* he attacked the vulgarity and deformity of life in general and of serfdom Russia in particular: he revealed Russia to herself. The romantic in him now took revenge by laughing more maliciously than in any of his previous works. And the method used was again that of realistic *Klein-*

1. Translated by George Reavey, in the Novel Library (Hamish Hamilton).

malerei. He once complained that the critics who 'dissected my literary talent were not able to find the essential traits of my nature. Pushkin alone was able to see them. He used to say that no other writer was endowed with my capacity for bringing out all the trivialities of life and for opening one's eyes to those trifles, which, as a rule, remain unnoticed.'

Vulgarity and drabness, presented in *Dead Souls*, are thus symbolic in the very intensity of their realism which seems to imply that something must be wrong with the transcendental core of life. Vulgarity as something immanent in existence became Gogol's *idée fixe*—an obsession which he added to his growing moral hypochondria. Conscious of his own defects, he was aware of all that was negative and nasty in the world with which he could never come to terms. Hence the restlessness of a man who was impelled to be eternally on the move, as though trying to escape from himself without knowing where or why. After 1836 he lived mostly in Italy, but he travelled also in France, Switzerland, Germany, feeling everywhere a stranger and a prey to his own ennui. 'Before the eyes of all there only grows the gigantic figure of Tedium,' he wrote in 1847. 'It grows and assumes infinite dimensions day in, day out. O Lord! Empty and terrible is Thy world!'

Gogol's aggressive realism became directed against this Tedium. Yet his fight with defects in the world around was in essence a fight with himself.

> While attacking some bad trait of mine, I presented it in a different role and tried to make it appear in my own eyes as a deadly fiend who has injured me terribly. Then I persecuted it with malice and irony, with anything I could. But had anyone seen those monsters which came from under my pen in my first drafts, he would have shivered with fear.

The subjective root of his realism is thus more than obvious. On the other hand, once Gogol's art had become a weapon of this kind, then a conscious moral purpose or even moral mission in general, bestowed as it were by God Himself, was likely to be one of his dangerous temptations. This was what happened to him after he had witnessed the chastening effect of *The Government Inspector* and *Dead Souls*. In order to be worthy of such a high mission, he now did all he could to deserve God's grace by rigorous ascetic practices— such as the ones described in the revised second part of *The Portrait*. Unfortunately, this mood coincided with a period when his artistic inspiration was at an ebb. Hence he increased his didactic propensity and, as if anxious to force the grace of God, began to talk as one having authority even concerning things about which he knew little or nothing. At a time when the Russian intelligentsia was fighting for a more liberal and progressive system of life, Gogol the incurable romantic continued to look upon such institutions as State, Church, serfdom, autocracy, and education in a bigoted conservative and patriarchal spirit. To make things worse, he decided to enlighten his readers upon these matters. In the hope that the whole of Russia would listen to his sermons with the same enthusiasm as she had hitherto welcomed his literary works, he published (in 1847) his *Selected Passages from Correspondence with My Friends* (*Izbrannye mestá iz perepíski s druzyámi*).

This book was responsible for the most painful shock in Gogol's life. Instead of resounding all over Russia like a prophet, he was now mowed down under the attacks, criticism and derision, which came not only from radical-minded intellectuals but even from some of his own friends in the conservative Slavophil camp. The most slashing blow came, however, from his former admirer Belinsky, who in a letter—the most famous private letter in Russian literature—called Gogol a preacher of the knout, an apostle of ignorance, a defender of obscurantism and darkest oppression. 'You are only bemused and not enlightened, you have understood neither the form nor the spirit of contemporary Christianity. It is not the truth of Christian teaching that your book breathed, but the fear of death, of the devil, and of hell.' This was largely true. The violent attacks on *Selected Passages* helped to raise and partly to clear certain problems in the light of which Gogol's own position grew worse and even somewhat ridiculous. Unable to parry the blows, he wrote to his friend the author Sergey Aksakov:

> Impatience made me publish my book. Seeing that I would not be able to master my *Dead Souls*, and genuinely grieving over the colourlessness of modern literature which indulges in empty discussions, I hurried to say a word or two on the problems I was interested in; the problems which I had wanted to develop or else embody in living images and characters.

And this brings us again to *Dead Souls*.

Gogol had intended to follow up the success of the first volume of this novel (which is a complete work in itself) by another two volumes, thus turning the whole into a kind of *Divina Commedia* of Russian life—with a 'message' attached to it. The first part, presenting only the negative side of Russia was to be its *Inferno*. The second part was planned, like Dante's *Purgatory*, on a higher moral level, while the third would deal with Chichikov's complete moral rebirth, or even with a possible rebirth of Russia. Such a task required convincing portraits of positive characters, but these were beyond Gogol's powers, since his source of inspiration was confined to indictment and ironic laughter. In the five chapters, which survived quite by chance, of the second volume of *Dead Souls*, on which he laboured for eleven years, the virtuous characters look artificial and stilted, whereas the negative ones are portrayed with vigour, even if Gogol's former verve was cooling down—a process which seriously perturbed the author himself.

8

In his letter to Aksakov, Gogol acknowledged that he had hastened to publish *Selected Passages from Correspondence* partly because he felt unable to cope with the creativity demanded of him by *Dead Souls*, and so he wanted to give Russia at least the benefit of his moral and social message. Gogol the Teacher, severed from his art, had, however, little to say, and what he did say was neither new nor particularly interesting. The very fact that he published his precepts in such a shape was proof that he was beginning to doubt his former artistic power. And since he regarded—quite in the romantic spirit—his literary genius as a special gift from on high, he was bound to interpret the drying up of his inspiration as being tantamount to a withdrawal of God's grace in punishment for his 'sins'. Morbidly conscious of certain weaknesses which were due partly to his underdeveloped sex, he considered himself a great sinner. He repented, prayed, mortified his flesh, and in 1848 even undertook a pilgrimage to Palestine, but it was all to no purpose. Neither the glow of literary creation nor that of religious fervour was now granted to him. What Gogol called his religious feeling was in essence atavistic fear of the devil and hell, to which Belinsky had alluded. Gogol himself wrote in a letter before his departure to Palestine (12 February, 1848): 'It even seems to me I have no religion. I confess Christ only because my reason commands me to. I only have the will to believe and, in spite of this, I still dare go on a pilgrimage to our Saviour's tomb. Oh, do pray for me!'

The cry, 'Oh, do pray for me!' became even more frequent after his journey to Jerusalem which had left him inwardly as cold, frightened, and bewildered as ever. His state of mind was aggravated by forebodings of imminent death. Was he ready for it? What answer would he give to the inexorable Judge? While in the throes of such moods and torments, he fell under the spell of a despotic priest, Father Konstantinovsky, who, playing on Gogol's fears, bullied him into spiritual submission. It was probably due to his influence that on the night of 11 February, 1852, Gogol burned the more or less completed manuscript of the second volume of *Dead Souls*.

In that night he prayed with great contrition, after which he called his servant boy and wandered through the rooms, in each of them making the sign of the cross. Finally, he took out of the portfolio his manuscript (the second volume of *Dead Souls*), threw it into the fireplace and lit it with the candle. The boy protested, but Gogol's only answer was, 'This is not your business—you ought to pray.' When the sheets were burned, he crossed himself, kissed the boy, shuffled to his bedroom, fell upon the divan and began to cry. A few days later, on 21 February, he died—probably from physical exhaustion due to ascetic practices.

9

Less studied abroad than some other Russian authors, Gogol nevertheless occupies one of the most important places in the fiction of his country. It was the heritage of Pushkin and of Gogol that determined the character as well as the trend of modern Russian literature. Whereas the Apollonian genius of Pushkin bequeathed to it its lucidity, simplicity and plastic power, Gogol was responsible for its disturbing subjectivism, inner quest and vexation of spirit, in which he anticipated both Dostoevesky and Tolstoy. He laid stress on the portraiture of characters at the expense of a well-constructed plot, and finally sanctioned the 'little man' as a subject worthy of literary treatment—two features which were adopted by the majority of subsequent Russian authors. The 'natural school', championed by Belinsky, took from Gogol above all the realism of ordinary life and of 'small facts' as well as that humanitarian note of pity which was stressed in Gogol's *The Greatcoat* and assumed, later on, such gigantic proportions in Dostoevsky's works. Overlooking the subjective character of Gogol's writings, Belinsky had in view Gogol's art at its best when he put forward his own 'natural (i.e., realistic) school' of literature as a contrast to the artificial and bombastically romantic current of the period. Yet while championing the description of life as it is, he also demanded that the authors should expose the evils of life (such as serfdom, for example) in the name of a better existence. His 'natural school' thus implied both critical realism and the humanitarian idea that literature should be in the service of life—not as preaching, but as good art and good literature in its own right. Belinsky, an admirer of Gogol, thus indicated the direction taken by the majority of the Russian writers from the 1840's on.[1] 'We have all come out of Gogol's Greatcoat,' Dostoevsky said of the writers of his generation when Russian realism was already on the way to being a great literary power. Akaky (the hero of *The Greatcoat*) certainly had a long literary progeny of the 'insulted and the injured', beginning with Dostoevsky's own *Poor Folk* (1846). Even Dostoevsky's 'pathological' trend, from *The Double* onwards, has one of its sources in Gogol's *The Diary of a Madman*. Gogol's Petersburg stories introduced (together with Pushkin's *Queen of Spades* and *The Bronze Horseman*), that 'irrational' atmosphere of the tsarist metropolis which was later expanded and deepened by Dostoevsky.

Gogol's peculiar attitude towards life and the world influenced a large number of Russian writers. His realism of a wounded romantic idealist is conspicuous in the works of such authors as Pisemsky and Saltykov-Shchedrin. Goncharov took on and continued Gogol's realism of *petits faits*. In addition, the two principal characters (Oblomov and Stolz) in Goncharov's novel *Oblómov* are obviously a further elaboration of Tentetnikov and Konstanzhoglo in the second volume of *Dead Souls*. Gogol's agitated prose was continued mainly by Dostoevsky. Its rhythmical and ornate character was investigated and further developed by the modernist Andrey Bely, who, together with Alexey Remizov, was responsible for some interesting experiments on similar lines.

Last but not least, it was in Gogol's works and in his 'laughter through tears' that literature made a decisive attempt to become a moral and social force in life—a tendency which was endorsed by the authors who came after him: from Nekrasov to Tolstoy, and from Saltykov-Shchedrin to Gorky.

10

Strangely enough, Gogol proved to be one of the main stimuli even for such a sane, balanced author as Sergey Aksakov (1791-1859) whose work and style are the exact opposite of Gogol's. Aksakov was born at Ufa and spent much of his early life on his grandfather's estate—Aksakovo, called in his books Bagrovo

---

1. As far as foreign influences were concerned, that of George Sand, with her philanthropic bent and her problem-novels, was prominent at the time.

—in the Bashkirian steppe. After his University studies at Kazan, he became a civil servant first in Petersburg and then in Moscow. Here he associated with literary and theatrical personalities. In 1832 he was deprived (by order of Nicholas I) of his post as censor. In the same year he met Gogol whom he befriended and whose belletristic works he admired without reserve. Five years later he bought some land and a house at Abramtsevo in the environs of Moscow. Here he lived the life of a lover of Nature, a sportsman, as well as an author who started writing rather late in life. After an unpretentious book about fishing (1847) and two books about hunting (in 1852 and 1855) he suddenly won a high place in Russian literature by two works, *A Family Chronicle* (*Seméinaya khrónika*, 1856) and *The Years of Childhood of Bagrov's Grandson* (*Détskie gódy Bagróva vnúka*, 1858), both of which are Russian classics.

The first is a delightful narrative about Aksakov's grandparents and parents at Ufa and Bagrovo. The second is a book of reminiscences about his own childhood in the same district. In those distant regions the serf-owning squires used to live in a broad, if somewhat autocratic patriarchal style. Aksakov's grandfather, as presented to us in *A Family Chronicle*, was an old-world patriarch of this kind. Lording it over his serfs with a good conscience, he was conscious not only of his rights but also of his duties, although his rights came first. The author is not blind to the darker side of serfdom at the end of the eighteenth and the beginning of the nineteenth century. Still, the family picture he presents is one of placid patriarchalism in the midst of broad and idyllic landscapes, described by Aksakov in a masterly way.

Richer in incident is *The Years of Childhood*. This is an autobiographical work: a memoir of Aksakov's own early years and impressions in the same region, but diversified by contacts with Nature and with people outside his family, not to mention excursions to all sorts of villages and landed estates. Introspective as it is, the book abounds in a child's psychology presented unobtrusively with spontaneity and freshness. Among other things we witness the illness and the death of Aksakov's grandfather at Bagrovo. This fascinating book about the growth of a child is written in the same leisurely, pure and homely Russian which makes his previous *Family Chronicle* such a delight to read. As for Aksakov's other memoirs, his *Literary and Theatrical Reminiscences* (1858) as well as his unfinished *History of My Acquaintanceship with Gogol*[1] are full of interest. In Gogol, whose writings he was among the first to admire, he saw the gap between the artist and the man, and was able to appreciate one without being enthusiastic about the other. Still, as far as literature is concerned, it is Gogol the writer that matters. Literary fashions come and go, but he stays. All that is significant and vital in his work has remained part and parcel of the literary heritage of Russia.

1.   It was written in 1854 and first published in 1890.

CHAPTER EIGHT

Lermontov

I

Born in 1814, Mikhail Yuryevich Lermontov was fifteen years younger than Pushkin, but he belonged to a different generation and lived in a different atmosphere. In the 1820s, at the height of his creative power, Pushkin represented the very apex of that period of Russian culture with its leadership still in the hands of the aristocratic and social élite. But after the fatal 'Decembrist' revolt, engineered by the liberal-minded members of the nobility, an élite which formed a compact cultural group and a leading force was hardly possible. So it was gradually replaced by the emerging intelligentsia—an amalgam of liberal upper-class intellectuals and educated commoners. They both shared a high standard of cultural and moral values, and an unwillingness to adapt themselves to the 'leaden rule' of Nicholas I. The great poet Lermontov, who belonged to this post-Decembrist generation, was the least adaptable of them all. Hence his isolation, which was more tragic than that of Byron's, however much he, too, may have displayed 'Childe Harold's cloak'. Besides, in an early poem Lermontov himself insisted that, although exiled from the world like Byron, he was yet different from him and 'endowed with a Russian soul'. The truth is that Lermontov's *mal du siècle* sprang not only from social but also from what might be termed spiritual causes. His romantic nostalgia is like that of a denizen from a different and timeless realm who still remembers it and therefore finds adjustment to the world he lives in impossible. When he was only seventeen, Lermontov wrote a poem called *The Angel*, which may provide something of a clue to the undercurrents of his romanticism :

> An Angel flew through the midnight sky
>   And gently he sang on high.
> And the moon, and the stars, and the clouds in a throng
>   Were entranced by that holy song.
>
> He sang of the bliss of the souls without sin
>   The heavenly tents within,
> Of the great God he sang, and all the while
>   His praise was pure, without guile.
>
> A young soul he carried in his embrace
>   To this world of grief and disgrace;

And the wordless song he sang on the way
　In the young soul then echoed for aye.

And long were the years alloted to her
　Of a strangely pining despair;
And the tedious songs of this world would in vain
　Try to silence that heavenly strain.[1]

The poem could well serve as an epigraph to Lermontov's work. It explains at least one of his differences from Byron, while shedding some light upon the character of his own pessimism amidst the reality he had to endure. Lermontov was the first significant poet in Russian literature to turn the bulk of his work not only into direct or indirect inner autobiography, but often into a kind of passionate self-confession.

2

Despite his 'Russian soul', Lermontov had some Scottish blood in his veins. One of the Learmonths entered the Russian military service at the beginning of the seventeenth century, settled in his adopted country and altered his ancestral name to make it sound Russian. (In two of his early poems, especially in *The Wish*, Lermontov alludes to Scotland as his homeland.) His father was an impoverished landowner who had married the daughter of the wealthy but capriciously overbearing Mme Arsenyeva and was always treated by his mother-in-law as a 'poor relation'. As his wife died after a few years of marriage, Mme Arsenyeva took her little grandson to her own estate where he was brought up until the age of twelve. Spoiled by his grandmother's adulation and at the same time deprived of congenial companions, the boy must have felt lonely during those formative years. Nor could he help being puzzled by the family quarrels between his father and his grandmother. Gradually he became a self-centred dreamer, anxious to conceal his passionate nature under the mask of aloofness, and his innate idealism behind the pose of disdain. His poetic gift, which remained his principal means of self-expression, began to develop in him surprisingly early and was fostered by two circumstances: his visit to the colourful Caucasus at the age of eleven, and his education in a privileged Moscow boarding school (from 1827 onwards) which was not devoid of literary interests. Under the guidance of such teachers as the poet Merzlyakov and the Schellingist philosopher Raitch, the young Lermontov was initiated into the works of Russian literature as well as those of Byron, Moore, Goethe, Schiller, and Scott. He was much impressed by Thomas Moore's biography of Byron, while his own translations from Byron helped him to work himself into the fashionable Byronic moods. At the same time he cultivated aloofness to such a degree that even on entering (in 1830) Moscow University he showed little inclination to mix with his fellow-students. He paid hardly any attention to the fact

1. Translated by J. L.

that after 1830 the University of Moscow, with its debating circles, had become a lively cultural centre. The Stankevich circle in particular, with the subsequent critic Vissarion Belinsky as one of its members, was exploring all sorts of literary and philosophic problems. The youths gathering around Alexander Herzen showed, however, a keener interest in social questions, the radical 'Decembrist' spirit still hovering over their debates. German philosophy, notably the ideas of Schelling and those of Hegel were strong influences at the time. Another stimulus came from the French Utopian Socialists (Proudhon, Cabet, Fourier), as well as from George Sand. Their theories were later combined by quite a few firebrands (Belinsky included) with 'left' Hegelianism, and the two together helped to kindle or even to shape the revolutionary thought among the young Russian radicals of those days.

Lermontov did not belong to any of these groups. In 1832 he even left the University and went to Petersburg where he entered a military school and, after two years of training which he hated, obtained a commission in the Guards. In 1837 he was transferred (or rather, exiled) to a Caucasian regiment on account of his invective, The Death of a Poet (Smert' poéta), written after Pushkin's tragic death. The poem could not be printed as long as Nicholas I was alive,[1] but as it was read in countless written copies, it made Lermontov's name known practically all over Russia. In the Caucasus, which was fated to be strangely connected with his life, his work, and also with his death, he met another poet, the banished 'Decembrist' Prince Alexander Odoevsky—one of the few people he really befriended. Owing to his grandmother's influence, Lermontov was allowed to return (at the end of the same year) to his old Hussar regiment. By this time, as he was already regarded as a poet in his own right and a possible successor to Pushkin, he made a considerable impression in St Petersburg. Admired and lionised, especially by the society ladies, he still felt as bored and lonely as ever. Like Byron before his Guiccioli period, he mixed a life of dissipation with poetic activities, although he did not care to make himself popular either in society or among his fellow-officers. And as for literary men, he seemed to avoid them on purpose. After a duel in February 1840 with the son of the French historian and ambassador, M. de Barante, he was arrested and sent to the Caucasus once more, where he engaged in some dangerous expeditions against the mountain rebels and often displayed reckless courage. One of the engagements he took part in—the battle on he river Valerik (on 11 July, 1840) —he described in a beautiful poem of the same name. In the spring of 1841 he made a brief visit to St Petersburg in the hope of being allowed to remain there, but without success. On his return to the Caucasus he stopped at his favourite spa of Pyatigorsk. The place was full of society people, including some of his old acquaintances. One of these, a certain Major Martynov, whom he tactlessly ridiculed in the presence of a lady, challenged him to a duel. The duel took place outside Pyatigorsk on July 27, 1841, and the poet was killed on the spot. He died at the age of twenty-seven, ten years younger than Pushkin at the time of his death.

1.   It first appeared in print in 1856, in Herzen's Polar Star (Polyárnaya zvezdá), published in London. Two years later the poem came out in Russia.

3

The best of Lermontov's work is second only to Pushkin's, with certain reservations. Pushkin showed even in his early verse great technical skill and finish. In Lermontov, however, it is only the mature work—roughly from 1836 onwards —that really counts. His youthful writings, whether poems or plays, compare with his later products chiefly as a series of exercises and experiments. He was perfectly aware of this and kept returning to some of his themes again and again, until they received an adequate final shape. Yet however much he differed from Pushkin in his outlook and temperament, he could not work without Pushkin's influence. He even at first approached Byron through Pushkin. His two immature tales in verse, *The Circassians* (*Cherkésy*) and *The Prisoner of the Caucasus* (*Kavkásskiy plénnik*), both written at the age of fifteen, were imitations of Pushkin's Byronic tales, with the Caucasus as their romantic setting. After a more thorough acquaintance with Byron's work Lermontov wrote his longer Caucasian tales in verse, *Ismail Bey* (1832) and *Hadjí Abrék*, the latter being the first of his narrative poems to be printed (in a periodical, 1835).

Meanwhile he tried his hand at plays. These are flamboyant, redolent of Schiller's 'storm and stress' period, very juvenile and with an obvious tendency towards self-dramatisation. *Men and Passions* (to which, for some reason, he gave a German title—*Menschen und Leidenschaften*, 1830) and *A Queer Fellow* (*Stránny chelovék*, 1831) must have been written under the impact of the family squabbles at home. His later drama in verse, *The Masquerade* (*Maskarád*, 1835), overstated though it may be, is more impressive in its portrayal of blind jealousy (the influence of *Othello*) on the one hand, and the conflict between a self-centred individual and society on the other. His less important play in prose, *Two Brothers* (*Dva bráta*), is partly biographical, and reflects his distress on hearing that his youthful love, V. A. Lopukhina, had married in 1835.

Whereas Pushkin the poet could and did rise to that affirmative attitude which made him look with tolerance upon life at large, Lermontov the romantic was too much inclined to see the whole of life in terms of his own frustrated ego, and he treated it accordingly. The language of many an early poem may seem somewhat blurred. Yet he gradually developed a rich imagery in words, and the vigour of his descriptive passages vies at times with that of Pushkin himself. On the other hand his realism often seethes with rancour and disgust against the world.

Lermontov's unfinished realistic tale *Sáshka* (1836), for example, is an offspring mainly of Byron's *Don Juan* and, to some extent, of the first canto of Pushkin's *Onégin*. It is an almost obscene satire against the landed gentry in their process of moral decomposition. The realism of another tale in verse, *A Treasurer's Wife from Tambov* (*Tambóvskaya kaznachéisha*, 1837), may have been partly modelled on Pushkin's *Count Nulin*, but with a bitter and biting inflection. It gives a picture of provincial officials, one of whom gambles away his pretty wife to an army officer. Lermontov sometimes reached Pushkin's simplicity and detachment, for example, in such a poem as *Borodino* (1837).

Here he rendered to perfection the tone, the manner and also the grumbling humour of a veteran warrior who talks to a youngster about Napoleon's first defeat during his invasion of Russia in 1812. And if the realism in some of his poems, such as *The Cossack Cradle Song* (*Kazáchya kolybél'naya pésnya*) can be rather poignant, it acquires a dynamic matter-of-factness in the description of the battle on the Caucasian river Valerik. The pathos of his *Testament* (*Zaveshchánie*) is again due to the discrepancy between the tragic situation of a soldier dying of wounds and the almost jokingly casual tone in which he expresses his last wishes to a comrade due to go home on leave.

> But if someone questions you
>> About me as they may :
> Just say a certain bullet flew—
>> My chest was in the way.[1]

The height of poetic detachment was reached, however, by Lermontov in a poem of a different order: in *The Song about Tsar Ivan Vasilyevich, the Young Body-Guard and the Brave Merchant Kalashnikov* (*Pésnya pro tsaryá Ivána Vasílyevicha, molodógo opríchnika i udalógo kuptsá Kaláshnikova*). This is one of the finest examples of a literary adaptation of the historical folk-songs (formally resembling the *byliny*) of the Russian people. Here the poet came as close, if not closer, to the spirit of the folk genius than Pushkin did in his poetic transposition of Russian fairy tales. But this is Lermontov at his best. Essentially subjective though he was, he succeeded during the last few years of his life in turning even his most personal moods and attitudes into great poetry, notably when face to face with nature, as in the poem beginning with the line, 'When o'er the yellowing corn a fleeting shadow rushes'. The same can be said of some lyrics about his unfortunate love for Mlle Lopukhina.

His awareness of the discrepancy between the world to which he was chained, and the timeless realm of the spirit (as he felt it) was too painful to make him accept his temporal fate. No wonder he derived his poetic power principally from protest, rebellion, and from that proud isolation which repudiates anything tainted with the stigma of the 'human-all-too-human'.

> Oh gloomy and dreary! and no one to stretch out a hand
>> In hours when the soul nears disaster ...
> Desire! but what use is an empty desire without end?
>> And the years, the best years, but fly faster.

> To love! yes, but whom? It is nothing in time's little space,
>> No love has an endless tomorrow!
> Just look at yourself : what is past does not leave any trace.
>> They are nothing—both pleasure and sorrow.

> What is passion? That sickness so sweet, either early or late,
>> Will vanish at reason's protesting;

1 Translated by V. de Sola Pinto.

And life, if you ever, attentive and cool, contemplate,
Is but empty and meaningless jesting.[1]

Thus the mood of *The Angel* kept recurring in some aspect or other in Lermontov's poetry, like a continuous echo of his own life. And since both his pessimism and rebellion were due to his latent metaphysical nostalgia, they gave him that almost elemental force of negation and challenge which came out in his two principal works, *The Novice* (1840) and *The Demon* (1841).

4

These two tales in verse represent the climax of Lermontov's romanticism and poetic genius. *The Novice* (he gave it the Georgian name—*Mtsýri*), is a glowing assertion of freedom, abounding in wonderful imagery of nature and is, moreover, narrated in such a bracing tempo that there are no feminine rhymes (rhymes with a soft ending) in its four-footed iambics. The theme itself goes back to Lermontov's early period. He began to work upon it in 1830. Five years later he embodied it as one of the motifs in his somewhat confused romantic tale in verse, *The Boyár Orsha* (*Boyárin Órsha*), and completed its final draft in the last year of his life. The tale is in the form of a confession on the part of a young Caucasian mountaineer, who as a child had been captured by the Russians and, having fallen ill, was then left in a Georgian monastery where he grew up and became a novice. But the monastery walls did not obliterate the memories of his childhood and his yearning for freedom. Determined to return to his native place in the mountains and to enjoy a free life once again, he escapes, wanders amidst the splendid Caucasian scenery, but in the end is found dying of exhaustion not far from the spot where his flight had begun. Having completed the circle, he is brought back to the monastery in a dying condition. He knows that his hours are numbered, but his spirit refuses to surrender. In words burning with passion he confesses, like the hero of Byron's *The Giaour*, to an old monk the reason for his escape, thus stressing his defiance and love of freedom to the very end.

Tragic, but in a different sense, is Lermontov's 'Eastern Tale', *The Demon*. He had started working at it as far back as 1829 and 1830, took it up once more in 1833, then again during his stay in the Caucasus in 1837, and completed it in 1841. The demon of this tale is Lermontov's own double, projected into the spiritual realm of man's consciousness. He is an exiled rebellious angel who still remembers his one-time bliss, but is doomed to be imprisoned in his own isolation till the end of time. The theme bears some influences of Byron's *Heaven and Earth*, of Thomas Moore's *Loves of Angels*, or even of *Eloa* by Alfred de Vigny. In spite of this, it remains Lermontov's typical and intensely personal creation. For it combines, in a symbolic manner, all the features of his own nature: his feeling of isolation, his rebellious pride, his secret wish (as well as his inability) to come to terms with life. The exiled and gloomy Demon soared above the sinful world, while memories

1.   Translated by C. M. Bowra in *A Book of Russian Verse* (Macmillan).

Before him brooding vision whirled
Of days when in the light of grace
A cherub bright and pure he shone,
When in the swift, unending race
The comet turned its smiling face
To greet him as they hastened on.[1]

And since this is an 'Eastern Tale', the Caucasus is introduced as the only adequate setting for such a spirit. It is the Caucasus Lermontov had known and admired since his boyhood.

Then o'er the high Caucasian maze
The banished angel slowly rose,
Kazbek with glinting lights ablaze
Stood clad in everlasting snows.
And deep below, an inky track
Like a dark serpent's hiding-crack,
The winding Darial met his gaze.

The Terek like a lion bounding
With shaggy mane upon the peak
Set all the hollow vales resounding;
And beasts upon the mountain bleak
And birds aloft in heaven's light
Both harkened to its thundered word;
And golden clouds in endless flight
Sped with it northward undeterred.

It is amidst this scenery that the Demon suddenly beholds Tamara—the most beautiful of mortal maidens, and falls in love with her. But Tamara is waiting for her bridegroom who, accompanied by a whole caravan, is hurrying to the wedding. She and her girl-friends while away the time with innocent pleasures.

Their palms in gentle measure clapping,
They sing, and then the young bride takes
Her tambourine, which, gently tapping
Above her head, she gaily shakes
With a lily hand that faintly quakes.
Now lighter than a bird she dashes,
Then, pausing, she will fix her gaze
While two moist eyes are seen to blaze
Beneath their jealous tapering lashes;
Now she will raise her brows with pride,
Now suddenly her form incline,
Then o'er the patterned floor will glide
Her foot. . . .

1. All the passages are taken from Gerard Shelley's translation of *The Demon* (the Richards Press).

The demon sees to it that the caravan of the travelling wedding guests is dispersed, while the bridegroom himself is killed. In despair, Tamara retires to a convent; but here the Demon begins to tempt her in her dreams. He does this with no evil intentions, for Tamara's beauty has made such a change in him that he hopes his love for her might save him at last from the curse of isolation. Invisible, he whispers to her:

> The gentle prayer of love unending
> I bring to thee with heart aglow,
> On earth my spirit's first unbending,
> The first tears from my eyes to flow,
> O let them not unheeded go!

He sincerely wishes to be reconciled through this love to God and God's world, but this is not granted him. When, finally, he embraces Tamara, she dies from the kiss of an immortal. Her soul is taken away by a messenger of God, while the Demon is left in the same cosmic loneliness as ever.

> Again he roamed in desolation,
> The haughty exile of creation,
> On whom no hope or love shall gleam.

With its intensely romantic theme and setting,[1] this poem remains one of the masterpieces of Russian literature. Lermontov expressed in it symbolically his own frustrated love and also the depth of his isolation as only a poet of his kind could have done. Yet, as the plane of such poetry was far removed from the actualities of the day, he decided to tackle the contemporary isolated or uprooted individual from a more realistic angle, and in prose. This he did in his novel, *A Hero of our Time* (*Geróy náshego vrémeni*, 1840).

5

Lermontov warns us (in the preface to the second edition of this work) not to confuse Pechorin—the hero of the novel—with the personality of the author. The truth remains, however, that he analysed in it above all his own negative propensities. In portraying himself, he also portrayed, to a large extent, the generation to which he belonged. In this manner he wrote his own counterpart to Alfred de Musset's *La Confession d'un enfant du siècle*—a book he must have been hardly less familiar with than he was with *Adolphe* by Benjamin Constant. Like the two works mentioned, *A Hero of our Time* is both a psychological novel and a confession in disguise. Its importance is further enhanced by the fact that it is written in a lucid and flexible prose, the most perfect Russian prose of that decade.

Pechorin himself is a literary descendant of Pushkin's Onegin. But unlike Pushkin's hero who belonged to the early 1820s, he is an Onegin of the late 1830s, psychologically dissected and presented to the reader as an up-to-date

1.   The Russian composer A. Rubinstein turned it into an opera.

variety of the 'superfluous man'.[1] A preliminary portrait of Pechorin can be found in Lermontov's unfinished early novel, *Princess Ligovskaya* (*Knyagínya Lígovskaya*, 1836), where he combined self-analysis with a picture of cold and callous Petersburg society. But what was here only a sketch and a promise, became in *A Hero of Our Time* a fulfilment. Consisting of five stories, all of which can be read independently, the first two narratives (*Béla*, *Maxím Maxímych*) show Pechorin as he is seen by others, and the subsequent three parts (*Táman'*, *Princess Mary*, *The Fatalist*) as he sees and describes himself in his diary. The background is again the Caucasus; only the plot of *Táman'* (one of the best stories in Russian) is set in the hardly less exotic Crimea.

The final impression Pechorin makes upon the reader is one of tragic failure. He has all the marks of a strong and superior nature, but can never apply his strength to anything worth his while, since in the Russia of Nicholas I no creative outlet was possible for people of Pechorin's kind. All his strength thus turns against itself and becomes vindictively destructive. He is a potential idealist by nature, whereas by conviction he is devoid of any faith and is unable to believe in any ideals. As he cannot even think of an adequate task or mission in life, he is doomed to remain sterile in whatever he does or undertakes.

> I have never been able to discover my mission, so I have succumbed to the temptation of futile and ungrateful passions. Out of their furnace I have issued hard and cold as steel, but I have hopelessly failed to pluck the most beautiful flower of life—the fire of noble impulses. How often have I been no more than an axe in the hands of fate. Like a death-dealing instrument, I fell upon the heads of the predestined victims, often without angry feelings, but always without regret.[2]

In other ways, too, Pechorin is a self-divided 'modern'. He is full of the will to live, to enjoy life, while at the same time his sceptical double continually watches, analyses and undermines all his best impulses. Such self-division makes him increasingly inhibited—until the only real feeling still accessible to him is that of power, which he exercises as an end in itself. Other people, especially women (Bela, Vera, Princess Mary) whom he fascinates, are victimised by the spell he casts over them. He himself is aware of this, painfully aware at times, and the only thing in his favour is that he is candid enough to acknowledge it. He says in his diary :

> I see the sufferings and joys of others only in relation to myself; I regard them as food to nourish my spiritual strength. It has become impossible for me to do foolish deeds under the influence of passion. In me, ambition has been crushed by circumstances, to assume another form. For ambition is nothing but the thirst for power, and my chief delight is to impose my will upon all with whom I come in contact. To inspire fear, what is it but the first sign and the greatest triumph of power? To be for some one a

---

1. It would be of some interest to compare Pechorin with Julian Sorel, the hero of Stendhal's novel, *Le Rouge et le noir*, written about the same time.
2. Translated by Eden and Cedar Paul (Allen & Unwin).

cause of suffering or joy, without the least right—can pride know sweeter food than this? [1]

Little wonder Pechorin himself comes to the conclusion 'Substantially I was a cripple.'

Thwarted strength is doomed to turn against itself or else to degenerate into the nihilistic 'will to power' for power's sake. Such was the inner tragedy of Lermontov himself. Through his masterly analysis of the tragedy of a *déraciné* he became the creator of the psychological novel in Russian literature; one of the first to tackle some of these aspects of individual self-division and frustration which afterwards were further developed in so many other Russian novels.

The 'demoniac' pride and self-assertiveness of Dostoevsky's heroes, such as Raskol'nikov and Stavrogin, have some of their roots in Lermontov. Whereas one aspect of Dostoevsky's work goes back to Gogol, the other points to Lermontov, and via Lermontov to Byron—however distant the affinities may seem to be. By his frankness and his refusal to indulge in any cant or rosy expectations, Lermontov was an example of that psychological and moral honesty which often verged on recklessness. Both as poet and novelist he was one of those who inaugurated the dissecting vertical direction in Russian literature. It was he who made it *conscious* of depth at a time when the more horizontal 'natural school', championed by Belinsky, was already branching off into a number of trends which were to form the bulk of subsequent Russian prose. Apart from this, Lermontov provides some of the best clues to the inner *cul de sac* of a romantic mind. It is idle to speculate what he might have achieved had he lived longer. All one can say in conclusion is that whatever his failings, he never gave up his intense longing for freedom and beauty. And since the language of these aspirations is universal, Lermontov the poet belongs to the family of those whose significance is universal.

1. Translated by Eden and Cedar Paul (Allen & Unwin).

CHAPTER NINE

Ivan Turgenev

I

Ivan Sergeyevich Turgenev was the first Russian author to become generally known and admired beyond the boundaries of his native country. It was through him that Russian fiction began to penetrate into Europe as one of the major literary influences. And for good reason, since he successfully combined his 'Russianness' with impeccable literary manners and with a technique perfect enough to challenge comparison with any prose-writer of the West. He loses only if compared with such geniuses as Dostoevsky and Tolstoy who were sufficiently great to be a law unto themselves.

Turgenev belongs to what might be called the well-ordered Mozartian—or, for that matter, Pushkinian—type of creator. Whatever subject he took up, he handled it first of all as a perfect artist. External reality, including its topical aspects and problems, was for him but raw material which he distilled into works of beauty. Keenly interested in the political, social and cultural struggles of the period, he had his own convictions, sympathies and antipathies; yet he never let them interfere with the aesthetic side of his writing. This did not exclude, of course, that unconscious discrimination which determines beforehand one's choice of certain themes and characters in preference to others. In this respect Turgenev remained a typical manor novelist, steeped in the 'Nests of Gentlefolk', at the very height of the intelligentsia period of Russian culture and literature. Although a member of the intelligentsia and a sincere liberal with a Western outlook, he had the ancestral manor not only in his memory but in his very blood, and in contrast to the more radical intellectuals from among the 'commoners', who looked towards a better future, Turgenev the artist could not help being rooted in the past even when fighting it in the light of the vital problems of the day. The company of the impetuous 'commoners', so conspicuous in the ranks of the intelligentsia during the 1860s, hardly made him feel at ease. At any rate, when at the beginning of that momentous decade a split between the 'gentlemen' and the 'commoners' took place within the precincts of *The Contemporary* (*Sovreménnik*, the principal organ of radical intelligentsia), Turgenev was one of those who walked out of the editorial premises.

After that split, the 'commoners', under the leadership of Dobrolyubov and Chernyshevsky, practically monopolised the journalistic and pamphleteering activities, whereas the 'gentlemen' concentrated more on works of literature.

With the exception of Dostoevsky and Leskov, both of whom were of mixed social origin, the principal authors of the 'fifties, 'sixties and 'seventies, dealt mostly with the manor or country-house and its residents. This applies above all to Turgenev, who belonged to a class which had a past but could no longer look forward with confidence to a future. It is in connection with the prevailing moods of the representatives of this class that we can see Turgenev's life and work in their right perspective.

Turgenev was born on 28 October 1818 at Oryol (Orël), the youngest of three boys in a not very happy family of the landed gentry class. His father, a dashing but impoverished cavalry officer, who had married only for money a wealthy tyrannical woman six years his senior, died when Ivan was sixteen. While watching his mother's brutal treatment of her five thousand serfs the boy was already full of disgust with a system in which such things were possible. After his early education at home on the estate of Spasskoe near Oryol he was sent to Moscow, where later he entered the University. But he soon passed on to the University of St Petersburg and, after graduation, went to Berlin in order to complete his studies. Here he stayed for about three years (1838–41) and was so impressed by European culture that he remained a convinced liberal Westerner to the end of his days.

On his return from abroad he started writing poetry. He achieved some success with a tale in verse called *Parásha* (1843), obviously influenced by Pushkin's *Onégin*. It was followed by three narrative and a number of lyrical poems, but the bulk of his lyrical verses scarcely rose above the good average. He seemed to waver for a while between poetry, drama and fiction. His plays, such as the now famous *A Month in the Country* (*Mésyats v derévne*, 1850) and *A Provincial Lady* (*Provintsiyálka*, 1851), are not without originality, especially the first which, devoid of the usual plot, anticipated the dramatic technique of Chekhov. But an even more startling note was brought by Turgenev into his prose by those stories and jottings which began to appear in 1847 and were issued in book form in 1852 as *A Sportsman's Sketches* (*Zapíski okhótnika*).

The title looked innocent and reassuring enough: a collection of impressions recorded by a roaming sportsman. Yet in the process of reading it one soon becomes aware of the actual theme of the book—the serf and the squire. We meet here the serf in his everyday surroundings and in his normal everyday contacts with the serf-owner. As the liberation of the serfs was then generally expected, such a theme was topical and had already been introduced in a tendenciously realistic and humanitarian manner by Dmitry Grigorovich. But in contrast to Grigorovich's *Village* (*Derévnya*, 1846) or *Antón Goremýka* (1847), Turgenev followed his own artistic instinct even when dealing with the evils of serfdom. Without distorting either the truth to life or that to art by any sentimental considerations, he depicted a great variety of serfs and peasants simply as human beings with their own ways of thinking, with their own individual defects and virtues, on a par with everybody else. The same balanced objectivity comes out in his portraits of the landowners; and it was not Turgenev's fault if many of these appeared to be humanly less valuable than their serfs. The whole of it expands into a mosaic of Russian rural life, and some of his pictures—the exquisitely drawn children in *The Bezhin Meadow* (*Bézhin lug*), or the superb story called *The Singers* (*Pevtsý*), for example, are unforgettable. In this particular story we are taken to a dingy village tavern where two peasant singers compete with their voices for a pot of beer and are eagerly watched and listened to by the admiring village audience. This is how Turgenev describes one of the singers:

> He gave a deep sigh and began to sing. . . . The first sound of his voice was faint and unequal and seemed not to come from the chest, but to be wafted from somewhere far off, as though it had floated by chance into the room. A strange effect was produced on all of us by this trembling, resonant note; we glanced at one another, and Nikolai Ivanych's wife seemed to draw herself up. The first note was followed by another, bolder and prolonged, but still obviously quivering, like a harpstring when suddenly struck by a stray finger it throbs in a last, swiftly dying tremble; the second was followed by a third, and gradually gaining fire and breadth, the strains swelled into a pathetic melody. 'Not one little path ran into the field,' he sang, and sweet and mournful it was in our ears. I have seldom, I must confess, heard a voice like it; it was slightly hoarse, and not perfectly true; there was even something morbid about it at first; but it had genuine depth of passion, and youth and sweetness and a sort of fascinating, care-less, pathetic melancholy. A spirit of truth and fire, a Russian spirit, was sounding and breathing in that voice, and it seemed to go straight to your heart, to go straight to all that was Russian in it.[1]

Still, it all ended in a rowdy drunken brawl.

In his description of landscapes, Turgenev knows how to be impressive with a kind of reserve which never takes liberties with Nature. Hence his preference for nuances and for that discreet lyrical intimacy with the rural scenery in which the mellowness of colour and of verbal music serves as an evocative accompaniment to the atmosphere demanded by the situation. Tur-genev's scenery is no longer a mere background for the characters—it merges with them as a vital part of the action itself. The Russian countryside found in him one of its best impressionistic interpreters. With regard to his characters, too, Turgenev is above all an observer with a sharp eye for those significant trifles through which he can describe a person or a whole crowd of people by means of a few dexterous touches. Here is one of his quick portraits:

> His face, plump and round as a ball, expressed bashfulness, good-natured and humble meekness: his nose, also plump and round and streaked with blue veins, betokened a sensualist. On the front of his head there was not a single hair left, some thin brown tufts stuck out behind; there was an ingratiating twinkle in his little eyes, set in long slits, and a sweet smile on his red, juicy lips. He had on a coat with a stand-up collar and brass

1.   *A Sportsman's Sketches*, translated by Constance Garnett (Dent).

buttons, very worn but clean; his cloth trousers were hitched up high, his
fat calves were visible above the yellow tops of his boots.[1]

As his descriptions are never dissociated from experience, we see his
characters as living beings and seem to know them as if we had been acquainted
with them personally for years. With the same balanced sensibility he tackles
social and political problems without making any *faux pas* at the expense of art.
Paradoxically enough, he discredited the iniquity and cruelties of serfdom
precisely by treating them as artist and not as preacher, and by this very technique he made the implied social-humanitarian 'purpose' all the more effective.
When the sketches appeared in book form, they impressed the Tsarevich (the
subsequent Tsar Alexander II) so strongly as to increase his determination to
abolish serfdom—a conspicuous example of the influence of art upon history.

2

Turgenev's vision, like that of Pushkin, is always concrete. He remains above
all an observer even when he is introspective: in his *Diary of a Superfluous
Man*, for instance, or in *Arya*. As his admirer Henry James put it in one of his
notes, he 'has no recognition of unembodied ideas; an idea, with him, is such
and such a nose and chin, such and such a hat and waistcoat, bearing the same
relation to it as the look of the printed word does to its meaning'. And Turgenev himself said in a paper that he 'had never attempted to create a type
without having, not an idea, but a living person, in whom the various elements
were harmonised together, to work from'. In contrast to Dostoevsky, who saw
all characters mainly from within; or to Tolstoy, who knew how to combine
his incredible plastic power with an acute analysis, Turgenev confined himself to the surface, but without being superficial. His characters are often as
much alive as any of those created by Tolstoy or Dostoevsky, although their
range may be smaller and less complicated. Unlike many Russian authors,
Turgenev was endowed with a rare sense of construction, proportion, and of
the carefully worked-out plot. All these things he perfected by learning from
Pushkin and Lermontov rather than from Gogol. The first two stories he wrote,
Andréy Kólosov (1844) and *A Reckless Fellow* (1847), bear the stamp of Pechorin
in Lermontov's *A Hero of Our Time*. Even in *A Sportsman's Sketches* one can
feel that architectonic sense which achieved veritable triumphs in his longer
stories, and especially in his novels: *Rúdin* (1856), *A Nest of Gentlefolk
(Dvoryánskoe gnezdó,* 1859), *On the Eve (Nakanúne,* 1860), *Fathers and Children (Ottsý i déti,* 1862),[2] *Smoke (Dym,* 1867) and *Virgin Soil (Nov',* 1876).

In Turgenev's novels one encounters again and again the effete gentry-
class types unable to cope with the task of adjusting themselves to the changing
conditions of the age in which they live. The 'Childe Harold-Onegin-Pechorin'
tradition of the 'superfluous man' is therefore bound to play a conspicuous

1. Translated by Constance Garnett. *Op cit.*
2. The title of the published English translation is *Fathers and Sons.*

part in them. As early as 1851 Turgenev wrote his *Diary of a Superfluous Man* (*Dnevník líshnego chelovéka*), and from that time on this unheroic hero remained one of his ever-recurring figures. Rudin, the first full-size portrait of this kind, in the novel bearing the same name, is one of Turgenev's amazing feats of characterisation.[1] We are introduced to Rudin in the drawing-room of an 'up-to-date' country-house, where he impresses everybody by his intelligence and rhetorical idealism (the style of the period). Then, to our surprise we learn that this brilliant talker and idealist is a parasite and a sponger, although we are eventually compelled to revise this opinion as well. After a number of contradictory features quickly following one upon another, he is subjected to a crucial test in his love for the hostess's daughter Natasha who has fallen in love with him. But here he shows his complete lack of backbone and even of ordinary courage. The author makes us alternately waver between admiration, spite, pity and affection, and each new feature of Rudin perplexes us as if it could not belong to the man we already know. Yet after a while all the contradictions adjust themselves, and we have before us an intensely real and complex character whom, for all his vagaries, we seem to like. Full of the best intentions, but as helpless in practice as a child, this pathetic *déclassé* is unable to find an active link with life. He is doomed to remain the victim of his own dreams, and his intelligence remains sterile, however rich the material of which he is made.

If Rudin is a restless descendant of Onegin 'gone to seed', Natasha has affinities with Pushkin's Tatyana. Like Tatyana, she is stronger than the man she loves, and after her initial disappointment, finds her place in life. The existence of Rudin, on the other hand, is only one long series of escapes—from life as well as from himself. He is the very embodiment of the woolly idealism which was so often to be found among upper-class intellectuals of the 1840s. And so it is almost with relief that we learn of his death on the barricades in Paris, during the Revolution of 1848.

The note of frustration is even stronger in Turgenev's next novel, *A Nest of Gentlefolk*. Here, too, we have a picture of gentry-class life, with several subtly contrasted characters, among whom the love between Lavretsky and Liza assumes a truly tragic turn. Lavretsky, a disillusioned married squire whose lewd wife is enjoying herself in Paris, is a solid hard-working man, but in essence as 'superfluous' as Rudin. During his wife's absence he falls in love with Liza—a woman with a profound religious sense of duty and, in spite of their mutual reticence, he knows that his love is reciprocated. Suddenly Lavretsky reads in a French newspaper that his wife has died. The situation is changed at once. The two lovers acknowledge their real feelings with the tacit hope that now they could become man and wife. But here Mme Lavretsky unexpectedly turns up, the rumour of her death in France having been false. She actually comes back with the diplomatic intention of obtaining her husband's forgiveness and more money for her further adventures. Unable to disentangle himself from the grip of his depraved wife, Lavretsky surrenders to his fate, whereas his wife soon goes again to France and back to her life of a

---

1. Rudin is supposed to be a portrait of the famous revolutionary Bakunin, whom Turgenev had known during his student years in Berlin.

'Muscovite Parisienne'. Liza, on the other hand, buries her own life in a convent. Here, after a considerable lapse of time, both lovers meet again in a scene which forms the very height of Turgenev's artistic tact and restraint. For not a single word is exchanged between the two—they pass each other like two pathetic ghosts, and yet the reader is fully aware of their feelings.

Needing delicate handling on account of its pitfalls, the subject-matter is worked out in a symphonic manner: with numerous secondary motifs, episodes, and characters held together by the basic theme. The contrasted and mutually complementary characters, the background, and the plot itself are so well blended that here the truth to life is unquestionably deepened and intensified by the truth to art. Even Turgenev's mood of gentle fatalism, which pervades the book, is so well sublimated as to cease to be personal. As for Liza, she may be idealised, but this does not prevent her from being alive and real—a thing which can be said even more so of Helena, the heroine of *On the Eve*.

In this novel Turgenev portrayed the generation of the 1850s, that is of the years which saw the Crimean Campaign and the death of Nicholas I. In anticipation of the reforms which were soon to come, these were years of expectation. But were the Russian intellectuals equal to the tasks ahead? Turgenev's answer was in the negative, at least with regard to the men. The heroine of this novel is represented (on the very eve of the Crimean Campaign) as the new active woman, capable of an heroic task without any heroic pose or self-admiration. Surrounded by intelligent talkative admirers, she falls in love not with a member of her own class or even of her own nation, but with the somewhat angular Insarov: a Bulgarian fanatically devoted to the idea of freeing his country from the Turkish yoke. But if Helena remains convincing in spite of idealisation, Insarov is presented as too much of a one-track mind to be truly alive. One admires his firmness rather than his personality, but in the end it is his dogged firmness and active idealism which makes Helen marry him. It is worth noting that even this novel, in which Turgenev was so anxious to portray a strong man, has an unhappy ending. Insarov dies in Venice, while on his way to foment a rising in his own country oppressed by the Turks.

It was only in his next and greatest novel, *Fathers and Children*, that Turgenev succeeded in giving a convincing portrait of the strong new man (this time a Russian) for which the age was clamouring. And since the author was doubtful of the members of his own class, he had to look for him among the 'commoners'. He found him in the person of the nihilist Bazarov, whose prototype was a young Russian doctor Turgenev had actually met. It was not without malice that he transferred Bazarov to a 'nest of gentlefolk', confronting him with the fossilised representatives of the 1840s. Devoid of any respect for traditions, conventional ideas and class-distinctions, Bazarov is frankness itself: always matter-of-fact, inconsiderate, even aggressive, but at the same time hard-working and full of courage. One can well imagine that the role he plays in the genteel 'Victorian' country-house of his hosts is none too pleasant for either party. Various conflicts, hidden and open, arise almost at once. They are caused not so much by the differences in manners as by those imponderable subconscious attitudes towards certain things in life which are often a stronger class-barrier than rank or wealth. Turgenev surpasses himself in the fineness of touch and delicate humour precisely when dealing with such imponderables. He himself may admire Bazarov, but does not really like him and feels more at home with the tame 'gentlefolk'. Yet he realises that the future is with Bazarov rather than with Bazarov's hosts, whom the 'nihilist' [1] cannot stomach. Bazarov was in fact the type of 'commoner' who emerged among the leading figures of the intelligentsia of the 1860s and with whom the 'gentlemen' had to put up, whether they liked it or not.

From a purely formal standpoint, *Fathers and Children* is as well constructed as *A Nest of Gentlefolk*, but its texture is richer, while the interplay of characters is even deeper. The 'tame' Arkady (with whom Turgenev himself must have had quite a lot in common), Arkady's father, the immaculately aristocratic uncle, Bazarov's pathetically simple parents, the shy Fenitchka, the self-possessed (and undersexed) Mme Odintsova, her gentle sister Katya—they all fit perfectly into the pattern devised by the author and are alive even in their casual words and movements. The finale is again a tragic one. Yet the scene of Bazarov's death from blood-poisoning is powerful because of its very reserve. The contrast between Bazarov's manly stoicism and the frantic state of his parents who are so anxious to conceal their despair from their dying son, is one of those marvels of art which are more real than reality itself. Although the novel depicts the early 1860s, it is easy to perceive behind it the eternal tragi-comedy of human relations in general: those between parents and their grown-up children; between men and women; aristocrats and 'commoners'; dreamers and realists; leaders and followers. It is again a case of truth to life being deepened and enriched by truth to art.

3

The younger generation of the 1860s repudiated *Fathers and Children*. The storm raised by the novel brought so much disgust to its author that, for a while, he intended to give up literature altogether. Turgenev's irritation at the Russian life of the period came out with a great deal of bitterness in his next novel, *Smoke*. As if feeling that he himself was now becoming superfluous in his own country, he preferred to live abroad where he counted among his friends and admirers some of the foremost literary figures of the day: George Sand, Gautier, Sainte-Beuve, Flaubert, Renan, the brothers Goncourt, Taine, Daudet, Zola and Maupassant. Yet life seemed to have lost its flavour, its essence and intensity—even its *negative* intensity—so far as he was concerned. He regarded life's monotony as 'meanly-uninteresting and beggarly-flat'. Yet his weariness and pessimism may have been due partly to his strange infatuation for the singer Mme Viardot-Garcia. Turgenev had met her in his twenties, while at St Petersburg, and that virile, and, in her own way, brilliant woman remained his life-long love. Although their relationship seems to have been for

1. It was probably Turgenev who introduced the word 'nihilist' into literature.

the most part platonic, the enamoured author followed her all over Europe and spent his last years near her at Bougival not far from Paris where he died.

Because of these wanderings he must have felt all the more uprooted at times, but he was less out of touch with what was going on in Russia than many of his critics thought. Turgenev the artist may have been above parties, but as a citizen he was keenly interested in the political and social life of his country. Even after his quarrel with the 'commoners' in *The Contemporary*, his outlook remained that of a liberal Westerner, for which attitude the patriotic Slavophil Dostoevsky viciously lampooned him in the figure of the author Karmazinov in *The Possessed*. The controversy between the two factions found an echo in Turgenev's *Smoke*—a novel in which biting personal indignation and political satire, directed against all the factions of Russian life, loom large— sometimes even at the expense of the finely worked-out romance, or the renewal of an old romance, between Litvinov (another 'superfluous man') and Irina. The entire action of the novel takes place at Baden-Baden and Turgenev the portrait painter achieves here one of his great triumphs with Irina—a more sparkling, more complex and subtly evasive personality than any of his previous heroines. Edward Garnett is right in defining her (in his study of Turgenev) as a woman with

> that exact balance between good and evil which makes good women seem insipid beside her and bad women unnatural. She ardently desires to become nobler, to possess all that the ideal of love means for the heart of a woman; but she has only the power given to her of enervating the man she loves. She is born to corrupt, yet never to be corrupted. She rises mistress of herself after the first measure of fatal delight. And, never giving her heart abso- lutely to her lover, she nevertheless remains ever to be desired. Further her wit, her scorn, her beauty, preserve her from all the influences of evil she does not deliberately employ. Such a woman is as old and as rare a type as Helen of Troy.

Despite its occasional flaws, *Smoke* is one of Turgenev's masterpieces. His last novel, *Virgin Soil*, however, displays an even richer pamphleteering charac- ter. Here the author obviously wanted to prove that, although living abroad, he was able to understand and interpret the aspirations of the advanced currents in his native country. This time he tackled the populist current prevalent in the 1860s and 1870s especially among those 'conscience-stricken' gentry radicals who were eager to undergo any trials in order to help the masses and prepare them for the hoped-for revolution and a better future. In *Virgin Soil* we can follow the activities of a whole group of such enthusiasts up to their disappoint- ment or failure. Anxious to blend the social-political theme with the artistic side of the novel, the author created, besides a number of well-portrayed rebels, the streamlined high bureaucrat (of the 'liberal' brand), Sipyagin. He and his equally immaculate wife are depicted with plenty of ironical touches. As for the active revolutionaries, the balanced practical idealist Solo- min and the generously purposeful Marianna (a kind of twin-sister of Helena in *On the Eve*) seem to be made for each other. The love between the 'revolutionary Hamlet' Alexey Nezhdanov and Marianna is however a new variation of the Rudin-Natasha motif. The general mood of the novel is pessimistic about the populist movement, above all in the description of the abortive attempt of a rising among the local peasants. Turgenev's own conclusions hardly differ from the ending of Zhdanov's poem, A Dream, which contains the following, not exactly flattering, lines:

> 'The Peasants sleep like the dead; they reap and plough asleep, they
> thresh
> And yet they sleep. Father, mother, all the family, all sleep.
> He who strikes sleeps, and he who receives the blow!
> Only the tavern is wakeful—and never closes its eyes;
> And clasping a whisky-pot with a firm grip,
> Her forehead at the Pole and her feet in the Caucasus,
> Sleeps a never-ending sleep our country, our holy Russia.'

Turgenev described the various aspects of Russian life at a time when the sleeper, rubbing his eyes, was just about to wake up and have his say at last. What that say would be like remained a puzzle for Turgenev. Russia's riddle and destiny were too intricate to provide an adequate answer.

4

In spite of unavoidable changes in literary fashions, Turgenev remains one of the great artists in Russian as well as European fiction. Apart from his polished style, his delicate irony and his sense of construction, one admires in him that indefinable intimacy with which he impresses his characters upon us even before we are aware of it. However strange they may appear at first, we soon move among them as among personal friends whose misfortunes often disturb us almost as much as our own. He excels as a psychologist and poet of love. And whatever theme or plot he may choose for his novels and stories, he usually treats it as something deeper and more permanent than the show of a passing period. The variety of his characters is surprisingly large. This is true also of his women portraits, in spite of his predilection for the 'Tatyana' type. Take the hysterically exalted girl in A Strange Story (Stránnaya istóriya); his gallery of old maids; his worldly cocottes (Mme Lavretsky in A Nest of Gentlefolk, or Mme Polozova in the partly autobiographic Spring Torrents—Véshnie vódy); his blue-stockings; his enchantingly sensuous Irina in Smoke. Turgenev's weakness for Mme Viardot-Garcia may have been responsible for the large number of weak and frustrated men in his novels and stories. Yet his weaklings are more interesting, more complex, and more successfully worked out than his strong men. The intricacy of his own love is further reflected in his moody disposition reminiscent of an autumn afternoon, with gentle fatalism permeating the air.

A similar mood can often be felt in his stories which are deservedly considered among the best in European literature. A master of impressionism in

A Sportsman's Sketches, and a superb story-teller in such narratives as *First Love* (*Pérvaya lyubóv'*), *Ásya*, *A King Lear of the Steppes* (*Stepnóy koról' Lear*), *The Spring Torrents*, and so many others, he can stand comparison with any famous artist of the word. Most of his stories resemble well-organised reminiscences, told in the first person and vibrating with that vague nostalgia for the past which was typical of Turgenev himself. As a 'superfluous' and misunderstood member of an already superfluous class, he felt so homeless in the rapidly changing world that an atmosphere of doom eventually seemed to emanate from his very personality. Mme Herzen once compared the ageing Turgenev with an uninhabited room : 'Its walls are damp, and their dampness gets into your bones; you are afraid to sit down, afraid to touch anything, and you only wish to get out of it as quickly as possible.'

Disillusioned and tired as he was, he had a few lapses from his high standard when, in *Clara Milich* (1882) for instance he began to dabble in occultism. His exquisite *Poems in Prose* (*Stikhotvoréniya v próze*, known as *Senilia*), on the other hand, reflect the weariness and the resignation of an old man who has nothing to wait for except death. Turgenev the man died in 1883. But Turgenev the author continues to live as a world classic, belonging not to one, but to all countries.

CHAPTER TEN

Fyodor Tyutchev

I

Among the leading figures in Russian literature, the poet Fyodor Tyutchev (1803-73) is still merely a name in Western Europe. This is not surprising, for even in Russia it took two or three generations before his work was appreciated at its true value. As his early poems coincided with the Pushkin period, he is often mentioned among the members of the Pushkin *pléiade*. Some of his best verses actually appeared in Pushkin's periodical *The Contemporary* in 1836, while Pushkin was still alive. Apart from this, however, Tyutchev had no close connection with the group. Besides, on leaving Moscow University at the age of nineteen, he was attached, almost at once, to the Russian Legation in Munich and later to that in Turin.[1] His stay abroad lasted some twenty-two years. During that time his genius reached its maturity away from his native land and largely under foreign influences.

The city which for several reasons he liked and enjoyed most was Munich. King Ludwig I, himself a poet, had succeeded in turning the Bavarian capital into a meeting-ground for writers, artists and cultural workers in general. Tyutchev felt thoroughly at home in this atmosphere and made good use of it, maintaining many stimulating personal contacts. In 1828 he was in touch with Heinrich Heine, who in a letter refers to him as his 'best Munich friend'. At the same time he often saw Schelling, whose philosophy of nature, together with Goethe's pantheism, exercised a strong influence upon his own poetry. And when, in 1832, Goethe died, his Russian admirer dedicated to him a poem worthy of its subject.

Tyutchev was only moderately prolific. The total number of poems to his credit is somewhere between 450 and 500. Considering the fact that he reached the age of seventy, this is not an overwhelming amount. He felt somewhat in-different about his literary career, and it is significant that on his return to Petersburg, in 1844, he soon became famous as a brilliant society wit and causeur, whereas his poems were known only to the initiated few. Refusing to curry favour either with the critics or the readers, he had to wait until 1850 for the first competent appreciation (by the poet Nekrasov) of his work. But even after that he showed so little interest in the promise of a belated literary fame

1. Pushkin never met Tyutchev personally. It was Vyazemsky who, in 1836, brought to Pushkin a notebook of Tyutchev's poems, and he printed twenty-four of them in the *Sovreménnik* (*The Contemporary*).

that he took no part in the first printed collection of his poems in 1854: he left it entirely to the discretion of his friend, the novelist I. S. Turgenev. The truth is that he wrote only when he could not help it, under inner compulsion, and even then with apparent reluctance, for he realised the inadequacy of the spoken or written word and felt sceptical about it. In one of his finest poems, *Silentium*, he explains the reason for his own meagre output in these lines, known to every lover of Russian poetry:

> Heart knows not to speak with heart.
> Song and speech can ne'er impart
> Faith by which we live and die.
> A thought once spoken is a lie.
> Unbroken, undefiled, unstirred
> Thy fountain: drink and say no word.[1]

Fortunately, Tyutchev did not always adhere to this rule. There were moments when he could not abstain from singing, whether he wanted to or not. His intimate contact with Nature, in particular, was responsible for a number of those moments, as was his emotionalised thought, aroused by an intense and distressingly visionary cosmic feeling. The spell of a tragic love, which swayed him in his later years, was responsible for a last and final crop of poignant lyrics. And since he wrote only when he felt impelled to, he put into his verse all the artistic and human integrity of which he was capable. Turgenev once said that Tyutchev's poems are not redolent of anything laboured, but seem to have been written, as Goethe wrote, on the spur of certain moments: instead of having been made, they have grown of their own accord 'like the fruits on a tree'.

2

To the average poetry-reader in Russia Tyutchev is known mainly for his nature lyrics. These are less ethereal but more direct and incisive in their laconic impressionism than the lyrics of his younger contemporary, Afanasy Fet (1820-92). They are also imbued with frequent philosophic contemplation spontaneously arising out of his moods rather than imposed upon them. He may sing about plains and mountains, spring floods, sea-waves, seasons, mornings and evenings —the array of motifs used by thousands of poets before and after him; yet he does it in his own manner, and his voice is unmistakable. As a rule he selects a few details only, which he arranges in such a way as to suggest the whole picture in its striking aspects without any superfluous words. Even such an obvious nature poem as his *Spring Storm*, now known from textbooks to every Russian schoolboy, can serve as an example. It begins with the simplest lines imaginable:

> I like a storm at May's beginning,
> When Spring's first thunder with wild cries

1. Translated by R. M. Hewitt in *A Book of Russian Verse* (Macmillan).

As though in frolic gaily spinning
Rumbles around the pale blue skies.

The elements of the storm are then compressed into eight lines which are sufficient to show it in its fullness, with the 'jargon of the forests, brawl of the mountains—all echoing the thunder's roar'. A mental picture with an appropriate simile is added as a final touch and conclusion :

Hebe, you'd say, had seized a brimming
Cup from Jove's eagle in wild mirth,
And laughingly had dashed the swimming
Nectar from heaven across the earth.[1]

But Tyutchev's lyrics are not always as cheerful as in the poem above. His impressionism often assumes a disquieting meditative character, tinged with symbolic meaning. The symbolist and the impressionist methods generally converge in him, containing now and then a summing-up comment as they do at the end of these lines :

The light of autumn evening seems a screen,
Some mystery with tender glamour muffling
The trees in motley, cloaked and eerie sheen,
The scarlet leaves that languid airs are ruffling.
The still and misty azure, vaguely far,
Above the earth that waits her orphan sorrow,
And bitter winds in gusty fragrance are
Forerunners of a bleak, storm-driven morrow.

The woods are waning; withered in the sun;
Earth shows the smile of passing, meekly tender
As the grave shyness of the suffering one,
In noble reticence of sad surrender.[2]

The last three lines stress the meaning of the picture. The symbolism of the following motif—a willow leaning over the running water—is, however, transparent enough to explain itself without any comment :

Why, O willow, to the river
Leans thy head so low, and why
Dost thou with long leaves that tremble,
And that thirsty lips resemble
Catch the ripples dancing by ?
Though thy leaflets faint and quiver,
Mirrored in the fleeting stream,
Yet the current speeds and splashes,
In caressing sunshine flashes,
And but mocks thy empty dream.[3]

1. Translated by V. de Sola Pinto.
2. Translated by Babette Deutsch and Avrahm Yarmolinsky in *Russian Poetry* (Lawrence).
3. Translated by Walter Morison in *A Book of Russian Verse* (Macmillan).

In Pushkin's poetry the phenomena of Nature exist as a rule in their own right, objectively, and are described as such. Tyutchev, on the other hand, prefers to approach them either as vehicles of his own moods and thoughts, or else to look upon them as a cover for what is clandestinely working behind and beyond the surface. His original contributions to Russian literature are, above all, those verses in which Nature herself is interpreted as a veil hiding from man's eyes the deeper cosmic processes active at the root of being.

It was here that certain influences of German thought left their mark in Tyutchev's work. Under the impact of Goethe's pantheism and even more of Schelling's philosophy of the identity between Spirit and Universe, he came to consider Nature as a living organism—with a soul, a mind and language of its own. These are accessible, however, only when the clarity of the day is replaced by the irrational element of the night. During the day we see the surface of Nature in all her alluring and deceptive beauty. But when the day is gone, man's consciousness can be attuned to the darker mysteries coming from the depths of being. He is then able to partake of universal life, provided he surrenders to the point of forgetting or even obliterating his own *moi haïssable* (hateful self). Such pantheistic moods at the hour of approaching night are well rendered in Tyutchev's *Twilight*:

> Dove-blue shades have met and mingled,
> Colours fade and sound is sleeping—
> Life and movement all dissolve in
> Trembling twilight, far-off weeping.
> Moths upon their unseen journeys
> Murmuring through the darkness fall . . .
> Moment this of wordless yearning!
> All within me, I in all. . . .
>
> Gentle twilight, sleepy twilight,
> Penetrate my inmost soul,
> Tranquil, languid, full of odours,
> All suffusing, lulling all
> In a mist of self-oblivion
> Every feeling softly fold!
> Let me taste annihilation,
> Merge me with the sleeping world.[1]

Night and twilight, imbued with this mystical flavour, became Tyutchev's favourite motifs. Appealing to his cosmic sense even more than to his sense of Nature, they affected him accordingly. What during the day appeared as harmony and beauty, was bound to dissolve at night into a foreboding of chaos as the lurking primeval essence of the universe. If the beauty of Nature gave him moments of ecstasy, the magic of night, charged with the bigger mystery of the cosmos, filled him with *angoisse* and metaphysical horror. His pantheism thus assumed the dualistic aspect of Day and Night, the symbolic meaning of which he expresses in this key-poem:

1. Translated by Walter Morison. *Op. cit.*

Across the spirits' secret world,
Hiding the chaos and the void,
The great gods, lest we be destroyed,
A golden curtain have unfurled.
This radiant veil we call the Day,
The lustrous Day, whose golden weave
Gleams nimbus-like on all who grieve,
And jewels with his joys the gay.

But Day wanes: Night shrouded in dusk,
Stalks forward, and with gestures gruff
Crumbles and rends the precious stuff,
And casts it down like any husk.
Then the abyss is bared to sight,
Its terrors grim, its shadows vast;
We shrink back, desperate, aghast.
Hence men, beholding fear the night.[1]

3

Around the hackneyed antithesis of day and night Tyutchev spun some of his
boldest imagery, but always with emphasis on the night. The poetry of night
was in vogue among the romantics, especially in Germany where it had devotees
such as Novalis, Tieck, Eichendorff and others. Among its votaries in Russia
was the tender lyrical poet Vasily Zhukovsky. Yet it would be hard to find a
poet who knew how to render this 'shrinking back aghast' with such vigour as
Tyutchev. If one can speak of nocturnal metaphysics at all, we find it in his
verses. Moreover, it was not terror alone but also the fascination of the Night
that drew him irresistibly with its mystery and magic.

As ocean's stream girdles the ball of earth,
From circling seas of dreams man's life emerges
And at night moves in silence up the firth,
The secret tide around our mainland surges.

The voice of urgent waters softly sounds;
The magic skiff uplifts white wings of wonder
The tide swells swiftly and the white sail rounds,
Where the blind waves in shoreless darkness thunder.

And the wide heavens, starred and luminous,
Out of the deep in mystery aspire.
The strange abyss is burning under us;
And we sail onwards, and our wake is fire.[2]

1. Translated by Babette Deutsch and Avrahm Yarmolinsky. *Op. cit.*
2. Translated by Babette Deutsch and Avrahm Yarmolinsky. *Op. cit.*

Tyutchev's awe of the waves thundering in the 'shoreless darkness' instead of abating as time went on, only grew stronger. He felt lost and forlorn like an orphan in the face of it, and while singing of man's 'fateful heritage', often obliterated the dividing line between things visual and things visionary. His impressionism passed into strangely realistic symbols.

> The night was dark with indignation;
> With cloud the sky was shrouded deep;
> It was not threat nor meditation,
> But drugged uncomfortable sleep.
>
> Only the lightning's summer revels
> Flashed alternating, out and in,
> As if a horde of deaf-mute devils
> Were holding conference of sin.
>
> As if a sign agreed were given,
> Broad conflagration fired the sky,
> And momently from the dark heaven
> Woods and far forests met the eye.
>
> Then disappeared again the vision;
> In visible darkness all was pent
> As if some great and dire decision
> Were taken in the firmament.[1]

'A horde of deaf-mute devils holding conference of sin' is one of those pregnant phrases (Tyutchev's poetry is full of them) which, once read, cannot be forgotten. As an emanation of his *angoisse* it points to certain realities within his own mind which haunted him. For he found there the same conflicting tendencies as in the cosmic life at large, only more personal, more painful— with the chaotic 'nocturnal' element on top of them all:

> Oh, thou, my wizard soul, oh, heart
> That whelming agony immerses,
> The threshold of two universes
> In cleaving thee, tears thee apart.[2]

Self-division of this kind anticipated certain *fin de siècle* traits. The agony alluded to was rendered even more unbearable because of the threat of scepticism, to which he was no stranger. As far back as 1851, he described to perfection (in eight lines) the inner vacuum resulting from that disposition which was doomed to undermine the generation of the 'moderns'.

> No sickness of the flesh is ours to-day
> Whose time is spent in grieving and despairing;
> Who pray all night that night will pass away—
> Who greet the dawn rebelliously uncaring.

1. Translated by Anon, in *A Book of Russian Verse* (Macmillan).
2. Translated by Babette Deutsch and Avrahm Yarmolinsky. *Op. cit.*

Withered and parched by unbelief, the soul
Impossible, unbearable things is bearing.
We are lost men, and ruin is our goal,
Athirst for faith, to beg for faith not daring.[1]

Tyutchev, too, was in danger of being inwardly paralysed by such a state of mind, and he knew it. In fact, during the decade preceding the above verses he wrote surprisingly little. He might have become silent altogether, had not chance provided him with a new source of inspiration. What happened was that in 1850 he, a married middle-aged man holding a high post in the department of censorship, fell passionately in love with a certain Mlle Denisyeva—a niece of the headmistress of the exclusive Smol'ny Institute, where his daughters were educated. Far from being a short platonic affair, this love lasted some fourteen years (until Mlle Denisyeva's death in 1864) and had a profound effect on Tyutchev's life and work.

4

There have been many—too many—poets of first love, but Tyutchev is not one of them. He sings of his last love instead. And his mood is not one of joy but of the nostalgic sadness of a parting day, the very beauty of which is tragic, as we can gather from his poem, *Last Love*:

As our years sink away, how tender it grows,
Our love, and how filled with fateful boding . . .
Shine on us, shine, thou farewell glow
Of love's last ray, of the twilight's brooding.

Shades have reft half the sky away:
Westward alone the light still lingers.
Bide with us, charm of the dying day;
Withdraw not, enchantment, thy magic fingers!

Let the coursing blood grow thin as gall,
If the heart but keep its tender burning . . .
O last and latest love of all,
Thou art bliss unending, and hopeless yearning.[2]

Tragic also was the love of Mlle Denisyeva. The position of a young and pretty society woman, who gave birth to three illegitimate children while her lover's German wife was still alive, was by no means easy. The gossip, slander and social ostracism she had to endure can well be imagined. Nor was Tyutchev himself invariably tender; there were times when his temper became unbearable. Besides, neither of the two lovers seemed able to separate love from torment and subsequent self-torment. A lyric in which he gives a condensed history of

1. Translated by R. Christie in *A Book of Russian Verse* (Macmillan).
2. Translated by Walter Morison.

his last passion begins with the frank exclamation, 'Oh, how killingly we love; how in the reckless blindness of passions we are sure to ruin all that is dear to our heart!' The 'immortal vulgarity of men,' having chosen Mlle Denisyeva for its target, did the rest. And the result? Two wrecked lives, and a series of poignant love-lyrics. These are written in a realistic vein, with frequent colloquial inflection. In some of them Tyutchev castigates himself by putting into the mouth of his beloved grave accusations, as though the verses had been written not by him but by her—in order to reproach him.

> That, as before, he loves me, tell me never,
> Nor that he treasures me as in the days gone by . . .
> Oh no! My life's thin thread, he, ruthless seeks to sever,
> For all I see the blade his fingers ply.
>
> Now raging, now in tears, with grief and anger seething,
> Swept madly on, my soul plucked bare and raw,
> I ache, nor am alive . . . in him alone know breathing;
> And needle-sharp is every breath I draw.
>
> He measures me the air more grudgingly and sparsely
> Than one would mete it out to one's most hated foe.
> I still can breathe; though painfully and harshly,
> I still draw breath—but life no longer know.[1]

The contrition after each fit of harshness may have increased the depth and the sincerity of his more tender feelings, but continuous ups and downs of this kind were costly for both—costly emotionally and physically. After some fourteen years of such love, it was the woman who had to pay the price. A further glimpse of her (and his) agony can be obtained from this poem:

> All day unconscious she was lying there,
> And evening shadows came and wrapt her round;
> Warm summer rain fell soft upon the leaves
> In steady flow and made a cheerful sound.
>
> And slowly she returned into herself,
> And trained her sense the pleasant sound to hear,
> And listened long, her mind absorbed in thought
> That carried her away, yet left her near.
>
> Then, as one speaking to herself, alone,
> Now conscious of the sound and all beside
> (I watched her, yet alive, though death was near)
> 'How dearly have I loved all this!' she sighed.
>
> Oh how thou loved'st it! And to love like thee
> Has to no other in the world been given!

1. Translated by Walter Morison.

My God! and can I then thy death survive
And my poor heart in fragments not be riven?[1]

Her death was an irreparable blow to Tyutchev. 'Only in her presence was I a personality, only in her love, her boundless love for me, was I aware of myself,' he owned to one of his friends in October 1864. 'Now I am a meaningless, painfully living nonentity.' Before long his poetic gift, too, began to decline. But while his lyrical vein seemed to be in abeyance, there was a sudden increase in the output of his political and civic verse—the last group of his poetry still to be considered.

5

With very few exceptions, Tyutchev's political poems cannot be compared either in depth or in technique with his lyrics. They are primarily a register of the ideological attitudes typical of Tyutchev the Russian and the aristocrat. His earliest political poem—an answer to Pushkin's Ode to Liberty—was written as early as 1820. Tyutchev wrote it in the liberal spirit prevalent among the advanced aristocratic youths of that generation. Later, however, he changed his opinions and after the Paris rebellion of 1830, definitely sided with reaction and the ideas of the Holy Alliance. He also became an ardent Russian patriot (while still continuing to use in private conversation and correspondence French in preference to his native tongue). In 1841 he, moreover, paid a visit to Prague, whence he returned a convinced pan-Slavist of the Russian brand.

From now on he considered Russia to be the only guarantee for the old order, since the West seemed to be in a constant ferment which had reached its climax in the revolutions of 1848. As a scion of the old serf-owning nobility, he was so frightened by the revolutionary trend in Europe that he wrote four essays (in French) in order to 'enlighten' the world at large. The most important of these is La Russie et la Révolution (1849). The gist of it was summed up by him in one of his political poems. The Rock and the Sea, in which tsarist Russia is likened to a cliff surrounded by the waves of the revolution vainly dashing against its 'gigantic heel'.

In spite of his one-time friendship with Heine, Tyutchev now turned his back on everything men of Heine's stamp were fighting for. Having identified Europe with the revolution, he prophesied in verse and prose the decline of the West. He even propped up his imperialistic pan-Slavism with a rather sophisticated philosophy of history. Russia would, in his opinion, eventually become the leader of all the Slavs, and the universal monarchy she was destined to found would extend as far as the Nile and Ganges, with Constantinople as its capital. A pax russica would then stem for ever the fury of the revolution, fomented by the godless masses of the West. In his poem, Sunrise, he gives allegorical utterance to the adage of ex oriente lux—quite in the spirit of mili-

1. Translated by P. E. Matheson in Holy Russia and Other Poems (Oxford University Press).

tant Slavophilism. Little did he suspect that some seventy years later the irony of history would make Russia a communist country, whereas the West would desperately try to save what it could of the old order. It was for patriotic, rather than religious, reasons that Tyutchev now stressed also his allegiance to the Russian Orthodox Church. In one of his poems he mentions Christ wandering in a slave's garb all over Russia and bestowing blessing upon her—a symbol of that religious Messianism which was so dear to the Slavophils.

The setbacks of the Russian army during the Crimean Campaign had a sobering effect upon Tyutchev. The morass into which the corrupt Russian bureaucracy had plunged the country was something of a revelation to him, and after the Tsar's death (during the campaign) he frankly said in a poem what he thought of him. Tyutchev's patriotism was sincere but, as he viewed the destinies of his country through his semi-feudal and imperialist spectacles, he was bound to see things in a wrong perspective. One more proof that good poets are rarely good politicians.

6

Tyutchev's place among the great Russian poets is no longer contested. Dostoevsky once called him the first poet-philosopher in Russian literature. Leo Tolstoy, who otherwise cared little for poetry, rated Tyutchev even higher than Pushkin. Touching with one end of his development the classical eighteenth century of Derzhavin, Tyutchev anticipated with the other the Russian school of Symbolism. He was a 'modern' before his time, which may have been one of the reasons why he had to wait so long for recognition. In spite of the high tribute paid to him by such contemporaries as Nekrasov, Turgenev, Apollon Grigoryev, and even the ultra-radical critic Dobrolyubov, Tyutchev's work came into its own only towards the end of the last century.

The pioneering article by the philosopher and poet Vladimir Solovyov (in 1895) was followed by a crop of essays in which some of the leading Russian symbolists proclaimed Tyutchev one of their predecessors. The height of his popularity was reached, however, in 1913, when a complete edition of his works, prefaced by Valery Bryusov, was launched as a supplement to the widely read monthly, Níva (The Cornfield). Nor did it suffer an eclipse after the Revolution of 1917 and in spite of his political views, his poetry is still acclaimed by Soviet readers. Among the more recent editions of his works there is even a large one for Soviet children—surely a sign of popularity the poet could never have dreamt of in his lifetime.

CHAPTER ELEVEN

Goncharov

I

Ivan Alexandrovich Goncharov (1812–91) is chiefly known outside Russia for his novel *Oblómov* which is now regarded as a world classic. At home, however, its author is still looked upon as one of the pillars of Russian realism, quite on a par with the great trio of Tolstoy, Dostoevsky and Turgenev. He was born in the remote Volga town of Simbirsk (now Ulyanovsk) into a merchant family living in comfortable circumstances. The practical and sober bourgeois-merchant strain in him on the one hand, and the more indolent gentry-tradition on the other, were largely responsible for his personal outlook on life and affected the character of his writings. His secondary and University education took place in Moscow, but most of his life was spent in Petersburg. He started his career as a punctilious civil servant who secretly trained himself as a writer. But, as if diffident of his talent, he was reluctant to publish anything until the age of thirty-five. Once he felt ready, however, he made the venture worth while. In 1846 he met the critic Belinsky, whose views on literature as a reflection and interpretation of life affected his own type of realism. Yet he did not seem to be on good terms with Belinsky and his circle of radicals. Years later, when looking back to that period, he candidly confessed :

> From a literary standpoint I merged with the circle, but in much, especially in its extreme negations, I did not agree with its members. The difference in our religious views, as well as in some other ideas and attitudes, prevented me from being more intimate with them. Most of all did I sympathise with Belinsky's sound views on literature, love of art, and finally with the honesty and severity of his character.

When in 1847 Goncharov's first novel, *A Common Story* (*Obyknovénnaya istóriya*) appeared, it was Belinsky who welcomed it at once and indeed proclaimed it the best work of fiction since Gogol's *Dead Souls*. But this sudden success did not turn Goncharov's head; slowly and methodically he kept writing his next novel, *Oblómov*, which was not published until twelve years later. Meanwhile, in the autumn of 1852 he started on an expedition, a hazardous sea-journey to Japan on the Russian frigate 'Pallas'. This venture lasted over two years and took him practically round the world. The expedition, with some five hundred sailors aboard; had the task of concluding a trade agreement with Japan. Goncharov, who travelled in an official capacity, recorded what he saw in a number of letters, sketches and diaries all of which appeared in various periodicals and were later (1855–57) published in two large volumes under the title of *Frigate Pallas* (*Fregát Palláda*)—an interesting but deliberately pedestrian account of what he had seen. As though defying any romantic propensities, Goncharov avoids here all 'purple patches' and enthusiastic effusions. The exotic scenery of the East hardly moved him at all, and the majesty of the Pacific storms, he saw—or pretended to see—as mere disorder and chaos. He had a good eye, though, for the ordinary daily life of the countries and races he visited. There is much humour in his descriptions of the frigate's stay at Nagasaki. His impressions of Japan and the Japanese certainly form the most amusing section of the book.

In 1859 Goncharov's *Oblómov* appeared and secured him a place in the front rank of Russian authors. The critic Dobrolyubov wrote in *The Contemporary* a whole essay about it which is still considered a classic of interpretative criticism. There followed scores of other articles, reviews and polemics, but Goncharov was in no hurry to exploit his fame by further writings. He waited another ten years before bringing out his third and last novel, *The Ravine* (*Obrýv*, 1869). This work was a great success with readers, but not with the critics. The radicals in particular were now fuming at him on account of a portrait which was supposed to be a skit on the revolutionary younger generation.

Goncharov, who had retired by then from the civil service, defended himself, but without avail. Besides, as if feeling that he had given all he could, he was now retiring also from literature. Henceforth he wrote mainly various reminiscences and one or two pieces of criticism. He was not anxious to cultivate literary connections on a large scale, especially after some previous misunderstandings with Turgenev, and in the end he became a recluse, tormented by persecution mania. Half-blind and paralysed, he died on 15 September, 1891.

2

Goncharov's main contribution to Russian literature consists of his three novels. He himself once said that, in spite of their differences, the three of them were actually one single novel, the subject of which was Russia during the transition years between 1840 and the end of the 1860s—a period of reforms, after which Russia was bound gradually to adjust herself to a more modern system of life based on money and economics. A slow infiltration of this system had in fact been going on for quite a time even before 1861, when serfdom was relegated to the past.

The theme of Goncharov's first novel, *A Common Story*, was precisely the need of such a switch-over from the old 'patriarchality' to something that was more in tune with the spirit of the age. The very structure of the novel is built upon the contrast between the old and the new as experienced by the generation of the 1840s. The narrative opens with the setting of an idyllic 'nest of gentlefolk' on the Volga. Prosperity and affection at home, magnificent scenery around, a pleasant carefree existence—all this is in store for the young Alexander Aduyev, the hero of the novel. Yet in spite of his dreamy nature, Alexander finds his home devoid of any active life and prospects. Spurred on by vague ambitions, he decides to leave for Petersburg. Preparations for his departure are in full swing, and they offer Goncharov an opportunity for drawing excellent portraits of both masters and house-serfs as he had seen them on the estates of the Simbirsk district.

Then we are transferred to Petersburg where the newcomer is confronted by his uncle Peter Aduyev—a man of substance and a great success not only in the civil service but in industrial enterprises as well. A realist through and through, Aduyev senior is the opposite of his provincial nephew whom he scrutinises with a hardly concealed mixture of pity and contempt. But he gives him a chance. In a couple of years Alexander had adapted himself (at least externally) to the metropolitan style of life, yet he made no headway either in the service or in his private love-affair, and least of all in business. As a result, both he and his uncle come to the conclusion that, being a failure, he ought to go back to his country estate and be content with his lot.

And this is what he does. At first he finds it pleasant to be at home again but as time goes on he becomes a prey to restlessness and boredom. Having tasted of life in the capital, he can no longer adjust himself to the stagnant quiet of the provinces and there is no other alternative for him except a new flight to Petersburg. Only this time he returns to the capital with a resolve to follow in his uncle's footsteps and take up an active life. The metamorphosis becomes clear in the Epilogue where we see him (a few years later) puffed up with success and on the eve of contracting a profitable *mariage d'argent*. Ironically enough, he displays this bourgeois pomposity at the very moment when his uncle , too, has undergone a change—in the opposite direction. Under the influence of his recently wedded sensitive wife Aduyev senior begins to wonder whether his own wealth and position are really worth all the sacrifices they have cost him in the past. At the end of it all he feels distressed and unhappy like a man whose life has been wasted. The author thus concludes his novel with a secret ironical chuckle, as if guessing that the same kind of meagre harvest awaits Aduyev's smart nephew in the future.

This simple and unexciting plot of the novel is told in a calm colloquial language. Admired by critics and readers alike, *A Common Story* gave Goncharov a name to be reckoned with. Expectations aroused by it were more than justified by his next work, *Oblómov*.

3

Oblómov can be approached from three angles: the artistic, psychological, and social. As a work of art it is above all a great character study in slow motion. Its sentences are long and leisurely, while its background is all of a piece with the dramatis personae. The novel is based on the same motif as *A*

Common Story, on the struggle between the old and the new. But here the chief character, Ilya Ilyich Oblomov, does not triumph over the 'old'; he is engulfed by it instead. The process of his going to seed is the actual theme of the novel.

Like Alexander Aduyev in Goncharov's previous work, Oblomov was a product of the comfortable parasitic existence based on serfdom. His ancestral Volga estate was a 'series of picturesque, bright, and smiling landscapes' for some ten or fifteen miles around. All the needs of its owners were provided by some three hundred toiling serfs. But the result of generations of such easy living had been to undermine both stamina and will-power. Oblomov, like the younger Aduyev, went to Petersburg in order to make the usual career befitting a nobleman. Yet it did not take long before he gave up all his ambitions and, instead of facing the demands of life, began to drift in his placid way year in year out. With his sloppy and eternally grumbling valet Zakhar—also a product of the serfdom system but from the other end—he continued to vegetate in the Russian capital with that absolute passivity which cannot but lead to doom.

The very opening of the novel shows us Oblomov's predicament when, at eight in the morning, he wakes up and suddenly remembers that a disturbing letter, received from his steward, has to be answered. But he postpones the answer, as he has done on so many previous occasions.

> Then he made up his mind to get up and wash, and, after drinking tea, to think matters over, taking various things into consideration and writing them down, and altogether to go into the subject thoroughly. He lay for half an hour tormented by his decision; but afterwards he reflected that he would have time to think after breakfast, which he would have in bed as usual, especially since one can think just as well lying down. This was what he did. After his morning tea he sat up and very nearly got out of bed; looking at his slippers, he began lowering one foot down towards them, but at once drew it back again. It struck half-past nine.

Yet Oblomov, who was so afraid of work and indeed of the slightest effort, drifted along with a good conscience. In his opinion it was perfectly right that, in spite of his indolence, he should receive a regular income provided by his serfs. This privileged parasitism, moreover, raised him in his own eyes to the status of a superior human being. When on one occasion his valet Zakhar likened him to other people, Oblomov was touched to the quick and flared up with moral indignation.

> Comparing me to other people! Why, do I rush about or work? Don't I eat enough? Do I look thin and wretched? Do I go short of things? I should hope I have someone to wait on me and do things for me. Thank Heaven, I've never in my life put on my stockings myself! As though I would trouble! Why should I? And to whom am I saying this? Haven't you waited on me since I was a child? You know all this; you know that I have been brought up tenderly, have never suffered from cold or hunger or poverty, have never earned my living or done any dirty work. So how could you bring yourself to compare me with other people?

The strange thing was that Zakhar entirely agreed with his master—agreed not only from a sense of duty but from his innermost conviction that Oblomov was a superior being. Such was the effect the serfdom system had on its drudging victims. What its effect on Oblomov himself was like, is illustrated by the whole of this novel. Yet the material of which Oblomov was made was essentially good, as anyone who came into contact with him was bound to feel. This was why such a woman of character as Olga Ilyinskaya fell in love with him and did all she could to drag him out of his sloth. But her high demands upon him only made him the more painfully aware of his own passivity which he was both unable and in the end also unwilling to overcome. Hence the pathos of the last meeting between the two.

> 'Why has all been wrecked?' Olga asked, suddenly raising her head. 'Who laid a curse on you, Ilya? What have you done? You are kind, intelligent, affectionate, noble . . . and . . . you are doomed. What has ruined you? There is no name for that evil.'
> 'Yes, there is', he whispered almost inaudibly.
> She looked at him questioningly, with her eyes full of tears.
> 'Oblomovism', he whispered.[1]

And that was that. The disease inherited from his ancestors had become incurable in him. Even the loyal efforts of his enterprising friend Andrey Stolz proved as futile as Olga's love had been before. The half-German Stolz, who subsequently married Olga, was an efficient bourgeois counterpart of Alexander's uncle in *A Common Story*. He did his utmost to save his friend from 'oblomovism', yet it was in vain. Besides, when he appeared on the stage, Oblomov had already found a new shelter under the wing of the plump lower-class widow Agafya Pshenitsyna, in whose suburban house he had taken rooms. There he felt safe at last, since the affectionate Agafya was unable to resist either the spell of the infant or of the gentleman in Oblomov. He soon became her lover, had a child by her, eventually married her but

> the great thing was that all went on peacefully: he had no lump at his heart, he never once wondered anxiously whether he would see his land-lady or not, or worried as to what she would think, what he would say to her, how he would answer her question, how she would look at him—there was nothing of the kind. He had no yearnings, no sleepless nights, no sweet or bitter tears. He sat smoking and looked at her sewing, some-times he said something and sometimes he said nothing, and all the time he felt at peace, not needing anything, not wanting to go anywhere, as though all he needed were here. . . . It was as though some unseen hand had placed him as a precious plant in a spot where he was sheltered from the heat and the rain, and nurtured tenderly.

In this vegative suburban paradise Oblomov drifted to eternal sleep as peacefully as any mortal could wish to. And with him died a whole era of

1. Quotations are taken from *Oblomov*, translated by Natalie Duddington (Everyman Library, Dent, 1932).

Russian history, even if the aftermath it left behind proved to be of a complex and disturbing nature.

Oblomov himself is an unsurpassed portrait of the 'superfluous man' produced by the serfdom system. But he becomes something more than that if we look upon him as an image of man's inherent tendency towards escapism, arrested development and the line of least resistance, instead of coping with the difficulties and trials of life. On the other hand, Goncharov asserted through the active (though somewhat abstract) Stolz his faith in a progress without the ironic implications felt at the end of *A Common Story*. Some ten years later he was compelled, however, to check a great deal of his practical optimism, or at least to modify its perspective. This he did in his next novel, *The Ravine*.

4

The theme of *The Ravine* is also based on the struggle between the old and the new, between 'fathers' and 'children'. Unfortunately, there is a certain confusion of the periods in this novel: its general background is that of the 1840s, whereas some characters, conversations and incidents are typical of the 1860s. Although Raisky, the main character of the narrative, is first presented to us in Petersburg, the subsequent action takes place entirely on Raisky's Volga estate, Malinovka, ruled over by one of his relations—a remarkable old woman, commonly referred to as 'granny'. His two pretty nieces, Vera and Marfinka, live there under her watchful eye, but they differ in character as much as did the Mary and Martha of the Gospels. As Malinovka is in the vicinity of a Volga town (Goncharov's Simbirsk), the author parades before us some of its inhabitants: officials, old-world gallants, schoolmasters, 'emancipated' women, and even an exiled revolutionary—Mark Volokhov who lives there under police supervision.

The central figure at first is Raisky. He is an aesthetic dilettante devoid of real talent; or rather he is endowed with an abundance of talents which he is unable to exploit in a creative way. Vacillating all the time between literature, music, painting, and sculpture, he is another variety of the 'superfluous man' who—with all his good intentions—never achieves anything worth while. The emptiness of his life in Petersburg makes him leave for Malinovka whose quiet charm is a revelation to him—at first. He is equally impressed by 'granny', as well as by the beauty of his two nieces with both of whom he falls, consecutively, in love.

The 'granny', with her poise and wisdom, is one of Goncharov's great creations: a positive character whom he has made fully convincing and alive. In some respects she is a symbol of all that was solid, good, and honest in the traditions of old patriarchal Russia without being in the least unreal or stilted. As for the two nieces entrusted to her care, Marfinka is like her 'granny': active, uninhibited, dominated by traditions, and integrated with her background. Her older sister Vera, however, is determined to go beyond the narrow if pleasant sphere of Malinovka and join the stream of the progressive forces of the age; but she does not even suspect the price she might have to pay for such a step.

As it happens, Vera thinks she had found a representative of those new forces in the 'nihilist' Volokhov. In spite of some of his troublesome characteristics she becomes attached to him at the very time when Raisky, too, is—rather unsuccessfully—in love with her. During these peripeties the centre of gravity is transferred from Raisky to Vera whose surrender to Volokhov and her reactions to it form the climax of the novel. Having discovered, to her horror, that she has been in love not with a man but with a fake, she has a complete moral and physical collapse after her 'fall'. She begins to recuperate only after she has made an attempt to adjust her inner self to those values of life which were embodied in 'granny'. To make her recovery more certain, Goncharov even sends her another admirer in the person of Tushin: a new edition of Stolz—this time of pure Russian extraction. Determined to graft the progressive bourgeois-capitalist forces upon what was good and solid in the old Russian values, Tushin thus corrects, as it were, the one-sided tendency to ape the West blindly and uncritically. The proper course was to blend the best qualities of the two and thus produce something that would be Russian and European in one.

Such, approximately, was the *arrière-pensée* of Goncharov himself, although here too he was concerned with characters and human relations rather than with ideas. Needless to say, the *dénouement* of the novel is more or less happy for all concerned except Raisky. Feeling more superfluous than ever, he leaves Malinovka a sadder but hardly a wiser man.

5

The Ravine is richer in incident than Goncharov's other two novels. But it is often rambling and now and then marred by the author's outbursts against the followers of Western radicalism and materialism. He charged them with the crime of having 'degraded man to a mere physical being and rejected all that was not animal-like in him.' Volokhov was commonly interpreted as a deliberate caricature of the radical-democratic youths of the 1860s, and this put the novel among the reactionary works of the period.

Goncharov tried to explain Volokhov away in his autobiographic *Better Late than Never* (*Lúchshe pózdno chem nikogdá*, written in 1870), which had, however, little effect upon those who were determined to think otherwise. As if tired of the present, he now preferred to look back to the past. The changes that were going on in so many branches of life were much too sudden and too quick for him to be followed or properly assimilated. In spite of his hatred of serfdom, for example, he yet felt much more at home in the Russia he had known before 1861. *My University Reminiscences* (1870), *Notes about Belinsky's Personality* (1874), *At Home* (1887), as well as his *Old-Time Servants* (1888) are all based on his recollections of the past. His critical essay, *A Million Torments* (*Milyón terzániy*, 1872) is a brilliant analysis of Griboyedov's comedy

Woe from Wit, whereas in *A Literary Evening* (*Literatúrny vécher*, 1877) he uses a narrative frame in order to air his own opinions about literary trends and theories. Finally, Goncharov's posthumous autobiographic *An Uncommon Story* (*Neobykovénnaya istóriya*), written in the second half of the 1870s and printed only in 1924, contains a savage attack on Turgenev whom he wrongly accuses of having plagiarised *The Ravine*.

The bulk of Goncharov's art differs from that of his contemporaries by its sobriety, its common sense, and also its good-natured (almost English) sense of humour. In contrast to Dostoevsky, who revelled in the irrational or the abnormal, Goncharov had a flair for what was settled and normal. A keen observer and an analyst in one, he knew how to deal competently with human characters and human relations on the one hand, and with genre pictures on the other. In his style he combined the simplicity inherited from Pushkin with Gogol's attention to detail. The *diapason* of his creations may not be very broad, yet his work, such as it is, entitles him to a place of honour in Russian literature, while *Oblómov* links his name with the *belles lettres* of the world.

CHAPTER TWELVE

Nekrasov

I

The poetic activities of Nikolai Nekrasov (1821–78) coincided with those years when the 'golden age' of Russian poetry was already a matter of the past. There was no lack of younger poets, but the majority of them were not on a par with, say, Tyutchev who was still alive and active as a poet. Even Nekrasov, potentially the most original of them, had started his career as an epigone. Gradually, however, he struck out a path of his own, the novelty of which can be explained partly by his personality, and partly by the conditions in which he lived and worked. Born in 1821, he matured with the generation of the 1840s —the period of the rise of the intelligentsia. The Decembrist spirit was not yet dead, and there was a regular cult of those political martyrs who were still toiling in the mines of Siberia. Typical products of that spirit were members of the landed gentry such as Alexander Herzen and Mikhail Bakunin, both of whom contributed what they could to the radical thought of Russia and indeed of Europe. It was in the 1860s that the role of the commoners in the literary, cultural and political activities rapidly increased. But whereas the gentlemen, relying on their estates, had enough leisure to write without worrying about their daily bread, most of the commoners lived from hand to mouth as journalists and pamphleteers. At times they were compelled to be purveyors of *vaudevilles*, hastily written *feuilletons*, topical doggerel, and other commercialised genres.

Nekrasov had to do his literary apprenticeship at the end of the 1830s and in the early 1840s. It was a hard school and full of bitter experiences; the more so because his father, an officer and landowner of the old, brutal type, left him without any support at the age of seventeen. He had sent his boy from Yaroslavl' on the Volga to Petersburg with the intention of making him enter the army. But as the future poet refused to have anything to do with the Cadet Corps, he was deprived by his parent of all financial help and had to rely on his own resources. Starving and freezing in the streets of Petersburg, Nekrasov lived for a while the life of a down-and-out. Things were so bad that he often had to be sheltered by compassionate beggars in doss-houses. He never forgot the lessons learned during those trials, but he managed to get out of them comparatively soon. His first step towards something better consisted of journalistic hackwork. Prolific as he was in both verse and prose, he was not slow in acquiring a certain facility which he retained—often at the expense of good taste—throughout the whole of his literary career. The ambition to succeed as a poet made him write a volume of poems called *Dreams and Sounds*, which was published in 1840. This was a collection of immature conventional verses (with traces of Zhukovsky's influence). The critic Belinsky attacked it so violently that the book had neither literary nor financial success. Undaunted, Nekrasov looked for a more remunerative outlet as editor and publisher. He was introduced to Belinsky, and before long the two were friends as well as fellow workers. Early in 1846 Nekrasov edited the *Petersburg Miscellany*, with Turgenev's *Three Portraits* (*Tri portréta*) and Dostoevsky's first novel, *Poor Folk* (*Bédnye lyúdi*) as its pièces de résistance. The success was enormous. In the same year he was able to acquire (together with Panayev) *The Contemporary* which he turned into a periodical of the radical-minded democratic intelligentsia in Russia. In addition to the best authors of the day, he had among his contributors Chernyshevsky and Dobrolyubov—the two leading pamphleteers and critics after Belinsky.

The great decade of the 1860s began with the liberation of the serfs and some other far-reaching reforms, but the unfortunate Polish rising of 1863–64 marred a number of hopes. The suppression of the Poles by Muravyov, nicknamed the 'Hangman', was so brutal that the young Tsar Alexander II himself, who was under the influence of liberal advisers, felt disgusted and said so. Yet after the attempt on the Tsar's life (on 4 April, 1866) by A. Karakozov, the 'Hangman' who had been previously sacked, came into power once again, and this created considerable panic among the radicals. Nekrasov, known by then all over Russia as poet and editor, hoped to bribe Muravyov by writing some verses in his honour (which he himself recited at a banquet); but even such a shameful trick failed to work and *The Contemporary* was suspended in 1866. It was only two years later (1868) that Nekrasov managed to get hold of another important periodical, *The Fatherland's Annals* (*Otéchestvennye Zapíski*), in the editing of which he was soon joined by the satirist Saltykov-Shchedrin and the sociologist Mikhailovsky. Under their guidance the periodical became the principal organ of the populist trend of thought. Strangely enough however, Nekrasov managed to combine his editorial and literary duties with all sorts of excesses which required a great deal of money. He gambled, hunted, entertained on a lavish scale, kept expensive cooks and even more expensive mistresses. In the end he became involved (together with his mistress Mme Panayeva) in a shabby financial transaction which concerned the fortune belonging to the feeble-minded wife of the expatriate poet Ogaryov—all this, while he was writing deeply-felt poems about the people's woe and injustice. His double nature must have caused him a great deal of suffering. He was also afflicted, quite early, with an incurable disease in the throat, from which he died on 8 January, 1878. Accompanied to his grave by the populist generation of the 1870s, Nekrasov remained, whatever his private failings, their inspirational mouthpiece.

2

After his lack of success in 1840, Nekrasov found his own poetic voice rather late—towards the end of the 1850s and in the first half of the 1860s. As for the general trend of this poetry, it had a number of themes some of which had their sources in his experience at home and in Petersburg. In boyhood he witnessed the cruel treatment meted out to the serfs, as well as to his own mother (a Polish woman of some education and refinement), by his uncouth father. In Petersburg again he saw the very depths of misery bred by a big city. His opposition to everything that was connected with serfdom and autocracy made him write civic poetry, whereas his sympathy with the oppressed serfs drove him towards the people and was responsible for the voice of a 'repentant nobleman', with a strong guilt-complex, in most of his work. To this the realism of his 'big city' poems, dealing with the Petersburg he had learned to know, should be added. In one of them, beginning with the line, 'When I drive at night in a darkened street,' he describes with haunting directness a starving couple whose baby has just died. Both of them have been reduced to such straits in their garret as to be unable to buy even the coffin in which to bury their child. In the end the young mother is compelled to go out on the streets whence, later on, she returns—her eyes full of shame and despair—with money for the coffin. The extremes of such misery appealed to Nekrasov the poet as much as they did to Dostoevsky the novelist. And he was among the first to introduce the 'big city' motif to Russian poetry. His *Street Scenes* and pictures of Petersburg outcasts were further enlarged by social satires, by caustic scenes from bureaucracy and high life. These border, however, on his civic poems proper. Much of his civic and political verses can be dismissed as rhymed pamphleteering. If we want to find Nekrasov at his best and most original, we must look for him in the poems he wrote about the toiling people and frequently also in the manner of the people.

In order to appreciate his poetic work a few words should be said about some other gifted poets of his generation, such as Apollon Maikov (1821–97), Yakov Polonsky (1819–97), Afanasy Fet-Shenshin (1820–92) and others. Both Maikov and Polonsky wrote 'engaged' as well as 'pure' poetry. Whereas their social indictments are in the style of the period, their nature lyrics are often exquisite in their musical and evocative quality. Polonsky was the greater poet of the two and, as a partial follower of Lermontov, remained to the end predominantly subjective and romantic. The best lyrical voice of that group was, however, the voice of Fet—a champion of 'pure' poetry. He showed no marked interest in social or political questions, but his love lyrics and nature verses, as well as his philosophical poems (vibrating with a stoic acceptance of life), are unsurpassed by any of his contemporaries. Like Tyutchev, he came to be appreciated rather late: he was 'discovered' and taken up by the Symbolists at the end of the last century.

The poetic pattern of the Nekrasov period would not be complete if it did not include such widely different poets as Count Alexey K. Tolstoy (1817–75) and Nikolai Ogaryov (1813–77) on the one hand, and Ivan Nikitin (1824–61) and Nikolai Shcherbina (1821–69) on the other. Herzen's friend and helper Ogaryov was not only a voluntary exile, but a typical 'repentant nobleman' singing of frustration and nostalgia in his intimate as well as civic verses. Alexey K. Tolstoy, however, was from the very first an essentially cheerful and humorous poet whose polished lyrics are full of verve and a healthy joy of life. Although devoid of any democratic sympathies, he was no reactionary. In his satirical and intelligent nonsense verse he was, moreover, ready to deride or parody both friend and foe. The Works of Koz'ma Prutkov, 1855 (Sochinéniya Koz'mý Prutkóva), which he had written together with his cousins, the two brothers—Alexey and Vladimir—Zhemchuzhnikov, was a creditable achievement of this kind.[1] And so was his posthumously published (1883) History of the Russian Empire—a hilarious satirical parody in verse. As for Nikolai Shcherbina, who was half-Greek, his calm 'Parnassian' poetry conjured up serene images of the classical world. The commoner Nikitin, on the other hand, was a poet of gloom and despondency. He wrote some incisive nature lyrics; but he is at his strongest in realistic verses describing the people's misery, as he does in his best known narrative poem, The Usurer (Kulák).

The talents of these poets were on the whole greater than their craftsmanship which fell below that of the Pushkin generation. This applies even to such an exceptional man as Konstantin Sluchevsky (1837-1904). Complex and original as he was, he had plenty to say, but he said it in a fragmented manner and remained only the 'torso of a genius'. He, too, like Fet, was properly appreciated only by the modernists, one of whom (Valery Bryusov) made the apt remark that Sluchevsky stammered, but his stammer was like the stammer of Moses. Nor should be omitted the eclectic character of poetry in those days—a feature from which Nekrasov at his best escaped. And he was able to do this only because of his sympathy with the people and his feeling for the Russian folksong. Whatever one may think of Nekrasov's civic and political-didactic verses, there can be no doubt of the power and the melody he so often extracted from the folksong. Elements of such creative rapprochement with the people can be found before him—in Pushkin, Lermontov, and especially in Kol'tsov, but none of them went farther in this direction than Nekrasov. It may have been partly for this reason that the populist Chernyshevsky (not a reliable judge of poetry) put Nekrasov higher than Pushkin and Lermontov.

Nekrasov's flair for the melody of the folksong (with its peculiar rhythms and verbal instrumentation) was exceptionally strong. It was he, too, who cultivated on a large scale the dactylic endings typical of the bylíny and many other Russian folksongs. Through his peculiar blend of anapaests and iambics with dactylic rhymes he enlarged the scope and the melodiousness of Russian poetry, thus building a bridge between literature and the people. Having turned, on many occasions, against the accepted canons, he made the next step and tried to de-

1. Under the collective pseudonym, Koz'ma Prutkov, there appeared, from 1851 on, a number of satirical poems and plays in Nekrasov's Sovreménnik. In conjunction with another brother Zhemchuzhnikov (Lev) they even invented and published—in 1855—a fictitious biography with a lithographed portrait of Koz'ma Prutkov, who for quite some time was believed to be a real person.

poetise literary poetry by introducing all sorts of unpoetic and peasanty words.[1]
Yet it is the genuine folk-flavour that makes a number of his poems, including
The Pedlars (*Korobéiniki*), *The Green Rustle* (*Zelyóny shum*) and the whole of
his epic *Who can he Happy and Free in Russia?* (*Komú ná Rusi zhit' khoroshó?*),
almost untranslatable. Even the best rendering of the contents does not do justice
to such poems unless one catches all the peculiarities of Nekrasov's inflection,
rhythm and melody, and these are inseparable from the Russian language. So
much for Nekrasov's technique. Another strong point of his work is its village
realism which also deserves to be mentioned.

3

Nekrasov's 'big city' motifs were largely connected with his civic poetry and
owed a great deal to the 'natural school,' advocated by Belinsky. The same
holds good of his poems directed against his own class—the poems of a nobleman who, for moral as well as humanitarian reasons, became a defender of
the peasant and the village. One of such examples is his *Home*. It makes one
think of Lermontov's indictments and of Pushkin's poem, *In the Country*, with
the difference, though, that Nekrasov openly accuses himself, his ancestors
and particularly his own father. This is how it begins :

> Behold it once again, the old familiar place,
> Wherein my fathers passed their barren vacant days!
> In muddy revels ran their lives, in witless bragging;
> The swarm of shivering serfs in their oppression found
> An enviable thing the master's meanest hound.
> And here to see the light of heaven I was fated,
> And here I learned to hate, and bear the thing I hated;
> But all my hate I hid within my soul for shame,
> And I at seasons too a yokel squire became;
> And here it was my soul, untimely spoilt and tainted,
> With blessed rest and peace too soon was disacquainted;
> Unchildish trouble then, and premature desires,
> Lay heavy on my heart, and scorched it with their fires.
> Nay, from those younger years of harshness and rebelling
> No recollection brings one comfortable ray.[2]

Remembering the sad lot of the serfs, Nekrasov was never able to dissociate
it from the suffering of his own bullied mother, for whom he conceived (at
least after her death) a regular cult, as one can conclude from the following
lines in the same poem :

> Here is the dark, dark close. See where the branches thicken,
> What figure glimpses down the pathway, sad and stricken?

1. This process of de-poetisation was strongly marked in his civic verses (addressed
mostly to the 'populist' intelligentsia) and abounding in words taken from ordinary
journalese.
2. Translated by Oliver Elton in *A Book of Russian Verse* (Macmillan).

Too well the cause I know, my mother, of thy tears;
Too well I know who marred and wasted all thy years.
For ever doomed to serve a sullen churl untender,
Unto no hopeless hope thy spirit would surrender;
To no rebellious dreams thy timorous heart was stirred;
Thy lot, like any serf's, was borne without a word.[1]

In the end the poet—a descendant of serf-owners—experienced something like a moral satisfaction when seeing his ancestral home almost ruined. On the whole, the virulence of his indictment was always in direct ratio to his own repentance. Repentance, or rather a mood of ever-recurring moral masochism and self-castigation, may well have been needed by him even as a creative stimulus. This alone would be enough to throw some light on the quality of his behaviour during his years of prosperity; on the one hand the sumptuous living typical of a squire, and on the other his self-reproaches—turned into poetry. And the more he hated the remnants of the squire in him, the more acutely he felt also the people's tragedy and the people's cause, with which he was anxious to identify himself in his verses. After all, he called his Muse 'the people's sister'.

Nekrasov's realism of the countryside does not entirely concentrate on the negative and tragic side of village life. There are bright moments as well. What could be more delightful than the realism of his poem, *Peasant Children* (*Kres-tyánskie déti*), in which he describes a bevy of little village urchins clandestinely looking at him through a chink and making comments of their own! Here is the beginning:

Again in the country! A life full of pleasure,
I shoot; I write verses in solitude deep;
And yesterday, searching the moorland for treasure,
I came to a cowshed, turned in, fell asleep.
I woke. Through a crack in the wall had come prying
The sun's joyous rays, in profusion of gold,
A pigeon is cooing; some young rooks are flying
Just over the roof, in a chorus they scold.
Another bird raises an outcry uncanny,
I think by its shadow a crow it must be,
But hark! There's a whisper! And lo, through the cranny
A row of bright eyes gaze intently at me.
Yes, grey, black and blue eyes in earnest reflection
Are mingled together like flowers in a field.[2]

Equally delightful are some of his other poems—humorous, descriptive, didactic—dedicated to Russian children: *Uncle Jack*, for instance; or *General Toptýgin*, in which the frightened peasants mistake a run-away bear for an angry General; or *Grandad Mazáy*, who during a spring flood rescues a boatful

1. Translated by Oliver Elton. *Op. cit.*
2. Translated by Oliver Elton. *Op. cit.*

of hares and would not touch the bewildered creatures. He releases them instead, though with a warning:

> God speed you!
> Straight to shelter.
> But look, my friends,
> Though now I free you,
> When summer ends
> Don't let me see you:
> I raise my gun—
> Your day is done.[1]

Yet in the majority of his peasant or village poems the sad and gloomy disposition prevails. Nekrasov's verses about the people's woe always strike the right note and are particularly moving when he sings of the hard lot of the Russian peasant woman. The account in *Orína—a Soldier's Mother* of how a peasant woman's only son, a healthy young giant, had been forcibly conscripted, and after a few years returned home a complete wreck only in order to die of tuberculosis, is heart-rending in its tone and simplicity. Then there are the suffering toilers on the Volga and elsewhere, whom the poet asks at the end of his famous *Meditation at a Porch*, whether the only thing they have given to the world is their 'song resembling a groan', after which they are perhaps doomed to disappear for ever. Nekrasov himself may have wavered in his answer, but not for long. Behind the people's tragedy he felt also the people's vitality, as well as that broad, generous goodness which comes only from latent strength. And his admiration for them is testified by a number of his best poems, such as *The Green Rustle, The Pedlars, Vlas, The Red-Nosed Frost* and *Who can be Happy and Free in Russia?* It was in these poetic creations that Nekrasov identified himself with the very soul of the people in a more distinctive way than any other Russian poet of that period.

4

Take such a lyrical drama in miniature as *The Green Rustle*. The bracing rhythm of the opening verses is itself suggestive of the arrival of the spring. The manner, the accent and the imagery are those of the peasants. Even the blossoming trees are white as if someone had 'poured milk over them'. And then we listen to the monologue of a peasant who, on his return home from Petersburg (where he had been working), learned that his wife had been unfaithful to him. All through the Winter he had brooded resentfully and in the end sharpened a knife with which he intended to kill her. Suddenly the Spring arrived and drove all evil thoughts out of his mind. As though spell-bound, his heart could not resist the wave of generosity and forgiveness brought along by so much beauty. And this is the final note of the poem:

1. Translated by Juliet Soskice in *Poems by Nekrasov* (The World's Classics, Oxford University Press).

Love as long as you can,
Suffer as long as you can,
Forgive as long as you can,
And let God be your judge!

The Pedlars again is a series of poems about two enterprising Yaroslavl'
peasants, peddling their wares in the countryside :

Making profit with each mile;
Everything they chance to meet with
Serves the journey to beguile.[1]

In this series Nekrasov came so near to the accent and the spirit of the
people that its opening verses have actually become a folksong :

Oy! How full, how full my basket!
Calicoes, brocades, a stack,
Come, my sweeting, make it lighter,
Ease the doughty fellow's back.
Steal into the ryefields yonder,
There till night-fall I'll delay,
When I see thy black eyes shining
All my treasures I'll display.[1]

There follow the pedlars' jokes, arguments and adventures with the village
folk. As a contrast to their carefree gaiety the *Song of a Poor Pilgrim* is interpolated, but the wailing tune and rhythm of its Russian words can hardly be
rendered in any translation.

I pass through the meadows—the wind in the meadows is moaning :
  'Cold I am, pilgrim, cold I am.
  Cold I am, dear one, cold I am.'
I pass through the forest—the beasts in the forest are howling :
  'We're hungry, oh, pilgrim, we're hungry!
  Hungry, oh dear one, hungry!'

The whole of the unhappy, exploited peasant Russia is thus reviewed, and
each line ends with the refrain of either 'cold' or 'hungry', the slow repetition of
which in Russian (*khólodno, gólodno*) suggests the moaning of the wind or the
howling of beasts. The motif of desolation in these lines also prepares the reader
for the tragic end of the cycle. The two pedlars are murdered by a woodman
who robs them of their money and is, in his turn, arrested the same night while
carousing in a village inn.

The poem *Vlas*, which was much admired by Dostoevsky (he wrote about
it in *The Diary of an Author*), portrays a thoroughly Russian figure : a repentant
sinner after the people's heart. He is a former village *kulák* who without
mercy—

---

1. Translated by Juliet Soskice, *Op. cit.* The same applies to all the following quotations
from Nekrasov, except the last.

Snatched the bread from needy neighbours
While, in famine's hideous reign,
Not a coin would leave his pocket
Unrepaid by threefold gain.

But during a heavy illness he had the vision of hell—horrifying enough
to make him regret all his evil deeds and to become a new man. With the same
firmness of purpose with which he had formerly robbed his fellow-beings, he
now gave up his earthly possessions—

All his wealth in gifts bestowing,
Destitute did Vlas remain,
Wandered barefoot, homeless, begging
Money for God's church to gain.

Red-Nosed Frost (*Moróz-Krásny nos*, 1863) is another gem of Nekrasov's
poetry. Although written in conventional metres, it is a perfect blending of
poetic realism, peasant-mentality and folklore. The theme is simple. Prokel,
young Darya's husband, has died and, in severe wintry weather, is buried with
all the peasant rites and customs. After the burial Darya returns to her cold
hut. In order to make it warm for her two tiny children, she drives her horse
Savraska to the neighbouring wood. While she gathers logs, King Frost sees her,
swoops down, and makes her fall asleep. Freezing to death amidst the gorgeous
scenery of the snowy forest, she dreams of all the best moments connected
with her married life, her fields, her children Grishouka (Gregory) and Masha
(Mary). The following section of the poem is typical of Nekrasov's realism,
applied to the more idyllic side of a peasant's life and work :

In sparkling white hoarfrost encrusted
To cold overpowering she yields,
She's dreaming of radiant summer,
Some rye is still left in the fields—

It's cut though; relieved they are feeling,
The peasants are piling it high,
And she, in another allotment,
Is digging potatoes close by.

The grandmother too is there working,
And on a full sack at their feet
The pretty rogue Masha is sitting
And clasping a carrot to eat.

The big, creaking wagon approaches,
Savraska is turning her head,
And close to the bright, golden burden
Comes Prokel with ponderous tread.

'God keep you! And where is Grishouka?'
The father inquires, passing by,
'Among the sweet peas,' say the women,
'Grishouka, Grishouka!' they cry.

And meanwhile Grishouka comes running,
With garlands of peas he is bound,
A living green bush one might fancy
Is skimming along oe'r the ground.

He runs! Eh! ... As swift as an arrow!
He's burning the grass in his flight!
Grishouka is black as a raven,
His little head only is white.

He's shrieking with joy. There's a circlet
Of peas round his neck, like a wheel.
He gives some to mother and granny,
And sister. He twists like an eel!

From mother the mite gets caresses,
From father a sly little pinch,
And meanwhile Savraska's not idle:
She's stretching her neck, inch by inch.

She's reached them, the peas, sweet and juicy!
She's chewing and licking her lips
And raising her mouth, soft and loving,
The ear of Grishouka she nips.

5

There remains Nekrasov's central work *Who can be Happy and Free in Russia?*
(1873-76). This epic is unique of its kind and occupies in his writings a position
similar to that of *Onégin* in the work of Pushkin. If *Onégin* combines and
completes, as it were, all the ingredients of Pushkin's poetry, *Who can be Happy
and Free in Russia?* shows all the main features of Nekrasov the poet. Its
aim was to give a picture of the whole of Russia after the abolition of
serfdom in 1861, but it is written in the people's spirit, style and language.
The loom on which it is woven is that of a folk-tale, which does not prevent
the poet from displaying plenty of realism, indictment, satire, boisterous
humour, as well as the implied didactic purpose within the frame of the epic.
Seven poor peasants meet on a high road and begin to argue as to who is happy
and free in Russia. They go on arguing until they come to blows. Then they
capture a little peewit. The mother-bird, seeing this, offers them as ransom a
magic napkin which, at their bidding, will produce in a moment all the food
they ask for. They agree to it. Provided with such an unexpected gift,

The peasants unloosen
Their waist belts and gather
Around the white napkin
To hold a great banquet.
In joy, they embrace
One another and promise
That nought shall persuade them
To turn their steps homewards
To kiss wives and children,
To see the old people,
Until they have settled
For once and forever
The subject of discord :
Till they have discovered
The man who, in Russia,
Is happy and free.

Their Odyssey begins. In the course of it they encounter all sorts of people, take part in a rowdy village fair, get acquainted with such remarkable and truly strong characters as Klim the village Elder and the peasant woman Matryona—a worthy counterpart of Darya in *Red-Nosed Frost*. Uneven as a whole, the epic contains fine descriptive and lyrical passages, including a paraphrase of a folk song *About the Two Great Sinners* (*O dvukh velíkikh gréshnikakh*). The scenes at a village fair are grotesquely amusing. Both humour and satire are provided by the figures of the doddering old squire, Obolt-Obolduyev, who refuses to accept the reforms of 1861. His heirs, afraid of making him angry and thus forfeiting the expected fortune, have—through bribery—persuaded the peasants to behave, until the squire's rapidly approaching death, as though they were still serfs, which they do with much fun. Russia passes before us in a variety of aspects, and whatever her trials, she has enough vigour and vitality to overcome them all. So the epic, although unfinished, contains a note of faith and hope. An ambitious youth, Grisha, from among the commoners, sees in his poetic dreams what is in store for his country and people; dreams which are enough to chase away despondency and pessimism from the reader's mind.

His bosom was burning;
    What beautiful strains
In his ears began chiming;
    How blissfully sang he
The wonderful anthem
    Which tells of the freedom
And peace of the people.

Such was the apotheosis of Nekrasov's populism in poetry while this trend was still being followed by the majority of the intelligentsia as well. Finally, one should not omit his purely personal lyrics. Among them we find those dealing with the wrangles he was having with his mistress, Mme Panayeva (wife of his fellow-editor of *The Contemporary*), and those poignant verses which he wrote during the worst moments of his illness. Nekrasov was not a pleasant person to live with. Moody and sullen, be often would not say a word for days; and as for loyalty, he was no more addicted to it than the flighty Mme Panayeva. The years during which they lived together were by no means years of harmony. But Nekrasov tried to make up for it at the end by addressing his mistress as follows:

> Goodbye! Forget the days of wane,
> Dejection, bitterness and pain,
> Forget the storms, forget the tears,
> Forget the threats of jealous fears.
> But the days when the sun of love
> Uprising kissed us from above,
> And bravely we went on our way—
> Bless and forget not one such day.[1]

As for Nekrasov's poems which relate to the last phases of his illness, it is enough to say that in some of them his 'Muse of grief and vengeance' received a final touch. His satirical epic, *The Contemporaries* (*Sovreménniki*, 1875-76), on the other hand, dealing with the new bourgeoisie of bankers and speculators, completed his 'engaged' or pamphleteering poetry.

6

And what of Nekrasov's place in literature? Turgenev once said that the Muse of poetry had not spent a single night in Nekrasov's verse. With all respect for Turgenev's aesthetic sense, such a verdict no longer holds good. By turning against accepted canons, Nekrasov opened up new possibilities with regard both to contents and technique. By introducing a number of 'unpoetic' themes in a purposely depoetised language, he divested his verse of solemnity on the one hand and of 'prettiness' on the other. As a result, his directness made him accessible to a wider circle of readers. Even his journalistic verses performed a useful task in so far as they awakened and kept alive an interest in poetry among those readers who otherwise had little mental equipment for it.

This was why Nekrasov found so many ardent admirers among those commoners whose cultural background was smaller than that of the members of the intelligentsia. One of his recent critics, Kornei Chukovsky, is therefore justified in saying that Nekrasov wrote for a new type of political and social consciousness. His work served as a literary link between the intelligentsia and the masses.

Nekrasov failed to create a definite school of his own. Nevertheless, his attitude towards the village, the people and the folk-poetry acted as an inspiration for several poets who came—even long after him—from the people (the

1.   Translated by M. Baring in *A Book of Russian Verse* (Macmillan).

best known of them being Sergey Esenin). His attempt at marrying poetry to topical journalism may not have augured a happy union, but it had a strong following in Soviet Russia, where Mayakovsky and his group made—after 1917 —a series of further experiments of this kind. Nekrasov's technical devices, too, have drawn considerable attention of late. We may no longer think (as some of his contemporaries did) that he is greater than Pushkin. Yet with all his faults and virtues, he occupies one of the important places in the Russian Parnassus.

CHAPTER THIRTEEN

Dostoevsky and Tolstoy

I

When—in the 1860s and 1870s—Russian fiction reached its peak, it became clear that even apart from a considerable novelty of the material, it differed, or tended to differ, from European fiction as a whole. What must have astonished many a Western reader was the spaciousness, depth, frankness, as well as moral earnestness with which the Russian authors tackled the problems of life. From Gogol onwards, Russian literature showed an instinctive trend to go beyond mere entertainment or even beyond mere art. Besides, in a country where there was no freedom of the press, fine literature was the only realm in which it was still possible to exercise—at least by a clever use of the 'Aesop' language—that freedom of mind and spirit which was banned by the authorities. Writers were thus looked upon not only as artists of the word, but also as guides and teachers in a deeper sense. They were supposed to understand life better than ordinary mortals; so it was their duty to impart this knowledge to others in an appropriate shape and form. No wonder that many a Russian novel showed a propensity to combine fiction with moral, social and political ideas—not necessarily at the expense of art, but as one of the vital ingredients of art itself.

It is at this point, however, that a philosophical novel can easily degenerate into a mere philosophising novel of a didactic kind. For, in spite of their resemblance on the surface, the two are poles apart. In a didactic-philosophising (or, for that matter, propagandist) novel characters serve above all as pegs upon which the author hangs his own attitudes and ideas, usually with foregone conclusions. Instead of being embodied in the characters, these ideas are only stuck onto them. The characters themselves thus resemble cleverly manipulated puppets which may look quite lively at times without being really alive. In a truly philosophical novel, however, ideas are embodied in the characters organically, as an integral part of their inner lives and destinies, no matter whether the author himself agrees with them or not. The same applies, and even more so, to dramatic works. There is a world of difference between a lively dramatisation of a public lecture and a drama of thoughts and ideas clashing with each other on equal terms and, as it were, outside the author's own sympathies or antipathies. All this is obvious. Yet it may be worth mentioning in order to point out certain differences between Shaw and Ibsen, for example; or to take a more complicated case, those between Tolstoy and Dostoevsky—at least in so far as the last phase of Tolstoy's literary activities is concerned.

A comparison between these two greatest representatives of Russian fiction has become a frequent method since D. Merezhkovsky's pioneering study,[1] published in 1901. Others, notably the philosopher Lev Shestov and the novelist V. Veresayev, have explored some further aspects along similar lines.[2] Still, the fact remains that the very differences between Tolstoy and Dostoevsky are so complementary that it is almost impossible to talk of one without mentioning the other. Even as artists, great as each of them may be in his own sphere, they seem to stand at two opposite poles, a parallel treatment of which may be helpful.

To begin with, the writings of Tolstoy and Dostoevsky represent two different currents of Russian prose. Tolstoy, with his lucidly calm and outwardly simple manner, continued the Pushkinian tradition which he intensified with his own tremendous plastic sense. His art reached a climax in *War and Peace* (*Voiná i mir*, 1862-69)—a novel which gives a cross-section of the entire Russian nation, from the high aristocracy down to the humblest serfs, during one of the critical periods of its history. The way in which Tolstoy unfolds that period before our eyes verges on the miraculous. Against a continually varying background we watch hundreds of characters, each one moving about as a three-dimensional being, alive even in the most casual words and gestures. Equally remarkable is Tolstoy's epic broadness encompassing all modes and aspects of human existence within the range of his observation. For in Tolstoy observation comes first, which he then enhances or intensifies by his intuition. In Dostoevsky this process seems to be reversed: he prefers to show the man from within first and then from without.

While in *War and Peace* he presents the Russia of 1812, Tolstoy gives us the same wide range of more recent Russian life (life in the 1870s) in *Anna Karénina*, with the tragic adulteress Anna and her lover Vronsky at the centre. One marvels once again at his competence in dealing not only with high society and bureaucracy in Moscow and Petersburg, but also with the country manors, as well as with peasant types after 1861. It would be difficult to find a description of feminine beauty to equal Tolstoy's portrait of Anna. And in the very teeth of his moralising propensity (in the name of which he condemns and punishes Anna) one finds oneself in the company of the charming shallow *bon viveur* Stiva Oblonsky—a complete contrast to the brooding Levin, Tolstoy's double and the principal hero of the novel. No one who is interested in Russian life at certain periods can afford to ignore such novels as *War and Peace* and *Anna Karénina*. Yet the world described in them is intertwined with human elements which also transcend any strictly historical period. They belong to all times.

In contrast to Tolstoy, Dostoevsky the artist came out of Gogol. There is no Pushkinian calm or simplicity in his prose. It was Gogol's restless emotional

1. *Tolstoy and Dostoevsky.*
2. An interesting more recent study on comparative lines is George Steiner's *Tolstoy or Dostoevsky* (Faber).

style (often verging on pure rhetoric, yet still within the boundaries of art) that Dostoevsky inherited. Whereas Tolstoy was above all a great epic creator, the prose of Dostoevsky was of a dramatic kind. He is the author of some of the most dramatic novels in modern literature. And their very structure is held together by the tension arising from the author's basic approach to life. For unlike Tolstoy, who confined himself to what might be called the average or normal plane of life, Dostoevsky was interested in the psychic dimension which lies beyond such a plane. This means that even as seekers the two great novelists differed. Tolstoy was rational, or mainly rational, even when dealing with the irrational aspects of existence. Dostoevsky, on the other hand, was drawn from the outset to the area which is neither normal nor rational, let alone rationalistic. And in this he persisted to the end.

2

One of the causes of such a difference may have been the fact that in Tolstoy there was a certain gap between the artist and the moralising thinker, whereas in Dostoevsky thought and art were never quite severed or differentiated. Nor were art and psychology. It was above all as a profound psychological novelist that he became read all the world over. And not without reason. For, long before Freud, he had not only explored but illustrated (in a creative manner) man's unconscious mind and shown the irrational roots even of our rational behaviour. What he was mainly interested in as artist was the riddle of human personality and its place in the scheme of life or even of the universe. He was not concerned with the psychology of textbooks. His realm was that borderline where the normal and the abnormal elements of man's psyche meet and where their mixture may lead to unexpected contrasts, conflicts and crises in the face of which the rational self is utterly helpless. But this was not the whole of his task. To quote from a previous work of mine:[1]

> Dostoevsky introduced new themes and vistas into literature. He also replaced the leisurely broadness of such 'manor novelists' as Aksakov, Goncharov, Turgenev and Tolstoy, by a quickened pace and a dramatic tension hardly paralleled in modern letters. An epileptic, an unstable and unbalanced city dweller himself, he was anxious to unravel the chaotic urbanised man of our age—the man whose secret inner problems and contradictions he tried to explore to the end. With all this he combined a metaphysical attitude towards evil as one of the most mysterious and disturbing problems of existence. At the same time his spiritual thirst was directed towards 'the city of God' for which he fought all the more desperately the more his profoundly religious temperament was being undermined by his own scepticism or even latent nihilism. It was the clash between all sorts of opposite tendencies that drove him the more to his own daring psychological experiments during which he obliterated the line between the rational

1. *Dostoevsky* (Macmillan, 1946; Russell, N.Y., 1969).

and the irrational, between the normal and the abnormal. Deliberately, he placed his heroes in the most unusual situations and conditions in order to see how they would react and how much doubt and travail their spirit could endure. He thus hoped to extract the secret of man and life from the exceptional, from the abnormal rather than from the normal. The French author, Melchior de Voguë, called him the 'Shakespeare of the lunatic asylum'. But such a statement is too sweeping to be applied to Dostoevsky literally. The kernel of his writings is and remains not that of an alienist but of a philosophic seeker in the deeply tragic sense of this word.

3

It is hardly necessary to enumerate all those circumstances which contributed to the formation of Dostoevsky's mind. They are known to every student of literature. One ought to point out, however, at least some facts of his early life which may shed more light on the complexities of his work and character.

As a boy he seems to have conceived an instinctive loathing for his father —a hospital doctor and a miser who was later murdered by his own serfs. Dostoevsky's chronic 'guilt complex' may have arisen from an involuntary wish for his father's death. Owing to his own reckless nature, the young Dostoevsky —a military engineer by training—must have passed through penury, through endless personal difficulties and humiliations, before his first novels, *Poor Folk* (*Bédnye lyúdi*, 1846) and *The Double* (*Dvoiník*, 1847), both of them influenced by Gogol, made his name known. Those were the years when he stood close to the circle of Belinsky and also became a member of the revolutionary group of young atheists and followers of Fourier, organised by a certain Petrashevsky. Denounced by an *agent provocateur*, the members of this group were arrested. After months of imprisonment and investigation they were sentenced to death. In December 1849 they were all marched to the place of execution, but at the last moment were reprieved and sent instead to Siberia. Dostoevsky spent over eight years in Siberia: four among the most hardened criminals in the penal settlement at Omsk, and four in a line-battalion at Semipalatinsk on the Mongolian border. In 1859 he was allowed to return to European Russia. After an interval of some ten years, he thus resumed his literary activities. But he was now a changed man, with a strongly religious propensity, and full of a Slavophil enthusiasm for the Russian people and things Russian.

The first two narratives he wrote when freed, *The Village Stepanchikovo* (*Seló Stepánchikovo*)[1] and *The Uncle's Dream* (*Dyádyushkin Son*) in 1859, do not make a single mention of the terrible experiences the author must have gone through in Siberia. They are both boisterously funny and their grotesque types makes one think of Gogol and Dickens. The influence of Dickens—this time the humanitarian Dickens—is definitely felt in his first long novel, *The Insulted and the Injured* (*Unízhennye i oskorblyónnye*) which appeared (1861) in the short-

1. Foma Opiskin, the principal character in this narrative, is supposed to be a caricature of Gogol in his later years.

lived periodical *Time* (*Vrémya*) edited by Dostoevsky and his brother Mikhail. The novel contains some remarkable psychological passages—his analysis of the 'injured' child Nelly, of the cynic Valkovsky, or of the self-divided Alyosha; but as a whole the novel only proved that Dostoevsky was still groping for creative self-expression on a big scale. A much greater work was his *Notes from the House of the Dead* (*Zapíski iz myórtvogo dóma*, 1862), describing his life at the penal settlement. His remarks about the criminal mind, which he knew from personal observations, are invaluable. And the conclusion he arrived at was new indeed for that period, namely that great criminals are often endowed with unusual will-power, as well as talent, both of which have gone wrong. 'For I must speak my thoughts as to this: the hapless fellows there were perhaps the strongest and, in one way or another, the most gifted of our people. There was all that strength of body and mind lost. Whose fault is that?'

Even more provocative is he in his *Notes from the Underworld* (*Zapíski iz podpólya*), published in 1864. This work can serve as a key to many of his writings. It is a decidedly philosophic-polemical narrative directed against the positivist utilitarians of the 1860s (Chernyshevsky, Dobrolyubov, etc.). But the ideas expressed in it are above all the outbursts of a frustrated individual—of an ambitious man who has been rejected by life and by society and whose only compensation is his jeering criticism of all and sundry. For in jeering at them, he has at least a temporary illusion of his own superiority over those whom he ridicules in such a self-assertive manner.

Dostoevsky's main achievement in this work was to point out the contrast between the man of statistics and man as a living human being. For purposes of statistics, even utilitarian statistics aiming at the 'greatest happiness of the greatest number', each individual is interchangeable with other individuals in the same way as standardised articles are interchangeable with each other. In reality, however, each living individual is unique. Which means that his personal fate and suffering cannot be interchanged with those of anybody else. Nor can he serve as mere manure for the happiness and harmony of some future generations in which he himself will never share. At the same time the idea of a compulsory Millennium, established by science and reason, whether on Communist or any other lines, is equally improbable and hateful to Dostoevsky's man from the underworld.

> Does not reason err in estimating what is advantageous? May it not be that man occasionally loves something beside prosperity? May it not be that he loves adversity? Certainly there are times when man *does* love adversity, and love it passionately. Man is a frivolous creature, and like a chess-player, cares more for the process of attaining his goal than for the goal itself. Besides, who knows (for it never does to be sure) that the aims which man strives for upon earth may not be contained in this ceaseless continuation of the process of attainment—that is to say, in the process which is comprised in the living of life rather than in the aim itself, which, of course, is contained in the formula that twice two makes four? Yet, gentlemen, this formula is not life at all: it is only the beginning of death!

At all events, men have always been afraid to think that twice two makes four, and I am afraid of it too! . . . I should not be surprised if amidst all this order and regularity of the future, there should arise suddenly, from some quarter or another, some gentleman of low-born—or, rather, of retrograde and cynical demeanour, who, setting his arms akimbo, should say to you all: 'How now, gentlemen? Would it not be a good thing if, with one consent, we were to kick all this solemn wisdom to the four winds, to send those logarithms to the devil, and to begin our lives again according to our stupid whims?' Yet this would be nothing: the really shameful part of the business would be that this gentleman would find a goodly number of adherents. Such is man's way. . . . Whence do the savants have it that man needs a normal, a virtuous will? What man most needs is an *independent* will—no matter what the cost of such independence of volition, nor what it may lead to![1]

The whole of Nietzsche's subsequent philosophy of Will to Power could be derived from such a premise. But Dostoevsky did not stop at this stage of individual self-assertion. He saw only too well that such a stage by itself is also a blind-alley and a destructive one at that, when it does not take man beyond himself. The starting point made here thus invariably led to further questions: *What* is that individual self which insists so passionately on its own 'independent volition'? How and in the name of what values could this self go beyond its own narrow limits and fulfil its destiny in the truest sense? What, then, is its ultimate destiny and meaning? Or is it devoid of any meaning at all?

Such were the 'existentialist' problems Dostoevsky set out to tackle in his great novels, *Crime and Punishment* (*Prestuplénie i nakazánie*, 1866), *The Idiot* (*Idiót*, 1868–69), *The Possessed* (*Bésy*, 1871–72), *A Raw Youth* (*Podróstok*, 1875), and *The Brothers Karamazov* (*Brátya Karamázovy*, 1879–80). And, let it be stressed once again, he tackled them not merely as a thinker but as a creative artist.

4

Raskolnikov, the hero of *Crime and Punishment*, is a talented but frustrated youth—frustrated by poverty as well as by his own unadaptable character. Yet in his self-will he goes much further than the man from the 'underworld'. Full of spite and resentment, he divides (like Nietzsche after him) the whole of mankind into two categories: the 'herd' whose business it is to be ordered about and to obey, and a few exceptional individuals—such as Napoleon— who are clever and strong enough to command and be a law unto themselves. As a votary of science and reason, Raskolnikov rejects the very possibility of any absolute standard of good and evil; for such a standard could have been

1. All quotations in this chapter are taken from Constance Garnett's translation of Dostoevsky's works (Heinemann).

given only by an absolute Being (i.e., by God) in whom he does not and cannot believe. Since God does not exist, all values of good and evil are relative, man-made, and therefore fictitious. There is no such thing as either virtue or crime in itself. Nor is there any higher meaning in our existence. Man is nothing but a casual bubble produced by the blind laws of nature; and if he has become aware of this, why should he not take his destiny into his own hands? Why should he not ignore the laws (if he is clever enough not to be caught) and live according to his own whims and his own 'will to power'?

Working from this premise, Raskolnikov yet remained something of a Hamlet. He was not quite sure whether he belonged to the exceptions or to the 'herd'. So he decided to prove to himself that he was strong and daring enough to be an exceptional individual (who was 'beyond good and evil') by deliberately breaking one of the fundamental laws. He murders an old pawnbroker woman and does this in such a way that there is not the slightest evidence against him. Yet no sooner has the crime been committed than something strange begins to happen. Reason and logic, with its premise that all values of good and evil are man-made and therefore fictitious, had given him a full sanction to kill, that is to wipe out a stingy human 'louse'. It was only after the murder of the old woman (and accidentally also her sister) that his irrational self, with its own peculiar truth, reacted in such a way as inwardly to cut him off and isolate him from all living beings, even from his own mother and sister. He had murdered the old woman physically, but he himself was spiritually murdered by her. And he became terribly aware of this. It was not repentance but a complete inner vacuum—the vacuum of a living corpse—that constituted his punishment from within and made him so frantically restless after the crime. In the end it compelled him to make a voluntary confession and to surrender himself to the authorities, although even after such a decision he was logically not in the least convinced of being a criminal.

> 'Crime? What crime?' he cried in sudden fury at his sister. 'That I killed a vile, noxious insect, an old pawnbroker woman, of use to no one! Killing her was atonement for forty sins. She was sucking the life out of the poor people. Was that a crime? I am not thinking of it and am not thinking of expiating it, and why are you rubbing it in on all sides? I am further than ever from seeing that it was a crime.

Yet he gave himself up and accepted the punishment (Siberia) as a last hope that through suffering he might perhaps alleviate the unbearable inner void his deed had inflicted upon him, and thus be resurrected to life like Lazarus from the tomb. In short, his rational self had one truth, and his irrational self had another. But there was no bridge between the two.

5

It was the nature of the irrational that Dostoevsky tried to probe further when he wrote *The Idiot*. The title of this novel is ironical in so far as from a rational angle its hero Prince Myshkin, who is returning to Petersburg from a Swiss mental sanatorium helpless and naïve as a child, may actually resemble an idiot; yet he is all the stronger on the irrational plane, where his intuitive clairvoyance—in the midst of cunning hangers on—abounds even in flashes of genius. As one of the heroines (Aglaya) puts it: 'Even if your surface mind be a little affected, your real mind is far better than all theirs put together. Such a mind as they have never dreamed of, because really, there are two minds—the kind that matters and the kind that does not matter.'

Myshkin is provided with a mind that matters. He is also morally pure without in the least being prudish or improbable. What may diminish the value of his sexual morality is, however, the fact that according to certain allusions, he is physically unable to be anything but 'pure' in this respect. Otherwise he is one of the few Christ-like personalities in modern fiction; only he remains much too passive and therefore at the mercy of circumstance. Like the majority of Dostoevsky's heroes, he is self-divided. His inability to make a definite choice between his love for Nastasya and Aglaya becomes his undoing. After Nastasya has run away from him only to be murdered by the semi-mad Rogozhin, Myshkin cannot stand the inner convulsion caused by it all and ends by becoming an idiot—this time a real one.

The Idiot gives one the impression that the author had too much to say to put it all into one single novel. It does not take long, though, to discover that here, too, he was preoccupied with Raskolnikov's dilemma. The character who provides the link between The Idiot and Crime and Punishment is the consumptive nihilist Ippolit—an 'enlightened' youth of the 1860s. Believing neither in God nor in any higher meaning of man's existence, he sees life as a kind of 'dumb monster' which crushes human beings and makes them suffer mechanically, blindly, without even being able to take notice of it. More uncompromising than Raskolnikov, Ippolit refuses to accept life on such terms and sees in suicide the only logical and psychological answer. 'If I had the power to prevent my own birth, I should certainly never have consented to accept existence under such ridiculous conditions. However, I have the power to end my own existence.'

We will find the same conclusion, but this time turned into practice (by Kirillov) in Dostoevsky's next book, The Possessed—one of the most cruel novels ever written. Irreligiosity, destruction, and self-destruction meet in this work as in a focus, and all three prove to be interdependent. One of the Russian critics (A. Volynsky) referred to The Possessed as the 'book of great wrath'—directed against those ultra-radicals of the 1860s whose revolutionary activities could have been summed up as destruction for destruction's sake. But in attacking them, Dostoevsky went much further than Goncharov in The Ravine. He tried to unveil—whether rightly or wrongly—the metaphysical roots of revolution as a mere will to destroy, originating in a nihilistic (i.e., irreligious) view of life. Both Stavrogin and Peter Verkhovensky draw out of Raskolnikov's dilemma some ultimate conclusions. If life has no higher sense, then it should either be finished with, or else turned into a series of daring experiments upon one's own fate and that of others, no matter how much bloodshed and crime such sport might involve. It is all part and parcel of that orgy of destruction which ultimately becomes a demoniacal urge, an end in itself, or rather an obsession whose consequences are incalculable.

'Listen,' Peter Verkhovensky raves in front of Stavrogin, 'first of all we will make an upheaval. We shall penetrate to the peasantry.... On all sides we see vanity puffed up out of all proportion, brutal, monstrous appetites. ...Do you know how many we shall catch by little ready-made ideas? Oh! this generation has only to grow up. One or two generations of vice are essential now; monstrous, abject vice by which a man is transformed into a loathsome cruel reptile. That's what we need. And what's more, a little fresh blood, that we may get accustomed to it. . . . We will proclaim destruction ... We will set fires going ... We'll set legends going ... There's going to be such an upset as the world has never seen before ... Russia will be overwhelmed by darkness, the earth will weep for its old gods. Listen, Stavrogin, to level the mountains is a fine idea, not an absurd one. Down with culture! The thirst for culture is an aristocratic thirst. . . . We will make use of drunkenness, slander, spying; we will stifle every genius in its infancy. We'll reduce all to a common denominator. Complete equality! Only the necessary is necessary: that's the motto of the whole world henceforward.'

Starting with absolute license (mistaken for freedom), revolution on these terms is bound to end in that absolute tyranny of which Dostoevsky had given such an ominous warning to his generation. One of the nihilists, Shigalyov, parades a complete programme of such a totalitarian tyranny, while Kirillov, starting again with Raskolnikov's premise, arrives at self-destruction as the only logical conclusion. 'If God exists all is His will and from His will I cannot escape. If not, it is all my will and I am bound to show self-will. . . . Because all will has become mine.' But the acme of his own self-will is self-destruction as a protest against a world in which he sees only mockery and a universal 'vaude-ville of the devils'. And the alternative? Dostoevsky explored both sides of the problem in his last and greatest novel, *The Brothers Karamázov*.

6

Before embarking upon this masterpiece. Dostoevsky wrote the novel, *A Raw Youth*,—a subtle study of an adolescent's mind and at the same time a compendium of problems, some of which were of topical interest to his contemporaries. Intelligentsia and the people, Russia and Europe, culture and the elite, 'fathers' and 'children'—all this comes out in the conversations between the fastidious aristocrat Versilov and Arkady—his illegitimate son by a peasant woman. The main theme of the novel is the gradual adjustment between the two. Whereas Arkady is all youthful ferment, Versilov is an unusually cultured but inwardly 'mixed-up' character, unable to come to terms with himself or with life. By marrying Arkady's peasant-mother, the aristocrat Versilov hopes to conquer, as it were, the prospect of inner harmony and stability through being rooted in the people. After a series of hectic peripeties and crises the end is a conciliatory one. Several problems indicated in this and in Dostoevsky's previous novels were carried over to *The Brothers Karamazov*.

In this lengthy novel we see first of all two generations facing one another: the dissolute and morally disintegrating old Karamazov, and his children. Mitya, his eldest son, has inherited his father's formidable *libido*, but in a somewhat nobler aspect, however chaotic his impulses may be. In Ivan the father's vitality has become transmuted into a powerful intellect—disturbed by an instinctive hatred for his parent, as well as by his Hamlet-like broodings and doubts about all and everything. Cold and aloof, he is incapable either of Mitya's spontaneous generosity or of the equally spontaneous human sympathy typical of his youngest brother Alyosha. In Alyosha all has been sublimated into spirit, and he himself is a novice living in a nearby monastery. Then there is their illegitimate half-brother Smerdyakov (son of a beggar woman)—a rancorous physical and moral cripple who suffers from epilepsy and is employed as a flunkey in Karamazov's household. It should be pointed out that Ivan and Alyosha were sons of Karamazov's second wife from whom they have inherited certain traits different from those of Mitya who was a child of the first marriage.

The framework of the novel, crowded with incident and characters, rests above all on the rivalry between Mitya and his father for the favours of the elusive *femme fatale*—Grushenka: a rivalry in which the hatred between father and son comes out in all its ugliness, breeding scandal in the gossipy provincial town. At an opportune moment Smerdyakov takes advantage of the clash between the two and contrives to murder the old *roué* (whose hidden money he steals) in such a way that all the circumstances point to Mitya as the murderer. Mitya is arrested, tried, and sentenced to penal servitude in Siberia. While he is in jail, both he and the woman he loves undergo a profound inner change. Far from feeling rancorous about the injustice done to him, Mitya accepts suffering as a path towards a new life—better and cleaner than the life he has known hitherto.

Of particular interest are the different sorts of inner relationships and conflicts conspicuous in this novel. Ivan and Smerdyakov, for instance, like two opposite poles of humanity, were yet for some curious reason subconsciously drawn to each other. Ivan knows that the murderer was not Mitya but Smerdyakov. Smerdyakov even confessed to Ivan what he had done and handed to him the old Karamazov's money he had stolen during the murder. For he, too, was in the throes of a reaction he had never expected to take place.

I did have an idea of beginning a new life with that money in Moscow or, better still, abroad. I did dream of it, chiefly because all things are lawful. That was quite right what you taught me, for you talked a lot to me about that. For if there's no everlasting God, there's no such thing as virtue, and there's no need of it. You were right there. So that's how I looked at it.

The inner reaction in Smerdyakov is so terrible that in the end he finds the only escape from it by hanging himself. But Ivan, too, is aware of his share in the deed. Although only a theoretical accomplice, he now experiences the same kind of restlessness and punishment *from within* which Raskolnikov had felt after the murder. And, like Raskolnikov, he, too, decides to confess every-thing and give himself up, while yet not believing in such things as crime and virtue. This is why the devil he sees in delirium keeps taunting him :

> You are going to perform an act of heroic virtue, and you don't believe in virtue, that's what tortures you and makes you angry, that is why you are so vindictive . . . Why do you go meddling, if your sacrifice is of no use to anyone? Because you don't know yourself why you go! Oh! you'd give a great deal to know yourself why you go! That's the riddle for you.

Self-divided as he is, Ivan is drawn (for entirely different reasons) also to Alyosha. It is to him that he pours out some of his most painful doubts and ideas about man, God, the universe, and the future of mankind. For Ivan, in spite of his Hamlet-like nature, and intelligent though he is, realises that human intel-lect, such as it is, is incompetent either to affirm or to deny the existence of God and those ultimate values which depend on the solution of this problem. But even while admitting the possibility of God's existence, he repudiates Him and rebels against Him for moral reasons, because he feels profoundly dis-gusted with all the suffering and injustice in God's world. Having mentioned some revolting cases of cruelty inflicted upon innocent children in particular, Ivan exclaims with that kind of moral indignation which goes far beyond mere morality!

> 'Without suffering, I am told man could not have existed on earth, for he could not know good and evil. Why should he know that diabolical good and evil when it costs so much? The whole of knowledge is not worth a child's suffering. What comfort is it to me that there are none guilty and that cause follows effect simply and directly and that I know it? I must have justice or I will destroy myself . . . Surely I haven't suf-fered simply that I, my crimes and sufferings may manure the soil of the future harmony of somebody else. . . . . If I must suffer for the eternal harmony, what have children to do with it? It's beyond all comprehension why they should suffer, and why they should pay for harmony. Why should they too furnish material to enrich the soil of the harmony of the future? And if it really is true that they must share responsibility for their father's crimes, such a truth is not of this world and is beyond my comprehension . . . I don't want harmony. From love of humanity I don't want it. I would rather be left with my unavenged suffering and unsatis-fied indignation, *even if I were wrong*. Besides, too high a price is asked for harmony; it is beyond our means to pay so much to enter on it. And so I hasten to give back my entrance ticket, and if I am an honest man I am bound to give it back as soon as possible. And that I am doing. It is not God I don't accept, only I most respectfully return Him my ticket.'

And as for Ivan's conception of mankind's future, he unfolds in his *Legend of the Grand Inquisitor* such an appalling picture of totalitarian humanity, based on a pre-fabricated ideology for the sake of man's compulsory 'happiness' and 'harmony', as to outdo any nightmare. The painful implication behind this legend is the idea that the saviour of our chaotic and muddled mankind may eventually come not in the name of Christ, but of Antichrist who would fill their stomachs and lower their minds and consciousness to the level of happy infants. Ivan's own tragedy was that he had an insatiable thirst for faith in God whom he could not accept, and worse, whom he refused to accept because of his own intellectual and moral honesty. Yet without religion, that is without faith in some higher transcendental values and meaning of life, he could not go on living, since to his uncompromising conscience existence, such as he saw it, seemed utterly meaningless and idiotic. So where was the outlet? Once again we see the clash between the rational and the irrational truths in man without any real point of contact between the two. Even an intuitive acceptance of some 'higher' truth may only be an escape from logic into one's own wishful thinking and by no means a guarantee that such a truth really exists. Or can the idea of God, instilled in one's consciousness as an everlasting postulate, lead one to the conclusion that there must be something behind it? Ivan does not know the answer. Nor does Dostoevsky. Hence the religious outlet which he so forcibly imposed upon himself.

A counterpart to Ivan Karamazov is Alyosha's spiritual guide, Father Zosima. Dostoevsky puts into this *pater Seraphicus* some of his own ideas about Christianity which may not tally with any official denomination under that name. Zosima's Christian religion does not preach medieval (or any other) asceticism. Its ideal is that fullness and joy of existence which can only be attained by a religious conception based not on a repudiation of life, but on sympathy with all life. For only by recognising a higher sense in the whole of humanity and the cosmos can we also accept and love both. To repeat Zosima's words:

> God took seeds from different worlds and sowed them on this earth, and his garden grew up and everything came up that could come up only through the feeling of its contact with other mysterious worlds. If that feeling grows weak or is destroyed in you, the heavenly growth will die in you. Then you will be indifferent to life and will even grow to hate it.

This is only a brief definition of Dostoevsky's novels from a philosophical angle. As for his stories and short novels, in most of them psychology or pathology is conspicuous: in *The Eternal Husband* (*Véchmy muzh*), for instance, or in *The Gambler* (*Igrók*) with its matchless pictures of Dostoevsky's own gambling mania. The surprising thing is not that all the thoughts and ideas in Dostoevsky's novels spring from the innermost experience of the characters concerned, but that all the pros and cons are pitted in them against each other on equal terms. For Dostoevsky too, like Ivan Karamazov, was a clandestine unbeliever, but passionately anxious to overcome his scepticism and to arrive at some certainty. Yet as Ivan's nightmare devil aptly put it: 'Till the secret is revealed, there are two sorts of truth for me—one, their truth, yonder, which I know nothing about so far, and the other my own. And there is no knowing which will turn out the better.'

7

Dostoevsky felt at home most of all in that border region where rational and irrational elements mingle, where 'all contradictions exist side by side'. In this region Dostoevsky's thought and art always converged to strengthen each other. In Tolstoy, on the other hand, the two often seemed to be curiously severed. No one will deny Tolstoy's artistic genius. But, as has already been pointed out by Merezhkovsky, his is the clairvoyance of the body and of the emotional sphere as distinct from Dostoevsky's clairvoyance of the spirit. More than any other author, Tolstoy knew how to project into his characters all that touches upon the full-blooded instinctive, physical, and emotional side of existence. Here he goes to the very root of things with that integrity which cannot but amaze even the most exacting of readers. It was prominent in his very first effort, *Childhood* (*Détstvo*, 1852), in his short novel, *The Cossacks* (*Kazáki*, 1861), and reached the height of plastic and analytical power in his two central works, *War and Peace* and *Anna Karénina*. At the same time, his propensity to moralise, conspicuous even in his early *Sebastopol Stories* (*Sevastópol'skie rasskázy*) and particularly in *The Cossacks*, remained with him to the end and was always ready to interrupt Tolstoy the artist, to warn him, or to interfere —often in a somewhat distressing manner. However much Tolstoy the man was in love with life, the reasoning and didactic moralist in him demanded the meaning of life, or rather the meaning of death, since the full-blooded Tolstoy was afraid—instinctively and physically afraid—of death. His fear of death thus became only another aspect of his truly pagan love of life. He felt the horror—both physical and metaphysical—of dying to an almost incredible degree. That was why he entrenched himself in a moralising process which was an anxious search mainly for a 'rational' explanation and a justification of the fact of death.

In Tolstoy's early works one can detect this method of showing in a parallel manner the various aspects of one dilemma in such a way as to leave the reader in no doubt as to which of these is preferable, without exactly forcing the intended conclusion upon him. His story, *Three Deaths* (*Tri smérti*) is an example. It consists of three parallel pictures of death, each of them almost independent of the other, but differing in the amount of physical and moral torment involved. In the end it becomes clear what kind of death, and on what conditions, is the least painful and therefore preferable. In short, the less awakened the awareness of man's personal ego, the easier is the process of dying. The reader's conclusion is naturally expected to coincide with that of Tolstoy. As is well known, Tolstoy was amply endowed with all those temptations of the flesh of which his inherent morality did not and could not approve. Thus in his short novel, *Family Happiness* (*Seméinoe schástie*), he gives us a parallel analysis of a young woman's love before and after her marriage to a much older husband. And again the reader is led to decide 'independently' why non-sexual postmarital love is preferable to the passionate and intensely personal love in the first part of the novel. In *War and Peace* there are a number of themes, developing parallel with each other, or else intertwining as in a symphony, but for our purpose a comparison between the two principal seekers in the novel, Prince Andrey and Pierre Bazukhov, is of importance. They represent the two contending doubles in Tolstoy's own personality; yet here he knew how to integrate, as far as possible, their quest with their entire inner life and made them psychologically and artistically convincing.[1] He coped with the same task, though less objectively, when dealing with the inner torments of Levin in *Anna Karénina*. The antagonism between preaching and living life, which came to a head in his *My Confessions (Ispoved'*, 1879), that is after his so-called conversion, is here clearly anticipated. One feels that behind it all his moral consciousness kept watching, censoring, and shaking the rod, until—step by step—Tolstoy was compelled to repudiate all his instincts of the flesh. These he began to disparage vehemently precisely because he himself had been much too often at their mercy. His moralising was thus an inevitable struggle with himself. Tolstoy the moralist was at loggerheads with Tolstoy the man and the artist, both of whom he had to repress time and again in order to make way for the Puritan. Having reduced the meaning of life only to its *moral* meaning in the sense of an 'improved' Sermon on the Mount, Tolstoy, who once had known and enjoyed the throbbing fullness of existence in all its aspects, eventually postulated in his writings that life itself—his own and everybody else's—should be sacrificed to what he himself considered to be the meaning of life. According to him, the variety and broadness of human existence ought to be clipped down to those five moral rules to which he had reduced the Sermon on the Mount, even if all our cultural and technical achievements were doomed to perish because of it. In short, once Tolstoy had found the 'truth', he ceased to be a seeker and became a preacher, whatever the price. It was Tolstoy the preacher who now demanded the sacrifice of Tolstoy the artist. In this he largely succeeded—largely, but not completely.

8

Since the 'converted' Tolstoy was unable definitely to integrate his puritanical tendencies with the great artist in him, he was bound to be tossed between the two even after he had publicly condemned all art (his own included) which could not be stated on behalf and in terms of morals. His brilliantly misleading book, *What is Art (Chto takóe iskússtvo*, 1897) was a plausible but hardly convincing vindication of the moralist in him. Even less convincing was his furious *pogróm* upon Shakespeare.[2] Moreover, the forceful intrusion of the moralist

1. At the same time the whole of his reasoned and anti-individualistic philosophy of history is interpolated; this is something which could have been left out without any harm to the novel.
2. In his booklet, *About Shakespeare and the Drama* (1907).

into his works, could not prevent Tolstoy from stating whatever he had to say clearly; after all Tolstoy was Tolstoy. Sometimes he blended the two antagonists: in his didactic *People's Stories* (*Naródnye rasskázy*), for instance, which he wrote for peasants in the simple peasant style and language. In such powerful narratives as *The Death of Ivan Ilyich* (*Smert' Ivána Ilyichá*, 1886) and *Master and Man* (*Khozyáin i rabótnik*, 1895) the moral purpose is not imposed upon the theme but is inherent in it: the change undergone by human consciousness when facing unavoidable death and the mystery of death. The moralist may be strongly felt in Tolstoy's peasant drama, *The Power of Darkness* (*Vlast' t'my*, 1887) or in such a cruel tale of jealousy as *The Kreutzer Sonata* (1891); yet the climax in both is psychologically motivated with a technical mastery which could not but turn them into significant works of art. It was the reasoning puritan in Tolstoy who later added to his *Kreutzer Sonata* an *Epilogue* in which he demanded complete sexual abstinence even in marriage.

While suffering from the painful contradictions of his own ego, he saw the only way out in repressing his (or any other) personal self and dissolving it in the pre-individual mass and group-soul of humanity through what he regarded as 'Christian' love. His depersonalising tendency went so far as to repudiate any kind of purely personal resistance, even if this be resistance to evil. Hence also the prodigious number of tracts and homilies (*Gospels Explained*, *What I Believe*, *What then Must We do*, etc., etc.) which he kept pouring out. Yet it is not difficult to detect a utilitarian flavour, or rather a camouflaged utilitarian impulse behind them. In *What I Believe*, for example, he argues that Christ 'teaches life in which besides salvation from the loss of personal life, there will, here in this world, be less suffering and more joy than in personal life. Christ, revealing His teaching, says that there is true worldly advantage in not taking thought for the worldly life.' And in his Diary (13. VII, 1896) Tolstoy the preacher makes the astonishing admission that 'Christianity does not give happiness, but safety: it lets you down to the bottom from which there is no place to fall.'

9

One of Tolstoy's early ambitions, stirred in him during the Crimean War (when he was writing his *Sebastopol Stories*), had been to found a new type of Christian religion. What he eventually founded was in fact a short-lived minor sect known as Tolstoyanism. Yet even during his most strenuous years of teaching and preaching the artist in him could not but assert itself in at least a few works almost independently of the preacher. His satirical comedy, *The Fruits of Enlightenment* (*Plodý prosveshchénia*)—a skit on spiritism and the leisured upper classes, written in the late 1880s and published in 1890—is a work in which fun as such prevails. Some other writings of that period contain a moral purpose by implication rather than overtly, i.e., by homilies. Such a narrative as his magnificent *Hadjí Murád*, extolling the exploits and character of an intrepid Caucasian warrior, is told mainly for its own sake. The thoroughly amusing yarn, *False Coupon* (*Fal'shívy kupón*), may also be mentioned in this context; or even his *Father Sergius* (*Otéts Sergéy*) which is a fine but unfinished psychological exploration of spiritual pride in the guise of piety. Also unfinished was his drama, *The Live Corpse* (*Zhivóy trup*) whose main hero, Fedya Protasov, is a wayward, irresponsible yet thoroughly generous Russian character.[1]

There is no conspicuous moralising at the expense of art in the above-mentioned works. This cannot be said, however, of Tolstoy's last long novel, *Resurrection* (*Voskresénie*, 1899). Here the preacher came into his own, and with a vengeance. The theme of the novel is one of moral conversion (or resurrection). Prince Nekhlyudov seduced his aunt's domestic Katyusha Maslova who then had a child by him, lost her job, and after her baby's death became a prostitute. Eventually she was involved in the murder (with robbery) of one of her merchant customers. During the trial in the law-court Nekhlyudov, who is one of the jury, recognises Katyusha and learns the whole of her fate since the day she had been seduced by him. Appalled by it, he becomes conscience-stricken to the extent that he decides to redeem his guilt by saving her morally, even by following her (together with the other criminals) to Siberia—and, though scarcely credible—by wanting to marry her.

Katyusha, on the other hand, not only repudiates his intentions but actually feels bored by this 'are-you-saved' business. She even reproaches him that what he really wants is to save not her but himself: by calming his own guilty conscience. In the meantime the aristocrat Nekhlyudov has undergone a moral rebirth after the pattern of Tolstoy's own precepts and ideas. These have been obviously pasted upon him to such an extent as to turn him into a dummy. In the end he bores the reader as much as he bores Katyusha Maslova. One is not surprised that once she has contacted the political convicts, she begins to grope for something like a new life in the warmer and more charitable atmosphere of the exiled revolutionaries who must have seemed a relief to her after Nekhlyudov's cut-and-dried (however lofty) mission. Tolstoy the psychologist thus turned, inadvertently as it were, against Tolstoy the preacher. Moreover, apart from its 'edifying' side *Resurrection* abounds in excellent descriptions, portraits, ironical sallies and situations, since its author could not but remain a great writer even when the moralist in him was doing his best to spoil his art.

10

In contrast to Dostoevsky's dramatic way of telling a story, Tolstoy was predominently an epic narrator. Even his vexation of spirit, however poignantly recorded in his *My Confession*, is devoid of any dramatic explosions. The same can be said of his methodical inner quest. The difference between a passionate seeker and a preacher can best be seen in the contrast between Ivan in Dostoevsky's *Brothers Karamazov* on the one hand, and Nekhlyudov in Tolstoy's *Resurrection* on the other. And since the work of both Dostoevsky and Tolstoy

1. All these works were printed posthumously in 1911, one year after Tolstoy's death.

was 'engaged' also in the sense of being preoccupied with the fate and future of humanity, it might be helpful to draw a distinction between the two in this respect as well.

It is not hard to see that Tolstoy, with his rejection of history and civilisation, wanted to entice mankind back to a primitive communal existence, where there would be no room for individualism, no functional or any other separation between man and man. It was Rousseauism sifted through a 'corrected' Sermon on the Mount and reduced to absurdity. What he finally postulated was an amorphous human mass clinging together and toiling on the land in the name of that 'love' which constituted the Categorical Imperative of Tolstoyanism. Such a 'Kingdom of God' on earth was offered by Tolstoy the prophet as an alternative to civilisation. To put it briefly, instead of trying to overcome civilisation and its evils, he ran away from them—back to an undifferentiated and mythical past in which the very idea of history would be dead.

Dostoevsky, on the other hand, wanted to go not back, but forward—to a new kind of history and civilisation to be achieved through a change in man's consciousness by means of what he regarded as dynamic and creative religion. Otherwise he saw nothing but ruin for a world whose scientific and technical progress had become much too rapid to be matched by an adequate moral and spiritual growth. And he had no sentimental delusions about its result. He even foretold the possibility of civilised cannibalism : of the kind that has been practised *en gros* in the death factories at Auschwitz and elsewhere as a matter of daily routine and according to the last word of technical science.

Readers who are interested in these aspects of Dostoevsky's work should turn to his *Diary of an Author* (*Dnevník písátelya*), published in 1873, 1876–78, and resumed shortly before his death. Here we see what Dostoevsky was like apart from his novels and stories. What is more, his articles—like some of his private letters—provide many a clue to his novels, as well as to his personal attitudes with regard to the problems of the day, especially the problem of Russia and Europe. Like Alexander Herzen before him, Dostoevsky was appalled by the pettiness and callous philistinism of the European bourgeoisie. Yet his attitude towards Europe was, as we can see from his famous Pushkin speech (delivered in 1880), one of conciliation rather than hatred. Aware of the fact that mankind must either unite or perish, he aimed at a co-operation between Russia and the West even if his own conception of the so-called 'Russian Idea' was not devoid either of political prejudices or of hidden national pride and imperialistic chauvinism.

From a literary angle one is interested above all in those of his ideas which were embodied so organically in the characters of his works that it is almost impossible to separate their psychology from their ideology. If Tolstoy endangered his artistic genius at times by turning art into preaching, Dostoevsky knew how to turn even preaching into art. And in so doing he added a new dimension to Russian and European fiction as a whole.

CHAPTER FOURTEEN

Ostrovsky

I

While Russian realism was scoring its triumphs in prose, there was at least one dramatist whose work had affected the Russian theatre or theatres for generations, although his plays are still comparatively little known outside Russia. His name is Alexander Ostrovsky. Paradoxically enough, it was his very originality, his 'Russianness', that was the chief obstacle to an international reputation. His fifty-odd plays, with all their colourfulness, are too remote for foreign audiences who would probably miss in them some of the very points Ostrovsky's own countrymen most enjoyed and evidently still enjoy.

This is true of Ostrovsky's early works in particular. Born (1823) and bred in the old merchant quarter of Moscow, where his father was a lawyer, he served for a number of years as a clerk in the 'Conscience Court'[1] and then in the Commercial Court of Justice. The milieu he thus came to know best was that of the close-fisted patriarchal merchants who formed a social caste, indeed a peculiar world, of their own. It was here above all that Ostrovsky found plenty of material—most of it untapped—for his plays.

This strange world (now a matter of the distant past) was of great interest to Russian spectators, even though Ostrovsky's peculiar dramatic method required some adjustment. To begin with, he never cared for a closely knit, elaborate, or artificial plot. Nor was he keen on too much external action on the stage. In this respect his art was at the opposite pole of what Bernard Shaw understood by 'Sardoudledom'. It would be equally futile to look in his works for any cheap stunts, family triangles, or sexy bedroom scenes which were rampant in commercialised theatres all over the world. Like the great prose-writers of his country, Ostrovsky avoided any spectacular sensationalism for its own sake. He preferred to concentrate on a faithful but creative presentation of manners instead.

Having come out of Belinsky's 'natural school', he was unable to look upon the theatre merely as a place for amusement. The idea of civilised relaxation was, of course, taken by him for granted. But he also demanded that the stage and its repertory should be one of the most important social-cultural institutions in the life of a nation, providing it with really good plays. To quote his own words, each play ought to have a 'strong dramatic vein, a great deal of

---

1. This court had been established by Catherine II. Its special task was to settle all sorts of disputes between parents and their grown-up children.

humour, ardent and sincere feelings, and characters who are strongly alive'. Such was the principle to which he himself adhered. Instead of indulging in stock-in-trade artifices, he relied on the adequately organised *byt* (mores) or living material at his disposal.

2

Ostrovsky made his debut in 1847 when two scenes of his subsequent comedy, *It's a Family Affair* (*Svoí lyúdi sochtyómsya*, its original title was *The Bankrupt*), appeared in a Moscow newspaper. In this satirical comedy Ostrovsky followed in the footsteps of Fonvizin, Griboyedov, and Gogol. The *byt* or setting is that of a God-fearing patriarchal merchant family with a marriageable daughter who is as stupid as the heroine of Gogol's comedy *The Marriage*, but more mean and vulgar. Bolshov, the head of the family and owner of a number of prosperous shops, is rather busy. For he has devised how to arrange a would-be bankruptcy and thus get hold, with one stroke, of a big sum of money by not paying his creditors for the supply of goods. In all this he is helped by his equally fraudulent clerk Lazar Podkhalyuzin who has an eye on his boss's daughter Lipa. The gist of the scheme is as follows:

> *Bolshov.*   Now is the proper time; we have a great deal of ready cash, and all the notes have fallen due. What's the use of waiting? You'll wait if you please, until some merchant like yourself, the dirty cur, will strip you bare, and then you'll see, he'll make an agreement at ten kopeks on the ruble, and he'll wallow in his millions, and won't think you're worth spitting at. But you, an honourable tradesman, must just watch him, and suffer—keep on staring. Here's what I think, Lazar: to offer the creditors such a proposition as this—will they accept from twenty-five kopeks on the ruble? What do you think?
> *Podkhalyuzin.*   Why, according to my notion, if you are going to pay at the rate of twenty-five kopeks, it would be more decent not to pay at all.
> *Bolshov.*   Why, really, that's so. You won't scare anybody by bluff; but it's better to settle the affair on the quiet. Then wait for the Lord to judge you at the second Coming. . . . Why the devil should I scratch around for pennies. I'll make one swoop, and that's an end to it! Only God give us the nerve![1]

He did make the swoop. Despite his cunning he was naïve enough to trust his clerk (who, as a reward for collaboration, obtained Lipa's hand) and to settle fictitiously all his property on him. But once on horseback, the clerk forgot their amicable agreement—their 'family affair' as he styled it, and even refused to save his dear father-in-law from the debtors' prison.

When *It's a Family Affair* was published, in 1850, its invective against the practices of the merchant class was a pretext for the censor to ban the comedy

1. *Plays by Alexander Ostrovsky* translated by George Rapall Noyes (Scribner, 1917).

from the stage—the first performance took place only in 1861. The author was dismissed from the civil service and put under police surveillance. Meanwhile he achieved one stage success after the other, beginning with a comedy, *A Poor Bride* (*Bédnaya nevésta*, 1852), into which he introduced the background of petty officials and matchmakers, a 'substantial' aged wooer, and—to crown it all—the triumph of money over affection. A further success was scored by his *Poverty is no Crime* (*Bédnost' ne porók*, 1853). In this weaker and somewhat melodramatic comedy the merchant way of life is displayed once more to the full. Its invective is balanced, though, by a sudden conversion of the chief character, the bully Gordey Tortsov, who at the end of the play becomes quite human. In another comedy, *A Lucrative Post* (*Dokhódnoe mésto*, 1856), we are again in the world of officials, whereas in *The Ward* (*Vospítannitsa*, 1859) Ostrovsky gives us a picture of the landed gentry with their appalling self-will and lust for tyranny. To the same period belongs his amusing trilogy of comedies about the foppish minor clerk Balzaminov and his silly mother, in a typical lower middle-class setting.

It would be wrong, though, to look in Ostrovsky's plays of that period only for indictments. For one thing, he was associated from the outset with the Slavophil sympathisers who were prone, almost as a matter of course, to idealise everything Russian. He felt close to Apollon Grigoryev's idea of an artist's duty to be rooted in the soil and the spirit of his nation. True enough, some of Ostrovsky's comedies, especially those dealing with the 'dark kingdom' of the commercial bourgeoisie, are rather gloomy, and for good reason. 'We find in it no light, no warmth, no space,' commented his critic Dobrolyubov; 'the dark, narrow prison reeks of dampness and putrefaction'. Yet Ostrovsky kept attacking as an optimist who believed in his homeland and in man's potential decency. In *Poverty is no Crime*, for instance, the drunkard and wastrel Lyubim Tortsov displays a wealth of inner nobility and kindness almost in the style of the proverbial *âme russe*, supported by an excess of folkloristic and ethnographic details (folksongs, ritual songs, etc.). Ostrovsky, like Apollon Grigoryev, actually stood somewhere half-way between the Slavophils and the *naródniki* or the populists. But he was too much of an artist to sacrifice his plays to any ideology or to mere plots as such. What he cared for was life expressed in terms of the stage. Whenever he had to choose between truth to life and the conventions of a dramatic plot, he sided with the former. In his plays it is often baseness, vulgarity, and rascality that triumph even at the expense of poetic justice: as in *It's a Family Affair*, *A Poor Bride*, or *The Ward*; but this is surely what happens so often in life itself.

Whatever Ostrovsky touches, he is anxious to transform it into life on the stage, even if this be in terms of farcical scenes or of the queerest and craziest of characters. In fact, he is fond of buffoons by nature (especially if there is a tragic undertone in them). And however sad the subject-matter, he likes to relieve it, wherever possible, with humour. Life, *byt*, and character—such are the three pillars of his art. They are reflected also in his racy language which differs not only according to the individuals, but also according to the social categories to which they belong. And as for dramatic contrasts, he likes to confront the old-fashioned *samodúrs* (bullies) of both sexes with tender, weak, or fatalistic characters, as he did in one of his best plays, *The Storm* (*Grozá*).

3

This work appeared in 1860 and marked Ostrovsky's temporary passage from comedy to a drama whose realism is charged with a strong poetic and tragic atmosphere of its own. The scene of action is a merchant family in a God-forsaken Volga town. Its most respected (and feared) citizen, the merchant Dikoy, knows only one law of life. 'If I choose I spare you; if I choose I trample you under foot.' Not less of a tyrant is the old Kabanova whose sensitive and lovely daughter-in-law, Katerina, is the heroine of this drama. The general level is aptly summed up by the artisan Kuligin :

> They are a coarse lot, sir, in our town, a coarse lot! Among the work-ing people, sir, you'll find nothing but brutality and squalid poverty. And we've no chance, sir, of ever finding our way out of it. For by honest labour we can never earn more than a crust of bread. And everyone with money, sir, tries all he can to get a poor man under his thumb, so as to make more money again out of his working for nothing.[1]

Katerina, a repressed, deeply religious and inhibited young beauty, has been compulsorily married to Kabanova's son whose personality is entirely squashed by his bullying mother. Suffocating in the atmosphere of that 'dark kingdom', Katerina is in revolt against it; yet she is too much under the spell of inherited moral taboos to take an independent step. Her husband's kindness towards her only makes things worse, especially when she has fallen in love with Dikoy's charming but spineless nephew Boris. While her husband is away, she surrenders to Boris, but the sense of guilt which grips her after her husband's return is too heavy for her to bear. Pursued by her mother-in-law, by her own mental and moral ghosts, even by the stormy heaven, she vainly tries to escape from it all and in the end drowns herself in the Volga.

This simple plot is worked out by Ostrovsky with a great deal of poetic and dramatic power. The play excels in its beauty of language which—in Kat-erina's case—has the ring of the people's speech at it's most authentic. The high quality of this drama was recognised at once. No one gave it greater praise than the critic Dobrolyubov. And in 1898 Edward Garnett summed up his impressions of the play, in his preface to its first English edition, in these words :

> *The Storm* will repay a minute examination by all who recognise that in England to-day we have a stage without art, truth to life, or national significance. There is not a superfluous line in the play : all is drama, natural, simple, deep. There is no falsity, no forced situations, no sensational effects, none of the shallow or flashy caricatures of daily life that our heterogenous public demands. All the reproach that lives before us in the word *theatrical*

1. *The Storm*, translated by Constance Garnett (Duckworth, 1898).

is worlds removed from *The Storm*. The people who like 'farcical comedy', and social melodrama, and 'musical sketches' will find *The Storm* deep, forbidding, and gloomy. The critic will find it an abiding analysis of a people's temperament. The reader will find it literature.[1]

4

The Storm was partly connected with the 'literary expedition' that was sent in 1856 by one of the Ministries to the Volga region in order to collect linguistic and ethnographical material. Ostrovsky, who took part in it mainly on the upper Volga, found the journey stimulating. He himself asserted that the 'best school for any artistic talent is the study of one's own people whose recreation in terms of art is the finest emporium for one's activities'. Following up this principle, he cultivated his affinity with the people and made ample use of their idioms, sayings and proverbs in his writings, or in the very titles of his plays : *Poverty is no Crime, Don't Sit Down on Someone Else's Sledge (Ne v svoí sáni ne sadí')*, *Every Wise Man Can Be a Fool (Na vsyákogo mudretsá dovól'no prostotý)*, etc.[2] No wonder Apollon Grigoryev claimed him to be a true *póchvennik*, a man of the soil.

A further outcome of Ostrovsky's journey on the Volga was a cycle of historical dramas in verse, mostly about the 'troubled period' (1595-1613). They are not on the same level as his other works, and their pathos often reminds one of the cheap patriotic plays by Kukol'nik—a contemporary of Gogol.[3] They are certainly inferior to Alexey K. Tolstoy's historical trilogy—*The Death of Ivan the Terrible (Smert' Ivána Gróznogo, 1866), Tsar' Fyódor (1868)*, and *Tsar' Borís (1870)*—in which portraits and the well-suggested background of the period strengthen each other. A success on the stage, however, was Ostrovsky's dramatised fairy tale in verse, *The Snow Maiden (Snegúrochka, 1873)*. Inspired by folklore, it is a kind of Rousseauesque-Slavophil idealisation of the people. Rimsky-Korsakov used it later for his famous opera of the same title.

In spite of such digressions, Ostrovsky never forgot that his proper medium was the satirical comedy of manners. His favourite themes remained those about the merchant *byt*; yet he turned against the landed gentry as well, particu‐ larly in his *Forest (Les, 1871)* and *Wolves and Sheep (Vólki i óvtsy, 1875)*—two comedies which have inherited the spirit of Fonvizin's satires. The principal character in each is an autocratic woman bullying a helpless and bewildered human 'sheep'. 'Wolves' and 'sheep' actually became one of Ostrovsky's favour‐ ite dramatic contrasts. His 'sheep' may be snatched from disaster in the nick of time, but only after they have been thoroughly mauled and mangled by human 'wolves'.

After the reforms of 1861, the old-fashioned merchant caste was being

1. The famous Czech composer, Janáček has turned this play into a successful opera, known as *Kátya Kabánova*.
2. Some fifteen titles of his plays are based on popular sayings.
3. Ostrovsky also provided the librettos for two operas on historical themes : one by Tchaikovsky and the other by Serov.

gradually replaced by industrialists, speculators, or simply by reckless financial gamblers of a modern variety. These, too, figure in Ostrovsky's plays: in *Easy Money* (*Béshenye dén'gi*, 1870) for example, or in one of his strongest plays, *Dowerless* (*Bezpridánnitsa*, 1879). Peasants qua peasants, however, are hardly noticeable in his works, although he wrote two comedies about the people's *byt*: *Do not Live as You Want to* (*Ne tak zhiví kak khóchetsya*, 1854) and *A Lively Spot* (*Na bóikom méste*, 1865). Nor does he portray any memorable representatives of the intelligentsia. On the other hand, he wrote a few plays about actors. Two of these emerge—very much apropos—in *The Forest*. The comedy, *Talents and Adorers* (*Talánty i poklónniki*, 1882), and the somewhat melodramatic 'Volkstück', *Guilty without Guilt* (*Bez viný vinovátye*, 1884), are about strolling actors in the provinces.

Towards the end of his life Ostrovsky's dramatic vein began to decline.[1] As if aware of this, he increased his practical work on behalf of the theatre instead. One of his cherished dreams was to establish in Moscow a People's Theatre, accessible to the masses, yet at the same time preserving a high artistic standard. After having been rather shabbily treated by the government for years, he became, in 1885, director of the Moscow State Theatres and of the School of Dramatic Art. It was an appointment after his own heart. But just when he was beginning to develop his new activities, he died on 2 June, 1886.

5

The first thing which is likely to strike any student of Ostrovsky's plays is that practically all of them, with the exception of his 'Chronicles' and *The Snow Maiden*, can be classed as a combination of the comedy of manners and critical realism. His satire, though, was not an aim in itself, but rather a by-product of the *byt* which was his main concern. For him *byt* was more important than either the plot or any psychological disquisitions. It was within this frame that he tackled—Russian-fashion—all sorts of moral and social values. And however critical his mood may have been at times, he preserved his broad common sense and, together with it, his faith in man and life.

Last but not least, Ostrovsky is the only significant Russian author who gave the whole of his life to the stage. His manner and technique put him somewhere half-way between Gogol and Chekhov. Like Chekhov he often replaced the plot just by a sequence of 'scenes of merchant life', 'scenes of Moscow life', 'scenes of village life'. Yet despite his technical innovations, he still preserved such an old expedient as the monologue. His practice of making the names of many of his characters suggestive of their defects or virtues is also a remnant which goes back (via Gogol) to Fonvizin and eighteenth-century drama.

However much attracted by life in terms of the stage, Ostrovsky was fond of unsophisticated characters (even when these were a bit 'crazy'). In this

1. A mention should also be made of Ostrovsky's translations, which ranged from Plautus to Shakespeare (*Antony and Cleopatra*, *The Taming of the Shrew*), and from Cervantes to Goldoni.

respect he was worlds apart from the types of another famous Russian drama-tist : his contemporary Alexander Sukhovo-Kobylin (1817–1903). Kobylin's three plays—the only ones he wrote—*The Wedding of Krechinsky (Svád'ba Krechínskogo*, 1855), *The Death of Tarelkin (Smert' Tarélkina*, 1869), and *The Process (Délo*, 1869) are highly grotesque and contemptuous indictments of institutions and human beings alike. *The Process* in particular is among the most cruel satires on corrupt bureaucracy and judges in any language.

It stands to reason that Ostrovsky's love of the deepened truth to life on the stage called for a perfectly natural style of acting. This style soon found a galaxy of fine interpreters, such as Sadovsky, Martynov, Lensky, Ermolova, Varlamov—right down to the members of Stanislavsky's Moscow Art Theatre. In the same way Ostrovsky left his imprint on a number of dramatists who came after him : Chekhov, Naidyonov, Gorky and others. As for his own plays, they have been and still are the mainstay of Russian theatres big and small. It is not unfair to say that even in present-day Russia there are two great play-wrights whose popularity with the Russian theatregoers remains unchallenged, albeit for entirely different reasons. One is Shakespeare, and the other Ostrovsky.

CHAPTER FIFTEEN

Populists and others

I

Whatever its trials, Russian literature has always shown the courage to face the vital problems of life, whether in its social, political, or spiritual aspects. The difficulty which often arose was how to integrate such problems with art instead of treating them in a pamphleteering or didactic manner at the expense of art. Among the 'accursed problems' looming into prominence were the problem of serfdom, the problem of Russia and Europe, and that of the intelligentsia and the people. Of these the dilemma of Russia and Europe was responsible for two rival factions: European-minded Westerners and the patriotic Slavophils symbolising the divided Russian consciousness after Peter I. The great Slavophil sympathiser in literature was Dostoevsky. In poetry it was Tyutchev who—in addition to Yazykov—could claim to be on the side of the Slavophils, while Khomyakov (one of the Slavophil leaders) was occasionally a good poet rather than a great one. Generally speaking, the Slavophil trend produced some interesting historical and cultural-political theories and polemics by Ivan Kireyevsky, Alexey Khomyakov, and the brothers Konstantin and Ivan Aksakov. But Slavophilism eventually degenerated into the kind of arbitrary Byzantinism which was preached by Leontyev, into the plain imperialism of a General Fadeyev, or 'biological' nationalism of N. Danilevsky—the author of the once sensational book, *Russia and Europe* (1869).

An interesting example of a pro-Westerner being converted to an opponent of the West is that of Alexander Herzen (1812-1870), one of the most intelligent Russians of the last century. This happened in a way which had some far-reaching consequences. An illegitimate son of a rich landowner, Herzen was given a good education and studied at Moscow University in the early 1830s when the famous debating circle of Stankevich was one of its stimuli. Strongly influenced by the rebellious spirit of the 'Decembrists', Herzen and his friend, the subsequent poet Nikolai Ogaryov, had sworn as teenagers to fight autocracy and serfdom. Herzen certainly kept this promise. In 1847 he achieved considerable success with his problem novel *Whose Fault* (*Kto vinovát*) in which the influence of George Sand was evident. In the same year he emigrated to Western Europe whence he hoped to fight for a freer Russia more efficiently than if he stayed at home. Yet having witness in France, Italy and elsewhere the failure of the revolution and the triumph of the bourgeoisie in 1848, he lost his faith in Europe. In 1852 he settled in London where he founded the Free Russian

Press (for publishing books prohibited in Russia). From 1857 on he also edited the radical Russian periodical *The Bell* (*Kólokol*) which was being regularly smuggled into Russia and which, through its disclosure of abuses, soon became the nightmare of tsarist bureaucracy.[1]

It was after his disappointment in the West, a disappointment which he vented in his brilliant book of essays, *From the Other Shore* (*S togó bérega,* 1851), that Herzen directed his hopes onto the less civilised Russian people in whose *mir* or *obshchína* (the village commune), with its collective ownership of land, he saw the promise of an agrarian socialism based on the peasants, as distinct from a socialism based on the industrialised proletarians. In this he discovered the possibility for the Russian people to achieve their own type of socialist way of life without first passing through a capitalist phase in the Western style. Such was one of the principal sources of that Populism or *naródniki*-movement[2] which was destined to play a prominent part among the Russian intellectuals from the 1860s onwards.

Populism shared in some respects the Slavophil cult of the people, but without the people's Orthodoxy, or without any religion at all, since the majority of the Populists were steeped in Western science and positivism. The Slavophils and the budding Populists were in fact opponents; yet in some respects they were complementary to each other. As Herzen himself put it in his reminiscences:

> Yes, we were opponents but very strange ones. We had one love, although it differed. They and we succumbed from our earliest years to one powerful irrational feeling—the feeling of limitless all-embracing love for the Russian people ... To them the Russian people was above all Orthodox, i.e., closest to the heavenly city; to us it was above all a social entity, i.e., closest to the earthly city.

The populist trend was more than likely to attract the 'superfluous' radical-minded *déclassés* on the one hand, and the 'repentant noblemen', with their strong guilt complex, on the other. If the first wanted to get rid of their isolation by merging with the people, the second were determined to atone for the transgressions of their serf-owning ancestors by helping the people, however great the social distance between the landed gentry and the toiling masses may still have been even after the liberation of the peasants in 1861. The same distance divided the people and the intelligentsia as a whole. Incidentally, the man who above all was doing his best to bridge this gap was Dostoevsky, after his return from Siberia in 1859. It was with such a plan in view that he founded the *Time* (*Vrémya*) and, after its suppression in 1863, its successor *The Epoch* (*Epókha*). Supported by the poet and critic Apollon Grigoryev (1822-64), he called the intellectuals back to the soil and the people; and since the Russian word for soil is *póchva*, the sympathisers with this movement were called

1. The prestige of this periodical fell among the Russians during and after the Polish rising in 1863 because of Herzen's open sympathies with the Poles. In 1865 Herzen transferred it to Geneva where it kept appearing for another two years (in French) and then came to an end.

2. From the word *naród* (people).

póchvenniki, the 'rooted ones'. They actually might have formed a link between the Populists and the Slavophils but for Dostoevsky's Orthodox-religious and monarchic bias which could not and did not appeal to the advanced minds of the period. The intellectuals with populist inclinations found their own leaders in such radicals as Dobrolyubov, Chernyshevsky, and later on in Mikhailovsky whose influence was at its height in the 1870s—the actual decade of Populism.

The two commoners, Nikolai Chernyshevsky (1828-89) and Nikolai Dobrolyubov (1836-61) were, together with the 'nihilist' of aristocratic birth—Dmitry Pisarev (1840-68), the principal champions of revolutionary democracy in the 1860s. That was the age of emancipation, of scientific materialism and of that active utilitarianism which was embodied in Chernyshevsky's tendentious novel, *What is to be Done? (Chto délat'*, 1863). Radical journalism, represented by thick monthlies, was to a large extent in the hands of commoners who revelled in criticising all the negative aspects of Russian life. Even their literary criticism was social rather than aesthetic. This applies to Chernyshevsky's *The Age of Gogol*, to Dobrolyubov's essays on *Oblómov* and on Ostrovsky's plays, while Pisarev went so far as to want to dethrone Pushkin himself in the name of a ruthlessly utilitarian attitude towards art.

The next radical decade, the decade of the 1870s, was one of the populist ideology proper—represented above all by young noblemen sincerely anxious to redeem the evils perpetrated upon the people by their serf-owning forebears. That was why hundreds or even thousands of aristocratic youths and girls were now voluntarily giving up their comfort in order to live among peasants and workers whom they wanted to help and prepare for a revolution in the name of that future agrarian socialism in which they believed. It was a kind of moral and social epidemic in the best sense of the word.

These young *narodniki* found an inspiring leader in Nikolai Mikhailovsky (1842-1904). Partly influenced by Stuart Mill, he was a utilitarian social thinker who went beyond any narrow-minded Utilitarianism and remained a consistent champion of an individualistic approach to sociology. His attitude towards literature, too, was broader and much more cultured than the one upheld, say, by Pisarev. He was in fact quite a good critic in his own right. Another thinker who gave plenty of ideological and moral support to that generation was Peter Lavrov (1823-1900) whose anthropological approach to evolution was expounded in his *Historical Letters (Istorícheskie pís'ma*, 1870)—a vigorous apology for the role of the individual in history.

There was something pathetic and at the same time naively honest in those young men and women who were ready to sacrifice everything for the sake of the people. But the irony of it all was that they were frequently denounced to the authorities by those very peasants and workers whom they were so anxious to help. The fact that their efforts were, moreover, often futile was recorded in Turgenev's novel *Virgin Soil*. Here the author portrayed—in the person of Nezhdanov—a type of 'superfluous revolutionary' who, in spite of his good-will, was yet unable to believe in those activities, and in the end committed suicide.

The most radical group of the populist movement assumed the programmatic slogan of the 'People's Freedom' in the name of which its members were ready to use terrorist methods when necessary. They were actually responsible for the assassination of Alexander II (on 13 March 1881) which was followed by a period of dire political reaction during the next two decades. Still, at the beginning of the 1890s the populist trend was renewed under the name of the Social-Revolutionary Party—a rival of Marxism. It played a considerable role during the revolutionary events of 1905-06; but in the upheaval of 1917 it was entirely ousted by its Marxist-Leninist opponents.

2

The Populist trend had a fairly strong echo in Russian literature, not to mention the vast amount of pamphleteering on its behalf. Alexander Herzen himself is remembered above all by his book of reminiscences, *My Past and Thoughts* (*Bylóe i dúmy*), written between 1861 and 1867. A classic of memoir literature —one of the finest books of this kind in any language—*My Past and Thoughts* is a summary of Herzen's life from the earliest days he could remember until middle age. The author's personality stands out as that of a fighter and a sterling character—against the shabby background of the Europe he lived in and of the shabbier Russia he contended with. But he was not blind to possible remedies. The way in which he shows the atmosphere that prevailed among the young Moscow idealists of the 1830s is unique. And so is the series of meetings not only with crowds of political refugees, but also with such people as Garibaldi, Mazzini and other famous men he had known. Among the radicals of all nations he met during those wanderings was the swashbuckling German poet Herwegh, who callously seduced Herzen's wife Natalia—one of the tragic personal chapters recorded in *My Past and Thoughts*.

Of the great authors it was Tolstoy who came very close to the Populists, whereas Dostoevsky's sympathies remained on the side of the Slavophils. As early as 1865 Tolstoy maintained that 'the world task of Russia is to provide a social structure devoid of the individual ownership of land'. And on one occasion he acknowledged his admiration for Herzen himself in a talk with Gorky: 'The main point in which I am close to him is his love for the Russian people and for the character of the Russian people'. Moreover, Tolstoy's sympathetic descriptions of the Russian peasants, as well as his later efforts to identify himself in his dress and ways of life with the toilers on the land are a matter of general knowledge. Of the minor authors who persevered their belief in the Russian *muzhik* and regarded such institutions as *mir* and *artél'* (the artisan co-operative) not only as social but also as powerful moral factors, Zlatovratsky and Zasodimsky could be mentioned.

Nikolai Zlatovratsky (1845-1911) stressed the ethical qualities of the Russian peasant in his works, the best known of which is his long populist novel, *Foundations* (*Ustói*, 1875-82). Of considerable interest are his memoirs of the 1860s, *How it All Happened*. His sincerity, mixed up with wishful thinking, was, however, much stronger than his critical sense. This was also one of the failings of Pavel Zasodimsky (1843-1912). He knew the Russian peasant and the village commune, but his invariable tendency was to idealise both. Of a higher calibre were the writings of Gleb Uspensky (1840-1902). In addition to being an acute observer he was endowed with a critical acumen which in the end undermined any idealising propensity. In his first important work, *Manners of the Rasteryayeva Street* (*Nrávy Rasteryáyevoy úlitsy*, 1866), he depicted—with occasional comic relief—the mire of the slums in a big provincial town; but as a convinced Populist or *naródnik* he gave his main attention to the peasant. His best work of this kind was the novel, *The Power of the Soil* (*Vlast' zemlí*, 1882). Being, however, fully aware also of the power of money, he could not help seeing the gradual deterioration of the village under the impact of capitalism and the materialistic chase after gain. His high moral standards made him increasingly sceptical, as well as isolated—the state of mind in which he committed suicide.

Another victim of his own moral sensitiveness was the talented short-story writer Vsevolod Garshin (1855-1888). His *Four Days* (*Chetýre dnya*)—an excellent though gruesome tale from the Russo-Turkish war of how a wounded Russian soldier spent four days alone beside the corpse of the Turk he himself had killed—was one of Garshin's stories to bring him fame. Prostitution, merciless exploitation of the workers, ineradicable human misery and helpless compassion for the 'injured and offended' provided the material for his further stories, told in a nervously agitated yet vigorous style. In his narrative *The Artists* (*Khudózhniki*) a young painter abandons art and becomes an ordinary teacher in order to help the exploited masses; but neither he nor those he wants to help derive any benefit from his sacrifice. The only person who dies in the delusion that evil can be and has been eradicated is the madman in the little tale, *The Red Flower* (*Krásny tsvetók*). Unable to endure the atmosphere of the 1880s, Garshin too put an end to his own life. The misery of the village and the inadequacy of the intelligentsia provided the main themes for N. J. Petropavlovsky-Karonin's (1857–1892) tales. A sunnier and more optimistic air pervaded the work of another Populist author, Vladimir G. Korolenko (1853–1921).

After the death of Mikhailovsky, Korolenko the man and writer became a moral force among the Populists and was closely connected with their monthly, *The Russian Wealth* (*Rússkoe Bogátstvo*), which began appearing after the suppression of the *Fatherland's Annals* in 1883. As a young revolutionary, he had been exiled for several years to Yakutia, the coldest region of Siberia, and his first story, *Makar's Dream* (*Son Makára*, 1885), is on a Yakutian theme, with a Siberian background. A very humane narrative is his *The Blind Musician* (*Slepóy muzykánt*)— the story of how a blind boy was trained in music so successfully that, despite his handicap, he became adapted to life as a professional virtuoso. Korolenko's tale *In the Night* (*Nóchyu*) shows a great understanding of children's mentality, while his *Day of Atonement* (*Súdny den'*) is full of humour combined with a friendly attitude towards the Jews who, in those days, were being persecuted both by the authorities and the populace. The lyrical overtones in his descriptions of nature continue the tradition of

Turgenev and are at times almost overdone. Yet he knows how to make the life of nature blend with the lives of human beings: in his narrative *The Rustling Forest (Les shumít)*, for instance, where nature's background blends perfectly with a grim crime-story. His biggest and most soberly written work is his *History of my Contemporary (Istóriya moegó sovreménnika)*—an auto-biography in disguise, the first part of which appeared in 1910 and the rest in 1922. It is a reliable introduction to the mentality and the problems the younger generation had to face and cope with before 1880.[1] He spent the later years of his life in the Ukrainian town of Poltava where he was left in peace even after 1917, in spite of his anti-bolshevist attitude.

Another Populist sympathiser was Alexander Ertel' (1855–1908) whose novel *The Gardenias (Gardéniny*, 1888) abounds in a series of vivid peasant portraits presented with raciness and humour. Here, as well as in his other novels, such as *The Change (Sména)* or *Strúkov's Career*, he championed man's deeper spiritual cravings, but devoid of any dogmatic 'isms'. He himself, though, was mildly influenced by Tolstoyanism. Close to the Populists also stood D. N. Mamin-Sibiryak (1852–1912). In his best-known novel, *Privalov's Millons (Priválovskie miliyóny*, 1883) he described the predicament of the Ural miners and the ravages of money in the hands of ruthless speculators portrayed also in such regional novels as *Gold, Bread*, etc.

A brief mention should be made of Pavel Mel'nikov-Pechersky (1819–83), who wrote about the Russian people in a way that secured him a place of his own. His early work, *The Krasílnikovs* (1852), was a realistic indictment of bureaucrats and landowners. His *opus magnum* that followed consists, how-ever, of two rather long but highly interesting novels with the simple titles *In the Woods (V lesákh*, 1871–75) and *On the Mountains (Na gorákh*, 1875–81). Both are semi-ethnographic panoramas depicting a peculiar branch of the Rus-sian people: the same Old Believers whose ancestors, exhorted by the archpriest Avvakum, had once defied the reforms of the Patriarch Nikon and remained loyal to their old religious customs and traditions. Scattered in the wooded regions of the Upper Volga and the mountainous Urals, they were steadily persecuted by the tsarist regime. This made them, however, all the more attached to their own God of fear, as well as to their hidden shrines, convents and monas-teries, especially when the latter were threatened by such destruction as is described in *On the Mountains*. Pechersky wrote down only what he saw. But he portrayed some amazing characters, beginning with the village merchant Potap Maksimych and his sister—the abbess Manefa. In the novel *In the Woods* the death of one of the female characters (Nastya) is followed by a detailed description of an old-world Russian burial with funeral songs and customs of which probably nothing is left in the rapidly changing modern world. These two long novels, so rich in documentary material and presented at a leisurely narrative pace, hold the reader's attention on account of their authenticity and novelty.

---

1.   In the first half of the 1890s there also appeared *Tyoma's Childhood, Grammar-School Boys and Undergraduates* by N. Garin (N.G. Mikhailovsky 1852-1906). This is an interesting and well-written trilogy about the education of youths of the intelligentsia of that period.

3

In contrast to the Populists there were writers with a strong upper-class consciousness. Evgeny Markov (1835–1903) was one of them. His novels *Squirelings* (*Barchukí*, 1875) and *Black Earth Fields* (*Chernozyómnye polyá*, 1878) were an aggressive defence of the squire's rural mission as against the encroachment of the town. Among the authors writing especially for the radical and liberal-democratic intelligentsia, A. K. Scheller-Mikhailov (1838–1900) was notable for his many novels and narratives, but they are now practically forgotten. The work of his equally prolific liberal-minded contemporary, Peter Boborykin (1836–1921), is more significant. He was an able chronicler not only of the intelligentsia but also of the rising bourgeoisie which, after 1861, played an increasingly important part in Russian life. One of Boborykin's favourite themes was the metamorphosis of an aristocrat into a businessman: in his novel *Kitái-Górod*, for instance, with its rendering of the Moscow atmosphere of the 1880s. Familiar with the trends of the age he lived in, he was, however, more a versatile than a truly creative master of realism. The quantity of his work (he wrote over one hundred volumes) could not help growing at the expense of quality. He was too fluent to be profound.

One of the conspicuous features of the period was the emergence of the general reader, largely among the petty bourgeoisie. What this kind of reader demanded from literature was above all relaxation, amusement and pleasant escapism. And since a comfortable escape can always be provided by the historical past, it is not surprising that the historical novel became quite popular in Russia at the time, even though its quality may not have been very high. The principal purveyors of this genre, Grigory Danilevsky, Count Evgeny Salias and Vsevolod Solovyov, did not disappoint their readers. Count Salias's *The Pugachov Men* (*Pugachóvtsy*, 1874) was a best-seller. A great favourite was *Prince Serebryany* (*Knyaz' Serébryany*, 1862) by Count Alexey K. Tolstoy. It dealt with the epoch and the character of Ivan the Terrible, but its frequent pseudo-archaic passages and forced folkloristic flavour are less likely to appeal to a modern reader.

The historical novel may have been popular in the 1870s; yet as its standard kept falling, it did not play a conspicuous part in literature. The big names of that decade were the realistic authors who had begun their careers in the late 1840s or soon after. Leo Tolstoy, Turgenev and Goncharov were still alive when the assassination of Alexander II in 1881 suddenly changed the political and social climate of Russia. The gloomy decade of the 1880s, with its 'Chekhovian' despondence, was looming on the horizon. It was bound to have a strong impact on literature even though such a man as Korolenko refused to succumb to the general mood of despondency. The same could be said of another and even more interesting writer of that period—Nikolai Leskov.

CHAPTER SIXTEEN

Nikolai Leskov

I

The vogue of Russian realism in the second half of the nineteenth century is known abroad through the works of Turgenev, Dostoevsky, Tolstoy, Goncharov, and Chekhov. But important though they be, these authors do not exhaust either the wealth or the pattern of that prodigiously creative period. One of its major representatives, Nikolai Leskov (1831–95), for instance, is only now finding, slowly but surely, due appreciation abroad. At home, however, his reputation stands high indeed. No less a person than Maxim Gorky said of him (in the preface to one of Leskov's stories) that as a literary artist, Leskov can beyond any doubt be placed on a level with the great masters of Russian literature. According to this verdict, Leskov's talent is in no way inferior to theirs, and what is more—in his broad variety of themes he even surpasses many of his contemporaries. His knowledge of Russian is supreme; and so is his gift of narrative for its own sake, not to mention his understanding of human beings as they are. He may and does shape his characters by a method different from, say, that of Tolstoy. On the other hand, he makes them speak for themselves in such a way that in the end they are as convincing and even physically tangible as the characters created by other famous authors. Gorky further refers to him as the 'most truly Russian of all Russian writers' and 'entirely free from outside influences'.

A younger contemporary of the great realists, Leskov occupies a place of his own in Russian fiction: a fact which can perhaps be explained partly by the peculiar conditions he lived in. Whereas a number of the old leaders of Russian *belles lettres* came from the gentry, Leskov counted among his ancestors priests, traders, and minor officials. This may explain the wide range of his themes, his lack of any social bias, as well as his general approach to life. Socially he stood nearest to those commoners who came into their own in the active 1860s. On the other hand, Leskov was much too independent, both as man and artist, to be pigeon-holed into any of their groups or doctrines. Least of all was he inclined to indulge in the enthusiastic but often somewhat adolescent radicalism of that decade. Moreover, he openly defended religion at a time when scientific materialism was considered the hall-mark of progress and fashion.

The same independence was shown by Leskov in his style, in his choice of subject matter, even in his attitude towards the accepted literary language.

Not unlike Nekrasov in poetry, it was he in particular who broadened Russian prose by grafting upon it the authentic pattern and inflection of the people's speech at its best. No prose-writer of his period was endowed with so strong a flair for the spoken word as he. The word as such was something more than just a means to him—it assumed a value of its own, which he learned to feel and to appreciate through contact with the simple folk. He also enlarged the area of Russian literature by introducing a number of new themes.

2

Born in the town of Oryol (Orël), the environs of which were made famous by Turgenev in his *A Sportsman's Sketches*, Leskov breathed from his childhood the atmosphere of that provincial Russia which later became inseparable from his writings. While still at Grammar School, he witnessed the loss of the family fortune—a blow which compelled him to interrupt his education and fall back upon his own resources. Full of vitality and common sense, he took his courage in both hands and went into the world. Eventually he worked in Kiev (in the 1850s) under a Briton—a certain Mr Scott, manager of the vast estates belonging to the Perovsky and the Naryshkin families. In the capacity of Mr Scott's agent, Leskov travelled all over Russia and especially in the Volga provinces, thus widening his own experiences, his knowledge of people and of the world. His British chief also discovered in him a potential author and urged him to write. Having made his debut in 1860 (when he was nearly thirty years old), Leskov soon gave all his energies to literature and settled down in Petersburg. Here he wrote for several periodicals, including Dostoevsky's *Time* (*Vrémya*) whose peculiar brand of Populism must have appealed to him.

It should be borne in mind that the 1860s were a period of wrangles between political groups, notably between the patriotic Slavophils on the one hand, and the liberal or radical pro-Western intellectuals on the other. But whatever the differences between them, the intelligentsia as a whole had hardly any real contact with, or understanding of, the peasant masses. Dostoevsky saw, or foresaw, the deeper implications of such a state of things and never wearied of pointing out that the Russian intellectuals should take root in the soil and the people of their native land—a call which was endorsed by Apollon Grigoryev in essays, by Alexander Ostrovsky in drama, and by Leskov in fiction. Incidentally, Grigoryev was one of the first critics to welcome Leskov's talent, which blossomed out in the second half of the 1860s and continued to enrich Russian literature for a period of over thirty years. During that time Leskov wrote a vast amount of works which can be roughly divided into novels, chronicles of provincial life, stories pure and simple, didactic legends, apocrypha, and lastly the so-called *skaz*—a sort of narrative connected mainly with his name and technically quite an important genre of his writings.

Leskov's two bulky first novels, *The Impasse* (*Nékuda*) and *At Daggers Drawn* (*Na nozhákh*), are mainly political and touch upon the problems the generation of the 'sixties was called upon to face and to cope with. The first novel appeared in 1864 and can be regarded as an attempt on the part of the author to clear up his own attitude towards the radical currents among the younger intelligentsia of which he was rather critical. For this reason it is often included, though less so than *At Daggers Drawn*, in the series of 'reactionary' novels comprising Goncharov's *The Ravine* and Dostoevsky's *The Possessed*. As it happened, two years before the publication of *The Impasse* Leskov had written in Bulgarin's conservative 'Northern Bee' (*Sévernaya pchelá*) an article about the epidemic of mysterious conflagrations in Petersburg, ascribed by the police to the activities of the 'nihilist' section among the students. Although written in defence of the students,[1] the article was misinterpreted by the radical press as an accusation of them; which was a pretext for discovering in Leskov an ideological enemy and raising a hullabaloo against him. In spite of his liberal opinions, the author was thus driven into the opposite camp. As a result he adopted in this novel an aggressive attitude towards his accusers. But *The Impasse* was a diagnosis rather than a direct attack. Leskov did not conceal in it his sympathy with the true and sincere idealists among the revolutionaries, while condemning without mercy the frauds, fools, and opportunistic camp-followers of radicalism. Like Dostoevsky in *The Possessed*, he saw in the extreme left section of the intelligentsia an uprooted and purely destructive element, unable to grasp either the real needs or the real tasks of Russia after the abolition of serfdom. It is a pity that he cheapened the plot by showing the revolutionaries as dupes of Polish Jesuits in disguise—supposedly preparing the ground for the rebellion in Poland (in 1863) by fomenting internal troubles in Russia herself.

Although vivid and full of incident, this work does not surpass the average novel of the period. It falls far below the level of such an apocalyptic book as *The Possessed*. The hue and cry it caused among the radicals was quite out of proportion to its real merit. Leskov was, from now on, either ignored or else slandered by the radical press. But this only made him adopt a more aggressive attitude towards his own opponents. He gave vent to it in his second political novel, *At Daggers Drawn* (1871), after which a reconcilation was out of the question. Still, it should be noted that he never took part in any reactionary activities and was as outspoken about the excesses on the right as he was about those on the left. In a number of narratives he attacked the bureaucracy of the State and the Church with such virulence as to risk—in 1883, for example an open conflict with the authorities. In 1889 one of his works was even confiscated by the police on account of its harmful tendencies.

Some of Leskov's earlier writings could conveniently be left out but for the fact that they point to certain questions of nineteenth century Russia—questions which transcend mere politics. The already mentioned problem of the relationship between the uprooted intelligentsia and the people was one of them. Leskov himself—a true Russian if ever there was—broached the theme of the 'superfluous man' rather originally, in *The Islanders* (*Ostrovityáne*). Its principal character is a gifted but unaccountable Russian artist, shown against the

---

1.   What Leskov demanded in this article was that the police should deny that the students had started the fires, or else punish the actual offenders.

background of the ultra-respectable German settlers in Petersburg, whose milieu produced *déracinés* of its own (illustrated by the heroine of the novel).

Leskov would probably have continued to write in the vein he had started, had he not come to the conclusion that after the hostile reception of his two political novels his literary future lay not in the novel at all. He was on the look-out for something new, as one can gather from his next two works, *Cathedral Folk* and *The Sealed Angel*.

3

Cathedral Folk (*Soboryáne*, 1872) is not a novel in the usual sense of this word. It is a chronicle of life in a Russian cathedral town—with the clergy as its prominent feature. Leskov introduced into Russian literature this thematic element with such competence as to have added the two principal figures described, the archpriest Tuberozov and his assistant Akhilla, to the memorable characters of Russian fiction. The contrast between the dignified, tactfully active idealist Tuberozov and the impulsive Akhilla (a Cossack who by some mistake had joined the Church but could never quite fit into his profession) abounds in comic as well as pathetic incident. Akhilla worships his superior with the unquestioning admiration of a child and behaves like a jealous woman whose love, although appreciated, is studiously ignored. The amusingly colourful account of events is obscured by Tuberozov's troubles with the Church bureaucracy and ends in a sad note—the death of the archpriest himself and, not long after, of the turbulent Akhilla as well.

The whole of this narrative is admirably interwoven with the life of a provincial town and the surrounding district. Some of its passages (the storm in the forest, for example) are among the gems of Russian prose. With the same competence are rendered the peculiarities of the archaic speech used by the clergy. But while showing the vanishing patriarchal life in a sympathetic light, Leskov lays bare, and most scathingly too, the dry, pedantic opportunism of the higher Church authorities. With even greater relish he caricatures the unscrupulous sham-radicals and the would-be 'new men' of the 1860s.

But since *Cathedral Folk* is referred to as a chronicle and not a novel, it is essential to show the difference between the two (although they may overlap, as they do in Tolstoy's *War and Peace*). Briefly, a novel is based on a plot the pattern of which is decisive for its structure. A chronicle, on the other hand, is a sequence of happenings arranged in the way they occur in real life. Here the structure of the narrative is more loose than in a novel, and single incidents can often be added or deleted without impairing the whole. In 1875 Leskov wrote about the artificial and unnatural form of the novel, and pointed out the fact that in life things happen differently. 'A man's life is like the unfurling of a scroll, and I am going to use the same method,' he said. Moreover, he endowed each of his characters with a voice and intonation corresponding to his profession and social status. This itself led him to the *skaz*—a story told by a man of the people or by a lower middle-class person, with all the idioms, inflections and popular etymologies typical of the narrator and of the social stratum to which he belongs. At the same time Leskov preferred to render the traits of his characters not so much by means of analysis as by an accumulation of incident and anecdotes. This method brought him, in turn, close to the picaresque story which he often blended with the *skaz*.

Less than a year after *Cathedral Folk*, another of Leskov's masterpieces, *The Sealed Angel* (*Zapechatlénny ángel*), appeared. This is one of his finest and alas! least translatable works. It combines in a striking manner his innate religious sense with the *skaz*, and is told by an artisan from among the dissenters or 'Old Believers' with that admirable use of the people's idioms and phrasing, the mastery of which became at the beginning of this century something of a test for a writer's verbal skill. While keeping to the chronicle-pattern in some of his other works, notably in his long narrative *A Decayed Family* (1875), Leskov preserved the *skaz* and gave full scope to its form in such bracing stories as *The Enchanted Wanderer* (*Ocharóvanny stránnik*), *The Amazon* (*Voítel'nitsa*), *The Steel Flea*,[1] and *The Hare Chase* (*Záyachiy remíz*). The first of these is a picaresque tale of adventure told by an ordinary Russian who, after years of roaming, is on his way to a monastery and shares his reminiscences with a few pilgrims. The story is not only an illustration of the vitality and stoicism of the character concerned, but also of Leskov's narrative talent. Some of the scenes, such as the dance of the gypsy belle (whose tragedy is interwoven with the story) are described with an intensity of vision and feeling which takes one's breath away.

The Amazon is another *skaz*. It is told by a lower middle-class matchmaker who, in the broadness of her character, becomes a procuress; yet in spite of this, there is so much warmth and generosity in her simple heart that in the end one cannot help liking her. The hero of the hilarious *Steel Flea* is a left-handed smith from Tula whose sagacity outstrips even the inventive genius of England; but, as was so often the case in old Russia, his skill leads to no constructive or practical purposes. This *skaz* (perhaps the best known Russian specimen of its kind) also reflects what might be called the instinctive attitude of the Russian masses towards the English—an attitude of benevolence and admiration, but hardly devoid of the spirit of rivalry. The story itself was suggested to Leskov by the popular Russian saying: 'The English made a flea of steel, but our artisans of Tula shoed it.' As for *The Hare Chase*, first published in 1917, it is a life-story told in the inimitably comic mixture of Russian and Ukrainian by an upstart who came to grief. Devoid of brains and scruples, but full of 'zeal' for the powers-that-be, he wormed his way into the position of a police officer employed in the chase of revolutionaries. Eventually he lost both his career and his reason through having failed to catch a most dangerous rebel who, during all that time, had been employed—cleverly disguised—as his coachman. *The Hare Chase* sparkles with fun and with that satirical spirit which marked Leskov's writings in the 1880s and 1890s, often bringing him close to Saltykov-Schedrin—the Russian Swift of those days.

1. This is the title of its English translation. Its Russian title is *Levshá* (The Left-handed Man).

4

Even if Leskov was not the actual inventor of the *skaz* (its beginnings go back to Gogol and Pushkin), he nevertheless became its first undisputed master and brought it to such perfection as to secure for it a high place in Russian fiction. But he can be equally relied upon in the straightforward traditional story which he imbued with quick and vivid action. A good example of this kind is his *Lady Macbeth of the Mtsensk District* (*Lady Macbeth mtsénskogo uyézda*, 1865).[1] Taken from the *milieu* of the patriarchal merchant class in the provinces, it depicts a woman's blind passion—an obsession rather than a passion—and the crimes resulting from it, with brutal yet powerful directness. The colours are plain, while the inner logic of the crime and the punishment that follows is as inexorable as is the sway of carnal lust—the cause of it all. Needless to say, Leskov here made splendid use of the people's language. In this story, too, the characters are alive above all in terms of incident.

This method can be studied in a number of other narratives, especially those in which he keeps to the *skaz* type. The whole of *The Amazon*, for example, is but a string of episodes and anecdotes arranged in such a manner as to make the woman of the story as real as if we had known her personally. The same can be said of *The Enchanted Wanderer*; or of *An Iron Will* (*Zheléznaya vólya*): a humorously ironical portrait of a German engineer in Russia. Leskov's experience of life was so rich indeed that several of his jottings were left in the state of raw anecdote and semi-documentary reportage. Nor did he mind using the actual names of people, historical or otherwise, who had taken part in some of the happenings told. *Cheramour*, Leskov's lower middle-class counterpart of Turgenev's *Rudin*, is an instance. So is *The Immortal Golovan* (*Bessmértny Golován*) based, like *Cheramour*, on his reminiscences of a person the memory of whom still lingered in Leskov's native town of Oryol. To this category can be added *On the Edge of the World*: an account of the hair-raising experiences of a Russian bishop (The Bishop of Yaroslavl') whose life was saved, during one of his diocesan journeys in the Arctic wastes, by the loyalty and devotion of a pagan, while a Christian convert of the same tribe behaved like a cad. But since the implications of this story point to another group of Leskov's work, we can pass to those narratives which touch upon religious and ethical problems.

5

It is known that in the 1880s Leskov became temporarily interested in Tolstoy and Tolstoyanism. Tolstoy, in his turn, commended the essential 'Russianness' of Leskov and this helped, as far as possible, towards the latter's literary re-habilitation. However, the gospel of the much-too-conscious self-perfection

---

1. The Soviet composer Shostakovich made use of this story for his well-known opera under the same title.

on the part of Tolstoy was hardly likely to appeal without reserve to Leskov whose Christianity (based on spontaneous warmth and goodness rather than on parading one's contrition, or moral book-keeping) was nearer to the people than that of Tolstoy. This attitude found an expression in his parables and legends—some of them paraphrased from the old Church-Slavonic *Prologue*, while others were taken from folklore, or else from the general stock of East-European Christian tradition. Such legends as *The Juggler Pamphalón*, *The Mountain*, *The Fair Azra*, deal with the early Christian period in Alexandria, but they lay stress on charity in Leskov's sense rather than on rigid morality in the sense of Tolstoy.[1]

In Tolstoy the uncharitable moral element was stronger than his religious consciousness, and it often thrived at the latter's expense. Leskov, on the other hand, was endowed with a religious instinct spontaneous and warm enough to save him not only from any lack of charity, but also from conscious or unconscious moral exhibitionism—the pitfall of many a frowning Puritan. If Leskov's art harbours a message at all, to which our (or any other) period might listen with profit, it is the simple truth that the thing most needful is human warmth and sympathy, as a preliminary condition for everything that makes life worth while. Leskov himself did not lack this virtue. In his attitude towards the world there was nothing reminding one either of Gogol's rancour and mistrust, or of Tolstoy's severe moral judgment. On the contrary, he found life attractive precisely because he approached it in the spirit of broadness, tolerance and charity. He was one of those Russian realists who were able to depict good characters—take his Tuberozov—without being stilted, rhetorical or moralistic.

6

Novels, naturalistic stories, *skaz*-tales, legendary and folklore themes, anecdotic reminiscences, intensely documentary pictures of the serfdom period (*The Beast*, *The Make-up Artist*, *The Vale of Tears*, etc.)—all these contributed to the variety of Leskov's work without impairing either its artistic or human integrity. 'He narrates, and in this art he has no equal,' says Gorky. Gorky who, incidentally, learned a great deal from Leskov, also points out Leskov's profound love of Russia. Nor was it a small merit that Leskov preserved this love —together with his faith in life—even at the time of the despondent 1880s and early 1890s.

Ignored or else deprecated by the critics while alive, Leskov yet succeeded in creating quite a large reading public for his works. But he really came into his own at the beginning of this century, when he was taken up by a number of modernists. Alexey Remizov, a modernist virtuoso of the *skaz*, followed Leskov (including his legendary and hagiographic motifs) in his own writings. Another modernist, Evgeny Zamyatin, excelled in the *skaz* manner both before

1. Yet one of the stimuli under which Leskov wrote those legends came from Tolstoy's *People's Tales*.

and after the revolution of 1917. Quite a few elements have been taken from Leskov by some of the Soviet authors during the early phases of Soviet fiction. A popular representative of the *skaz* was the Soviet author Mikhail Zoshchenko, many of whose shrewdly stylised sketches have been translated into foreign languages. The fact that, in spite of literary and other changes, the influence of Leskov's work persisted even after 1917, is the best proof of its vitality.

CHAPTER SEVENTEEN

Pisemsky and Saltykov-Shchedrin

I

The 'natural school' of fiction, as championed by Belinsky, insisted on showing up the negative aspects of Russian life in order to arouse the reader's social and moral indignation. And Russia offered an author plenty of causes for indictment and indignation even after the abolition of serfdom. The entire bureaucratic apparatus with its plague of graft, bullying and bribery was a case in point. The crowd of self-made profiteers and speculators whose greed for money knew no limits was another. The appalling poverty of the village presented a further evil one had no right to ignore. And as for the rootless intellectuals, they were more than inclined to indulge in passive wishful thinking on the one hand, or in all sorts of destructive tendencies on the other—both harmful to a degree.

Such a state of things could not but invite observant writers to exercise their critical or satirical vein upon what they saw around them and turn their art into a realism of indictment. Saltykov-Shchedrin was one of them, and so largely was his slightly older contemporary Pisemsky. Both of them were excellent observers, severe judges, and fluent narrators. Yet in their critical attitudes towards the whole of Russian life they took two different directions. While Shchedrin waged a relentless war against the present in the name of a better future, Alexey T. Pisemsky (1821–81), a wounded and frustrated idealist, remained a sceptic for whom there was nothing much to hope for or look forward to. He was endowed with a powerful capacity for scrutiny and was never afraid of calling a spade a spade. Stylistically he was often rather careless. This did not prevent him, however, from being a good psychologist and story-teller, especially when he could pour into his pages plenty of gall. Upper-classes in their process of decay, corrupt officialdom, crafty speculators, ambitious upstarts—they all found in him a merciless castigator, even in his early narratives written towards the end of the 1840s and at the beginning of the 1850s. In his *Boyárshchina*, for instance, we follow the tragic lot of an unhappily married woman victimised by the uncouth and debased way of life typical of the provincial land-owning nobility. His grimly satirical attitude towards that class did a great deal to debunk the myth about the idealistic 'superfluous gentleman'. Thus his *Muff* (*Tyufyák*) is a study of an Oblomov-like sluggard, but it would be futile to look in him for an inkling of Oblomov's potential or actual good qualities. Or take the heroine of *An Old Man's Sin*. Here an elderly disillusioned official falls in love with a much younger 'educated' woman. When she is in financial difficulties, he helps her out with some government money which she promises to bring back in time. But instead of doing this, she squanders it with her gigolo without giving a thought to what might happen to her benefactor who then vainly tries to borrow from his acquaintances the money to repay without which he is a doomed man.

Pisemsky's principal work is however his long novel, *A Thousand Souls* (*Týsyacha dush*, 1858), which was proclaimed by the critic D. Pisarev the best novel of the period. This is a work of scathing criticism of life combined with fine psychological portraits. Kalinovich, the main character of the novel, is an impecunious (and for this very reason all the more ambitious) commoner who thinks of nothing but money and success. Obsessed by vanity, he sacrifices even the woman he loves and instead marries a wealthy semi-cripple who owns a thousand 'souls', i.e. serfs, but is connected with people who matter both financially and socially. Taking advantage of this, he strides from success to success, until he reaches one of the highest rungs on the bureaucratic ladder. Yet once he has gratified his ambitious dreams, he cannot but see the emptiness and mockery of it all. At first he tries to redeem his own careerism by strict integrity as a high-ranking civil servant. But attempts of this kind only make him see all the more clearly the corruption of the tsarist officialdom in which any counter-measures are doomed in advance. In the end he gives up everything and goes back—a reformed character—to the woman he once had loved. In her affection he finds at least compensation for the shocks and disappointments he has had to endure while running after worldly advantages.

Intensely critical of Russian life as a whole, Pisemsky yet found some relief in describing the peasants. These he treated in a sympathetic light, even though he was by no means blind to their failings. He wrote the excellent peasant drama (or rather tragedy), *A Bitter Lot* (*Gór'kaya sud'bína*), which appeared in 1859, i.e. less than two years before the abolition of serfdom. Its theme is the love between a squire and the beautiful wife of one of his serfs, followed by the disastrous reaction of the deceived husband. Together with Leo Tolstoy's *The Power of Darkness*, this is one of the best realistic plays about Russian peasants. Pisemsky himself regarded the peasants as better human material than the intellectuals, especially the radical intellectuals whom he attacked in his novel, *The Storm-tossed Sea* (*Vzbalamúchennoe móre*, 1863). As though venting his personal rancour against them, he reduced a number of characters concerned almost to the level of animals. This discredited him, however, with the liberals of the period, in consequence of which his gloomy disposition only increased. The novels and several plays he wrote after 1861 are, on the whole, of minor importance. As though trying to make up for his former 'reactionary' attitude, he adopted in some of them, especially in the novel, *In the Whirl* (*V vodovoróte*, 1871), an anti-bourgeois attitude, but without much effect. On the other hand, this work impressed Leo Tolstoy enough to make him send its author a letter (3.III,1872) in which he said: 'I read your novel again, and the second reading only strengthens the impression I mentioned to you. The third part, which I had not read at the time, is as excellent as the first two by which I was enchanted at the first reading.' It should be remembered that a number of long or longish Russian novels used to be printed in thick periodicals before they were issued in book-form. Thus Pisemsky's *In the Whirl* appeared serially in the periodical *Beséda (Discourse)* in 1871.

2

Pisemsky's radical counterpart, Mikhail Saltykov-Shchedrin (1826-92), was equally merciless in his realism but his principal weapon was laughter, of the kind he inherited from Gogol. He wavered continuously between satirical fiction and satirical pamphleteering, and was fond of mixing the two. In both he exercised his gift of irony and invective to the full. In order to get round the censorship he became a past master at making use of the proverbial Aesop language, not only in his political *Fables* in prose. He, too, started writing in the late 1840s under the wing of Belinsky. Because of some 'dangerous' utterances in his early stories he was exiled to Vyatka where he remained for seven years but without being deprived of his post as a civil servant. Moreover, he gradually rose high in the State service. This did not prevent him, however, from collecting all the imbecilities of that provincial existence upon which he soon took due revenge as a first-rate satirist.

The facts observed provided all the nourishment he needed for his attacks. He made good use of them in his *Provincial Sketches (Gubérnskie ócherki,* 1856-57) published in Katkov's *Russian Messenger (Russky Véstnik)* which, in those days, was not yet a conservative organ. He caricatured provincial officials and patriarchal old-world merchants whom he also paraded for what they were in his satirical comedy, *The Death of Pazúkhin* (1857). Nor were his *Innocent Tales (Nevínnye rasskázy,* 1863) as innocent as the title might imply. In 1862 he joined the radical *Contemporary;* and when, four years later, this periodical was clamped down, Shchedrin became one of the principal contributors to the *Fatherland's Annals,* whose editor in chief was the poet Nekrasov. To this journal he contributed, from now on, prolific belletristic and pamphleteering material decrying the manners and morals of his country. There was hardly any negative aspect of Russian life during the 1860s and 1870s, that evaded his pen. One of his best known works, *History of a Town* (1869-70) is a parody of the past and present of a town called Glupov (Sillytown) with the entire pageant of its inhabitants reflected as in a crooked mirror. His *Pompadours Male and Female (Pompadúry i Pompadúrshi,* 1863–74) is an onslaught upon the then fashionable pseudo-liberal phrase-mongers with reactionary leanings. In *The Gents from Tashkent* (1869-72) he chose for his target the unscrupulous dealers anxious to get rich by hook or by crook, whether speculating at home or in recently acquired parts of Russian Asia. Many of Shchedrin's writings are too topical and require a certain amount of comment to be duly appreciated by present-day readers. There is, however, one work which is overwhelming and clear enough not to need any comment: his great novel, *The Golovlyov Family (Gospodá Golovlyóvy),* which he wrote between 1875 and 1880.

3

This work has been proclaimed, and perhaps rightly so, the gloomiest novel in Russian literature. It deserves this qualification for its portrayal of provincial landowners immediately after the liberation of the serfs. In the whole novel one could look in vain for a single positive or pleasant character.

This time, too, the action takes place in a nest of gentlefolk, but—what a nest! The two main characters of the novel are the bossy former serf-owner Arina Petrovna and her hypocritical and knavish offspring Porphíry—nicknamed Yudushka (Little Judas). While referring to their position after 1861, the author points out that, like so many other members of the provincial gentlefolk of that era, the Golovlyovs had no contact with public life, with duties or obligations of any kind; degenerate as they were, they continued stagnating in their decayed country houses. Arina, who was unable to give up her autocratic habits even after the abolition of serfdom, now practised her tyranny upon members of her own family, particularly on her decrepit old husband.

White like a corpse and wearing a nightcap he lay dozing on his bed covered with a white quilt. When his eldest son Stepan came back bankrupt from Moscow he was met by Arina with her customary malice.

> 'Aha, you've been caught in the old hag's clutches', he [the father] called out when his son kissed his hand. Then he crowed like a cock, laughed again, and repeated several times: 'She'll eat you up! She'll eat you up!'[1]

And she did. Later, however, the power in the entire household was usurped by the unctuous Yudushka—'a hypocrite of a purely Russian sort, that is simply a man devoid of all moral standards, knowing no truth other than copy-book precepts. He was pettifogging, deceitful, loquacious, boundlessly ignorant, and afraid of the devil.' An arch-liar, bigot and babbler in one, he was yet cunning enough to deprive his 'dear friend mamma' of any authority, after which he ruled the estate like a tyrant. He reduced Arina herself to the role of a gossipy parasite. By methods of his own he even contrived to become the wealthiest landowner in the district. A cheat by nature, he was yet unable to do any cheating without God's name on his lips. His meanness had caused the death of two of his sons. When his third son, after having gambled away some government money, implored him to help him with the sum needed, he turned his back on him and drove him to suicide. Then there were Yudushka's two young inexperienced nieces. Both wanted to become actresses in order to escape from the Golovlyov atmosphere but were unable to escape from the provinces in whose morass they eventually sank to the level of prostitutes. After an ugly law-case one of them took her own life. But her sister—ill with consumption—returned to Yudushka's manor at a time when its aged owner was already a half-crazy recluse and drunkard. Moreover, in his old age the voice of conscience was beginning to stir in him—a process he was unable to face. As if guessing

1. Quoted from *The Golovlyov Family*, translated by Natalie Duddington (Everyman's Library, Dent).

what was going on in his mind, his niece caroused with him simply in order to annoy him in his drunken state and thus make his and her own torments even worse.

> Yudushka groaned and, consumed with anger and restlessness, with fever-ish impatience waited for the evening, not only to get drunk like a brute but to drown his conscience in vodka. He hated the wench who so coldly and impudently probed his wounds but was irresistibly drawn to her as though something still remained unsaid between them and there were more wounds to be probed.

Eventually he became aware that something must have gone hopelessly wrong with the whole of his life which, at that late hour, was beyond repair. And in this mood he died. It is not surprising that Yudushka has passed into the history of Russian literature as a nickname on a par with the characters of Gogol's *Dead Souls*.

Like Pisemsky, Shchedrin too sympathised with the people and dreaded the arrival of the *kulák* (the village usurer) as much as he did the political pressure from above. Some of these fears were adequately expressed in his satirical narrative *A Contemporary Idyll* (1883). Finally his last important work, *The Old Years in Poshekhonie* (*Poshekhónskaya Stariná*, 1887-89) ought to be singled out both for its literary and its documentary value. As in so many of his writ-ings, critical realism is mixed up with pamphleteering. This is another chronicle of a noble family living in the old serfdom days in one of the remote corners of Russia. It is told in the first person. The narrator begins with reminiscences of his earliest years in an *usad'ba* or manor where cruelty, bigotry, greed and meanness of all kinds prevailed. Serfs, especially women, were being exploited in the most inhuman fashion and were punished for the slightest offence. There are grotesquely amusing portrayals of members of the family, of acquaintances, of Moscow relatives, etc. The whole of it is, however, a powerful indictment of the evils of Russian life presented as a memento of days past.

4

Two other exponents of the art of indictment, in a condensed form, were the talented but prematurely deceased writers Nikolai Pomyalovsky (1835-1863) and Fyodor Reshotnikov (1841-71). Pomyalovsky, a priest's son, was endowed with an ultra-democratic outlook. He wrote some narratives in that spirit, but he is remembered only by one work—his *Seminary Sketches* (*Ócherki búrsy*) which appeared in 1863 and presented a scathing naturalistic spectacle of education in an old-world clerical school for prospective priests. The majority of the pupils were, like the author himself, priests' sons, but the atmosphere in which they were being prepared for their vocation was worse than a night-mare. The author, who wrote from personal experience, said with brutal direct-ness all he had to say about an institution of this kind. But he became also one of its victims and died—from poverty and drink—at the age of twenty-eight.

The same fate was in store for Reshotnikov whose naturalistic novel *The People of Podlípnaya* (*Poplípovtsy*, 1864) appeared when he was barely twenty-three. This is an intensified picture of utter misery in a far away Ziryan village of northern Russia. The life of the non-Russian villagers, as here described, is more savage than human. Anxious to improve their lot, some of the peasants depart in order to work on a distant river as boatmen. But this step, too, comes to nothing once they have lost their leader in a catastrophe. Like Pomyalovsky, Reshotnikov showed a strong class consciousness and was among the early Russian authors to write about proletarians and factory workers.

As light relief a memorable book by another commoner can be mentioned for its freshness, good humour and the lively way in which it is written. The book is called *Nikolái Negórev* (1871), and its author was Nikolai Kushchevsky (1847-76): a young Siberian, who came to St Petersburg in search of suitable literary work, but found only disappointments. His hero Negorev, though, is luckier. Even as a boy he showed the makings of Pisemsky's Kalinovich, but without the latter's callousness. He is a lower-class opportunist of a fairly harmless brand: a fellow who lives and lets live. What he achieves may not be anything exceptional, but it is enough to make him preserve the cheerfulness of a 'gay Russian'. The author introduces, with the same humorous inflection, several other characters whose good or bad fortunes we follow with unflagging interest. The sparkling quality of this novel is the more remarkable because its destitute author wrote it while lying ill in hospital. Like Reshotnikov and Pomyalovsky, he became a victim of alcohol and disease, which sent him to a premature grave.

CHAPTER EIGHTEEN

Anton Chekhov

I

The era of monumental Russian realism came to an end after the death of Dostoevsky and Turgenev in the early 1880s—a decade which was not at all favourable to the development of art and letters. After the assassination of Alexander II the reign of his successor, Alexander III, was frankly reactionary. It was, moreover, accompanied by a rapid growth of capitalism and financial speculation with a gospel of 'get-rich-quick'. Everything that the best representatives of the intelligentsia had been working for since the years of Nicholas I now seemed to be threatened. Hence the atmosphere of gloom and defeatism among them. The prevalent state of mind was of mental and moral stagnation on the one hand, and of social frustration on the other. Vsevolod Garshin's stories reflect the mood of that decade. So does the poetry of Nadson (1862-87). Semyon Nadson was not a great poet; yet in his civic and personal verse he expressed the gloomy disposition of the period which can also be felt in the music of Tchaikovsky and in the nostalgic poetry of A. N. Apukhtin (1841-93). But to find a consummate artistic interpretation of those years, we must turn to the writings of Anton Pavlovich Chekhov—past master of the short story and the *novella* even before he was recognised as one of the pioneers of modern drama.

Born on 17 January, 1860, at Taganrog (a port on the Sea of Azov), where his father had a grocery shop, Chekhov had to put up with many difficulties in his boyhood and early youth. As a schoolboy he witnessed the bankruptcy of his father's business, after which the family settled in Moscow, but he himself remained in Taganrog in order to finish his grammar school studies. On matriculating he obtained a small scholarship which enabled him to enter Moscow University and study medicine. As the family (his parents, three brothers and one sister) lived in rather poor circumstances, Chekhov—as a young medical student—started writing humorous stories and potboilers. This he did (under the pseudonym of Chekhonte) mainly in order to ease the financial burden of the family. His contributions to comic papers, above all to Leykin's *Splinters* (*Oskólki*), aroused considerable attention. Before long he was invited to write for the wealthy and widely read *Nóvoe Vrémya* (*New Times*) whose founder, Alexey Suvorin, became one of his friends and admirers.

It was from that time on that the young Chekhov, now a doctor, began to shift to serious literature at the expense of his medical profession. As he himself put it: 'Medicine is my legal wife, and literature is my mistress. When

I get tired of one, I spend the night with the other.' Yet he kept spending more and more time with his 'mistress,' especially after having started writing plays. He bought the small estate of Melikhovo not far from Moscow, but as he was already suffering from consumption, he had to think of a more congenial climate. Eventually he settled near Yalta in the Crimea. At the height of his fame he married (in 1901) Olga Knipper, one of the leading actresses of the Moscow Art Theatre. But in spite of their mutual affection they had to live apart: he in the Crimea—his 'warm Siberia'—because of his health, and she in the snowy north because of her profession. When all efforts to get rid of his illness had proved futile, he went, together with his wife, in the summer of 1904, to Badenweiler in the Black Forest. It was here that he suddenly died on 2 July at the early age of forty-four.

2

What is striking in Chekhov's writing is his integrity and artistic conscience. In a period of social and spiritual gloom he refused to look for any comfortable shelter by false pretences. He preferred to face the situation as it was without forcing himself to adopt anything he could not believe in, whatever the consequences. In one of his letters to A. Suvorin he compared himself and some other authors of his time with those of the previous era of whom he said:

> The best of them are realistic and paint life as it is; but because every line is permeated, as with a juice, by the awareness of a purpose, you feel, besides life as it is, also life as it ought to be, and this captivates you. And we? We paint life as it is, and beyond that—no 'gee up' nor 'gee down'. . . . Beyond that, even if you lashed us with whips, we could not go. We have neither immediate nor remote aims, and in our souls—a great emptiness. We have no politics, we do not believe in revolution, we have no God, we are not afraid of ghosts, and personally I have no fear even of death and blindness. He who desires nothing, hopes for nothing, and is afraid of nothing, cannot be an artist. Whether it is a disease or not, the name does not matter; but it must be owned our situation is worse than bad. . . . I am at least clever enough not to hide my disease from myself, nor to cover up my emptiness with borrowed rags, such as the ideas of the 1860s and so on. I shall not, like Garshin, throw myself down a flight of stairs, but neither am I going to delude myself with hopes of a better future. I am not to blame for my disease, nor am I called to cure myself, since this disease has, it must be supposed, some good purpose of its own hidden from us, and has not been sent in vain.[1]

The last line evidently leaves a loophole wide enough to prevent him from falling into utter pessimism. It made him preserve a glimmer of hope which kept smouldering in spite of all. He showed some interest in Tolstoy's teaching,

1. From *The Life and Letters of Anton Chekhov*. Translated and edited by S. S. Kotelian-sky and Philip Tomlinson (Cassell).

but only for a while. As an artist he felt, though, a certain affinity with Turgenev. It was above all Turgenev's emphasis on uprooted or 'superfluous' individuals and his art of conjuring up 'atmosphere' that was brought by Chekhov to perfection. Like Turgenev, he too was interested in the tasks and problems of the day without committing himself to any of them personally. He was explicit about this in another letter to Suvorin (1888) in which the passage in question runs as follows:

> To deny that artistic creation involves problems and purposes would be to admit that an artist creates within premeditation, without design, under a spell. Therefore if an artist boasted to me of having written a story without a previously settled design, but by inspiration, I would call him a lunatic. You are right in demanding that an artist should take a conscious attitude to his work, but you confuse two conceptions: *the solution of a question and the correct setting of a question.* The latter alone is obligatory for an artist. It is for the judge to put the questions correctly; and the jurymen must decide, each one according to his taste.

True to this attitude, Chekhov abstained from ideologies, 'missions', and from political or any other parties, thereby preserving his creative freedom to the end. In a further letter we read:

> Pharisaism, stupidity, and arbitrariness reign not in shopkeepers' houses and prisons alone. I detect them in science, in literature and in the younger generation ... For this reason I nurse no particular partiality for gendarmes, or butchers, or savants, or writers, or the younger generation. I look upon trademarks and labels as prejudices. My Holy of Holies is the human body, health, mind, talent, inspiration, love and the most absolute freedom—freedom from violence and falsehood in whatever they may be manifested. This is the programme I would follow if I were a great artist. (4 October 1888).

3

Having such pronouncements of his at our disposal, we can more easily approach the spirit and the general character of Chekhov's work. Formally he became, almost from the start, one of the most economical and disciplined writers. To that simple naturalness which was the core of his own nature, Chekhov added the kind of artistic restraint which tends to express a maximum of contents by a minimum of means. And he always knew how to make the psychology of his characters fit into the background of his tales whose principal cementing factor gradually became that 'atmosphere' which is unalienable from his art. His first longer narrative, *The Steppe* (1883), is an impressionistic description of what happened during a journey through the Ukrainian steppe and how it was enjoyed by the fresh perception of a boy of nine. There followed, in quick succession, a number of longer stories, each of them significant and displaying

Chekhov's manner at its best: *A Tedious Story* (1889), *The Duel* (1891), *Ward No. 6* (1892), *The Tale of an Unknown Man* (1893), *The Black Monk* (1894), *A Woman's Kingdom* (1894), *Three Years* (1894), *My Life* (1895), *Peasants* (1896), *In the Ravine* (1900). And as for his numerous motifs, one can feel even in his earlier humorous stories and miniatures a great deal of social satire with all its anti-bourgeois and anti-philistine undertones. Many of his tales are full of that whipping laughter which is due not so much to inherently funny types or situations as to the author's dismay at the coarseness, corruption and other evils rooted in all walks of life. But even when his social and humane pathos took the upper hand, his humour did not vanish, although his laughter may have turned into a wistful smile instead.

Take Chekhov's story about an ordinary Moscow cabby who has just lost his only son. While serving his passengers on a frosty winter night, the cabby is anxious to alleviate his grief by trying to talk about his son's death to one client after another, but none of them cares to listen. Finally, late at night, when back in the stable, the grief-stricken cabby stands in front of the horse and begins telling him in detail how his son died. In this grotesquely tragic situation the listening horse appears to be more humane than the humans to whom the cabby had tried to open his heart before.

A perplexed sadness emanating from life and too intricate for any solution is felt in several longer narratives by Chekhov, beginning with *A Tedious Story* (*Skúchnaya istóriya*). An elderly professor of medicine, who has tasted fame and success, knows that he is mortally ill and, like Tolstoy's Ivan Ilyich, feels alienated from all and sundry, his wife and daughter included. The only human being still dear to him is his young ward Katya who has passed through her own tragic experiences and is restlessly seeking for a meaning or a direction in life. With the hope of finding it in the old savant, to whom she is deeply attached, she comes to him again and again only to discover that, with all his knowledge and wisdom, he is as helpless in this respect as everybody else. He has nothing to offer, least of all a 'general idea' which might be able to guide her through the problems and puzzles of existence. And so in spite of their mutual attachment the two part, almost like two hostile beings, unable to help each other.

This kind of tragic impasse became one of the recurring themes in Chekhov's stories and plays. There was no 'general idea' to give one a reliable outlook in this world. As though in search for some deeper truth about life and human beings, Chekhov embarked in 1890 upon an eight-month journey to the island of Sakhalín where he interviewed and investigated thousands of convicts in one of the most wretched places on earth.[1] But he came back tired, ill, and hardly less puzzled by life than before. He was now even more aware of the old truth that certain people are crushed by life simply because they are too sensitive to be able to put up with the coarseness and vulgarity around them. Take his Dr Ragin, hero of *Ward No. 6* (*Paláta No. 6*), who is in charge of a

---

1.   The record of his impressions, under the title *The Island of Sakhalin* (*Óstrov Sakhalín*) appeared in the periodical, *The Russian Thought* (*Russkaya mysl'*, 1893-94) and in book form in 1895.

lunatic asylum in the provinces where he finds nothing but chronic disorder, abuse, ignorance, and such semi-savage relations between human beings as his own nature cannot endure. Lonely as he feels, he becomes somewhat indifferent even to his professional duties and looks for an escape in philosophic books and vodka. Among his patients in the asylum he finally comes across a lunatic who happens to be the only intelligent man in the town. He gets interested in him, and before long the two discuss all sorts of problems and ideas that matter. The doctor spends hours and hours talking with him until he himself is looked upon as a lunatic. This is a welcome opportunity for his assistant—a robust vulgarian—who locks him up as a patient in the hope of replacing him as chief of the hospital. Fortunately, during this process Dr Ragin dies of a stroke.

Sensitiveness versus vulgarity is one of Chekhov's favourite motifs. And vulgarity always wins. In *The Teacher of Literature* (*Uchítel slovesnosti*, 1894) a young schoolmaster in the provinces marries the girl he loves. He is at the height of happiness. But his wife, who has been brought up in the traditions of bourgeois philistinism, cannot help disappointing him even sooner than expected. This is what he writes only one year later in his diary :

> Where am I, my God? I am surrounded by vulgarity and vulgarity. Wearisome, insignificant people, pots of sour cream, jugs of milk, cockroaches, stupid women. . . . There is nothing more terrible, mortifying and distressing than vulgarity. I must escape from here, I must escape to-day, or I shall go out of my mind.

A much more complex tragedy is *The Black Monk* (*Chórny monákh*). A young philosopher experiences moments of abnormally intensified consciousness. He is exalted and happy in the awareness of his own genius, especially when confronted, time and again, by the apparition of a legendary black monk who encourages him in his aspirations to lead humanity to a higher destiny. His happiest moments are those in which he talks to his ghostly visitor. In this pathologic state of mind he marries the woman who sincerely loves him and is devoted to him. But one night when he talks again to his phantom, his wife awakens and is seized by despair at the thought that her husband is mentally ill. Full of loving care, she and her father consult the doctors and take all sorts of measures to make their adored patient healthy and normal—in which they succeed. But once deprived of his abnormal moments, the patient has also lost the exaltation of a genius and has become just an ordinary mortal, a nonentity. Conscious of this, he turns his resentment against his wife and his father-in-law by ruining the lives of both. Utterly frustrated he dies of consumption —in the arms of another woman—in the Crimea. While dying he sees again the apparition of the black monk, but only to be rebuked by him.

The element of frustration, of tragic disharmony between man and man, between man and life, is usually distilled by Chekhov in a unique and subtly symbolic manner. Such cruel stories, on the other hand, as *Peasants* (*Muzhikí*) and *In the Ravine* (*V ovráge*) seem to have been devised in order to debunk the populist illusions about the muzhiks whom Chekhov knew well from personal experience. Yet when describing sensitive and tender people, he himself can be tender, even while being amused by them as he is in *The Darling* (*Dúshenka*, 1898). This is the story of a simple woman whose maternal need of loving makes her quite indiscriminate in her choice of men she loves and marries. Finally she adopts a little boy on whom she lavishes all her affection.

To sum up, Chekhov's subtle and yet simple short-hand method of telling a story makes any diffuse and long-winded realism of the past look obsolete. 'After your stories, however insignificant, everything appears crude, as though written not by a pen but by a cudgel,' Gorky once wrote to Chekhov and remarked that Chekhov's art was actually slaying realism in the old sense. In addition one could say of Chekhov the author what Anatole France had said when writing of Maupassant's stories, namely that Maupassant possesses three great virtues: the first is clarity, the second is also clarity, and the third is clarity once more.

5

The impact of Chekhov on world literature seems in some respects stronger than that of any other modern Russian author after Dostoevsky. This applies to his plays even more than to his stories,[1] since he happens to be one of the reformers of the modern theatre and drama. Chekhov himself proclaimed (in one of his letters) the theatre of his time a 'skin disease, a world of muddle, of stupidity and high-falutin' which should be swept away with a broom.' He did not mind being such a broom even in the late 1880s when the only conspicuous reformer in this respect was Henrik Ibsen. Chekhov's inauguration of drama devoid of traditional plot and big theatrical gestures, not to mention the old declamatory pathos, was a courageous feat in those days, although he may have faltered now and then under the weight of his own experiments. His *Ivánov*, for example, was given a brilliant first performance in the Alexandrinsky theatre at St Petersburg on 31 January, 1889. Its reception was favourable, which, however, could not be said of his next play, *The Seagull* (*Cháika*), produced in October 1896. Chekhov felt so depressed by its failure that he thought of giving up the theatre altogether. But on 17 December 1898, a very successful production of *The Seagull* took place in the Moscow Art Theatre. Less than a year later another triumph was scored in the same theatre by Chekhov's *Uncle Vanya* (*Dyáyda Ványa*)—a modification of his less pessimistic play *The Wood Demon* (*Léshiy*).[2]

Chekhov thus became closely connected with the Moscow Art Theatre, run by Stanislavsky and Nemirovich-Danchenko. In 1900 he wrote for it *The Three Sisters* (*Tri sestrý*) and in 1903—roughly one year before his death—he completed *The Cherry Orchard* (*Vishnyóvy sad*). In addition, he was responsible for several one-act plays some of which are dramatised short stories. They

1. In England it was Katherine Mansfield in particular who wrote her stories under Chekhov's stimulus.
2. This play which, incidentally, has a happy ending, was subsequently excluded by Chekhov from the collected edition of his works.

abound in farcical situations, quite in the tradition of the old vaudevilles which were always great favourites with the Russian audiences. Such of his one-act plays as *The Proposal* (*Predlozhénie*) and *The Bear* (*Medvéd'*) are of international repute.

Chekhov's plays, like so many of his stories, depict the blind-alley of the rootless and decaying intelligentsia either against the background of their country estates, as in *Ivanov*, *The Seagull*, *Uncle Vanya*, and *The Cherry Orchard*, or against the provincial town atmosphere as in *The Three Sisters*. His characters are 'superfluous' individuals in a more acute sense even than those of Turgenev. They do not know what to do with themselves, and their minds are further complicated by the strange inner barrier separating them even from those whom they had once regarded as their nearest and dearest. Such is Ivanov, the principal character of the play under the same title. Treplev in *The Seagull*, Voinitsky, Dr Astrov, and Sonya in *Uncle Vanya* belong to the same category, not to mention, Masha, Olga and Irina in *The Three Sisters* (first performed on 31 January, 1901).

According to Chekhov a sensitive person, confronted by the rough and ready style of life he has to face or contend with, is almost doomed to failure, and a failure of this kind, morally speaking, may not be to his credit, since success is only too often a prerogative of pushful vulgar types. This is why Chekhov looks with sympathy upon those *hommes manqués* who have been crushed because they expected from life more than it could give. Some of them still cherish hopes for a better future by trying to believe that the price they have to pay is not entirely in vain. Maybe they are paying the bill for the happiness of future generations whose lives will be less muddled and stupid—a thought which by no means alleviates their own ordeals, but may at least prevent them from slamming the door on the last glimmer of hope. Still, Chekhov's characters have to foot the bill. Quite a few of them accept the bill in this spirit simply in order to avoid the danger of utter nihilism and despair.

> Those who will live a hundred or two hundred years after us, and who will despise us for having lived our lives so stupidly and tastelessly—they will, perhaps, find a means of being happy, but we. . . . There is only one hope for you and me. The hope that when we are asleep in our graves we may, perhaps, be visited by pleasant visions.[1]

Such is Dr Astrov's comment in *Uncle Vanya*. But the same emergency faith is voiced by Vershínin in *The Three Sisters* and by Trofímov in *The Cherry Orchard*. Amidst all his despondence Chekhov himself arrived at a solace of this kind, as one can judge from his letter to Diaghilev (December, 1902), in which he says:

> Modern culture is but the beginning of a work for a great future, a work which will go on, perhaps, for ten thousand years, in order that mankind may, even in the remote future, come to know the truth of a real God—

1. All quotations from Chekhov's plays are taken from Constance Garnett's translation of Chekhov's works (Chatto and Windus).

that is, not by guessing, not by seeking in Dostoevsky, but by perceiving clearly, as one perceives that twice two is four.

6

Flashes of such faith did not redeem, however, that quagmire of Russian reality which Chekhov had to endure and which he used as the raw material for his stories and plays. The surprising thing is that he was able to transmute it into perfect art, the devices of which are also worth studying in connection with his dramatic technique.

Chekhov did his best to 'de-theatralise' the theatre by depriving it of everything 'heroic', noisy and artificial. But in doing this he increased the effect of his plays in a strangely suggestive manner. In his early play, Ivánov,[1] he still depended on tradition, albeit he purposely abstained from a worked-out plot and made use of what he called the 'belletristic', as distinct from the dramatic, method in the old style. 'Each act I finish as I do my stories,' Chekhov says in a letter; 'I develop it quietly and calmly, but at the end I give a slap to the spectator. All my energy is centred on a few really strong passages, but the bridges connecting these passages are insignificant, weak and old-fashioned.' The main hero, Ivanov, is an unheroic 'superfluous' intellectual—a victim of those Russian circumstances he is unable to overcome. He has lost his hold upon life and feels, at the age of thirty-five, an old man.

> Exhausted, overstrained, broken, with my head heavy and my soul indolent, without faith, without love, without an objective in life, I linger like a shadow among men and don't know what I am, what I am living for, what I want. . . . My brains do not obey me, nor my hands, nor my feet. My property is going to ruin, the forest is falling under the axe. My land looks at me like a deserted child. I expect nothing, I regret nothing; my soul shudders with the fear of the morrow. . . . What is the matter with me? To what depths am I making myself sink? What has brought this weakness on me?

But there is no answer. Surrounded by fools and nonentities, Ivanov—an essentially decent fellow—sinks deeper and deeper into the morass of his own despondence. In his bewilderment he does not mind offending even his consumptive wife who adores him and whom he used to adore. After her death he is free to marry Sasha, who had been secretly in love with him all that time; but for no apparent reason he shoots himself, when on the point of taking her to the altar. His is the tragedy of a sensitive man doomed to failure, although he himself does not know why. There is no plot in the play and even the normal logical causation (the 'bridges' connecting the passages) seems to be absent; yet as a picture of life transformed into art the play is convincing and impressive.

1. Chekhov's first long and not very successful play Platonov (1881) remained in manuscript, but some of its characters and themes served for his other plays, especially for Ivanov.

In *The Seagull*, written some eight years later, Chekhov's peculiar technique is more pronounced than in *Ivanov*. This time, too, the plot is replaced by a string of seemingly casual happenings, cemented by that lyrical 'atmosphere' which became—both in his plays and narratives—the principal if not the only unifying factor. Here the tragedy of frustration in Treplev and Nina is the more poignant because of all the trivialities leading up to it. While Nina, after her disappointments, finds shelter in the profession of an actress, Treplev cannot fill the void of his life even with his initial success in literature. These are his parting words to Nina, after she had vainly deserted him for the writer Trigorin who cared for her as little as for a shot seagull:[1] 'You have found your path, you know which way you are going, but I am still floating in a chaos of dreams and images, not knowing of what use it is to anyone. I have no faith and I don't know what my vocation is.' Chekhov once again made use of the 'belletristic' method, but was not quite sure whether to approve of it or not, and he said so in a letter to Suvorin (November 1895): 'I began it *forte* and finished it *pianissimo* against all rules of dramatic art. It came out like a story. I am more dissatisfied than satisfied with it, and, reading over my newborn piece, I became once more convinced that I am not a playwright at all.' He certainly was not a playwright in the traditional sense, some further proof of which he gave in *Uncle Vanya*, *The Three Sisters*, and *The Cherry Orchard*.

In *Uncle Vanya* we meet the same type of intellectual gentleman victimised by a trivial existence, as in *Ivanov* and *The Seagull*. The plot as such is replaced by a series of 'scenes of country life in four acts'. The 'atmosphere' is all important, while the subject-matter is as simple as it can be. A famous but now retired university professor, suffering from conceit and gout, comes with his beautiful second wife Elena to settle down on his estate, where his brother-in-law, Voinitsky (Uncle Vanya), and his daughter from a first marriage, Sonya, have been toiling for years in order to add to his income. Much admiring the professor's fame and learning, Voinitsky has spent the whole of his adult life in serving him—only to discover at the age of forty-seven that the supposedly great man was nothing but a puffed-up ignoramus. Voinitsky, now a weary middle-aged man, realises his mistake, but the lost years cannot now be retrieved. To make things worse, he is in love with Elena, who is too indolent to respond even to the advances of the younger and more interesting wooer, Doctor Astrov—a man still in the process of going to seed. As though lost in his own void, Voinitsky is frightened of the present and the future. 'I am forty-seven. If I live to be sixty, I have another thirteen years. It's a long time. How am I to get through those thirteen years? What shall I do? How am I going to fill them up? . . .' In his rancour he fires two shots at the pitiably frightened celebrity and, having missed, thinks of suicide. But it all ends *pianissimo*, that is peacefully. The learned professor and his frigid wife depart. Life returns to its old routine. Both Sonya (whose love for Astrov is now frustrated for good) and Voinitsky find a questionable escape in accountancy and petty drudgery about the estate in order to increase, once again, the professor's income.

1. The tragedy of Nina with Trigorin was partly based upon an actual love affair of the singer Lika Mízinova (one of Chekhov's friends) and the writer Potapenko.

The Three Sisters is written in a similar vein, but with a greater amount of lyrical touches. Again there is no plot. We are introduced to three sisters—members of the intelligentsia. After the death of their father (a cultured high-ranking officer) the sisters and their brother have remained stuck in a provincial garrison town which they loathe. Their determination to return to Moscow, where they were born, only expresses their desire for a fuller life. But the provincial mire is stronger. Neither they nor their brother, who is preparing for a university career, succeed in extricating themselves. Instead of living, they are compelled to vegetate. 'I am nearly twenty-four,' complains Irina. 'I have been working for years, my brains are drying up, I am getting thin and old and ugly and there is nothing, nothing, not the slightest satisfaction, and time is passing, and one feels that one is moving away and being drawn into the depths. I am in despair and I don't know how it is I am alive and have not killed myself yet.' It is no fault of theirs that all their efforts are futile and that things go from bad to worse. Their brother, moreover, marries a mean and vulgar *petite bourgeoise* who openly deceives him with another man. And as in *Uncle Vanya*, Chekhov ends this play *pianissimo*, with apparent resignation camouflaged by hard work.

The tone is somewhat gayer in *The Cherry Orchard*—a cleverly dramatised string of comic and semi-tragic incidents. The bankruptcy of the irresponsibly carefree, or rather careless, Ranevskaya and her brother Gáyev is here symbolic of the inner as well as the outer inefficiency of that landed-gentry class which, not so long ago, had dominated Russian life. Ranevskaya's country-house, together with its magnificent cherry orchard, is bought by the self-made businessman Lopakhin—the son of a former serf. And the first thing the new owner does is to fell the orchard in order to make room for a suburban housing-estate, planned out on a most profitable basis. Lopakhin thus emerges as the new social force—a capitalist on a large scale. But the 'eternal student' and revolutionary Trofimov has little respect for him. 'I can get on without you. I can bypass you.' He and the girl he loves are still young enough to flatter themselves with the illusion that they, and not the money-grabbing Lopakhin, are in the front rank of humanity; nevertheless Lopakhin is the only one who triumphs at the end of the play.

The Cherry Orchard was written especially for Stanislavsky. But Chekhov himself did not approve of the interpretation the Moscow Art Theatre gave it. He actually complained in a letter to his wife that its two directors, Nemirovich-Danchenko and Stanislavsky, had never read his plays properly, and least of all *The Cherry Orchard*.

7

Chekhov's technique stands outside that tradition of the Russian dramatic art which goes from Fonvizin—via Griboyedov—to Gogol's *Government Inspector*, although his small farcical pieces may be reminiscent of Gogol. On the other hand, his 'belletristic' method had an interesting Russian precedent in Turgenev's *A Month in the Country* which, like *Uncle Vanya*, could be called 'scenes from country life' rather than a play in the traditional style. Finally, the playwright Alexander Ostrovsky contributed certain elements to the Chekhovian drama, however different Ostrovsky's aims and reasons may have been from those of Chekhov's. As an innovator Chekhov also had some features in common with Ibsen, but with reservations.

Like Ibsen in his later plays, he reduced the external action to a minimum. He replaced it not so much with Ibsen's psychological inner tension as with an accumulation of those lyrical-impressionistic touches which keep the seemingly disjointed incidents together. But the similarity between the symbolic use of the seagull in Chekhov's play of the same title and that of the wild duck in the well-known drama by Ibsen is hardly accidental. Analogies could also be found elsewhere, especially in Chekhov's frequent use of the double dialogue, the spoken words of which serve only as a mask for what one wants, or rather does not want, to say. However, there are essential differences between these two pioneers of modern drama. As a rule Ibsen relegated the tragic guilt of his main characters to the past (i.e. to the time before the play began) and gave all his attention to the psychological *dénouement* as seen through the workings of the hero's conscience, tossed between two contradictory sets of values. Even in his realistic middle-class dramas he was still rooted in the romantic tradition. His characters show a strong will opposing or fighting the surrounding conditions to the end. Thus Stockmann in *An Enemy of the People* is the bourgeois equivalent of such a heroic-romantic figure as Brand. The ex-Pastor Rosmer in *Rosmersholm* is also a romantic idealist. Even Nora in *A Doll's House* rises to the stature of a rebel determined not to put up with her position of a doll petted by a smug philistine husband. And as for the master-builder Solness, Borkmann, and the sculptor Rubek, they all perish in an attempt to assert their own will and freedom against fate; but their very defeat, however catastrophic, can be regarded as a romantic self-affirmation. In each case we watch how the inner change of the hero is due to a sudden perception of a truth which gives a new direction to his will even if he may no longer be destined to live up to it.

Chekhov proceeds differently. Having discarded the old plot, he does not replace it by a conflict of values in the manner of Ibsen for the simple reason that his very point of departure is the bankruptcy of all values. Nor do we find in him that logical and psychological consistency of characters in which Ibsen excelled. Chekhov depicted a disintegrating life in that seemingly casual way to which Tolstoy once referred (with disapproval) as a 'scattered composition'. Tolstoy himself greatly admired Chekhov's stories, but was somewhat critical of his plays. 'As you know,' he once told him, 'I do not like Shakespeare; but your plays are even worse'. . . . Yet there was a system in Chekhov's method of cementing the 'scattered' bits and slices of life together and he did so with a skill in which he proved to be master of his art.

By his method of showing the tragic nature of everyday existence in its ordinary everyday conditions Chekhov also made a contribution to the new style of acting. The success of Chekhov's plays depended and depends largely on all sorts of nuances, of psychological imponderables, not to mention the importance of pauses, of tempo, as well as of the deeper 'symbolic' side of words, gestures and inflections. After all, it was not for nothing that Chekhov was proclaimed by Andrey Bely a precursor of Russian symbolism.

Chekhov's symbolism is more vague and elusive than, say, that of Ibsen. Also his characters are too fatalistic or else too pathetic in their passivity to be tragic in Ibsen's sense. They have neither enough faith nor enough stamina to fight for, let alone shape, their own destinies. The originality of Chekhov is in fact due more to the way in which he showed that the very drabness of life can be turned into significant art. And he did this not only in a new light, but also with that peculiar understatement which, together with his short-hand realism, could not help influencing a number of other literary and dramatic creations of our era.

CHAPTER NINETEEN

Maxim Gorky

I

The span of time dividing us from Maxim Gorky's death is now long enough to allow us to see his life-work in its proper perspective from a literary as well as from a social point of view. In his case it would even be difficult to separate the two, since the pathos permeating his writings was not so much of an aesthetic as of a social and reformatory order. His very choice of themes was conditioned above all by his protest against the kind of life he saw around him. But instead of feeding on a rancorous negation of life, he permeated his writings with his strongest urge—the urge to turn the whole of our existence into something of which human beings need no longer feel ashamed. Gorky's literary work can, therefore, best be understood in conjunction with the role he played as a writer in the social and political life of Russia during the most fateful transition years in her history. The uniqueness of his role was increased by the fact that he was the first major Russian author to start life as a proletarian, if not exactly an outcast. Apart from a few months in an elementary school at Nizhny Novgorod (now Gorky), he knew only one other school—that of life. But he made such good use of it that, at the age of thirty, he was already one of the most popular authors in his country, and before long his name became a household word not only in Russia but the world over.

This alone puts Gorky among the arresting figures of our time. Yet if we care to gauge the full value of his work and personality, we must approach him in the light of social conditions prevailing in Russia at the beginning of the 1890s, when he (at that time a proletarian of twenty-four) had his first story printed. The tsarist Russia of that period was one of the most class-ridden and caste-ridden countries in Europe—a state of things which was further aggravated by her rapidly expanding industry. The abolition of serfdom had made the peasants independent of their former owners; but as it had not given them enough land to subsist on with their growing families, the surplus village population continued to emigrate to Siberia or else flooded the town-factories, where they often had to work under the most appalling conditions. It was among the proletarian factory workers that the Marxian type of socialism took root. The Russian Socialist-Democratic Party, whose early leader was Plekhanov, began to spread its activities in Russia in the later 1880s.

As far as Russian intellectuals were concerned, the majority had become by then a rather fluid and bewildered body suffering from the effects of the reactionary regime of Alexander III. Among their literary representatives there emerged in the 1890s a strong modernist movement with an interest in the 'decadent' art-for-art's sake school, taken over largely from the French. This group was more or less detached from the social and political struggles of the day. But parallel with it there existed another group of writers—whether 'commoners' or otherwise—who still had a sense of social responsibility and social service. Some of these were bound to look for a contact with the proletarians who were gradually consolidating their own organisations both politically and professionally. It was in connection with this particular process that Maxim Gorky's talent was soon to blossom out and to affirm itself. So much so that, at the beginning of this century, he became one of the principal literary and moral forces inspiring the best elements in the working-class movement in Russia. These activities reached their first climax in the abortive rising of 1905–6, and their rather complicated victory in the Revolution of 1917. It is the background of the two revolutions, with all the toil which preceded, conditioned and followed them, that can provide one with a reliable approach to such a phenomenon as Maxim Gorky.

2

Born in 1868 into an artisan family at Nizhny Novgorod, Alexey Peshkov (Gorky's real name) was soon taken to Astrakhan' where his father was employed. After his father's sudden death the boy went to his native town to stay with his grandparents. His sadistic grandfather, who had a dye workshop, went bankrupt, and the boy—hardly more than ten years old—had to earn his living. He was first employed in a footwear store, from which he escaped. For a while he served as a dish-washer on a Volga steamer, but this was only the beginning of an endless series of odd jobs: from sweated worker in a baker's shop to a street pedlar; from a fisherman on the Caspian Sea to a railway worker at some god-forsaken stations; from a petty clerk in a lawyer's office to a debutant in literature; and from a provincial journalist to a world-famous author. In the course of all these changes and peregrinations it was in Kazan' alone (where he mixed with the radical-minded undergraduates) that Gorky found a congenial atmosphere, but not for long. There were times when he was actually starving. In 1887 he made an attempt at suicide, but his life was saved by the skill of a hospital surgeon. His frequent companions in those days were social outcasts. Yet far from avoiding or despising them, he tried to understand their fate and to fathom through it his own attitude towards life. Years later he confessed to having felt among them 'like a piece of iron in glowing coal—every day filled me with a mass of sharp, burning impressions. I saw before me people nakedly greedy, people with rough instincts—and I liked their bitterness about life, I liked their ironically hostile attitude towards everything in the world, and also their carefree attitude towards themselves.' There was a great deal of moral and social callousness among them, but Gorky's actively idealistic and reformatory temperament—the most typical feature of his character—was his surest guide through the vicissitudes of life. He also realised that before taking any part in the fight against the ugliness and cruelty of existence he had much to learn. So he missed no opportunity to make up for his deficient education. Even after his first story, *Makár Chúdra* (1892), had appeared in a Caucasian newspaper at Tiflis, Gorky was not yet quite sure whether writing was his true vocation. He continued his literary apprenticeship while working for the most part on some Volga papers, and his talent kept maturing at such a pace that in 1898 he was already able to publish the first two volumes of his collected stories. Their success was immediate. Many people were shocked by the novelty of Gorky's themes, by his tone and manner, but they all read him. And they realised there and then that a new literary force had arisen which could be either accepted or rejected but by no means ignored.

The significance of this force was the greater because the decade preceding Gorky's debut was one of tiredness and disappointment. Capitalist investment, 'business' and industry, had made (especially under the leadership of Count Witte) such strides in those days as to turn even a large portion of intellectuals into their votaries. A number of these adopted a philistine indifference to everything except comfort and money. No wonder they were soon to be challenged by Maxim Gorky. The whole of Gorky's work can in fact be described as one long challenge. But it was also a tonic—a tonic potent enough to stir up a new will and a new hope even among those who had hardly ever dared either to will or to hope.

3

Gorky's first and second periods of literary activities, roughly from 1892 until 1901, bore the stamp of romantic defiance against the forces and conditions which tend to cripple life and dehumanise the majority of human beings. For this reason he chose a somewhat loud and flowery language, charged with the fury of a 'stormy petrel', as he was named from the outset. He also introduced into his stories such characters as were likely to voice his own defiance and protest. We find among them gypsies, Tartar shepherds, ragged tramps and vagabonds, smugglers, thieves, fishermen, and people from the 'lower depths' in general— people who had not the slightest reason to be in love with the existing order of things. Resentful, as well as provocative in action, most of them kept to the philosophy of safety last. At the same time they had their own ideas of human worth which did not necessarily tally with those of their social betters, about whom they had no illusions.

Consciousness of the class-division and class antagonism thus reached in Gorky's characters a new climax which was not devoid either of pride or dignity. Some of Gorky's critics were inclined to see in him at first a kind of Nietzsche from the gutter. But this was a superficial judgment. Gorky, who had passed through the gutter and had risen high above it, was anxious to abolish the gutter of life altogether. In this lay his strength and also his weakness: strength, because such an aim increased his creative élan, and weakness, because it imparted to him a didactic and, at times, even dogmatic 'purpose'. Thus he worked in two parallel directions. One of these was the way of protest in the name and on behalf of the victims of life; and the other took the form of a series of pictures of the gutter peopled by 'creatures who once were human beings' but were doomed to become—to use the pregnant Russian phrase—*bývshie lyúdi* (ex-humans).

Most of Gorky's early material was taken from his own experiences and observations. He knew how to describe his characters in a provocative as well as didactic manner. This applies particularly to his pictures of the 'lower depths,' where his realism of indictment had full sway. For no matter how degraded were the people portrayed, he lost no opportunity to stress at least the potential excellence of the human material thus crushed and wasted by life. One of his expedients, that of intensified characterisation, provided the kind of paradox one finds in his early story, *Chelkásh*. Its hero, a thief and outcast, has no respect for anybody or anything; yet at bottom he is a broad, generous type—a potential aristocrat by nature. His ally in a risky criminal adventure is a pious little yokel, who in the end turns out to be a worm—ready even to murder his companion in order to gratify his own greed for money. As a result the outcast Chelkash proves to be of much better human material than the acquisitive God-fearing peasant who can think in no other terms except those of property.

Nowhere, however, is Gorky's faith in the latent value of the social outcast stressed to better purpose than in his story, *Twenty-six Men and One Girl* (*Dvádtsat' shest' i odná*, 1899). Twenty-six 'creatures that once were human beings' toil like slaves in a filthy suburban bakery. They are mercilessly exploited by their boss and despised even by those workers whose pay and status are slightly higher than theirs. The only ray of light in that squalor is a pretty innocent girl who passes every morning by their den in order to collect some pretzel buns. All the twenty-six slaves fall in love with her—ideally and chivalrously, since she embodies that element of decency and beauty of life which still secretly smoulders at the bottom of their hearts in spite of their misery. But even this last illusion is gone when, one day, they find out that she has succumbed to the charms of a swaggering vulgarian.

It was not for nothing that the author of such a narrative called himself Maxim the Bitter (*gor'kiy* means 'bitter' in Russian). But since his bitterness only fostered his fight against the filth and cruelty of life, he could not help being didactic even to the extent of turning many of his characters into spokesmen for his own aims and ideas. Hence his frequent preaching, his love for instructive formulae, his exuberance and—in contrast to Chekhov—his use of glaring colours. One of the chief faults of his early writings was overstatement, which he naively mistook for strength.

It may have been for this reason that, in a letter, Chekhov referred to Gorky's art as carrying 'much unnecessary ballast' and 'provincialism'. In another letter, addressed to Gorky himself (in December 1898), Chekhov expressed his friendly and at the same time severe criticism of Gorky's style in these terms:

In my opinion you do not use sufficient restraint. You are like a spectator in the theatre who expresses his rapture so unreservedly that he prevents both himself and others from listening. Particularly is this lack of restraint felt in the descriptions of Nature with which you interrupt your dialogues; when one reads those descriptions one wishes they were more compact, shorter, put, say, into two or three lines. The frequent mention of tenderness, whispering, velvetness, and so on, gives to these descriptions a certain character of rhetoric and monotony—and chill the reader, almost tire him. Lack of restraint is felt also in the description of women and in the love scenes. It is not vigour, nor breadth of touch, but plain lack of reserve.[1]

This is fair criticism, especially of Gorky at his worst. But one should not forget that Gorky was a self-made author who wrote for a new type of reader, emerging from among the working classes. This reader needed a different approach, as well as a style more accessible to him than that offered by the avant-garde literature of the period.

4

Gorky certainly proved to be a great stimulus in this respect. And when he was at the height of his success, not only did he not dissociate himself from the toiling masses but, on the contrary, took a lead in their movement, knowing that his voice was likely to be heard far and wide. This demanded, however, an enlargement of his themes which soon included a deeper criticism of society and life, beginning with his first longer work, *Fomá Gordéyev* (1899). The background of this novel is the close-fisted but already decaying commercial bourgeoisie in a Volga town. Realising the emptiness of such an existence with its opulent animality, the principal character Foma, a member of the same class, feels out of tune with it. One can see in him a not entirely successful transposition of the 'superfluous man' from the gentry to a different social layer. For Gorky's Foma is, despite his bouts of drunken violence, almost the only effete character in the novel : much less impressive than his enterprising godfather. And he ends up as an idiot. Critical realism, inspired by faith in man and aiming at a renewal of life, was and remained Gorky's basic attitude. This was partly the reason why he tried his strength in dramatic activities as well. Aware of the influence that could be exercised on the stage, in 1901 he wrote his first play, *The Philistines* (*Meshcháne*). Here he challenged the philistinism of the more prosperous artisan-class, the only redeeming feature of which he found in the younger generation anxious to work for a new and better era to come. About a year later Gorky's second play, *The Lower Depths* (*Na dné*), became a world success—largely because of its subject-matter. The author introduces us here to the inmates of a doss-house. He shows us the misery and degradation of 'ex-humans' in whom one can still perceive sparks of humanity, strangely

1. *The Life and Letters of Anton Chekhov* (Cassell).

mixed up with their search for truth (however devious) and their dreams of an existence worthy of man. The resentment permeating the play is social and moral; and the author's brutal frankness about the depths of human misery can have an overwhelming effect, if well acted.

Gorky was by then a member of the Russian Social-Democratic Party which he joined in 1902. He became something of a focus for the revolutionary activities before and during the eventful year of 1905, which did not prevent him, however, from finishing two topical plays, *The Holiday Makers* (*Dáchniki*) and *Children of the Sun* (*Déti sólntsa*), tackling the problem of the intelligentsia and the people. Gorky's attitude towards the intellectuals of his time was, on the whole, negative. He thought the bulk of them effete and all the more 'superfluous' because they were despised by the people themselves who saw the emptiness of their isolated existence. In another piece, *The Barbarians* (*Várvary*), two intellectuals—this time engineers, building a railway through a distant provincial town—succeed in corrupting the whole place as if it had been invaded by savages. The only hope Gorky could see was in the new intellectual, arising from the masses and courageously working for better times to come. This, at any rate, is the leading idea of *The Holiday Makers* which—let it be said in fairness—is not a good play. The problem is treated somewhat differently in *Children of the Sun*. Here we see the élite of the mind; but since this élite is severed from the people and the masses, the danger of its being cut off and ousted from life is there and abounds in ominous possibilities. Finally, in *The Enemies* (*Vragí*, 1906) he considered the proletariat and its struggle against capitalism the only guarantee for a better future. Gorky's plays were being staged all over Russia at a time when Chekhov's dramas enjoyed great success in the Moscow Art Theatre. Yet Gorky, whose loud, explosive manner is so different from that of Chekhov, aimed at adopting Chekhov's technique. It was a risky step; and more than once, instead of Chekhov's discreet pastel, he produced somewhat glaring didactic oleographs. At his best, however, he managed to get away with it—in his *Lower Depths*, for instance.

5

Gorky's early dramatic works coincided with his publishing ventures which marked a further stage in his endeavour to make literature itself an active and creative ingredient of life. At a time when the slogan 'art for art's sake' was fashionable all over Europe, he became the promoter of the publishing firm *Znánie* (Knowledge): a gathering point for those authors who were anxious to preserve the good traditions of Russian realism and make their own works socially significant—in plain defiance of 'highbrow' writers. The success of this venture surpassed all expectations. A number of talented young authors—Kuprin, Andreyev, Shmelyov, Veresayev, Bunin—wrote for *Znánie*, association with which soon became an entrance-ticket to fame.

Gorky's influence had by then grown strong enough to make the authorities perturbed. Having already been in prison on several occasions, he regarded further ordeals of this kind as a matter of course. After the blood-bath on 9 January, 1905, when a peaceful procession of workers (wishing to lay their grievances before the Tsar) had been massacred by the troops almost within the Winter Palace, Gorky was arrested once again. His fame was, however, so great by then that violent protests followed from all over the world, under pressure of which he had to be released. But he remained incorrigible. In October 1905 he founded the socialist paper *New Life* (*Nóvaya zhizn'*) which, edited by Lenin himself, existed for some five weeks before it was closed by the police. It was in this paper that Gorky's vigorous series of attacks on modern bourgeois mentality appeared. He played one of the leading parts in the Moscow rising. And when the Revolution of 1905-1906 proved a failure, Gorky gave all his support to those who were determined to continue the fight underground. He travelled in Europe and America in order to increase the funds of the party. Then he settled in Capri, where he worked for a resumption of the struggle and finished his revolutionary novel *The Mother* (*Mat'*, 1907-08)—his first big, although artistically inferior, work since 1905.

An important social document and a propaganda novel rather than a pure work of art, *The Mother* depicts the Russian workers' struggle for their rights at the beginning of this century. The events described actually took place in 1902 in the factory district of Sormov near Nizhny Novgorod, and the two leading characters of the novel—the young worker Vlasov and his widowed mother—were among Gorky's personal friends. The early chapters, which are the best, show the low level of the old-time factory workers with their sloth, apathy, drunken rows, and hooliganism. Then, step by step, a new set of social values and ideals with which some of the workers became imbued, brought about an almost miraculous change, which was soon translated into an active effort to work for the future. Gorky makes us follow the various phases of this process. We see how revolutionary organisations are formed from within. We witness the clashes between workers and employers, as well as the onslaught of the reactionary powers-that-be. The struggle goes on, but the tenacity of the workers grows in proportion to their setbacks. What impresses one in this novel is the vitality of the Russian workers, once they have embraced a cause in which they can believe. Yet it was here in particular that Gorky's didactic propensity asserted itself to the utmost: propaganda is *mixed* with (rather than sublimated by) art. In spite of its faults the novel made a strong impact upon the working-class movement in Russia, as well as abroad, notably in France and Germany; and this at a time when the liberal bourgeoisie of those two countries had already turned against Gorky.

6

Less than a year after *The Mother*, Gorky published one of his strangest books, called simply *A Confession* (*Ispoved'*). Written in Capri, it reveals a typical Russian roamer: not the anarchic vagabond of Gorky's earlier stories, but a character who is rooted in his country and united through a kind of *participation mystique* with the eternally toiling, eternally yearning and seeking, God-seeking, folk masses. Its pages vibrate with that innate love for the land and its people which is a matter of one's instinct rather than any ideologies. The beauty of the spacious Russian landscape is conjured up here with all its charm. It is a poetic book about Russia, probably inspired by the exiled Gorky's nostalgia for his native land. The distance which lay between Capri and Russia, however, made him see also the negative side of Russian life more acutely than ever. This itself was responsible for his increased realism of indictment—such as we find in his narratives, *The Town of Okurov* (*Gorodók Okúrov*) and *The Life of Matvey Kozhemyakin* (*Zhizn' Matvéya Kozhemyákina*, 1909-11).

These two works are interdependent. *The Town of Okurov* is called (like Leskov's *Cathedral Folk*) a chronicle. It deals with the same remote provincial Russia as Leskov's famous work; but as it shows only its shady side, it is more in the line of Saltykov-Shchedrin's invectives. The hero of the narrative is the town itself. There may be a difference between its 'respectable' quarter and its slummy suburb, yet life is equally drab in both, equally senseless and squalid. The only diversion that now and then interrupts its monotony is crime, or the kind of shabby drama that forms the climax of the narrative at the moment when echoes of the Revolution of 1905 are beginning to stir even this God-forsaken hole. Another typical chronicle is *The Life of Matvey Kozhemyakin*. Here Gorky takes a lower-middle-class citizen of the same town, Okurov, and unrolls before us his existence during some fifty years of continuous frustration. Sapped from the outset, Kozhemyakin is yet all the time groping for something worth living for, though without guidance and without even any tangible results. Feeling utterly 'superfluous' in his surroundings, he is unable to cope with their weight. His death, which is only the last act of a long process of stagnation, takes place when the revolutionary outburst of 1905 seems to promise a different and better era. To quote an entry from Kozhemyakin's own diary shortly before he died :

> New workers have now appeared in our life—with hearts full of love for this earth which we have besmirched; they are living ploughs which will furrow God's field deeply, down to its very heart and will make it glow and blossom up with a new sun, warm and kindly to all men, bringing to them a happy life.

After some three hundred pages of futility, depicted with Gorky's rugged indignation, the final note of this work is one of faith and hope. Such an attitude was typical of Gorky even during the stifling era after 1905-6. His criticism of Russia became increasingly violent, and so did his insistence on radical change. In the same way as he had always disagreed with Tolstoy's gospel of pseudo-Christian non-violence, he was now utterly opposed to those advanced intellectuals (many of them former Marxists) who in 1909 came forward with the miscellany *Milestones* (*Vékhi*, edited by M. O. Gerschenzon) with its call back to religious or even 'church' values. This publication caused havoc among the ranks of the intelligentsia; but Gorky—a stranger to Church and religion—only increased his demands that concrete humane improvements should take place in all aspects of life. Even his excellent literary achievements, *Childhood* (*Détstvo*) and *In the World* (*V lyúdyakh*)—the first and the second parts of his autobiographic trilogy—are an indictment of those conditions which can so easily cripple one's tender years, as had largely been the case with Gorky himself. The only bright spot in the nightmare of his early life was his grandmother whose portrayal in *Childhood* is a marvel of Gorky's skill.

Thanks to the amnesty on the occasion of the tercentenary of the Romanovs in 1913, Gorky was allowed to return to Russia. He stayed there all through the First World War. But he was far from being enthusiastic either about the war or about its motives and his subversive activities continued. In the winter of 1915 he started a monthly, *The Annals* (*Létopis'*), the spirit of which was anti-bourgeois, anti-war and anti-imperialistic. Then came the Revolution of 1917 which, with all its horrors, seemed at first to promise the very things Gorky had all the time been fighting for. His two bugbears, the decayed capitalist bourgeoisie and the decayed section of the intelligentsia, were swept away by the tidal wave of the upheaval which, at last, unleashed the untapped energies of the Russian masses inhabiting one sixth of our globe. To quote Gorky's own words, 'Now the entire Russian people is taking part in history—this is an event of cardinal importance, and it is from this angle that we ought to judge all the bad and good things, all our joys and sorrows.'

This does not mean that Gorky approved of everything that was taking place in those fateful days. In the periodical, *New Life*, which he resuscitated, he carried on a series of disputes with the Bolsheviks and with Lenin himself. Appalled by the excesses let loose by the Revolution, he insisted on raising the cultural level of the masses and, after his reconciliation with Lenin in 1918, did all he could towards this end. He was one of the principal organisers of aid to writers, artists and savants regardless of their political allegiance—not a small matter in those days of general shortage and famine. Gorky, moreover, stepped in as a defender of cultural continuity at a time when a number of victorious revolutionaries were advocating a purely proletarian culture. It was he in particular who turned against any narrow-minded sectarianism and demanded that the best elements bequeathed by the former culture and the literature of the gentry and intelligentsia should be assimilated by the Soviet masses and creatively blended with what they themselves could give to the world. And so even before the duress of the Civil War was over, he set up a far-reaching undertaking. Its aim was to present the masses with the classical works of world literature, translated and commented by experts. In this manner he became a bridge not only between the Soviets and the former Russian culture, but also between Soviet Russia and the culture of the world.

Whether or not Gorky welcomed certain single aspects connected with the birth-pangs of this New Russia does not really matter. What matters is that he fully realised the impact of the new direction given to world-history by the Revolution of 1917. After all, tsarist Russia had been a diseased organism in need of a surgical operation, and—as we know—operations performed by history are done without anaesthetics. Hence we must not be surprised that, in spite of several initial polemics and misunderstandings, Gorky—for reasons of his own—threw in his lot with the Soviet system despite the fact that he was aware of its faults. Several years later he explained this step of his in a private letter as follows:

> Do I side with the Bolsheviks who deny freedom? Yes, I do, because I stand for the freedom of all people who work honestly, but I am against the freedom of parasites and harmful babblers. I used to argue with the Bolsheviks and to oppose them in 1917, when it seemed to me that they were unlikely to win over the peasants driven by the war into anarchy, and that a conflict with them threatened to ruin the workers' party itself. Then I came to the conclusion that I was wrong, and now I am fully convinced that the Russian people, however much it be hated by the governments of Europe and whatever its economic difficulties as a result of that hatred, has entered upon the phase of its regeneration.

7

All these activities on the part of Gorky were so much hampered by bad health (lingering tuberculosis) that in 1922 he undertook a cure abroad, first in Germany and later in southern Italy. He returned to Russia in 1928 and again in 1933: this time for good. During all those years his literary output remained as abundant as ever and included some of his maturest works: *My Universities* (Moí universitéty), his novels *The Artamonov Business* (Délo Artamónovykh) and *The Life of Klim Samgin* (Zhizn' Klimá Samginá), as well as his play *Yegor Bulichov and Others* (Yegór Bulichóv i drugíe).

My Universities refers to Gorky's hard school of life during his years of adolescence and early manhood. It completes his autobiographic trilogy and (like the first two parts) is crammed with incident, portraits and descriptions. Like the previous two volumes, it is invaluable for an understanding of Gorky's development in general. As for *The Artamonov Business* (1925), the very title of this novel suggests that, once again, we are taken back to the moneyed bourgeoisie of the old regime. Stained by a crime at its beginning, the factory founded by the energetic ex-serf Artamonov soon expanded into a prosperous concern. But the disintegrating process set in with the second generation, while in the third the Artamonovs were ruined by the Revolution of 1917. The firm became national property, and a different era came in to stay. A similar motif must have been in Gorky's mind when he planned his unfinished dramatic trilogy of which *Yegor Bulichov* was to be the first part. Here, too, as in *The Artamonov Business*, we see the new era knocking at the door of a prosperous but corrupt firm; only this time the starting point is the chaos prevailing during the First World War and the Revolution. The cunning, unscrupulous Yegor is something of a symbol of the old system and, like the system itself, suffers from an incurable disease. When at last the song of the rising masses bursts from the street into the room of the dying invalid, he knows that his time is up. 'What is it? The burial service singing me out of the world!' And so it is;

the burial service singing out of the world the entire historical period represented by him.

There still remains *The Life of Klim Samgin*—in all evidence the most
ambitious of Gorky's works. It is in four parts, the last of which remained
unfinished. At a first glance it may look like a more detailed intelligentsia counterpart of his petit-bourgeois chronicle, *Matvéy Kozhemyákin*. But it turns out
to be something much more important: a chronicle of Russian life during some
forty years, roughly from 1880 until 1917—a subject which in some respects
was almost too big even for him. Gorky attempted to give here a cross-section
of practically all the Russian classes as seen by that offspring of the intelligentsia,
Klim Samgin. Klim himself serves as the central figure of an amazing variety
of characters, many of them in the course of their development, or else depicted
in their reactions to all the phases of Russian history during those years. Particularly good is the first part, showing the early development of a whole generation in a big provincial town. The second and third parts, dealing with the Russo-
Japanese War and the events of 1905, are rather drawn out (by lengthy discussions), but they are of great documentary value. The same can be said of the
unfinished fourth part, which brings events up to the February Revolution of
1917. Such a long and ambitious chronicle of Russian life is bound to be uneven,
yet quite a few of its single portions show Gorky the critical realist at his best.
At the same time one can feel in him (here perhaps more than in any of his
former writings) an active idealist aiming at a transformation of the old pattern
of existence. In addition to his descriptive passages he excels as a portrait painter
and psychologist. In no other work did he give such a number of complex
characters, beginning with Klim Samgin whose life is an abbreviated and somewhat symbolic image of that liberal intelligentsia whose unfulfilled historical
mission was terminated by the Revolution. It was in this novel that Gorky
tried to show not only the external but also the inner reasons why the intelligentsia proved unable to lead the country and the nation through the most
fateful crisis in Russia's history. Hence he had to describe—in retrospect—the
entire development of the generation represented by Klim as its typical specimen. We see him first as a child growing up in an intelligentsia family with
'populist' traditions. After his grammar school years in a provincial town, we
follow him as a student to St Petersburg, to Moscow, then as a lawyer in the provinces, as a tourist abroad, finally again to St Petersburg where he watches
the Revolution of 1917 and becomes one of its victims. He is an example of the
bourgeois intelligentsia in the process of its Hamlet-like doubtings and decay.
Gorky shows how, step by step, everything disintegrated in that particular
stratum: family, love, sex, culture, literature, politics, while events in Russia
seemed to go on as though urged by an irresistible logic of their own. The final
issue is, in fact, Intelligentsia and Revolution. It is an answer, or at least Gorky's
answer, to the question why it was that the old intelligentsia was bound to be
so cruelly eliminated by the cataclysm of 1917.

8

Even a brief survey such as this should not omit Gorky's pamphlets, diaries, articles, essays, and especially his excellent reminiscences of Tolstoy, Korolenko, Chekhov, and Andreyev. Those of Tolstoy, in particular, however brief, are among the best short accounts ever given of that puzzling genius. Instead of analysis Gorky gives us here only a string of anecdotes and impressions; but these are chosen in such a way as to make Tolstoy (without the slightest hagiographic touch) intensely human and intensely alive.

Last, but not least, Gorky was the initiator and the first theoretician of Socialist Realism, which from the mid-thirties became—often in a distorted bureaucratic variety—the official literary trend in Soviet Russia. But in Gorky's opinion Socialist Realism presents, or should present:

> Being as action, as creation aimed at the unbroken development of the finest individual traits of man, that he may triumph over the forces of nature, that he may realise the joy of living on earth, which by his ever-increasing requirements he is induced to transform into a splendid place for all mankind united into one single family.

This trend implied by its very nature what might be called Socialist Humanism, which, indeed, became closely connected with Gorky's name. A system founded on the struggles and the hatred of classes necessarily requires countless victims and personal frustrations, by virtue of which the individual inevitably regards himself as an enemy of society. This feeling of hostility grows together with one's isolation and the ensuing brand of pessimism. As Gorky himself pointed out, 'in the twentieth century pessimism degenerated into a philosophy of complete social cynicism, into a complete and decisive denial of humanitarianism of which in former times the bourgeois of all countries boasted so much.' He saw the only remedy in a society based on a pattern which would form a synthesis of Socialism and Humanism. A synthesis of this kind is in fact the great problem of today and tomorrow. Here literature, as Gorky thought, could be a powerful medium. This was why, only two years before his death, he said in one of his talks:

> I want literature to rise above reality and to look down on reality from above, because literature has a far greater purpose than merely to reflect reality. It is not enough to depict already existing things—we must also bear in mind the things we desire and the things which are possible of achievement.

This last sentence is typical of Gorky's work as a whole. In a number of his writings he proved to be the very embodiment of Socialist Humanism with its respect for human personality—not isolated and self-centred personality, but one directed towards, and consciously working for, its integration with society, with mankind as a whole. No wonder that he became the idol of the new readers as well as of the new intellectuals from among the Russian working-classes whose tastes and requirements often differed from those of the former intelligentsia.

The results can be judged by the astronomical sales of Gorky's writings. According to the *Literary Gazette* (June 15, 1946), his works have appeared, only between 1917 and 1946, in sixty-six languages, and sold in 42,000,000 copies. According to the latest statistics 99,000,000 copies of his works have been sold in the Soviet Union alone. It is doubtful whether any modern author anywhere else on earth could dream of such an achievement. Even the fateful years which have passed since Gorky's death in 1936 do not seem to have impaired his stature in Russia. Having come from the people, he is still regarded as the people's author in the best sense of the word. And lastly, his own will and vitality seem to have become symbols of a nation which has shrunk from no hardships, no sacrifices, and even no mistakes and blunders, in order to shape a life different from and better than the life of the past. It is for history to say what its final outcome will be.

CHAPTER TWENTY

Leonid Andreyev

I

There are literary works whose symptomatic significance is often greater than their artistic value. Typical not so much of the whole of their own epoch as of some of its single trends or fashions, the authors of such works are usually overrated during their lifetime, and underestimated once they are dead. Such was largely the fate of Leonid Andreyev (1871-1919) who, between 1902 and 1910, was one of the most discussed writers in Russia and, for a time, rivalled in popularity even Gorky himself. Nor is it without interest that the first literary successes of Andreyev were partly connected with Gorky's name, although later he became hostile to almost everything Maxim Gorky stood for. While Gorky worked for a new era, a new community and a new set of readers, Andreyev preferred to apply his undoubted talent to the avant-garde of decaying Russian intellectuals in order to reflect, as in a magnifying mirror, their mentality during the last few years before their passing out of history in 1917. From about the middle of the 1890s the influence of certain 'Dostoevskian' moods and thoughts increased among those sceptics who were inclined to let politics take care of itself and were more or less indifferent even to a clash with the forces of reaction. But when, in 1905–6, such a clash did occur, reaction won a victory so brutal and so complete that practically the entire intelligentsia was thrown into a slough of despond, or rather into a vacuum in which escapist novels, 'mystical' stimulants, detective stories and thrillers were much in demand.

This was why Sherlock Holmes became one of the most popular heroes with a whole category of Russian readers. Others preferred the bracing adventure tales supplied by Jack London—a great favourite of the Russian public. Readers with more fastidious tastes were on the look-out for mental, spiritual and aesthetic expedients strong enough to take them away, at least for a while, from the things they wanted to forget. There was a considerable hankering after esoteric cults, especially the more spurious ones. Finally, there were erotic tales which were particularly welcomed as sensual stimulants, no matter whether they had been manufactured at home or abroad. The vogue of the sex-ridden Polish decadent, Stanislaw Przybyszewski, was extremely strong in Russia at the time. An idol of the younger generation was the German playwright, Frank Wedekind. And as for Russian stimuli of this sort, the artistically unimportant but very 'sexy' novel, *Sánin*, by Mikhail Artsybashev became a best-seller as soon as it was published in 1907. There were, of course, other provocative and, in their own way, escapist best-sellers, especially those which came from the pen of Leonid Andreyev. They were of a different kind and often even of a high literary value.

Apart from his early stories, the majority of Andreyev's writings deal with 'big' themes and subjects, treated in that modernist style which, for all its pretentious garb, is generally accessible and therefore likely to flatter the less tutored readers by giving them the illusion of being on a par with the 'highbrows'. But this alone would hardly have brought Andreyev to the pinnacle of fame and prosperity, had he not sponsored some of those topics which were bound to appeal to the bulk of the intellectuals of the period in question.

2

Born into the family of a petty official in the provinces, Andreyev hardly had a background spacious enough for his talent. On finishing his University studies, he became a lawyer's assistant—a profession he gave up when he discovered (in 1897) that he could make a living by his writings. In his first stories the echoes of Chekhov, Korolenko, and Gorky were noticeable. Soon the influences of Dostoevsky and Tolstoy were added, and later also that of Edgar Allan Poe. In his early period he was realistic, with a social or humanitarian under-current, but invariably ending in a minor key. The final note of his Little Angel (Angelóchek, 1899), for instance, is one of gloom and disillusionment. So is the ending of Petka in the Country (Pét'ka na dáche, 1899)—the story of a boy of ten slaving in a Moscow barber shop. For the first time in his life he is taken for a holiday in the countryside; but just when his impressionable mind has opened up with enthusiasm to all the beauties of nature, he is forced to go back to the same tedious drudgery in the slums without the prospect of anything better.

Even when Andeyev became a contributor to Gorky's publishing firm Znánie, he made only few concessions to the social and humanitarian optimism of that group. One of these was his story In the Basement (V podvále), obviously implying—like Gorky's Twenty-Six Men and One Girl—that even the hearts of the 'ex-humans' still retain sparks of true humanity which may flare up if given a chance. One of Andeyev's best early stories, Once there Lived (Zhíli-býli, 1901) was partly inspired by Tolstoy's Death of Ivan Ilyich. The action takes place in a clinic where there are several patients knowing they are doomed to die; but the atmosphere of death is handled, this time, with Chekhov's technique and, what is more, with Chekhovian understatement—a rare thing in Andreyev's writings. A different propensity is noticeable in his longer story In the Fog (V tumáne, 1902). Here Andreyev tackled the tragedy of awakened sex in a school-boy who contracts venereal disease and eventually murders a prostitute and commits suicide. The story caused much uproar and can serve as a proof of the author's growing hankering for morbid themes, worked out in a dramatic (or even melodramatic) manner. This was particularly the case when he came under the spell of some of Dostoevsky's ideas and problems. As the latter were sometimes too big for his pen, he tried to compensate by raising the tone and filling his pages with overloud symbolist clichés designed to surprise, or rather to stun his readers by means of paradoxical logic. This brought a forced hyperbolic note into some of his writings, charged with pseudo-symbolism: a genre clearly anticipated in sketches such as *Silence, The Wall, The Tocsin, The Abyss*, and *The Thought*—all of them written between 1900 and 1902 in a mood of futility. The blind-alley of existence was taken up by Andreyev with relish, but he turned it into a substitute for religion. He even equipped it with the theology of the fashionable 'mystical anarchism', and his solemnly hollow incantations were but a camouflage for his own fear of life. The apotheosis of this fear became Andreyev's 'purpose' (one could almost say—moral purpose) which he cultivated as the very essence of his type of modernism.

Always an individualist, Andreyev was strongly attracted by the pose of a rebel. But as he felt more and more the fascination of Dostoevsky's metaphysical rebels, he too became one of them without even believing in metaphysics. He prostrated himself before the principle of negation which he pushed to the verge of grotesqueness. Like some of Dostoevsky's heroes he saw (or forced himself to see) in life only a 'vaudeville of the devils'; but instead of searching for something beyond it, as Dostoevsky did, he often derived from the very hopelessness of such a disposition a peculiar and almost ecstatic kind of pleasure.

3

One of his first successful longer narratives, imbued with this brand of nihilism, was his *Life of Father Vasily Fiveysky* (*Zhizn' ottsá Vasíliya Fivéyskogo*, 1903). The problem tackled here is the eternal problem of evil, but the questioner in Andreyev's story is a village priest whose unconditional faith in God is being undermined by the horrors of life he sees around him. Like a modern Job, Father Vasily passes through a series of misfortunes, including the birth of an idiot son. He looks for comfort in his own Christian faith, but his reiterations of the formula, 'I believe, O Lord, I believe,' are answered only by the imbecile laughter of his stinking little idiot and by an increase of evil—personal and otherwise. Outraged in his moral sense of justice, the priest hurls at last a mad challenge to God, but this time he himself is crushed by it, or rather by the emptiness of a Godless and senseless world.

Senselessness is further canonised in Andreyev's story, *Phantoms* (*Prízraki*, 1904)—obviously a literary descendant of Chekhov's *Ward No. 6*, with the action taking place in a lunatic asylum. The author analyses the imaginary phantom existence of the inmates in whose minds the boundary line between the normal and the abnormal has been obliterated. But life outside the asylum (especially in the fashionable night-club, where the doctor-in-charge spends most of his free time) is implied to be equally phantom-like; so there is not much to choose between the two. Or take *The Red Laugh* (*Krásny smekh*, 1905) —the would-be written monologue of an officer who lost both legs in the Russo-

Japanese War, the 'madness and horror' of which continue to haunt him in his invalid bed to the point of insanity. In Andreyev's allegorical narrative, *Thus Was It, Thus Will Be* (*Tak býlo, tak búdet*, 1905), the futility of revolutionary upheavals is marked by the clock of Time; or by its indifference to the happenings on earth, the history of which remains the same blood-stained farce for ever, no matter what antics and atrocities may be performed by human puppets. With no less emphasis Andreyev stresses in another story, *My Memoirs* (*Moí Zapíski*, 1908), the nothingness of freedom and—by implication—of the fight for freedom. To crown it all, his turgid *Lazarus* (*Eleázar*, 1906) brings such a nihilistic attitude to a head. Lazarus, after having been resurrected by Christ, has brought back from the tomb some horrid truth of his own. He is now a walking corpse, paralysing those with whom he comes into contact, since the mystery peering out of his eyes reminds them that life itself is only a form of death.

Yet if his 'metaphysical' themes often outstrip his talent, Andreyev fares much better when concentrating mainly on psychology. One of the best stories of this kind. *The Governor* (*Gubernátor*, 1905), is told with economy and with an almost Tolstoyan matter-of-factness. The hero of the story is the governor of a province who in the turmoil of the revolution gives the order that a gathering of workers should be fired on and dispersed. Because of the many victims, he receives an intimation from the local terrorists that they have sentenced him to death. The certainty of impending doom then hangs over him like fate itself, until the inevitable happens. Andreyev at his best also succeeded in skilfully combining psychological observations with some deeper idea which enhanced the value of his story. In his *Christians* (*Khristiáne*, 1904), for example, he unmasks with unflagging irony the hypocritical character of our Christianity, seen from the angle of a prostitute who, feeling her sinfulness, obstinately refuses to take a Christian oath, to the indignation of the no-less-prostituted but otherwise respectable citizens—a mark of Tolstoy's influence.

More involved is the story, *Darkness* (*T'má*, 1907). Once again, Andreyev attacks morality, but this time from an unexpected and as if supramoral angle. A revolutionary terrorist, whose whole life has been one long struggle for freedom and justice, is hiding from the police. The circle of his pursuers has grown so narrow that the only refuge where he still feels safe for a while is a house of ill-fame. As he has never been in such a place before, he is staggered by the human degradation he finds there. In his struggle for a better world he has always kept himself pure and had never touched a woman. Now, too, he would have nothing to do with the prostitute in whose room he is hiding. But having guessed who he is, and feeling offended by his purity, the prostitute asks him rather impertinently what right he has to be pure and moral while she and millions of other human beings cannot help wallowing in utter filth. The problem unexpectedly sinks into his mind and, step by step, produces an unexpected reaction. Unable to behave like a moral prig amidst so much mud and mire in the world, he begins to feel uneasy about his own 'white robes', until he is actually ashamed of them. In the end he becomes conscience-stricken on account of his own chastity. In this state of mind he is impelled (by a strangely twisted *moral* impulse) to degrade himself deliberately and as though with vengeance. He falls so low morally that even the gendarmes, who at last get hold of him in the brothel, are disgusted—without even distantly suspecting the inner cause of his self-degradation.

4

Andreyev can be good, even excellent, when he is preoccupied with the story as such and tells it without affectation. The two of his longer, though widely different, narratives of this kind are *Judas Iscariot and Others (Iúda Iskariót i drugíe*, 1907) and *The Seven that Were Hanged (Rasskáz o semí povéshennykh*, 1908).

The first is ambitious not only because it is connected with the Gospel, but also because it concerns the ever-mysterious personality of Judas himself. What were the motives behind his betrayal of Jesus Christ, since greed alone is too paltry an explanation? Did he want to protect Jesus, hoping that, if imprisoned, He would be beyond the reach of the infuriated Jewish mob? Or was he anxious that Jesus should thus be compelled to fulfil His great mission without vacillating and proclaim His glory to the world? Without bothering about any previous explanations of the motives, Andreyev took a provocative line of his own. His Judas is something of a self-divided misanthropist whose double nature is marked by the very shape of his ugly head. Endowed with far greater intelligence and knowledge of life than all the other disciples put together, he is suspicious and cynically scornful of human beings. He does not think much of the noisy plebeian Peter or of the smugly virtuous John, let olone the feeble-minded simpleton Thomas. But he knows how to conceal his spite, as well as his cruel wisdom, behind the mask of a clown. There is only one person before whom he bows unconditionally and with fanatical devotion, namely Jesus. Judas the cynic would not question for a moment the Master's moral and spiritual greatness. The point about which he felt sceptical, though, was the assertion of Jesus that He was the Son of God, since the clever doubter Judas could hardly presume the existence of a God behind such an idiotic world. Puzzled as he was, he decided to betray Jesus mainly in order to arrive at some certainty at least with regard to this matter. He reasoned that if God existed at all, He would not allow the vulgar scoundrels to triumph over His beloved Son. A miracle was sure to happen, proclaiming the Saviour's glory to all. But even if God did not exist, the Master's hour of trial might still become an hour of triumph, because the mob, callous and cruel though it be, would surely recognise in Him the noblest being that ever trod the earth.

And so the betrayal took place. Insults were piled on Jesus. He was ridiculed, maltreated, tortured, spat upon, yet God remained silent: no miracle happened. And the howling mob, which not so long before had shouted Hosanna in the streets of Jerusalem, now clamoured for the malefactor Barrabbas to be set free instead of Jesus. During the Master's agony on the cross Judas, too, went through a crucifixion of his own. With anguish past endurance he watched the last hours of Jesus at a time when all the other disciples, prudently hiding from the authorities, were able—to Judas's disgust—even to eat and sleep. But of what account were the disciples now that everything had crumbled to pieces! The only thing left was to fling the money back into the faces of the pompous worthies responsible for the Master's fate and then out of a world in which such things are possible.

The Seven that Were Hanged is more topical. It was written during the worst days of the Stolypin regime, when, after 1906, hangings of revolutionaries were a daily occurrence.[1] Andreyev obviously wanted to join Tolstoy and Korolenko in their protest against this routine phenomenon (*bytovóe yavlénie*)[2] of Russian life. But instead of a pamphlet he presented the world with a grue-some and in its own way intensely moving story about seven people—five revo-lutionaries and two ordinary criminals—condemned to die on the gallows. The thoughts, moods and emotions of each of them, from the death-sentence to the moment of their execution, are described with powerful directness and with warmth, although even here Andreyev is interested in the revolutionary per-sonalities rather than in the revolution as such. This time he paid due tribute to the fighters who sacrificed their lives for the sake of a better world about which he himself was so sceptical.

The dilemma of a selfless terrorist forms the subject-matter of Andreyev's only real novel, *Sáshka Zhegulyóv* (1911). Sashka is a young intellectual who, in the years of upheaval, joins the revolution out of sheer altruism. He forms a band of terrorists, but in practice criminal and revolutionary motives and activities become so intermixed that in the end it is impossible to tell one from the other. Under duress the band dissolves, while its few remaining members are surrounded and killed. The novel bears the mark of Andreyev's weakening talent. As though feeling that his narrative zest was subsiding, he turned more and more to the theatre and drama.

5

Andreyev began writing plays after the success of Maxim Gorky's *Lower Depths*. As his popularity at the time was not far behind the popularity of Gorky, it was natural that he should have emulated Gorky on the stage where he soon became prolific. Towards the end of his life he wrote plays almost ex-clusively. These can be divided into a realistic and a philosophical group, with the addition of a few clever pot-boilers of the kind that were sure to please the public. And, like his stories, most of them reflect Andreyev's problem-hunting and nihilism *à outrance*.

In his first dramatic work, *To the Stars* (*K zvezdám*, 1905), he tackled the Nietzschean problem of love for one's 'far ones' as being something incom-patible with the love for one's neighbours. His realistic *Sávva* and his abstractly 'expressionist' morality-play, *The Life of Man* (*Zhizn' chelovéka*)—both written

1. The hangman's rope was ironically referred to as 'Stolypin's cravat'.
2. Such was the title of one of Korolenko's vigorous pamphlets against executions.

in 1906—testify to an even greater despair about man and life than his stories. 'I survey with my eyes the earth,' says Savva, 'and I see that there is nothing more terrible than man's life.' Savva is soaked in that negative revolutionary mood which wants to destroy mainly for the sake of destruction. Since history and civilisation have proved such a failure then the best thing we can do is to scrap the whole of it and start afresh—perhaps with more success. The drama, *King Hunger* (*Tsar' Gólod*), is again revolutionary in its protest against the capitalist minority. The enslaved workers who rebel are crushed by the technocratic élite, but the muffled threats of the slain that they will come back do not augur well for the future of that élite, On the whole, this is one of Andeyev's weakest plays. As in *The Life of Man*, or even more so, he mistakes allegory for symbol, especially in the last scene, whose forced artificiality is positively painful.

In *The Black Masks* (*Chórnye máski*, 1908) the theme of a self-divided personality occurs—this time in the shape of a 'surrealist' nightmare, taking place in a brain which is already in the grip of madness. *Anáthema* (1909), on the other hand, belongs to the 'titanic' genre. It is an allegorical melodrama, with overstatements from the first to the last line. Vaguely allegorical also is *He Who Gets Slapped* (*Tot kto polucháet poshchóchiny*, 1915). Here a former intellectual luminary has become a circus clown, celebrated for the prodigious amount of slaps he is able to endure. Intellect itself (in the garb of a clown) is being lustily slapped in a circus to the delight of a gaping and laughing crowd —such is the hidden meaning of this play.

Among Andreyev's plays intended for the public at large *The Days of Our Life* (*Dni náshey zhízni*, 1908) and *Gaudeamus* (1910), about the life of students, were great box-office successes. In the spicy *Anfíssa* (1909), however, he piled up morbid elements, including incest, to the extent of verging on a naturalistic parody. *Katerína Ivánovna* (1912), *Professor Storítsyn*, and *Thou Shalt not Kill* (1913) recorded the vulgar mentality of an epoch in which there was little or no room for values of a higher order. A new departure in the direction of humorous satire was Andreyev's play, *The Pretty Sabine Women* (*Prekrásnye Sabinyánki*, 1912)—a somewhat heavy satire on the opportunism of Russian liberals. In one of his last plays, *Sampson in Chains*, Andreyev tackled, once again, the drama of self-division.

During the First World War Andreyev, for all his previous nihilism, suddenly became a patriotic liberal. After the Revolution of 1917, moreover, he developed a violent hatred of Bolshevism. About two years later he died of a stroke in his lonely villa in Finland. But had he lived longer, he could not have added much to what he had already said. As the mouthpiece of that layer of the intelligentsia which was already decayed to the extent of revelling in the prospect of its own death, he himself could not but share the same fate, once the old order was swept away by the Revolution. Yet no modern author of his calibre has paid a heavier price for literary success *à la mode* than Andreyev.

CHAPTER TWENTY-ONE

Bunin and Kuprin

I

Among those authors after Chekhov who preserved in their writings a high level of prose Ivan Bunin (1870–1953) deserves to be mentioned. For it was Bunin who continued to stick to the tradition of classical realism during the very peak of modernist experiments, with all their 'isms', and managed to get away with it. As a poet, too, he stood aloof from the numerous fashionable cliques and followed the classical heritage without forfeiting thereby his own significance or originality. For some ten years he was connected with Maxim Gorky's *Znánie* team of writers; but even so he did not commit himself to any political, social or literary propaganda. In an Autobiographic Note which he wrote for the English edition of his novel *The Village (Derévnya)*,[1] Bunin proudly confessed: 'I took no part in politics; I belonged to no particular literary school, called myself neither decadent, nor symbolist, nor romantic, nor naturalist, donned no masks of any kind, and hung out no flamboyant flag.' In this respect he was considerably more neutral than such members of the *Znanie* group as V. Veresayev, I. Shmelyov and A. Serafimovich, let alone the less important authors of that set: E. Chirikov, S. Yushkevich, S. Skitalets, etc. Even when he emigrated, during the Civil War, he did this not for any ideological reason but simply because he felt a stranger in the Soviet Union arising out of the shambles of the Revolution.

Such a step was not surprising in his case. As a descendant of an old, though impoverished, noble family, Bunin was never able entirely to shed the ways and habits of the class into which he had been born. His early years were passed in a country-manor or *usad'ba* which, despite its decay, still retained the flavour of the old 'nests of gentlefolk'. Because of his family's difficult financial position he had to give up many an advantage youngsters of his class took for granted. Even his education was cut down to only four years at the Grammar School in Elets—a small provincial town not far from Voronezh (where the poets Koltsov and Nikitin came from). Whatever Bunin's early plans or ambitions may have been, they were thus frustrated from the outset. He spent a couple of years at home on the family estate which, anyway, was already going to rack and ruin largely owing to the carelessness of Bunin's father. But the boy was far from being idle. Keenly interested in literature, he read a great deal, learned English and, before long, started writing poetry. He

1. *The Village* by Ivan Bunin. Translated by Isabel Hapgood (Martin Secker, 1923).

was only sixteen when he saw his first poem printed in a newspaper and another in a well-known respectable monthly. This was a decisive step in his life. It made him think of literature as a vocation: the more so because he was a distant relative of the romantic poet and Pushkin's friend Vasily Zhukovsky —an illegitimate son of Afanasy Bunin and a captive Turkish girl.

For a while he joined one of his two elder brothers who was employed as a statistician at Kharkov. After a certain amount of wandering he worked on the editorial staff of a newspaper at Oryol. Here he fell in love with a doctor's pretty daughter (Lika) who joined him and shared his life in the Ukraine, but eventually left him. Later, in 1895, Bunin came to St Petersburg and was connected at first with the populist monthly, *The Russian Wealth*. In 1897 a collection of his stories came out, and their author was welcomed as a fresh and promising talent. Before long he found encouraging friends and supporters in Chekhov and Gorky. It was in fact in the miscellanies of Gorky's *Znánie* that Bunin's two successful novels, *The Village* (1909) and *Sukhodól* (1912), came out. These two masterpieces were followed by a number of stories some of which—*A Cup of Life* (*Chásha zhízni*, 1913), for instance, and particularly *The Gentleman from San Francisco* (*Gospodín iz San Francisco*, 1915)—were translated into several European languages. He also wrote a great deal of poetry and was, moreover, responsible for excellent Russian versions of Byron's *Cain*, *Manfred*, and *Heaven and Earth*, as well as of Longfellow's *Song of Hiawatha* and Tennyson's *Lady Godiva*.

After the Bolshevist victory he left Russia in 1919, since he could not stand the confusion and chaos all around him. As he says in the above-mentioned Autobiographic Note: 'What the Russian Revolution turned into very soon, none will comprehend who has not seen it. This spectacle was utterly unbearable to any one who had not ceased to be a man in the image and likeness of God, and all who had a chance to flee, fled from Russia.' He had to pass through plenty of ordeals before he was able to settle in France (mostly at Grasse) where he continued to work as indefatigably as ever. During his voluntary exile he wrote some of his best works, the short novel *Mitya's Love* (*Mítina lyubóv'*) and his autobiography *Life of Arsenyev* (*Zhizn' Arsényeva*) included. In 1933 he was awarded the Nobel Prize for literature. This made his financial position better, but did not save him and his wife from hard times during the Pétain regime after 1940. He died in Paris in 1953.

2

Bunin is above all a born story-teller who, with a few dexterous touches, plunges the reader into the heart of the matter. Take *The Sunstroke* (*Sólnechny udár*) for example, which is one of his best short stories. It is about a casual meeting of two strangers, a man and a woman, on a Volga steamer, and the spontaneous passion between them. These are the lines introducing the reader to all the happenings that follow :

After dinner they came on deck out of the brightly lit dining-saloon and stood by the rail. She closed her eyes, laid the back of her hand against her cheek, gave a lovely unaffected laugh—everything about this very young woman was lovely—and said: 'I feel as though I were drunk. . . . I must be crazy. Where did you come from? Three hours ago I had no idea that you existed. I don't even know when you came on board—was it at Samara? But what does it matter—I am happy with you! Am I giddy or is our boat really turning round?'

Darkness and light loomed ahead. Out of the darkness a strong gust of warm wind beat against their faces. The lights were sweeping past some-where to the side. The steamer in true Volga style was making for a small landing stage in a wide graceful sweep.[1]

Apart from being a superb narrator, Bunin was also a painter in words, with a strong sense of colour and a sharp eye for people and things. That was why he preferred to remain on the surface of what he saw, without indulging in psychological dissections. Even at his best he was evocative rather than analytical. His descriptions of Russian and Ukranian scenery were particularly good. And so were his renderings of exotic landscapes. For he was a great traveller, familiar with North Africa, Ceylon, Egypt, Palestine and Turkey, which figure in a number of his sketches and stories.

Always in love with the beauty of the world, he also loved the variety of life, but without closing his eyes to what was negative and evil. A strong pes-simism permeates his first novel, *The Village*. Bunin gave in it a picture of Russian life in the province he knew best—the province of his birth. He makes us acquainted with some striking characters, two of whom, the brothers Tikhon and Kuz'ma Krasnov, are in the centre of all events. Tikhon is a keeper of a pub, a ruthless speculator and *kulák*. His brother Kuz'ma, on the other hand, represents a more sympathetic side of the people. He is something of a Tolstoyan, a restless seeker for truth and justice, and even a bit of a self-taught poet *à la* Kol'tsov. But there was little to be done or to sympathise with in a village shortly before, during and immediately after the disturbing year of 1905. The picture we witness is one of poverty, savagery and muddle. Nor was the little country town nearby better off, although it was situated in the very heart of the fertile black-loam soil three feet deep. 'The town was famous throughout all Russia as a grain mart—but not more than a hundred persons in the whole town ate their fill of the grain. And the Fair? Beggars, idiots, blind men, cripples and such monstrosities as made one frightened and sick at the stomach to behold.'[2]

The compact and beautifully told *Sukhodól* is a longer short story rather than a novel. It is an absorbing account of Bunin's ancestral manor: about what happened to it and in it during the period of its going to rack and ruin—the fate of so many other manors of the impoverished landed gentry. Remem-bering this process, the author exclaims: 'And we wondered, how suddenly

1. Translated by E. M. Walton in *Representative Russian Stories* (Westhouse).
2. Translated by Isabel Hapgood. *Op. cit.*

it came! Is it possible, we thought, that its cause was the abolition of serfdom and the ties binding the serf and the squire? Incomprehensible seemed the very pace with which the old nests of gentlefolk were disappearing from the face of the earth.' In their early youth Bunin and his sister revisited the manor only to witness its decay. They found it in the charge of their dotty old aunt and her equally dotty old former serf-maid, Natalia, a foster-sister of Bunin's father. And it was Natalia who in a wistful manner told the two young visitors of the once prosperous and varied life of which nothing was left but remembrance. Gorky called *Sukhodól* a Requiem, and he was right. It is a Requiem of the old manor life, and largely also of manor literature.

Of the many narratives, long and short, written by Bunin, *The Gentleman from San Francisco* is a masterpiece which brought him international reputation. It is also one of his most sober and detached stories behind whose merciless realism there is yet a subtle symbolic meaning. Its hero is an American tycoon, a financial maniac in fact, who until his fifty-eighth year had slaved without ceasing only in order to accumulate enough money to reach the level of those financial barons 'whom he had taken as his ideals.' Once he had succeeded in this, he decided to set out with his wife and daughter for Europe where he intended to spend some two years of pleasure. The boat on which they travelled to Naples was, with all its pretensions, only for the exclusive financial and social élite. Everything was arranged so as to make the journey as pleasant as possible. The dinner, for instance,

> lasted two whole hours, to be followed by dancing in the ball-room, whence men, including of course the Gentleman from San Francisco, proceeded to the bar; there, with their feet cocked up on the tables, they settled the destinies of nations in the course of their political and stock-exchange conversations, smoking meanwhile Havana cigars and drinking liqueurs till they were crimson in the face, waited on all the time by negroes in red jackets with eyes like peeled, hard-boiled eggs.[1]

The first stop of the Gentleman from San Francisco, of his spouse and daughter, was in a luxurious hotel at Capri where the same round of expensive shams continued. But one evening, while at dinner, he suddenly had a stroke, collapsed and died. The proprietor of the hotel was furious that such a death could not be concealed from the carousing guests. But the important thing was to get rid of the body as quickly as possible by sending it to Naples. And since at Capri no ready coffin was available, the body was sent away in a large soda-water container at night, when the tourists were fast asleep.

> Having been subject to many humiliations, much human neglect, after a week's wandering from one warehouse to another, it was carried at last on to the same renowned vessel which so short a time ago, and with such honour, had borne him living to the Old World. But now he was to be hidden far from the knowledge of the voyagers. Closed in a tar-coated coffin, he was lowered deep into the vessel's dark hold.[1]

1. *The Gentleman from San Francisco and Other Stories.* Translated by D. H. Lawrence, S. S. Koteliansky and Leonard Woolf (Hogarth).

3

The hero of this unemotional story can be interpreted as a kind of Everyman representing that large portion of humans whose senseless life, sacrificed to material things, leads to an equally senseless death. Incidentally, *The Gentleman from San Francisco* was one of the last stories published by Bunin before he left Russia. As for his works written abroad, *Mitya's Love* narrates the tragedy of a young student who is profoundly in love with a girl (Katya) working for a theatrical career—the dream of her life. The student's love is fully reciprocated, or so he thinks. But the director of the theatrical school where Katya is being trained is a notorious debauchee who chooses his victims from among the girl students. Every summer he takes one of them with him to the south of Russia or abroad in order to have an enjoyable holiday. His usual bait is the promise of a brilliant theatrical career which, as a rule, is too tempting to be resisted. Mitya leaves at the beginning of the summer for his parents' country house. He languishes for his sweetheart's promised letters, but in vain. Exasperated by it all, he has an affair with a married peasant woman, when—at last— he receives a brief note from Katya. 'I have cast my lot: I am leaving—you know with whom. . . . You are sensitive, you are intelligent, you will understand me and yourself! Do not write to me a word, it's useless.' The result of such a letter can be guessed.

The background of this short novel is Moscow, and a country estate before 1914. It abounds in descriptive passages and gives the impression of being partly autobiographical—in the way *Werthers Leiden* was autobiographical of Goethe: a personal love tragedy sublimated by art. Bunin's *Arsenyev's Life*, on the other hand, is frankly autobiographical. It deals with the author's own development until he was twenty. His reminiscences of the years of childhood in the atmosphere of a country manor are full of that poetic flavour which is inseparable from the early phase of one's existence. Then we witness his work at the Grammar School, his first literary efforts, wanderings in Russia, journalism at Oryol, and finally his pathetic love affair with Lika which ended with Lika's death.

As a writer of stories Bunin was among the best after Chekhov's death. His excellent episodic sketches were also much relished by his readers. And as for the erotic motifs in such a collection as his *Dark Avenues* (*Tyómnye alléi*), one of the last books he wrote, they are treated with tact and that reserve which does not allow him to gloat over them in the manner of an Artsybashev. Yet when all is said and done, the world of Bunin is still the world of the pre-1917 days. It found in his works one of its last nostalgic echoes.

4

Bunin's friend, Alexander Kuprin (1870–1938) was another conspicuous writer of the same period, but of a different kind and origin. His father (a minor civil servant, married to a Tartar woman) died when his son was an infant. As a boy Kuprin was sent to the Cadet School in Moscow and on finishing it became an ensign in the army. Disgusted with the bullying methods typical of tsarist officers, he left the army in 1893 and embarked upon a precarious and erratic existence. He passed from one employment to the other, all of them equally casual. For a while he was a down-at-heel provincial actor, but finally decided to adopt writing as his vocation. This was a lucky choice. For even some early products of his pen were striking enough to draw the attention of Gorky, Chekhov and Bunin, all of whom became his friends and even admirers. What helped him most of all was, however, the verdict of Leo Tolstoy who, on reading one of Kuprin's stories, paid a public compliment to its author.

Kuprin, too, adhered in his narratives to the good old tradition. But, unlike Bunin, he never acquired a solid literary culture. Still, his talent was big and robust enough to help him out even in some of those cases when his taste could not be quite relied upon. He was at his best as a straightforward matter-of-fact observer who organised his material without any embellishments. What appealed to him was the broad and raw kind of life, wherever he found it. He had a particularly sharp eye for socially fluid types and for the lower class ambient in general. Both play an important part in his stories. This is how one of them—called *Pirate*—begins:

> He went by the name of the 'beggar with the dog'. No more details about him—his life, his family or his thoughts, were known to anyone; but then no one took any interest in him, anyway. He was a tall thin old man with shaggy grey hair and with the face of a confirmed solitary drinker. His shaking form was clad in rags and impregnated through and through with the smell of spirits and beggars' vaults. When, with his timid step, he entered some low-class pothouse with his brown half-blind dog crawling behind him, cringeing with fear and its tail between its legs, he was recognised at once by the habitués. 'Oh, there's the chap with the dog!'[1]

Kuprin is at his best when he is factual, that is describing what he himself has seen or gone through. Since he had once been a cadet and a minor officer, military motifs inevitably play a considerable part in his writings. Yet his reminiscences of the tsarist army were not to the latter's credit. Nor had he any intention to hide its brutal, humiliating aspects. His first major work, *The Duel* (1905), which appeared in a *Znánie* miscellany, was exclusively about the army. Owing to his first-hand knowledge of both officers and soldiers, the characteristics recorded by him were authentic. And the frankness with which he paraded all sorts of negative features of military service made this novel the more topical because of the Russian defeats at that time in the Far East.

Kuprin excelled in stories of adventure for adventure's sake, provided they smacked of a raw and robust existence. He felt a certain affinity with Jack London who in those days was most popular with Russian readers. He admired Rudyard Kipling in spite of Kipling's imperialistic anti-Russian utterances. Kuprin was able to keep the reader's attention whenever he dealt with such themes as are tackled in *The River of Life, Gambrinus*, the grim *Horse-thieves*, or

1. Translated by D. Binyon in *Representative Russian Stories. Op. cit.*

the thrilling detective story, *Lieutenant-Captain Rýbnikov* (1906). This story is about a Japanese spy who, during the War, operated in St Petersburg and was so well disguised that everybody took him for a somewhat rough Siberian officer on leave, until one night he inadvertently disclosed his identity while sleeping with a prostitute. The story is told in a style and language adequate to the subject-matter.

Different but well told, is his *Bracelet of Garnets* (*Granátovy braslét*, 1911), although the motif of a poor clerk hopelessly in love with a society beauty already looked somewhat trite in those days. His long drawn-out narrative *Ditch* (*Yáma*), about the life of prostitutes and their customers in a brothel is however, disappointing. This naturalistic novel is not devoid of good portraits and sarcastic passages; but on the whole it has a didactic and at times even sentimental undercurrent. Nor is it well constructed. The author himself realised this when referring to it as being 'pale, crumpled, chaotic, cold, and justly blamed by the critics'.

Kuprin, who in 1919 emigrated to western Europe, had to put up with hard times abroad. Unlike Bunin he failed, though, to produce any major or significant writings in his voluntary exile. Frustrated and vainly trying to find a solace in drink, he came to terms with the Soviets and returned—rather ill—to Russia shortly before his death in 1938.

CHAPTER TWENTY-TWO

The Modernist wave

I

One of the striking features of Russian literature is its alternate succession of poetry and prose. The Pushkin period had been essentially one of poetry, and of very good poetry at that. Then, from the late 1840s until the beginning of the eighties, monumental prose prevailed. But in the early 1890s a number of gifted men started a wave of modernist poetry which, at its best, compared well with Western European poetry of the same period and type. At that time in Russia the transition to a capitalist-industrial economy was marked by the growth of the bourgeois middle-class whose materialistic outlook differed widely from that of the less practical intelligentsia. The 'superfluous' intellectuals were now deprived even of an outlet in populism, since after the assassination of tsar Alexander II, any conspicuous activity of this sort was out of the question. Factories and investments were growing at a rapid pace, while political reactionaries, headed by Pobedonostsev, were doing all they could to stifle any freedom of thought or action.

It was in an atmosphere such as this that a number of intellectuals sought outlets for escape in philosophic-religious speculations, in Tolstoyanism, or else in such modernist literary (notably poetic) activities as were already fashionable in the West. At the beginning of the 1890s a revival of interest in Dostoevsky also took place. Vasily Rozanov's remarkable study of Dostoevsky's mind and work, *The Legend of the Grand Inquisitor* (*Legénda o velíkom inkvizítore*), came out in 1890. In the same year was published an apology for individualism, *In the Light of Conscience* (*Pri svéte sóvesti*)—an enquiring work by the poet N. Minsky (N. M. Vilenkin, 1855–1937). It was followed, three years later, by Merezhkovsky's book of essays, dealing with the causes of the decline in contemporary Russian literature,[1] while his important study, *Tolstoy and Dostoevsky*, appeared at the turn of the century. Among subsequent pioneers of new thoughts and currents was Lev Shestov (L. Schwartzmann, 1866–1938), whose writings about Dostoevsky, Nietzsche, Tolstoy, etc. provided valuable contributions to the mental and spiritual ferment of the period.

As for works of *belles-lettres*, Merezhkovsky's *Julian the Apostate*—the first part of his questing trilogy under the general title of *Christ and Antichrist* —was published in 1896. It was followed by *The Gods Resurrected* (about Leonardo da Vinci), and *Peter and Alexis*. The trilogy is written in the spirit of

1. *O prichínakh upádka* (*About the Causes of Decay*).

Ibsen's idea of the 'third kingdom',[1] according to which Christianity and Paganism would be finally reconciled in a new kind of consciousness. But whatever the intention of this trilogy, artistically it was over-schematic and, with its abundance of facts, uninspiring. However, a truly impressive product of that period was the rich crop of modernist poetry which (together with its best prose works, beginning with Chekhov's stories) was remarkable enough to deserve the name of the Silver Age of Russian literature.

2

The early Russian modernists found their stimuli in Western, especially French and Belgian poets, from Baudelaire, Verlaine and Mallarmé to Verhaeren and Maeterlinck. In France the 'decadent' poets were above all rebels against the old poetic conventions and traditions. They aimed not only at new poetic forms and techniques, but also at new contents within the strict limits of art. In this respect Baudelaire, in his *Les fleurs du Mal*, enlarged the diapason of modern poetry more than any of his contemporaries. Exploring the realms of vice, depravity and evil in terms of art, he introduced into his poems all sorts of morbid, sadistic and demoniac motifs. These were soon to infect the modern Parnassus whose adepts were only too prone to indulge in various cults: from the cult of aestheticism with its art for art's sake to the cult of the fleeting moment, of amoral erotomania, of satanism, or even of death and decay. All this was often rendered by means of ingenious new images, new rhythms, nuances and allusions. Poetry became, moreover, a confession through which an author tried to voice and assert all that was connected with his modern self. Hence its intransigent individualism, or rather egotism, strongly influenced also by the philosophy of Nietzsche.

The Russian modernists of the 1890s followed the French lead; but to the above-mentioned influences those of Edgar Allan Poe and Oscar Wilde should be added, as well as some of their own older poets from whom they took over certain elements for their own use: Tyutchev, Fet and Polonsky.

Of the pioneers of Russian modernism, one of the most gifted, though in the classical garb, was Innokenty Annensky (1856–1909): a highly cultured poet and dramatist, imbued with pessimism and with that feeling of isolation which found shelter in so many escapist 'ivory towers', whether in Russia or in the West. It is significant, though, that the first modernist wave in Russia, with its 'decadent' features, actually made its debut as Symbolism. In 1892 Merezhkovsky himself published (after his scarcely original civic verses) a book of poems bearing the title of *Symbols* (*Símvoly*). At the same time three outstanding 'decadent' poets came to the fore: Konstantin Balmont, Valery Bryusov, and Merezhkovsky's wife Zinaida Hippius.

Konstantin Balmont (1867–1941) was above all an accomplished virtuoso of verbal music. Even his two early books of verse (published in 1890 and 1892) were, with his cult of the moment and of exuberant life, poetry for music's

---

1. Expressed in the drama *Emperor and Galilean*.

sake. Their wealth of sound, rhythm and alliterations was often quite astounding. Balmont certainly wrote his verses according to Verlaine's injunction, '*de la musique avant toute chose*'; but this very virtuosity proved to be a weakness, making him write poem after poem even when he had not much to say. His temperament often kept his innate love of life vibrating to the full; but in order to be up to date he too wrote of sin, crime and perversion. Incidentally, he was a voluminous translator. He translated (not without flaws) the whole of Shelly's poetic work, a fair amount of Whitman and Edgar Allan Poe. His Russian version of Poe's *The Raven* is unexpectedly good.

Totally different from Balmont was his rival, Valery Bryusov (1873–1924), although he, too, understood symbolism in the French sense : as a literary—and purely literary—current without any social, philosophic, religious or mystical connotations.[1] He adored Verlaine (some of whose poems he translated), but he was particularly close to Baudelaire in his horror of the ugly and commonplace in life, and in his fascination with sin and evil. Whether this was genuine or a mere fashionable pose, he knew how to express it in disciplined and polished verses. Persistent and provocative, he made himself notorious by his first issue of *Russian Symbolists* (*Rússkie simvolísty*), with its 'scandalous' contents, in 1894. Before long he published another two booklets under the same title, in which he gathered together the poems of a number of young followers of modernism after the Western pattern. Yet he himself achieved fame by such collections of his own as *Urbi et orbi* (1903) and *Stéphanos* (*Venók, The Wreath*, 1906). In both he asserted himself as an ambitious, complex, and technically very competent modern poet. In contrast to Balmont, he showed in his poetic creations an almost academic economy. He did not mind 'shocking the bourgeois,' especially when dealing with erotic motifs. Yet even in his early phases he also translated much of Verhaeren, thus introducing Verhaeren's urban motifs (as well as *vers libre*) into Russian modernism. He was, moreover, one of the founders of the publishing firm 'Scorpio' (Skorpion) and of the important symbolist periodical *The Balance* (*Vesý*, 1904–1909)[2] which he himself edited.

As for Zinaida Hippius (1869–1927), she was a poet by God's grace. As a child of her age, she was endowed with an intensely tormented or self-tormented, but always maliciously lively and searching, mind. She found an ade-

---

1. This did not prevent him from joining, after 1917, the Bolshevik regime and adopting for his poems civic themes as well.

2. It should be pointed out that none of the Russian modernist periodicals was long-lived. *The World of Art* (*Mir iskússtva*), with which Diaghilev was connected, existed for some five years (1899–1904). The *Golden Fleece* (*Zolotóe runó*), a periodical favoured by the modernists in Moscow (where there was a group of modernist poets and writers calling themselves Argonauts), ceased publication in 1906—after four years of existence Merezhkovsky's religious-philosophic and neo-Christian periodical, *The New Path* (*Nóvy put'*), had an even shorter span of life : 1903–4. A notable exception was Bryusov's *Vesy* which came to a voluntary end in 1909, after Bryusov had joined *The Russian Thought* (*Rússkaya mysl'*), edited by Peter Struve. Under Bryusov *Vesy* was the best informed and highly influential literary periodical. It counted among its foreign contributors such men as Rémy de Gourmont, René Ghil, Verhaeren, Charles van Lerberghe and Maeterlinck. In 1909 *Vesy* was replaced by *Apollo* (*Apollón*) which, under the direction of the poet Gumilyov, soon deviated from Symbolism and under its 'acmeist' label even took a hostile attitude towards it. *Apollo* came to an end in 1917.

quate expression for it in her poems, short stories, and a number of essays. Under the pseudonym of Anton Krainy she also exercised (in several directions) her biting critical talent—to the exasperation of a large number of her victims.

While omitting many a less important member of the first generation of Russian modernist poets, it would be impossible to bypass such a talented decadent *à la* Baudelaire as Fyodor Sologub (F. Teternikov, 1863–1927). Although of humble origin (his father was a shoemaker), he became one of the most conspicuous Russian literary figures in poetry and prose of that period. What strikes one in Sologub's work as a whole is his innate fear of life; not so much of life itself as of its deceptions, vulgarity, ugliness and evil without end. As a neo-romantic *par excellence* he reacted against it in two ways, one of which involved a revenge upon life, and the other an escape into the 'artificial para-dise' of his dreams. Firstly, he was anxious to show up all the worst and most vulgar aspects of life simply in order to justify his non-acceptance of existence. Secondly, however, he sought a shelter from life in aesthetic sanctuaries pro-vided by his own fancy. His fear and world-weariness made him, moreover, long for a final deliverance from it all. This was why he celebrated death in a number of his exquisite poems. Sologub was a sensitive and sophisticated 'decadent' who preferred poetic reticence, with its delicate shades and nuances, to any glaring colours. He, too, called himself a symbolist; and this at a time when the second generation of Russian symbolists (differing from the one to which he belonged) was in the ascendant. But before dealing with these it might be helpful to mention a few significant novels of the period: those of Fyodor Sologub, for instance, and *The Fiery Angel* (*Ógnenny ángel*) by Valery Bryusov.

3

Sologub's prose is remarkable not only for its quietly ornate style, but also for the way in which the author keeps the reader's attention alive. Like Gogol, by whose mental attitude he was strongly influenced, he seemed to be convinced that evil and vulgarity (he more or less identified the two) were the indelible essence of existence itself. Hence his fatalism on the one hand, and the relish with which he was anxious to disclose and expose the disgusting aspects of reality on the other. But this is how a romantic aesthete usually takes revenge upon life for its being what it is.

Even his first novel, *Heavy Dreams* (*Tyazhólye sny*), begun in 1883 and com-pleted eleven years later, is typical in this respect. Having been for years em-ployed as a schoolmaster in a sleepy provincial town, he was able to describe to perfection all the futility and frustrations of an intelligent young man living in such paralysing surroundings. The same provincial town was taken up by him in his principal novel, *The Petty Demon* (*Melky bes*). This time, too, the main hero, Peredonov, is a schoolmaster teaching in the local Grammar School. But he suffers from progressive persecution mania. He is, moreover, teased and tortured by the hallucinations of a tiny demon who drives him to pathologic fits in one of which he commits murder. The semi-mad schoolmaster is at the same time a symbol of all the vulgarity and evil which Sologub, with his pessimistic Baudelairean outlook, felt to be at the very core of life. This is how he defines Peredonov as a type:

> His feelings were dull and his consciousness was a corrupting and deadening apparatus. All that reached his consciousness became transformed into abomination and filth. All objects revealed their imperfections to him, and their imperfections gave him pleasure. When he walked past an erect and clean column, he had a desire to make it crooked and to bespatter it with filth. He laughed with joy when something was being besmirched in his presence. He detested very clean schoolboys and persecuted them. He called them the skin scrubbers. He comprehended the slovenly ones more easily. There were neither beloved objects for him, nor beloved people—and this made it possible for nature to act upon his feelings one-sidedly, as an irritant. The same was true of his meetings with people. Especially with strangers and new acquaintances, to whom it was not possible to be impolite. Happiness for him was to do nothing and, shutting himself in from the world, to gratify his belly.[1]

The philistine provincial town in which he lived, with its atmosphere of a boredom, gossip, slander, and drunken bouts, was a suitable emporium for a character of this kind. Yet as a relief Sologub conjured up an aesthetic-erotic contrast in which beauty of the human body, the joy of nakedness and youth, prevail—even though the spontaneous erotic play between Ludmila and the schoolboy Pyl'nikov is not devoid of a half-conscious perverse flavour. The same God-forsaken town is used as the background for one of Sologub's further novels, *The Created Legend* (*Tvorímaya legénda*, 1908–12), which comprises three parts. This is an ambitious and at the same time rather equivocal work. Its main character, Trirodov, is also a teacher: a former University lecturer who has established outside the town a school of his own with a colony of children educated by him in an ultra-Rousseauesque atmosphere of freedom, beauty and happiness.

The first part of this trilogy, with all its symbolic touches, is realistic. But the author says at the beginning of the novel: 'I take a fragment of life, rough and miserable life, and create out of it a delightful legend, because I am a poet.' And he is as good as his word. If the first part of this 'Legend' is a picture of stark reality, its second part is fantastic, with the Queen Ortruda presiding over an imaginary 'Kingdom of United Isles' somewhere in the Mediterranean. And in the third fanciful part Trirodov himself becomes the ruler of that kingdom. The novel thus turns into an escapist neo-romantic 'ivory tower', but it is well told and holds the reader's interest to the end. The same is true of Sologub's short stories, many of which are, with all their mannerisms, among the best of that period. Finally, behind the externally simple garb of his poetry there is a great deal of inner complexity which is bound to escape a superficial reader. His plays are of lesser importance. And his last novel, *The Snake*

1. Translated by John Cournos and Richard Aldington (Secker, 1916).

Charmer (*Zaklinátel'nitsa zmey*), published (1922) under the Soviets, is definitely weak.

4

Sologub is neglected or even ignored in Soviet Russia; but there can be no doubt of the part he had played both as poet and prose-writer during the 'decadent' spell of Russian modernism. His *Little Demon* remains one of the great novels, whatever his critics may say.[1] A similar verdict upon Bryusov's novel, *The Fiery Angel*, is not likely to be unanimous, for the very reason that its excellence is of a different kind. It has the garb of an historical novel; but the events taking place in fifteenth century Germany, as here described, are only a pretext for the irrational, especially the occult and satanic practices of the witch-hunting period of German history. These had proved attractive not only to old romantics, but also to many a modernist, including Bryusov himself who had made an extensive study of the subject.

Deliberately stylised like a fifteenth century manuscript, *The Fiery Angel* is composed in detached and sober but very readable prose, testifying to Bryusov's competence and erudition in occult matters. In the rather long-winded title (according to the fashion of those days) the supposed recorder of the events acknowledges that this is

> A True Story in which is related of the Devil not once but often appearing in the image of a Spirit of Light to a Maiden and seducing her to Various Many Sinful Deeds, of Ungodly Practices of Magic, Alchemy, Astrology, the Cabalistical Sciences and Necromancy, of the Trial of the Said Maiden under the Presidency of his Eminence the Archbishop of Trier, as well as of Encounters and Discourses with the Knight and thrice Doctor Agrippa von Nettesheim, and with Doctor Faustus, composed by an Eyewitness.

The title thus gives away the gist of the narrative whose heroine, Renata, suffers from sexual and religious hysteria—a predicament which leads her to the witches' Sabbath (described in detail), and finally to the convent of Saint Ulf, where she infects and corrupts most of the nuns. This is what the 'Eyewitness' has to say about the collective possession of those nuns during the Archbishop's vain endeavours to exorcise Renata's demon :

> Wherever the eye could reach, could be seen only women possessed by demons, and they ran about the chapel, in a frenzy, gesticulating, striking themselves on the breasts, waving their arms, preaching; or rolled about on the ground, singly, or in couples, twisting in convulsions, pressing each other in embraces, kissing each other in a frenzy of passion or, biting each other like wild beasts; or sat fast on the spot furiously distorting their features in grimaces, rolling out or in their eyes, thrusting out their tongues,

1. Its hero Peredonov has become a sobriquet, like some of Gogol's characters, Goncharov's Oblomov, or Saltykov-Shchedrin's Yudushka.

roaring with laughter, and then becoming suddenly silent, or suddenly falling backwards, striking their skulls against the stones of the floor; some of them screamed, others laughed, a third group cursed, a fourth blasphemed, a fifth chanted; yet others hissed like snakes, or barked like dogs, or grunted like swine;—it was like hell, more terrible than that which appeared before the eyes of Dante Alighieri.[1]

The curious point about this novel is that despite its detachment and objectivity, it conceals, in its own way, a personal feud between Bryusov and the poet Andrey Bely for the love of Nina Petrovskaya—an excitable beauty and a minor writer courted by both. The narrator, Rupprecht, is Bryusov himself, while Count Henry, his rival for Renata, bears certain features of Bely— one of the leaders of the second generation of Russian symbolists whose aims differed in more respects than one from those represented, say, by the early Russian moderns influenced by France.

5

What mattered to such symbolist poets as Andrey Bely, Alexander Blok and Vyacheslav Ivanov, was their refusal to put up with any blind-alleys in the Sologub style, whether aesthetic or otherwise. Close to Russian traditions and influenced by German idealistic philosophy, they even disclaimed any strong French influences. In the words of Andrey Bely,

> Russian symbolism is both deeper and more rooted. Its best representatives have a blood-link with our own literature and poetry. Dostoevsky, Gogol and Chekhov dispute their impact with Nietzsche, Ibsen and Hamsun. Fet, Lermontov, Baratynsky, Tyutchev have had a greater influence upon us than Baudelaire, Verlaine, Maeterlinck, Rodenbach and Verhaeren.

The members of this second generation were also passionate seekers— seekers for something in the name of which it might be worth living and creating. In these efforts they found a powerful stimulus in the philosopher and poet Vladimir Solovyov (1853–1900)—the spiritual father of what might be called Russian symbolism.

Solovyov was the most conspicuous figure in the religious-philosophic thought in Russia during the second half of the nineteenth century. But he was also a poet in his own right. His purpose was to work out an active synthesis of philosophy, religion, the beauty of creative art, and life. He believed in a regeneration of man and mankind through Love in a religious sense and through that fullness of existence which would exclude chaos and nihilism. Thoroughly versed in German romantic philosophy, in Plato, Gnosticism and Christian mysticism, he conceived the image of the divine Sophia as the feminine hypostasis of the deity or even as the eternally living World Soul. This made him all the firmer in his belief that 'all transient things are but symbols'—symbols of

1. Translated by Ivor Montagu and Sergei Nalbandov (Humphrey Toulmin, Caym Press, 1930).

deeper realities in the sense of Goethe's dictum in *Faust*: *Alles Vergängliche ist ein Gleichnis*. As Solovyov himself put it in one of his poems:

> All that about us lies
> is but the shade, the mirrored image
> of things not seen by eyes.[1]

Unable, as well as unwilling, to regard existence as something devoid of transcendence, he lived his own life as a thinker, a visionary and a poet. It was in the capacity of all three that he influenced the next generation of Russian symbolists to the extent of making them imbue their art with a *Weltanschauung*, or rather with the idea of a new religious consciousness, a new conception and way of life, while Bryusov still insisted that symbolism was only a particular school of poetry, and nothing more. A certain link with this group was formed by Merezhkovsky who, in 1902, started at St Petersburg the Religious-Philosophic Society attended by such 'God-seekers' as Sergey Bulgakov, Nikolai Berdyayev, Dmitry Filosofov, and the quasi-mystical sensualist Vasily Rozanov. These men were not poets, but they made their own contributions to Russian thought and literature as essayists and explorers of the deeper aspects or problems of modern man and life. It can be said that some of those aspects also found poetic expression in the works of the three poets mentioned at the beginning of the chapter. And since Vyacheslav Ivanov (1866–1949) was considerably older than the other two, we should perhaps begin with him.

6

Vyacheslav Ivanov joined the group of Russian symbolists rather late. His first collection of poems, *The Pilot Stars* (*Kórmchie Zvyózdy*) appeared in 1903 and made him famous overnight. Before this he had been a serious scholar, a pupil of Momsen and a specialist in classical history. As a poet, however, he was soon nicknamed Vyacheslav the Magnificent—mainly on account of his decorative style, reminiscent at times of the magnificence of Derzhavin. Like Blok and Bely, he too looked upon symbolism as a *Weltanschauung* and a way of life: that is as an antithesis of any destructive decadence.

Following in the steps of Solovyov, Vyacheslav Ivanov saw in the actual world only a veil of the hidden deeper realities. It was he who promulgated the slogan: *A realibus ad realiora* (From the real to the more real), aiming at a comprehension of the inner essence of things. Symbolism thus postulated an art modified and transformed by living experience as a result of man's new consciousness and vision. Its tendency was to unite poetry, philosophy and religion. According to Ivanov, art should by no means be separated from religion, since its main task is to create such beauty as would be able to transfigure life in a spiritual sense. Individual independence and self-realisation also played their role in all this. Together with a minor poet (George Chulkov), Ivanov even preached for a while a peculiar gospel of 'mystical anarchism', that is, absolute

1. Translated by R. M. Hewitt. *Op. cit.*

freedom of personality, and union with society and mankind through his conception of Eros or Love.[1] Although he had a number of disputes with other poets, especially with Bely, Ivanov's St Petersburg flat, known as the Tower (*báshnya*, on the seventh floor of a house facing the old Potyomkin palace, subsequently the Russian Parliament or Duma) became popular on account of its noisy but stimulating 'Ivanov Wednesdays'. It was here that for years modernist writers and poets gathered every Wednesday in order to discuss new literary products and currents.

Apart from poetry, Vyacheslav Ivanov had numerous essays and studies to his credit. Among these were a book on Dostoevsky and a complex investigation of Dionysus and the Dionysian cult among the ancients. In 1924 he emigrated to Italy where he eventually adopted Roman-Catholicism. Having witnessed the horrors of the Second World War, he died in a Catholic monastery at the age of eighty-three.

Ivanov's conversion to Roman-Catholicism was a proof that, with all its ingenious formulae, the symbolist movement, even as devised by such seekers as Bely, Blok, and Ivanov himself, was inadequate in its efforts to solve the riddle of man and life, whether in terms of art or otherwise. Overwhelmed by the intricacy of the problems themselves, Ivanov eventually preferred a ready-made emergency exit to the uncertainties a contemporary seeker of his stature had to face. Nor were the paths taken by Bely and Blok straight or smooth in this respect.

7

Andrey Bely (Boris Bugayev, 1880–1934) gives the impression of one of those personalities who are inwardly too rich and at the same time much too divided and restless to be able entirely to co-ordinate their talents, interests and propensities. He was not only a poet, but also a novelist, a thinker, an able theoretician of literature, a prolific essayist and critic, a virulent debater, and an author of excellent memoirs and travel sketches. With all this he remained an indefatigable seeker and experimenter, whether in matters of spirit, of literature, or of life as a whole. Having grown up in a cultured atmosphere (his father was professor of mathematics at Moscow University), he met, as an adolescent, Vladimir Solovyov whose nephew, the modernist poet Sergei Solovyov, became his life-long friend.

One of the prominent features of Bely the writer was his feeling of the potentialities latent in his mother tongue. He not only made ample use of its rhythmical wealth, but was responsible for a series of innovations in the realm of neologisms and 'orchestrations of sound'. His very debut, *The Northern Symphony* (*Sévernaya simfóniya*, written in 1900 and printed in 1902) was an example of highly rhythmical poetic prose. So were his further three Symphonies, the last of which, *The Goblet of Blizzards* (*Kúbok metéley*) appeared in

---

1. Ivanov's idea of Eros was not devoid of secret erotomania (under the cover of ancient Greece).

1908. Modelled on Gogol's ornate prose, they are full of stylistic extravagances and romantic reminiscences, of despondency, humour and satire.

In the meantime he published also his first collection of verse *Gold in Azure* (*Zóloto v lazúri*, 1904)—an apotheosis of his joy in the beauty of the world with its azure air and sky, its amber-red gold of sunsets, as well as its mountain heights full of great longings and expectations. But he did not have to wait long for disappointments. His second book of poems, which is technically his best, is called *Ashes* (*Pépel*, 1908). Reflecting Bely's mood after the abortive revolution of 1906, it contains some of his gloomiest verses about Russia and the conditions he saw. 'O Russia, whither shall I flee from hunger, pest and drunkards!' But evidently there was no escape. And so his third book of poems bears the title *The Urn* (*Úrna*, 1909). It is a book of resignation, of his buried hopes and love, as well as of his own buried self which he yet expects to awaken to true life once again.[1] In all these poems Bely continued his experiments with words, rhythms and rhymes. He subdued the traditional regular metre to the rhythm—one of the many changes achieved by the symbolists. The symbolist conception of the world, with its 'correspondence' between man's soul or spirit on the one hand, and the universe on the other, was bound to lead not only to new poetic images but also to new forms, to the breaking-up of old prosody. A great experimenter with verse and prose, Bely actually became a pioneer of the 'formalist' school represented in early Soviet litearture by Zhirmunsky, Tynyanov, Shklovsky and a few others.

During those years he continued having repeated quarrels and reconciliations even with his best friends, especially with Blok, and mostly for ideological reasons. After close contact with Ivanov, Bely made it clear enough that he utterly disapproved of the latter's 'mystical anarchism' as well as of his peculiar idea of the collective or universal Eros which struck him as coming dangerously close to universal sensuality. On the other hand, he stubbornly shared with Blok and Ivanov the conviction that Symbolism was something more than just a new literary school. A symbol, as Bely understood it, should be a unity of form and contents in individual experience deepened to a religious-philosophic act. This was how he hoped to combine art with theurgy and to make symbolism pass into the higher forms of consciousness and life without ceasing to be art. In 1910 the Moscow firm Musaget issued Bely's *Symbolism*—a thick volume in which he put forward (not without an impact of neo-Kantian philosophy) all the main tenets of the symbolist current in his own interpretation. But those years were responsible also for Bely's two novels, *The Silver Dove* (*Serébryany Gólub'*) and *Petersburg*, the quality of which is worth exploring.

8

The Silver Dove was first published in Bryusov's periodical *The Balance* during 1909, when Bryusov had already left it. A year later it appeared in book form

---

1.   After these three books of poetry Bely concentrated mainly on prose. Among his later poems his *First Meeting* (*Pérvaya vstrécha*, 1921), partly inspired by Vladimir Solovyov's poem *Three Meetings*, is full of freshness and spontaneity.

and became a literary event of the season. Told in vivid and ornate prose (very reminiscent of Gogol at times) the novel has a familiar theme: the problem of the intelligentsia and the people, but in a quite original form. Its hero, the young intellectual and poet Daryalsky (in some respects an *alter ego* of Bely himself) is spending his summer vacation in the countryside so as to be near his fiancée Katya who lives with her aunt in an old manor house. The remote district contains a representative collection of peasants, artisans, and small shopkeepers both in the village and the neighbouring little town.

Anxious to get as close to 'the people' as possible, Daryalsky becomes emotionally entangled with the peasant woman Matryona, the coarse and lewd wife of the local carpenter. She and her husband are, however, members of a secret sect calling itself 'Doves' and combining a pseudo-mystical obsession with debauchery, as well as with certain practices reminiscent of dark Asia.[1] Enslaved by Matryona's overwhelming sensuality, Daryalsky deserts his fiancée, joins the sect and even takes part in its weird revels, while working in the carpenter's workshop. But this kind of nearness to the 'people', far from solving any of his problems, only increases his own inner and outer confusion. He begins to realise that the sect is not Russia, but some horrid 'Eastern abyss threatening Russia' and so decides to abandon the Doves. But they already suspect him of treason and callously murder him.

The westernised intellectual Daryalsky perished in the 'Eastern Abyss' which threatened to undermine the irrational foundations of Russia. He himself made the comment that in contact with such a Russia any rational knowledge of books 'turns into dust, and life itself gets burnt out. On the day when the West is grafted onto Russia, it will be seized by a universal conflagration; everything that can be burnt will be burnt out, because only from the ashes caused by death will there soar out the heavenly spirit: The Fire-Bird.'[2] Bely had actually intended to write a trilogy of novels under the general title 'East and West'. But he never went beyond the second novel, *Petersburg* (1912), in which there is, however, no sign of such a miraculous Fire-Bird, and still less of the 'heavenly spirit'. On the contrary, the author makes us watch the Petersburg of chaos and disorder during the restless period of 1905. It is the 'abstract' city of regular geometrical prospects, streets and cubes inhabited by beings who are more like phantoms supervised, as it were, by the statue of Peter the Great: the demoniac Bronze Horseman who 'has been galloping through the ages of time and, reaching the present moment, has completed a cycle'.

The two principal characters, the mighty Senator Apollon Ableukhov and his son Nikolai are of distant Tartar (Eastern) origin. The young, westernised Ableukhov is connected with a band of terrorists, who ask him to kill his own reactionary father. He does not hesitate to say yes, since the two are far from being on affectionate terms. 'Whenever father and son came into contact with each other, they resembled two ventilators that had been turned on facing each

---

1. Bely collected his material for the novel while studying the sect of the Khlysty, among whom he seemed to have found also some elements of Rasputinism.
2. The *Zhar-Ptítsa* (Phoenix) of the Russian folklore.

other; and the result was a most unpleasant draught.'[1] The bomb is brought
to Nikolai to be secretly placed in his father's bedroom. But after second thoughts
he feels he cannot do it, and says so. Meanwhile the Senator notices the ticking
tin in his son's drawer (casually left open) and takes it into his own study in
order, at some time, to have a look at it. Nikolai is at a loss to explain the dis-
appearance of the bomb and leaves it at that. At night, when everybody is
asleep, the bomb—forgotten in the Senator's empty study—explodes, but no
one is hurt. Soon after this the Senator tenders his resignation and leaves Petersburg for the countryside. His son, who can hardly boast of an easy conscience,
undertakes a long journey to Africa. On his return he settles down to a vegetative existence on his distant and isolated estate. The whole of this novel is
divided into short chapters which, owing to Bely's rhythmical and verbal skill,
are easy to read in spite of his neologisms and occasional syntactic extravagances.

After a number of financial difficulties Bely married (not in the church)
Asya Turgeneva, a niece of Ivan Turgenev. They both travelled for several
months in Italy, Northern Africa and Egypt. Vainly hoping to reconcile his
inherited rationalistic mind with his irrational 'Russian' propensities and intui-
tions, Bely eventually joined, together with Asya, Dr Rudolf Steiner's anthro-
posophic movement at its centre in Dornach, Switzerland; but his enthusiasm
was of short duration. Feeling disillusioned, he returned to Russia in 1916, while
Asya remained (for reasons of her own) in Dornach. After the great cataclysm
Bely, like Bryusov, sided with the bolshevist regime, for which he was severely
condemned by the émigré writers, especially by Zinaida Hippius.[2] Even before
the revolution took place, Bely could not help seeing the crisis or even the gradual disintegration of Symbolism as a group movement. Yet he continued to
stick to some of its main tenets. And so in his own way did Alexander Blok
whose stature and peculiar destiny deserve special attention.

1. *Petersburg*, translated by John Cournos (Weidenfeld and Nicolson, 1960). A new Russian
edition of *Petersburg* appeared at Berlin in 1922. This final edition was reissued in 1927.
2. See the two volumes of her *Zhivýe lítsa* (*The Living Faces*, Prague 1925).

CHAPTER TWENTY-THREE

Alexander Blok

I

Strange though it may seem, Blok had only a vague idea of modern poetry before he was eighteen. The favourite authors of his youth were the dreamy Zhukovsky and those German romantics with whom he felt a certain affinity, while France and French culture were somewhat alien to him. Blok's early poems were imbued with a hazy medieval flavour, while Vladimir Solovyov was responsible for the trend and perhaps even for the final awakening of Blok's poetic genius. Like Solovyov, he too accepted the immanent mystical 'World-Soul' (or the gnostic Sophia) as the Eternal Feminine, from which he hoped for a transfiguration of all life. He believed in this with a fervour strong enough to blend his poetic, religious and erotic impulses in one powerful flame even when, as a teenager, he was courting the girl whom he subsequently married, Lyubov'— a daughter of the famous Russian scientist Mendeleyev. He could not separate his sweetheart from the realm of the Eternal Feminine; and so his awakened sex turned entirely within, to the symbols and phantoms of his own poetic imagination. He actually felt Love to be a key to the mystery of the Universe. What in an ordinary talent might have resulted in dreamy sentimental outpourings was transformed by Blok into his first and almost overmelodious romantic book of poems—*Verses About the Lady Fair* (*Stikhí o prekrásnoy dáme*, 1905).

In these poems, typical of his early period (roughly between 1897 and 1904), Blok combined Solovyov's yearning for the miraculous with the tenderness of Dante's *Vita Nuova*, while yet imparting to them a style and texture entirely his own. Evocative in a musical and magical sense, many of these poems sound like ardent prayers of a troubadour extolling the Eternal Feminine, symbolised in his own vision of the Lady Fair. But the distance between her and him was so immense that an approach seemed unthinkable. All he dared look forward to were a few fleeting moments in which her presence, with all the glory of a different realm or dimension of life, would descend, like God's grace, upon him. As if unaware of the world around, Blok sings—at this stage—like a man in a trance, or like a medium, whose very passivity fosters his poetic intoxication. His images, for the most part vague, are imbued with an uncanny 'aura', radiating, as it were, from so many of his early poems (he wrote about eight hundred of them before he was twenty-five). His language may still be reminiscent—now and then—of Solovyov, but the melody and the 'touch' are his own. And as for the wealth of his rhythms, his new musical and prosodic devices, they are enough to drive frantic even the most experienced of translators.

The guardian spirit hovering over Blok's poetry of that period was Solovyov the visionary and mystic. But Blok's raptures were not always as innocent as they looked. The prayer-like tone of his verses was often disturbed by his own secret double, i.e. by flashes of the opposite depth : those of spiritual descent, blasphemy, and rebellion. This modernist duality assumed in him the form of fear, of ominous forebodings.

> I am afraid of my double-faced soul,
> And I carefully conceal
> My diabolical and wild countenance
> Underneath this sacred armour.

The awareness of the danger made him cling all the more to his mystical Beatrice. But he knew that descent was imperative, even inevitable. Moreover, separated from the facts of actual existence, he realised that he had no right to serve his ideal apart and away from life. And since he, too, was a man and not a ghost, he could not but wonder what would become of his vision on the plane of life as it was and not as it presented itself to his romantic imagination. His misgivings came out in this poem (addressed at one of such moments to his own Lady Fair) in June 1901, that is some two years before his marriage.

> I have foreknown Thee! Oh, I have foreknown Thee. Going
> The years have shown me Thy premonitory face,
> Intolerably clear, the farthest sky is glowing,
> I wait in silence Thy withheld and worshipped grace!
> The farthest sky is glowing : white for Thy appearing,
> Yet terror clings to me : Thy image will be strange,
> And insolent suspicion will arouse upon thy nearing,
> The features long foreknown, beheld at last will change.
> How shall I then be fallen!—low with no defender :
> Dead dreams will conquer me, the glory, glimpsed will change,
> The farthest sky is glowing! nearer looms the splendour,
> Yet terror clings to me. Thy image will be strange.[1]

2

What happened before long was a complete change of 'her' image. Having heard the summons of actual life, the poet had no right to ignore it. But once he had abandoned the realm of idealistic heights, he had to be ready for any shock on the plane of reality. To follow this second period (1904-1907) means to watch the early stage of the tragedy between Blok the man and Blok the poet, when his spiritual maxim of 'all or nothing' comes into conflict with the world around him, including his own marriage. For his wife Lyubov' was soon

1. Translated by Babette Deutsch and Avrahm Yarmolinsky in *Modern Russian Anthology* (Harcourt, Brace & Co., M. Lawrence).

to prove that, being a woman of flesh and blood, she had nothing in common with Blok's Lady Fair. Moreover, on meeting her husband's friend, Andrey Bely, Lyubov' became rather infatuated with him. There followed a hectic and harrowing love affair between the two, which ended only in 1910—after Bely had married Asya Turgeneva. The liaison between Lyubov' and Bely could not but lead to violent quarrels between the poets. And when the affair was ended, Bely himself once referred to Lyubov' with the unambiguous label: a doll.

Blok's disappointment in married life, was, however, closely connected with his disappointment in existence as a whole. Eventually, earth began to seem to him 'but a marsh full of slimy imps and bubbles'. In a flowery essay, written in 1910 (i.e. during the growing crisis of Russian Symbolism), Blok gave a veiled explanation of what had taken place. He deals here with his inner experiences only. As these are treated in terms of poetic activities on the one hand, and of life as it is on the other, he touches upon the problem of Art and Life in some of its acutest aspects, but from an entirely personal angle. On the plane of concrete earthly love and earthly existence there certainly seemed to be no room for such a symbol as the Eternal Feminine. Here his Beatrice was a romantic phantom, a myth, which, instead of bridging the gap between the actual and the transcendental, only widened it. The two worlds—the world of spiritual values and visions, and the world of facts—proved incompatible. One seemed to exclude the other. There was even no guarantee that his previous ecstasies had not been mere indulgence in subjective fancies rather than flashes of intuition with a higher reality behind them.

In this state of doubt and bewilderment, Blok was assailed by a swarm of 'doubles' which had been dormant in him as an antithesis to his former aspirations. He found himself cut off from the 'streaming light' of those regions where his imagination had soared before. His Lady Fair became a ghostlike doll, and his former vision turned into a tragi-comic puppet show in which he and his likes were but actors and buffoons, whether they knew it or not. He confesses in the essay mentioned:

> Had I made a picture I would have depicted it in this manner: in the lilac dusk of an endless world there sways an enormous white catafalque, and on it lies a doll whose face is dimly reminiscent of the countenance which once had shone through the heavenly dawns. . . . And so all is finished: my miraculous world has turned into an arena of my personal acting—into a puppet show in which I myself am only one of the company of my strange puppets. In other words, my own life has become art . . . I stand before it all without knowing what to do either with the show, or with my life turned into art; for in my immediate presence there lives my own phantom-creation: neither alive nor dead—a blue ghost. . . . It is here that arises the problem of the curse of art, of a return to life, of service to the community.[1]

This state was further complicated by the fact that although he had lost his former romantic faith, his romantic temperament remained unchanged, and

1. Translated by J. L.

from now on played havoc with him. When such an incurable idealist is faced with the 'bubbles of earth', with the facts and conditions of real life, disappointments in love and friendship included, he has to react as Blok did. Romantic irony and indictment play the principal part in it as they did in Blok's poetry which, from now on, became a strange psychological document and a confession in one—a record of his own inner drama. His lyrical play, *The Puppet Show* (*Balagánchik*, 1905), was one of the first attempts to ridicule his former visionary phase by means of buffoonery. From the angle of life 'as it is', the whole of that phase now appeared to him a tragic farce. And if his Lady Fair was but a doll or a ghost, then his own acts of devotion, as well as those of similar romantic Pierrots, were no more real than the gestures of puppets made of cardboard. In his play *The King in the Square* (*Koról' na plóshchadi*) the incompatibility of reality and the ideal is stressed through grotesque allegories. In another little play, *The Stranger* (*Neznakómka*), he lets his Beatrice—symbolised as a star—fall onto our earth, where she becomes an ordinary prostitute. Romantic irony thus passed into romantic blasphemy. But the old nostalgia was still there and pursued him in haunting visions. In a poem under the same title, *The Stranger*, Blok wants to forget 'her' by means of alcohol, but in vain. 'She' hovers around him even as a courtesan in a suburban restaurant where, amidst unspeakable vulgarity, drunkards show their true nature, while befuddling themselves with bottles of wine. It is here that every night a demi-mondaine in the shape of a mysterious woman appears and sits down by the window.

Spellbound by her presence, the poet is transferred for a moment to the hazy 'magical shore' of the world with which he had once been familiar. And as his own drunkenness increases, he is ready to believe in the truth and reality of that world, knowing full well that this illusion, too, will vanish when the effect of wine is over.

> Now I am lord of deepest mysteries,
> The sun of another world is mine,
> My soul is glowing with its radiance,
> Filled with the bitter spirit of wine.
>
> The ostrich feathers nodding dreamily,
> Sway in my heart for evermore,
> Those fathomless blue eyes are flowering
> Upon a wondrous distant shore.
>
> In my soul there's hidden a treasury,
> It has one key—the key is mine,
> Yes, you are right, you drunk monstrosities—
> Now I know, there is truth in wine.[1]

Having become something of a rancorous Don Juan, Blok looked in his love-adventures, too, as he did in wine, for an escape from the drabness of existence. But even in the hectic love poems, in which he sings of real women

1. Translated by V. de Sola Pinto. In the original the first and third lines are also rhymed.

who had loved him, there vibrates the repressed nostalgia for his vanished Beatrice :

> Yes, I have loved. And the mad glowing
> Of love's drunk pain is at an end,
> The triumph and the overthrowing,
> The name of 'foe', the word of 'friend'.
>
> There have been many, but a single
> Charm bound them all in unity,
> One frenzied Beauty made them mingle :
> Its name is Love and Life to me.[1]

3

Aware of the 'puppet show' of life, Blok was now ready to face reality, while yet refusing to make any compromise with it. Respectable, conventional existence was outside his ambitions; moreover—outside his taste. Life meant to him above all intensity of experience, intensity at any price. And when he could no longer procure it through the ecstasies of the heights, he plunged into those of the depths—into the emotional chaos of the unconscious, tinged with his own pessimism and boredom. But even on this level Blok could not continue without a substitute for his former Beatrice. He thought he had found it in the actress Volokhova—a 'tall black lady' with whom he fell passionately in love in 1906. Yet into his own irrational and destructive whirl of passion he now projected another beloved whom he was willing to serve with the devotion he had once lavished on his Lady Fair. This new beloved, whose voice sounded to him like the 'song of Fate', was Russia—not the 'holy' but the broad mysterious Russia of endless spaces, winds and blizzards; of flying troikas; of maddening nostalgia, drunkenness, and chaos.

> I will listen to the voice of drunken Russia
> And I will rest under a tavern roof.

Snow-Mask (*Snézhnye máski*) is the title of his typical cycle of that period. Its main note is one of intoxication with blizzards, wine and passion. The ecstasy of self-annihilation rings in the accents of his intensely sensual *Faïna*. In the more virile verses of another section, *Enchantment through Fire* (*Zaklyátie ognyóm*) his wish to come to terms with life flares up, but only for a while. There follows a new surrender to psychic drugs. Eventually, he could not rely on these either : he had to look upon the world with a sobered mind and with more than sobered eyes.

The prevalent mood of that phase (from 1908 until 1917, that is between the two Revolutions), can best be defined as spiteful apathy. The filth and vulgarity of existence overpowered him to such a degree as to make all effort appear futile. The title of a collection of poems written in those years is itself signi-

1. Translated by C. M. Bowra in *A Book of Russian Verse* (Macmillan).

ficant: *The Horrid World* (*Stráshny mir*). In *Iamby* he tried to kindle his crushed
faith in life. In his romantic drama on a medieval Provençal theme, *The Rose
and the Cross* (*Róza i krest*, 1912), even his one-time devotion to the Lady Fair
in terms of an all-consuming and self-sacrificing love was revived. Yet the world
itself seemed loathsome in all its aspects. But the more deeply he felt the futility
of things the more intense he became as a poet. Having abandoned his trance-
like vagueness and verbal music, he adopted a vocabulary which was tersely
realistic and at the same time symbolic. These two short poems, both of them
written in 1912, convey his moods and technique during that period. The theme
is night in a big city. And this is what Blok has to say about it:

Night: the street, a foolish lamp giving
A dingy light, a druggist's store:
For a quarter of a century go on living,
No escape. All will be as before

You die: afresh you start life boldly,
Just as of old each detail repeat.
Night, the canal rippling so coldly,
The druggist's store, the lamp, the street.[1]

In the second poem the big-city nightmare is rendered as follows:

An empty street: light in a single window gleams.
The Jew apothecary is moaning as he dreams.
Before the cupboard labelled 'poison' he can see,
Intently bending down on ghastly creaking knee

A skeleton wrapped in a cloak, who all the while
Searches for something, twists his black mouth in a smile.
Finding it, he stumbles unaware and makes
A noise, then turns his death-head while the sleeper wakes,

Screams and rises in his bed, and falls on the other side,
But the visitor beneath his cloak can hide
The accursed phial for two noseless women there,
Waiting outside beneath the street lamp's cold white glare.[1]

An even more typical example of Blok's symbolic realism is the first poem
of his *Danses macabres*, some verses of which we quote in a paraphrase made
by R. M. Hewitt:

It's hard for a corpse in this world of men,
Better remain apart, alone,
You have to mix with them now and then
Or you'll never succeed in your career.
But oh! the fear that they might hear
The rattle of bone on bone.

1. Translated by V. de Sola Pinto.

Live men still sleep when the dead man rises.
His thoughts are black as the day is long,
Plods to the office, bank or assizes,
Where quills whisper a welcome song.

Hour by hour must the dead man labour;
At last he's free and puts on his coat,
Wags his haunches, grins at his neighbour
And feeds him a bawdy anecdote.

The rain has smeared with a nameless liquor
Houses and churches and humans grimy;
But the dead man drives where the mud is thicker,
Knowing a place that is still more slimy.

A gilded hall with mirrors about it.
Imbecile hostess and husband fool
Are glad to see him, who can doubt it?—
His evening suit was made by Poole.

The reception, the music and dance go on. The 'dead man' behaves in the proper style, dances and talks to an equally 'dead' woman. Then he approaches a young girl who is still alive and even radiates the ecstasy of 'life's desire'. He pounces upon her according to all the rules of conventional gossip and entertainment.

With fluent malice more than human,
He murmurs into her ear alone,
Just as a live man woos a woman.
'How clever he is, how kind and dear!'
But somewhere near she can faintly hear
The rattle of bone on bone.

Another cycle of poems, *The Life of My Friend* (Zhizn' moegó priyátelya), is written in the same vein. In his beautiful *Garden of Nightingales* (Solovyínny sad, 1915) Blok the dreamer emerged again with all the magic of his verbal art, but one of his recurring motifs during the whole of that period was his thought and love of Russia. When everything else had disappointed and betrayed him; when he was tormented by forebodings about the 'cold and gloom of the days to come', his love for Russia never faltered, although he was profoundly aware of her failings, enumerated in a poem which begins:

To sin unashamed, to lose, unthinking,
The count of careless nights and days,
And then, while the head aches with drinking,
Steal to God's house, with eyes that glaze...

There follows a long list of vices and transgressions, depicted with all their ungainliness. But as if aware of something different and deeper underneath it all, Blok exclaims in the end:

Dearer to me than every other,
Are you, Russia, even so.[1]

4

The mixture of disgust and despair (so much in tune with the atmosphere which followed the thwarted rising of 1905-06) was only the reverse side of Blok's incurable idealism, of his yearning for a total change of man and life. As if anxious to contend to the end with all the contradictory elements within himself, he started writing (after a journey to Italy and Germany) an autobiographic epic in four parts called *Retribution* (*Vozmézdie*, 1910-21). The death of his father, professor at Warsaw university (he died in 1909), may have been a further reason why Blok wanted to give a poetic description of his own inner development in connection with his ancestry and with Russia's recent history, especially with the events in 1905. He worked upon this epic until his death. Had he completed it, it might have become his greatest work.

Parallel with this he continued writing poems among which the cycle *Carmen* (1914) was inspired by his love for an opera singer whom he had heard in the role of Carmen. But the fire now burning came largely out of the ashes. He looked upon life with growing pessimism, as well as with the secret hope that an elemental catastrophe would come at last and cleanse the earth of its quagmire. His hopes turned into actual forebodings, especially with regard to Russia. These he uttered in a number of poems (*On the Field of Kulikovo*, etc.), one of which, *Russia in 1914*, ends with the lines:

Dumbness—and then the tocsin ringing:
Each mouth is sealed and so we wait;
In hearts that once with joy were singing,
There's now an emptiness charged with fate.

And when the crows in the sky shall hover,
Above us lying beneath the sod,
May there be better men to look over
This Thy Kingdom, O God, O God.[2]

Only an attitude such as this can explain why Blok was one of the first to greet the Revolution of 1917 with demands and expectations of his own. At last the gap between art and life (or service to the community) was likely to disappear so far as he was concerned. He sensed a deep significance even in the horrors of those years: it was a new Apocalypse whose very compass and intensity must have contained some meaning. Far from being perturbed by it, he identified it with that elemental 'spirit of music' which—according to him— is at the bottom of all creative revolutions. What he actually meant by it was analogous to Nietzsche's 'Dionysian spirit'. Both Nietzsche and Blok saw the

1. Translated by Babette Deutsch and Avrahm Yarmolinsky in *Russian Poetry* (Lawrence).
2. Translated by V. de Sola Pinto.

cause of the one-sided development of European civilisation in our 'Socratic' rationalism—severed from that irrational spring of life which Nietzsche labelled with the name of Dionysus and Blok with the 'spirit of music'. The divorce between Reason and Nature, between Reason and the Cosmos itself, was (in their opinion) responsible for many aberrations characteristic of mankind. Having lost his sense of the irrational, of the infinite and the timeless, modern man has been deprived of his true focus. He has been narrowed down to petty rationalism and even pettier materialism with its egoistic concerns, without even suspecting that life, real life, is born only where such bondage ceases, and the sway of the 'music of the universe' begins. This is what Blok says about it in his essay *The Downfall of Humanism* (1919):

> There are two kinds of time, one historical according to the calendar, and the other 'musical', without date or number. In the consciousness of civilised man the first kind alone is immutably present: but it is only when we realise how near we are to Nature, only when we abandon ourselves to the wave of music issuing from the chorus of the Universe, that we live in the second. For life in days, months and years no balance of our powers is necessary. And this absence of necessity for effort soon reduces the majority of civilised people to the state of mere dwellers upon earth. But balance becomes indispensable as soon as we live near the 'musical' reality of the world—near to Nature, to the elemental. For this we need above all to be well-ordered both in body and spirit, since it is only with the complete body and the complete spirit acting together that the 'music of the universe' can be heard. Loss of balance between the bodily and the spiritual inevitably makes us lose that music. It makes us lose the ability to escape from the time of the calendar, that is, from chronological days and years, into the other time that cannot be calculated. Epochs in which this balance is not destroyed may be called epochs of culture, in contrast to those when an integral perception of the world is beyond the bearers of an outlived culture, owing to the influx of melodies up to that time unfamiliar and unknown, which overcrowded the hearing. The influx may be slow if measured by the calendar, for new historical forces come into the consciousness of humanity gradually. Yet that which takes place slowly according to the laws of one kind of time can be completed suddenly according to the laws of the other. The movement of the one directing baton is enough to turn into a hurricane the drawn-out melody of the orchestra. The mistake of the inheritors of humanistic culture, the fatal contradiction into which they fell, originated in their exhaustion. The spirit of integrity, the 'spirit of music', abandoned them, and so they blindly put their trust in historical time. They failed to see that the world was already rising at a signal from a movement which was entirely new. While continuing to believe that the masses were acquiring freedom within the individualistic movement of civilisation, they naturally could not see that those very masses were bearers of a different, of a new spirit.[1]

1. Translated by J. L.

The old romantic in Blok thus came out in his attitude towards the Revolution, but this time with a definite view about the creative value of the hurricane which—according to him—brought into history a 'different, a new spirit'. Carried away by the sway of this spirit, he felt the stirring of new hopes and visions. It was in January, 1918, i.e. during the cruellest ordeals, amidst hunger, cold and chaos, that he wrote his *The Twelve* (*Dvenádtsat'*) and *The Scythians* (*Skífy*), both echoing the Revolution in a quasi-Apocalyptic manner.

5

The first of these two creations is the high-watermark of Blok's poetry. Simple at first sight, it is full of ingenious rhythms and devices, some of which were even taken from street jargon and factory ditties. Blok the romantic, the realist and the symbolist collaborate here on equal terms, accompanied by his bitter hatred of the old world, the collapse of which he had been more than ready to welcome.

> The wind reels, the snow dances;
> A party of twelve men advances.
> Black rifle-slings upon their backs.
> And flame, flame, flame upon their tracks.
> With crumpled caps, lips smoking fags,
> All should be branded as prison lags.

This is how the poet introduces the twelve Bolshevik guards, patrolling the streets of Petrograd, at night, during the days of turmoil and hunger. The poem has twelve parts, each of them composed in a different rhythm and adding different motifs. The language, too, is appropriate to 'prison lags', who mix it with half-digested revolutionary slogans and clichés. The narrative incident is deliberately crude and could have been taken from any police chronicle. One of the twelve patrolling soldiers, infatuated with the street-girl Katya (whose stockings are 'packed with Kerensky notes') accidentally shoots her dead—while aiming at his own rival in love. Throughout the poem we can follow his reactions to the crime, but this personal drama is cunningly interwoven with the ordeals of a bleak northern winter and the Revolution. The tension of the conflicting social strata is suggested by the rhythm, the tone and the accent of each verse, as well as by Blok's own sallies against the old 'bourgeois' order:

> The bourgeois, where the roads divide,
> Stands with his nose sunk in his fur;
> And, hairy, shivers at his side
> With drooping tail, a poor whipped cur.

> Like the dog, stands the bourgeois, hungry,
> A silent question to the sky;
> The old world, like a homeless mongrel,
> With tail between its legs stands by.

Nothing that belongs to the old world matters any longer. Even the 'Holy Russia' of yore can be blasphemed and, hooligan-fashion, trampled underfoot for the sake of a new era :

> Don't shrink, comrade, get your rifle out;
> Give Holy Russia a taste of shot.
>> At the wooden land,
>> Where the poor huts stand,
>> And her rump so grand !
> Aha, but no Cross !

The fury of destruction, with 'no Cross', fills the air. But however un-Christian its external ravages, a revolution in the name of justice and brotherhood may yet be based upon a Christian impulse, which in the end must win—provided the revolution itself be imbued with that 'spirit of universal music' of which Blok spoke in his essay. This is where the creative element of the revolution comes in, no matter whether the participants are aware of it or not. And so 'the twelve' (a reflection of the twelve Apostles) march on. And in the midst of all the desolation, crime and chaos they are suddenly joined by an apparition which confers upon the poem a final message and meaning :

> On they march with sovereign tread,
> With a starving dog behind,
> With a blood-red flag ahead—
> In the storm where none can see,
> From the rifle bullets free,
> Gently walking on the snow,
> Where like pearls the snowflakes glow,
> Marches rose-crowned in the van
> Jesus Christ, the Son of Man.[1]

6

The Twelve is pervaded with the pathos of revolution and yet remains elusive enough to be interpreted in a number of ways. Christ as protector and leader of the twelve Bolshevist guards may appear to some people a blasphemy and to others a *deus ex machina*—the more so because nothing in the poem makes one expect such a dénouement. On the other hand, He can be explained as a Messianic symbol of that creative era which ought to follow upon the Inferno of suffering, blood and destruction. A revolution devoid of inner meaning remains only a calamity which has not been deepened into a purifying tragedy; and a mere calamity is always crushing and sterile. Blok knew that an event of such magnitude as the cataclysm of 1917 could not have been of this sterile kind, and he said so. *The Twelve* was a final attempt on his part to regain his faith in humanity and life—an attempt expressed in strains of which only great poetry is capable.

1.   Translated by C. M. Bowra. *Op. cit.*

Less elusive and somewhat programmatic is his other poem, *The Scythians*.[1] It was written during the peace negotiations at Brest-Litovsk and represents a platform counterpart to *The Twelve*. Here Blok challenges the luke-warm bourgeoisie of the Western world to join the universal brotherhood inaugurated by the Revolution. In terms redolent of aggressive Slavophilism and speaking both as a revolutionary and a Russian, he reproaches the nations of the West:

> Yes, you have long since ceased to love
> As our cold blood can love; the taste
> You have forgotten of a love
> That burns like fire and like fire lays waste.

> Yes, Russia is a sphinx. Exulting, grieving,
> And sweating blood, she cannot sate
> Her eyes that gaze and gaze and gaze
> At you with stone-lipped love for you, and hate.

This 'stone-lipped love and hate' with regard to Europe had nothing to do with the past—it is turned to a future growing out of the Revolution. Hence Blok's appeal to the sceptical and reluctant West:

> Come unto us, from the black ways of war,
> Come to our peaceful arms and rest,
> Comrades, while it is not too late,
> Sheathe the sword! May brotherhood be blessed.

And in case the challenged Western nations should refuse to join, he threatens them with the 'Asiatic face' of Russia (or rather with the Asiatic half of her face), as well as with her indifference to their fate even if another Mongolian invasion, headed by an up-to-date Genghis Khan, should come from the Far East.

> We will not move when the ferocious Hun
> Despoils the corpse and leaves it bare,
> Burns towns, herds cattle in the church
> And smell of white flesh roasting fills the air.[2]

Little did he suspect that the 'smell of white flesh roasting' would—in a few years time—be practised not by the Asiatics, but by the inhabitants of 'Christian' central Europe. In the year of grace 1918 History was not yet fantastic enough to make the death-factories of Auschwitz, as well as other equally efficient institutions of the sort, look credible.

1.   There existed at the time a Society of 'Scythians', led by Ivanov-Razumnik and expecting (quite in the Slavophil spirit) that Russia—renewed and regenerated by her Revolution —would become a kind of Messiah and saviour of the world which was in the grip of capitalist materialism of the West.
2.   Translated by Babette Deutsch and Avrahm Yarmolinsky *Op. cit.*

7

'Life is only worth living when we make immense demands upon it,' Blok wrote in an essay at the time of his two revolutionary rhapsodies. 'All or nothing! A faith, not in what is not found upon earth, but in what ought to be there, although at the present time it does not exist and may not come for quite a while.' Approaching the Revolution with such an attitude, he saw its scope as nothing less than a gradual remaking of man and he world.

> A true revolution cannot aim at anything else, though we cannot yet say whether this aim will be accomplished or not. Its cherished hope is to raise a universal cyclone which will carry to the lands buried in snow the warm winds and the fragrance of orange groves, and will water the sun-scorched plains of the south with refreshing rain from the northern region. *Peace and the brotherhood of nations* is the banner under which the Russian Revolution marches on its way. This is the tune of its roaring flood. This is the music which he who has ears to hear should hear.[1]

Such was Blok's idea of the great 'cyclone' which he, an intellectual and a poet of genius, joined without hesitation. He also turned against those members of the intelligentsia who had not followed his example (and they were the majority). His own maximalist demands made him impatient to see the economic and political upheaval completed by an adequate inner change of men, but this change was either too slow, or else entirely different from what he had expected. It must have been the discrepancy between the external and the inner revolutions—a discrepancy which assumed unexpectedly ugly aspects during the ravages of the Civil War—that eventually damped Blok's hopes and enthusiasm.

Disappointment, apathy, and illness closed in upon him. He was practically silent during the last two years of his life. His untimely death on 7 August, 1921 coincided also with the complete disintegration of that Symbolist school in Russia of which Blok was the acknowledged leader.

1. Translated by J. L.

CHAPTER TWENTY-FOUR

Sergey Esenin

I

Russian Symbolism reached its climax and its crisis by 1910. A reaction against its 'mystical' other-worldliness and vagueness was not unexpected; but it took several directions. The so-called Acmeists, led by Nikolai Gumilyov, Sergey Gorodetsky, Anna Akhmatova and Osip Mandelshtam, were—together with the associated guild of poets—all out for more concreteness combined with consummate craftsmanship. The refined and sensual author of 'Alexandrian Songs' (1906), Mikhail Kuzmin, insisted above all on 'beautiful clarity' which he also practised. The editor of the leading Acmeist periodical, *Apollo* (1909–17), was Gumilyov [1] whose virile, adventurous poetry and technical skill won him a number of admirers. His ex-wife, Anna Achmatov (née Gorenko, 1888–1966), on the other hand, was an exquisitely feminine poet with an accent and suggestive reserve entirely her own. Love, nostalgic yearnings and frustrations fill her intimate lyrics—all of them short and incisive. Her early collections, such as *Beads* (*Chótki*, 1913), *The White Flock* (*Bélaya stáya*, 1917) and *Anno Domini MCXXI*, gave her a distinguished place in modern Russian poetry. Her subjectivity—anathema to the Soviet authorities—was much admired by the literary élite. More concrete was Osip Mandelshtam (1891–1942) whose talent and craftsmanship were apparent already in his first booklet of verse under the curious title, *Stone* (*Kámen'*, 1913). He published two more collections of poems, *Tristia* in 1922 and *Poems* in 1928 both of which further enhanced his poetic gift and fame. He also wrote several essays and sketches testifying to his exceptional taste and culture. Unfortunately, during the last few years of his life he was driven from one place of exile to another and finally died in a prison camp near Vladivostok.

Like the Acmeists, the Futurists too were a reaction against the Symbolist school—a reaction not only against its frequent esoteric obscurity, but also against the soft melodious femininity of so many of its products. Another conspicuous trend, represented by such village poets as Nikolai Klyuyev (1887–1926) and Sergey Esenin (1895–1925), was at first connected with Symbolism, but became independent during the gradual decay of that trend. This applies particularly to Esenin who, together with Mayakovsky, dominated the poetic scene of Soviet Russia for quite a few years. Yet what a contrast between these two gifted youths, both of whom ended in suicide!

1. He was 'liquidated' for conspiracy against the regime in 1921, at the age of thirty-five

Whereas Mayakovsky eventually became the poetic voice of the rising proletariat, the voice of Esenin turned into an elegiac lament for things connected with the old patriarchal, peasant Russia. He could hardly have made a different choice. Born and bred in the depths of rural Russia (the district of Ryazan'), Esenin was steeped in the soil and in peasant lore. Hence he was never able to detach himself inwardly from his native village, least of all when he tried to adapt himself to the bohemian life of the young metropolitan littérateurs, or to the spirit of the Revolution. It would be a mistake, though, to regard his rural poetry from the angle of mere folklore or idyllic local colour. It went deeper. It could be defined as poetic self-assertion and self-defence of the essential peasant against the encroaching industrialism, urbanism, and the mentality of a machine age. In this respect it was the opposite of everything the futurist current stood for. The village in its primeval, archaic character found in Esenin's verse and gift for song one of the truly poignant expressions in modern poetry. It was and remained the basic source of his inspiration.

Yet his poetry, like that of the slightly older glorifier of the village—Nikolai Klyuyev—took several devices from the symbolist movement. It even looked at first as though it would impart a new vitality to Symbolism itself when the latter was on the decline. This was perhaps one of the reasons why Esenin's path to fame was comparatively easy after his arrival in Petersburg in 1916. The more so because at his début he knew how to conceal a considerable amount of peasant cunning behind the pose of a 'gentle shepherd swain', all of which was taken for the real thing by the Petersburg intelligentsia. His one-time friend, the imaginist poet Mariengof, tells us (in a book about him) how Esenin used to put on an embroidered blouse, a peasant cap and top boots, after which he would play folk tunes on the accordion—to the satisfaction of the highbrows who thus came into touch with the 'people' without needing to leave their comfortable drawing-rooms. Esenin, who made good use of such comic-opera masquerades, probably chuckled at his audience with no less amusement than the 'little muzhik' Klyuyev may have done behind his own humble peasant mask during his first steps towards literary fame. But this apart, Esenin—like Klyuyev—was a genuine poet. Gorky once referred to him (whether rightly or wrongly) even as the greatest lyrical genius since Pushkin. More authentic in his poems than with his peasant blouses, top boots, and accordion, Esenin sang with a poignancy born of his nostalgia for the fields, floods and winds he had left behind.

> O land of floods and agony,
> And gentle spring-tide powers,
> Under the masters Dawn and Stars
> I passed my schooling hours.
>
> While in the Bible of the winds,
> I pondered o'er the words,
> Isaiah came and walked with me
> To keep my golden herds.[1]

1.   Translated by R. M. Hewitt in *A Book of Russian Verse* (Macmillan).

Esenin's pastoral motifs, far from being a repetition of hackneyed old melodies, vibrate with such freshness and sincerity that, in spite of his calculated experiments in poetic technique (new rhythms, forms and images), they sound as if extemporised. His original texture and inflection are strengthened by peasant imagery and peasant idioms which are his usual expedients. Religion, poetic superstition, naïve animism, and pantheism seem to vie with each other in creating that intimate, homely atmosphere which permeates the poems of his early period. But this was only one facet of Esenin's Muse. Another and, for a while, hidden aspect of his poetry was that potentially anarchic spirit of the steppe which, lurking in the unconscious, was much more typical of the pre-revolutionary Russian peasants than their indolent quietism, submissiveness and humility. Whereas in the West freedom is associated with the image of a disciplined community, in Russia it used to be inseparable from the idea of boundless spaces where everything could be let loose on a more lavish and anarchic scale than anywhere in Europe. This spirit was often responsible for all kinds of inner restlessness, as well as for excess in everything: in piety and sacrilege, in meekness and cruelty, in active idealism and callous destruction for its own sake. Esenin—an 'essential' peasant from those spaces which stretch into the heart of Asia—confessed in one of his lyrics: 'I cherish my secret purity of heart; but still I may murder someone to the whistle of the autumn wind. . .' It may be that the same unruly anarchic spirit rather than any ideological convictions made him hail the Revolution of 1917, although he, too, like Blok, expected from the latter a renewal of life. Sentimental-idyllic and turbulent elements were intermingled in him as if in a fugue, out of which there emerged some remarkable melodies.

2

Unhampered by education or abundant reading. Esenin—like Kol'tsov and Nekrasov before him—relied on the sureness of his poetic instinct which made him glean the right words, metaphors and images from the heart of folk-lore itself. Most of the themes and images in his early poems were connected with the archaic life of the village. The people's saints are often treated by him in a mythological sense, as something inseparable from fields and seasons, however unexpected some of his similes and associations may sound. God is referred to as a grey-bearded elder sowing stars like winter corn. Esenin's landscape has the meek eyes of a cow. The dawn over the cornfields reminds him of a cow licking her new born calf. The dawn on the roof is like a kitten washing her mouth with her little paws. The moon is a golden puppy, or else a 'curly lamb gambolling in a blue meadow'. One of his early poems consists of these four lines:

Where dawn is watering the cabbage rows,
Splashing red pails upon her mighty jamb,

A little nuzzling maple reaches up,
To suck the full green udders of its dam.[1]

In another poem he compares the Russian autumn to a chestnut mare
cleaning her 'rough mane'.

Her hooves' blue chatter sounds above the bank
Of the still river where the reeds are rank.
The monkish wind steps lightly, and retrieves
With idle fingers handfuls of dry leaves,
And where a rowan blooms he stoops to lean
And kiss the red wounds of a Christ unseen.

Or take these few characteristic lines :

In the clear cold the dales grow blue and tremble,
The iron hooves beat sharply; knock and knock,
The faded grasses in wide skirt assemble
Flung copper where the wind-blown branches rock.
For empty straths, a slender arch ascending :
Fog curls upon the air and, moss-wise grows,
And evening, low above the wan streams bending,
In their white waters washes his blue toes.

The 'essential' peasant was so strong in Esenin that he could not shed him
even after he had turned to entirely different themes and interests. While piling
up laurels and disillusionment in the two Russian capitals, he still regarded the
hut and the cornfields of his childhood as his only true home. And when the
Revolution came, Esenin welcomed it in a spirit different from that of Blok or
Mayakovsky. He hailed it neither as a dissatisfied intellectual who thought he
had found an outlet in the new Apocalypse, nor as a proletarian, exulting at
the ruins of the world, but exclusively as a peasant and villager whom the
Revolution has turned into a rowdy. It was the turbulent yet Utopian villager
in Esenin which jotted down, in 1919, the revolutionary paean *Inónia*—that
might have been written as a peasant counterpart to Blok's *The Twelve*.

3

Inónia, is, together with Blok's famous poem, a wishful, though poetically
inferior, Messianic affirmation of the Revolution. Louder and more exuberant
than *The Twelve*, it sings of a millennium ruled not by the proletarians and
their machines, but by the peasants inhabiting a free and universal Arcadia :
quite in the style of those 'Populists' who once dreamed of a Russia untainted
by the evils of capitalist industrialism. Revolutionary in its tone and language,
it thus seems to be anti-proletarian by its very theme.

If the finale of *The Twelve* can be likened to a vision welcoming a hoped-

1. This and the next two poems are taken from *Russian Poetry*, translated by Babette
Deutsch and Avrahm Yarmolinsky (Lawrence).

for messianic era, *Inónia* is delirium passing into emotional and rhetorical intemperance. As though intoxicated by his own words, Esenin here lets loose not only his Utopian moods, but also his latent turbulence, his spiritual hooliganism. The result is a strange torrent of poetry, imaginist extravagance and even verbal hysteria. 'I will shear the blue firmament like a mangy sheep of its wool,' he shouts as though with foam on his lips. 'I will bite through the Milky Way. I will raise my arms as high as the Moon and will crack her like a nut. With my firm hand I am ready to turn upside down the whole world. Eight wings are splashing in stormy blizzards from my shoulders.' One 'colossal' simile is thus hurled upon another. Forgetting the peasanty Saviour of his former days, Esenin the revolutionary now yells in a raucous voice: 'The body, the body of *Christ* I will spit out of my mouth.' But what he offers instead is his vague Arcadian idyll 'where the Deity of the living resides'; where there is faith in power, and Truth is to be found only in man himself. Abstract old phrases, repeated in a new *fortissimo*.

This poem marks the dividing line between Esenin's true lyrics and his 'imaginist' experiments, the limitations of which he recognised, however, soon enough. Russian imaginism (similar, in its own way, to Anglo-American imagism) was ushered into existence in 1919 with a manifesto which proclaimed images the aim as well as the means of poetry, regarding them as something self-sufficient to the extent of dispensing, when necessary, with logic and coherence. In their wild search for images, the adepts of this current often strained their fancy to the point of grotesque distortions. But in other respects the movement hardly showed much vitality, and, were it not for the fact that Esenin happened to be one of its temporary members, it might have passed unnoticed. Anyhow, Esenin himself soon repudiated imaginism as something unnatural and forced. 'Imaginism was a formal theory we wanted to affirm', he wrote in a subsequent autobiographical note, 'but it had no ground under it and died, leaving the truth behind that only organic images are of value'. Still, whether in or outside this or any other group of poets, Esenin's poetry reflected also the excesses which the bohemian and underworld Moscow of the NEP (New Economic Policy) period was able to provide.

4

Associated with a few other turbulent, though much less gifted, poets, Esenin must have felt strangely out of place in the turmoil of the Soviet capital. Yet he forced himself to fit into it and to satisfy at least the unruly element in him. He did all he could to outdo the bohemians on their own ground, and in this he succeeded. Jeeringly provocative, he walked about with his 'head unkempt and like an oil lamp', glad to welcome any scandal, any escapade. Night brawls, prostitutes, taverns, police stations, hospitals, irresponsible marriages and divorces—such was his record of those riotous years. To make things worse, he met the Irish-American dancer, Isadora Duncan, who, at the request of the Soviet government had come to Moscow in order to conduct a dancing school for children. Esenin, a handsome youth, proved so irresistible to Isadora that they got married, although both of them must have known how unsuitable they were for anything remotely connected with married life.

The consequences could have been predicted. In due course Esenin grew tired and irritated. In his fits of retrospective jealousy he often treated his easy-going wife *à la moujik,* until a time came when the only thing to do was to part. But even this was not done without scenes and scandal, a glimpse into which is provided by this passage:

> Some time later, one afternoon when Isadora sat in her room with some callers Esenin came again to demand his bust. He demanded it loudly and instantly, and finally forced his drunken way into the room. The bust, which Konienkov had hacked out of a huge block of wood, stoop atop a high bric-a-brac cabinet in one corner of the room. When Isadora refused to give him the bust and asked him to come back again some time when he was more fit to carry it away, he dragged a chair over to the corner and with shaky legs mounted it. As he reached the bust with feverish hands and clasped it, its weight proved too much for him. He staggered and fell from the chair, rolling head over heels on the floor, still clasping tightly to his breast the wooden image. Sullenly and shakily he rose to his feet; and then reeled out of the room to wander later about the byways of Moscow and lose the encumbering bust in some gutter. That was the last view Isadora Duncan had of her poet and her husband, Sergey Alexandrovich Esenin.[1]

But there was despair in all this. Esenin's buffoonery makes one think of a sentimental-romantic peasant boy who had come too soon into the bedlam of fame and of the big-city life and was crushed by both. Unable either to adapt himself to their grip, or to rise above their temptations, he wanted to drown his despair in the mire which he probably loathed yet which made him at least temporarily forget that he belonged to a totally different pattern of existence. A prey to his own sensitiveness, he would, perhaps, have collapsed sooner, had he not found a refuge in cynicism, alcohol and scandal. And when the trend of events after the Revolution took the direction of industrialism on a gigantic scale, Esenin, with his ideal of a rural Arcadia, felt more dismayed than ever. Crushed by it all, he arrived at the conclusion that, together with him, everything else was at its last gasp. The following verses convey aptly enough what he meant:

> The little thatched hut I was born in
>   Lies bare to the sky,
> And in these crooked alleys of Moscow
>   I am fated to die.
>
> No hope have I now of returning
>   To the fields where I played,
> Of hearing the song of the poplar
>   As I lie in the shade.

1. *Isadora Duncan's Russian Days* by Irma Duncan and Alan Rose Macdougall (Gollancz).

The city is senile and dingy,
    And drab, yet I love it!
The golden somnolent East
    Is brooding above it.

And at night when the moon is a-shining
    (A hell of a moon!)
I lurch through the slums till I come to
    My favourite saloon.

There all the night through there is riot,
    And babble and sin,
I read out my verses to harlots
    And treat bandits to gin.

Still fiercer and quicker my heart beats,
    This is all I can say:
'I am lost, you are lost, we are all lost,
    I don't know the way.'

The little thatched hut I was born in
    Lies bare to the sky,
And in these crooked alleys of Moscow
    I am fated to die.[1]

In moods such as this Esenin called himself the 'last of the village poets' and predicted that rapid mechanisation of the land which was to destroy the life he had known and loved in his boyhood:

I am the last of village poets;
A plank bridge croons but modest songs,
I celebrate the requiem mass
Of censer-swinging leafy birch.

The iron guest will soon appear
And pace the paths of azure fields,
His swarthy hand will snatch away
The oaten sheaves spilled out by dawn.[2]

Provocative in his manners and verse, Esenin paraded, at times, words and expressions which are banned from civilised intercourse. And when he could no longer rely upon his former inspiration, he continued to pile up images some of which were tiresomely laboured. Yet his poems of 'tavern Moscow' (*kabátskaya Moskvá*) have a genuine ring and produce at times the effect of lived hallucinations.

1. Freely paraphrased by R. M. Hewitt.
2. Translated by G. Reavey in *Soviet Literature* (Wishart).

5

It was during those years of irresponsible scandal and confusion that his nostalgia for his lost and therefore poetically embellished Arcadia became particularly painful. The more so because one can guess from his *Return Home* (1924), that the new Soviet village had left little or no room for his old dreams.

> Rain with arrows in a crowd
> Has convulsed my home with clod,
> Mowed the blue bud from the land,
> Trampled down the golden sand,
> Rain with arrows in a crowd.[1]

Even his sister, a fresh peasant girl, was found by him poring over Marx's *Capital* 'as if it were a Bible'. His idyllic Russia was gone. All that she left behind was the nervousness of a transition period, alien to his simple peasant instincts. For, with all his decadent ways, Esenin was much too simple for the age and the conditions he was now compelled to live in. Having tasted glory and adulation, anarchy and hooliganism, travels (together with Isadora Duncan) in America, Germany and France, he yet remained inwardly tied to the 'patriarchal' village—inert and soothing because of its very inertia. But while refusing to outgrow it, he suddenly saw himself stranded and as if left behind by the new 'sovietised' countryside which he refused to accept. Hence his aimlessness and bewilderment. His early fame had unbalanced him like strong adulterated wine indulged in by a child.

Too sensitive and much too weak to face the new realities around him, he remained hanging in the air—a stranger to the world in which there was no room for archaic dreams and visions. He took revenge upon life as upon himself through a kind of moral *harakiri*, and revelled in the process of gradual self-destruction. It is true that during the last two years of his life he had a few quieter intervals, but it was the quiet of tiredness and a surrender to his own dismay. He also managed to be at peace with the Soviet government. In 1922 he even wrote a dramatic poem about the rebel Pugachov. But spells of peace and resignation did not last long with him. Even in those moments when he was inclined to 'accept all without yearning for anything,' he still yearned : for his squandered youth and for the rural Atlantis submerged by the Revolution. He felt he was a walking anachronism out of joint with everybody and everything. All he could do was to translate his sorrow into lyrics, or else stifle it in riotous night life.

With regard to form, too, he now underwent a change. Having abandoned the eccentricities of his 'imaginist' phase, he chose for his model the genius of Pushkin. Once more he sang in simple intimate strains. In his *Persian Themes* he even caught something of Pushkin's serenity—at least for a short while. But before long he was wallowing again in a confusion in which the gap between fancy and reality was steadily widening. It was no use drugging himself with wine, women and scandal. Besides, he felt too tired for expedients of this

1. Translated by C. M. Bowra, *Op. cit.*

kind. At the age of thirty he was like a man who has nothing more to hope for, to work for, to look forward to. A victim of hypochondria, disgust, and self-disgust, he saw only one escape and took it. A juvenile melodramatic touch was lent to his death by the fact that he wrote his last poem in his own blood.

Such was the literary career of the poet whose personal fate was in a way symbolic of the transitional period between the two Russias—the old and the new; between the agricultural pattern of existence on the one hand, and the birth-pangs of the industrialised Soviet system on the other. The conflict involved by this transition found in Esenin a pathetic voice which, in its turn, appealed to thousands of readers and was responsible for his vogue during and after the Revolution. It was this nostalgia that found a ready response in such readers who regretted the passing away of rural Russia, and these consisted by no means of mere *kulaks*.

Each period has its own swan-song. The landed-gentry period of Russian life found it in Turgenev; the intelligentsia period in Chekhov; and the patriarchal peasant Russia in Esenin. Suspended over the gulf between the vanishing past and the much too complicated and problematic future, he could not help reacting in the way he did: by suicide. Some five years later his action was followed by another young poet, Vladimir Mayakovsky, whose personal fate, was, however, closely bound up with the Soviet system and with those very changes which had seemed so unacceptable to Sergey Esenin.

CHAPTER TWENTY-FIVE

From Mayakovsky to Pasternak

Apart from being the most prominent poetic voice of the revolutionary period, Vladimir Mayakovsky is something of a landmark in modern Russian poetry as a whole. As a champion of the Futurist movement in Russia he was bound to relegate traditional poetry to the irrevocable past. This does not mean, however, that Russian Futurism was either homogenous or even particularly original in its character. Indeed, what could there have been in common between the decadent ego-futurist Igor Severyanin (the type of impecunious provincial *parvenu* who dreams of smart women, motor-cars and champagne) on the one hand, and such a bellicose poet as Mayakovsky on the other?[1] Nor does the intensely talented but placid dreamer Velemir Khlebnikov (1885-1922), with his archaic and 'dadaist' (*avant la lettre*) experiments with words, endorse the real aims of that current. It would also be misleading to categorise the relatively small group of Russian Futurist poets with the Italian Futurists, who had their heyday between 1910 and 1915.

The Italian movement under that label, initiated and led by Marinetti (in Paris they called him Marionetti) was a noisy reaction to Italy's over-rich and somewhat oppressive cultural heritage, both in art and literature. The very name of Futurism implied a refutation of that humanistic past which was felt to be almost a brake and a burden in an age of technology, speed and machines. Hence the deliberate attempt to undermine all cultural tradition and turn art itself into a glorification of the mechanical values of life. Marinetti's revulsion was so complete in this respect that he tried to drag, with hysterical impetus, not only literature but all the arts from the plane of culture to that of an up-to-date technical civilisation, imbued with the spirit of a Darwinian struggle for existence and the survival of the fittest. It was Marinetti who anticipated (via d'Annunzio and a semi-digested, misunderstood Nietzsche) the elements of Fascism and of the 'dynamic' mailed fist. The characteristics of that tendency can be gathered from the *Initial Manifesto*, issued during the exhibition of Italian Futurist art in London in 1912. Here are some of its pronouncements:

> Literature has hitherto glorified thoughtful immobility, ecstasy, and sleep; we shall extol aggressive movement, feverish insomnia, the double quick-step, the somersault, the box on the ear, the fisticuff.
> We wish to glorify War—the only health-giver of the world—militarism,

1. Severyanin was in fact repudiated by the actual group of Futurists.

patriotism; the destructive arm of the anarchist, the beautiful ideas that kill, contempt for woman.

We wish to destroy the museums, the libraries; we fight against moralism, feminism, and all opportunistic and utilitarian meannesses.

Set fire to the shelves of libraries! Divert the courses of the canals to flood the cellars of the museums! Oh! may the glorious canvases drift helpless! Seize pickaxes and hammers! Sap the foundations of the venerable cities!

We stand upon the summit of the world and once more cast our challenge to the stars!'

The frothy rhetoric of these sentences speaks for itself. A psychologist could easily detect in it the fury of vainglorious but sterile minds anxious to lay the blame for their own sterility on the rich tradition of the past. In Russia, however, where there was little evidence of an abundant and over-ripe cultural heritage, the position as well as the task of the Futurists was essentially different. It is true that a new poetic technique, more appropriate to our modern pace and manner of life, was one of their aims. But since the overwhelming tradition of Russia's past was one of political oppression and the very negation of culture, her fight for the future had to start with a fight against those very evils. It also explains the curious paradox that, while in Italy Futurism degenerated into cultural nihilism and a staunch supporter of Fascist tyranny, in Russia it turned towards Revolution, which had discovered its principal poet in Mayakovsky.

2

The innovations introduced by Mayakovsky were directed not only against the canonised values of the past, but above all against the established poetic technique in general. What he demanded was not drawing-room poetry, but a new and robust manner which would sing without shrinking from any harshness of thought, emotion or expression. Hence his challenge :

My words
   are not used
      to caressing ears;
nor titillate
   with semi-obscenities
maiden ears
   hidden in hair so innocent.
I open on parade
   my pages of fighters,
pass in review
   their lineal front.
My verses stand
   in lead-heavy letters

ready for death
and for deathless glory.[1]

Russian Futurists, led by Mayakovsky and consisting largely of bohemian *déclassés*, started their activities in a warlike mood. Defying the prevailing public taste, they tried to revolutionise Russian prosody, word-formation, and syntax. Some of them, especially Velemir Khlebnikov, made interesting excursions into the realm of old-Slav or even 'pristine' words. Others, Kruchonykh for instance, invented a 'translogical' language[2] of their own, based not only on analogies but on the onomatopoeic suggestiveness of sound and rhythm. They went considerably further in this respect than, say, James Joyce during his last period. Mayakovsky's verbal experiments were less eccentric. In his attempt to create a type of poetry intended especially for the platform, he freed verse from its regular metre and based it on intonation, regardless of the number of syllables. His rhythmic system was thus divorced from the old lyrical melody. He was more concerned with the dynamic or dramatic value of single words instead. These he treated almost as independent units—with a new function for pauses, inflections, and also punctuation. The so-called spatial punctuation, in which patterns of peculiarly printed words extended over the whole page, had been started by the Symbolists, notably by Andrey Bely and Alexey Remizov. Mayakovsky adopted it for his own purpose as something obvious and brought it to perfection.

Having abandoned the former melodious and symmetrical verse, he proceeded to work out his loud staccato platform-technique by means of which a poem was often reduced to the equivalent of a poster or a cartoon—with a maximum of *striking* expressiveness. In contrast to the Symbolists, who were concerned with the inner reality of existence, he concentrated upon an intensified rendering of external things as such. Hence the harsh 'palpability' of his words, metaphors and similies, of his parallelisms and associations. He indulged in assonances and did his best to depoetise poetry by using common words, slang, and street and tavern-jargon. At the same time he made use of hyperbolism on a colossal scale. He refers to himself as walking about with the sun as his monocle and holding Napoleon on a leash like a terrier. Yet Mayakovsky's depoetised verse tends to be poetry of a new and forcefully suggestive kind. The *Prologue* to one of his longer works—A Cloud in Trousers (Óblako v shtanákh)—may serve as an illustration.

Your thought
that muses on a sodden brain,
as a fattened lackey on a green couch,
I shall taunt with my heart's bloody tatters;
satiate my insolent, caustic contempt.
Not a single grey hair streaks my soul,
not a trace of grandfatherly fondness!
I shake the world with the might of my voice,

1. Translated by George Reavey in *Soviet Literature* (Wishart)
2. *Zaúmny yazýk.*

and stalk—handsome,
twenty-two year old.

Gentle souls!
You fiddle sweet loves,
but the crude club their love on a drum.
Try, as I do, and wrench
yourself inside out and be engulfing lips!
Come and be lessoned—
prim graduates of the angel league,
from boudoirs lisping in cambric!
You who tranquilly finger your lips
as cooks page a cookery book.

. . . .

I do not believe in flowery Nice!
I sing once again
men crumpled as hospital beds
and women as trite as a proverb.[1]

Colloquial slang, satire, parody, a mixture of the trivial and the comically grandiose—such are Mayakovsky's frequent devices. Among his Parisian poems, for example, there is one in which he chats to the Eiffel Tower, trying to make it leave 'this Paris of prostitutes, poets, bourse, the gap-yawning boulevards,' and emigrate to Soviet Russia where it would presumably feel more at ease; he ends with the promise to get it a Soviet visa—not an easy matter in those days. Or take this 'Most Extraordinary Venture', which 'happened to me, Vladimir Mayakovsky, at the Rumyantsev Summerhouse, Mount Akula, Pushkino, on the Yaroslavl' Railway.' On a hot July day, the poet—in a joking mood—invited the Sun to come down for a while and have a cup of tea with him. But the Sun took the invitation seriously and began to descend:

Coming of his own free will,
Striding with great flaming rays
Across the field
And down the hill.
I don't want to seem afraid,
So I take a few steps back.
Now his eyes are in the garden,
He's coming up the garden path.
Through the windows
And the doors,
Through every crack
In the walls and the floors
The great flaming bulk
Of the sun's body pours
And pours.

1. Translated by George Reavey. *Op. cit.*

And in a deep voice makes this exclamation :
'I have turned my fires back, you see,
For the first time since creation.
I heard you calling me.
So here I am.
Come on, you poet, hurry up with that tea,
Come on, and I want some jam!'
Tears were pouring out of my eyes
With the heat.
I was quite unsteady.
But I got to work
And soon had the samovar ready.
'All right' I said,'
'Come on, old Shiner, and take a seat.'
It must have been the devil
Who gave me the cheek
To yell out that invitation.
There I sat sadly
On the edge of the bench
In the greatest trepidation.
You see I was very scared
That things would turn out badly.
But from the sun
A strange brilliance flared
And I soon forgot
My shyness.
And gradually I got into conversation
With his celestial highness.

I began to chat
Of this and that,
I was calling him, 'old boy,'
And I clapped him on the back.
And the Sun said : 'See here,
You and I, comrade,
Are a pair, that's clear.
Come, poet, come with me,
We'll soar and we'll sing,
And defeat the world's dingy curses,
Over all that trash my beams I'll pour,
You'll flood it with your verses!'
. . . .
To shine—
No nonsense, I say,
That's the sun's slogan,
And it is mine.[1]

1. Translated by V. de Sola Pinto. The poem is quoted with some omissions.

3

Whatever subject Mayakovsky embarked upon he filled it with his own vitality, and his sonorous voice seemed to be created expressly for mass meetings. In handling the spoken word he certainly had few equals. One of his critics, Roman Jakobson, actually says that the 'word of Mayakovsky is qualitative and different from anything that preceded him in the Russian verse, and no matter how many genetic links we may try to establish—the pattern of his poetry remains profoundly original and revolutionary'. But if so, it is the more interesting to watch how and why he eventually dedicated the whole of his talent to the cause of the working classes and of the Soviet experiment. Not that such a thing happened all at once, or that there was no other side to his work. On the contrary, it is enough to compare his poetry before 1917 with the verses he wrote after the Revolution in order to see that there were at least two Maya-kovskys whose interrelation was very much dependent on the peculiar circum-stances of his life.

He was born in 1893 in the Caucasus, where his father was a forest-ranger. He did not know poverty until 1906, about which year we read in his brief auto-biography: 'Father died. End of prosperity. After father's funeral we had three roubles left. Instinctively, feverishly, we sold our chairs and tables. Moved to Moscow. Why? Not even acquaintances there.'[1] In Moscow he settled down, together with his mother and two sisters, in a precarious proletarian existence. In 1908 he became a member of the Russian Social-Democratic Party, was arrested, and spent several months in prison. During solitary confinement in 1909-10 he started writing poetry. The same year is marked by the following passage: 'Entered School of Painting, Sculpture and Architecture. Only place that did not ask for a certificate of good conduct. Worked well. Was amazed to find imitators petted and original minds badgered. My revolutionary instinct stood up for the badgered ones.'

In the Art School Mayakovsky developed his talent for painting posters—an occupation which he continued (also in his verses) until his death in 1930. It was here that he met another dissatisfied youth, David Burlyuk, who appre-ciated Mayakovsky the poet before any of his verses were published. An amus-ing example of this friend's shock-tactics occurred after Mayakovsky had read to him, for the first time, some of his early products. 'In the morning, Burlyuk, introducing me to someone, trumpeted: "Don't you know him? My genius friend. Famous poet Mayakovsky." I tried to stop him. Burlyuk was adamant. Leaving me, he bellowed: "Now write or you will make me look a regular fool." '

A poor man himself, Burlyuk yet gave Mayakovsky half a rouble daily so as to help him write poetry without starving. Before long he introduced him to two other youngsters, and all of them together now formed the nucleus of Russian Futurism. But let us quote Mayakovsky's reminiscences once again.

Khlebnikov in Moscow. His quiet genius was at that time completely over-shadowed by the roaring David. Here, too, was Kruchonykh—Futurist,

1. Translated by Herbert Marshall in his *Mayakovsky* (Pilot Press).

Jesuit of words. After a few lyrical nights we gave birth to a joint manifesto. David collected the material, copied it, christened the manifesto and published *A Slap of Public Taste*.[1]

This juvenile venture was followed by a series of lectures and scandals in the two capitals and also in the provinces. Then the year 1913 was suddenly marked by the brief 'tragedy in verse,' *Vladimir Mayakovsky*, which was actually performed in St Petersburg with Mayakovsky himself acting the principal part.

4

As the narcissistic title indicates, this work is a 'grandiose' confession and self-dramatisation, natural enough in a youth of twenty and a gate-crasher in the temple of fame. At the same time it is a display of defiance born out of despair and from a wish to serve humanity, amidst which he still felt a stranger. Like Gogol, Mayakovsky too (to use his own words) 'crucified on a cross of laughter my own tormented groan'. But whereas Gogol's figures remind one of Hogarth, those of Mayakovsky seem here to be nearer to the surrealist fantasies of a Hieronymus Bosch. Among the allegorical accessories to Mayakovsky himself one has to watch an old man—thousands of years old—with dried-up black cats; a man without an eye and one foot; a man without an ear; a man without a head—all this in the same loud 'expressionist' style which he also adopted in his next three longer poems: *A Cloud in Trousers*, *The Backbone Flute* (*Fléita iz pozvonóchnika*), and *War and the World* (*Voiná i mir*).[2]

The original title of the first of these three works was *The Thirteenth Apostle*, but it was not passed by the censor. It is a vociferous poetic document which he composed after having been rejected by an Odessa girl whom he wanted to marry. Yet as in a fugue, Mayakovsky's frustrated personal love is here combined with his social indignation raised to the point of rebellion against the world order itself. In a preface to the second edition of this work (in 1918) he referred to it as a catechism of present-day art, but this can only be applied to it in a negative, destructive sense. 'Down with your kind of love! Down with your kind of art! Down with your system of life! Down with your religion!' Such are the slogans of its four parts. Its 'colossal' metaphors are deliberately heavy; and however strange it may appear on the surface, the inner association of the outwardly incongruous things is there. For all its extravagance, this is an effective achievement in which Mayakovsky's pathos of despair is expressed by a tonality and technique of his own.

This pathos is intense and tragic in his *Backbone Flute*, which is inwardly connected with the previous poem, or rather with the previous two poems. The intimate tragedy of his love is again one of Mayakovsky's *leitmotifs*—this time played as it were on a flute made of his own backbone. Here his unrequited love

1. Translated by Herbert Marshall. *Op. cit.*
2. Since the Russian *mir* means both peace and world, a difference between the two was made only in pre-1917 spelling. In the first edition of this poem Mayakovsky used the spelling which meant the world, not peace.

is treated as a curse and a punishment, a torment and self-torment, the only result of which is inner devastation. Such a note, aggravated by a foreboding of his own tragic end, can be felt also in his anti-bourgeois poem, *Man* (*Chelovék*, 1917), which is at the same time an ecstatic apotheosis of his own personality. But in *War and the World* (written, in 1916, under the impact of the War) the social momentum is stronger. Mayakovsky here displays a poetic poster, interpreting the world in terms of the blood-stained arena in the Roman Colosseum. Anti-militaristic as it is, it ends with the dream of a better and united world, inhabited by a new species of man.

> And such day has dawned
> That Andersen's tales
> Were crawling at its feet like puppies.

5

During the whole of this period Mayakovsky's source of inspiration was, above all, his unhappy love[1] which he 'clubbed on a drum' with the chaotic world around as its accessory. But he was a rebel by temperament, by his very instinct. And so when the Revolution of 1917 broke out, the wish to join it came to him as a natural impulse. He embraced the tasks of the Revolution in their entirety and became the poet of the rising masses—even if his voice and manner were often those of a poetic 'boss' or demagogue rather than a servant of the Revolution. Yet the very fervour with which he now voiced its cause may also have been prompted by a wish to 'crush underfoot' the melody of his personal love-drama which had only been put aside rather than abolished or sublimated.[1] Hence his propaganda poems and his play, *Mystery-Bouffe* (1918, a revised edition in 1921).

This deliberate parody of the old mystery-plays is called by Mayakovsky a 'heroic, epic, and satirical picture of our epoch'. It is done in the style of a cartoon and, like all cartoons, it lacks depth, however amusing the very coarseness of its surface may be at times. The poet's familiar patting of the cosmos here passes into music-hall jokes and blasphemies, and the whole allegory is typical of the author's attempt to 'restore to the theatre its spectacular character and turn the stage itself into a platform'. The figures include the Unclean ones (the proletarians), the Clean ones (the bourgeoisie and the social high-ups), mixed up with God, angels, and devils. After the flood has destroyed the old earth, the Unclean rebel against the Clean ones and relegate them to Hell. Then they visit the heavenly Paradise which does not impress them at all. In fact, they leave it with scorn and go back to the ravaged earth which they want to transform into the Promised Land of happiness, plenty and comfort for all. The finale is similar to that of Mayakovsky's *War and the World*, but this time the stress is laid on the working class—which through the triumph of socialism, work and technique—has become the ruler of our planet.

1. He was in love with Mme Lila Brik, the wife of his friend and early publisher O. M. Brik.

Mystery-Bouffe is Mayakovsky's polar contrast to Esenin's *Inónia*. He would hear of no idyllic peasant paradise on earth. For he is not afraid of the machine and technology, provided that man shall be their master, not their slave. It is all rather schematic and simplified, yet in the years of the Civil War it must have served its purpose well. No less simplified is his long allegorical poem, *150,000,000*. Written in 1919, it represents the muzhik Ivan in a single combat with President Wilson—the champion of Capitalism. The meeting and the combat are full of allegorical imagery on a gigantic scale; but the issue of the duel is, of course, a foregone conclusion—with the prospect of a classless communist society.[1]

Such loud, 'poster'-like poetry did not require a great deal of strain on the part of the audience, since it was offered to them with the flavour of satirical journalism. Much of Mayakovsky's work after 1917 is actually a deliberate mixture of the two. Even his travel poems (1924–25) about France, Mexico, and America are journalistic *feuilletons* in verse—full of quick observations, irony and political harangues. 'In my work I am consciously becoming a newspaper man,' Mayakovsky said at a time when he was pouring out countless propaganda limericks, rhymed slogans, and *agitkas* or 'agit'-verses exhorting the Soviet citizens to perform their daily tasks and duties. He even asserted that 'meetings, speeches, front-line limericks, one-day agit-prop playlets, the living radio-voice and the slogan flashing by on the trams—are all equal and sometimes valuable examples of poetry'. To crown it all, he eventually defined his own verses as 'Com-Party' poems and did not mind calling himself an 'agitator, loud-speaker-in-chief'.

6

Such became the character of Mayakovsky's poetry when the social-political propaganda element prevailed in it. Yet even his loudest voice was not loud enough to suppress in the long run the personal dilemma which he had tried to eliminate, or at least to silence. It kept troubling him even during his most active propaganda period. In his poem *I Love* (*Lyublyú*, 1922), for example, he confessed :

> In others I know the heart's abode
> is in the bosom as we all know.
> But on me
> anatomy has run amok,
> I am nothing but heart
> tingling all over.

A year later another love poem, *About That* (*Ob étom*), reminiscent of his pre-war poetry (especially of *The Backbone Flute*) contained the following motif :

1. Lenin's attitude towards this poem was ironical and negative.

'He' and 'she' is my ballad.
The terrible thing is that 'he' is I
and that 'she' is mine.

The years that came immediately after the Civil War were at first stimulating enough to fill Mayakovsky with social enthusiasm to the exclusion (a temporary one) of disturbing personal problems. That period was responsible for
his longest and best propaganda poem, *Vladímir Ilyích Lénin* (1924), on the
occasion of Lenin's death. With all its caustic references to capitalism and its
didactic passages about 'brother Karl' (Marx), the poem reads like a paean to
the Revolution and its leader whom, with his flair for hero-worship, Mayakovsky includes among the great historical figures.

His is earthly—
    but not of those
        whose nose
delves only into
    their own little sty.
He grasped the earth
    whole,
        all at one go,
saw that
    which lay hidden
        in time.

In his diatribe against the modern super-capitalist fellow as seen from
Soviet Russia, Mayakovsky comes to the conclusion:

You can't
    jump over him
        no how you dodge past,
Only one way—
        explode![1]

During those very years he did a lot of travelling, giving recitals of his
poems. About 1925, for instance, he wrote: 'Around-the-globe was a flop.
Firstly, was robbed in Paris; secondly, after half a year of travelling, rushed
back to the U.S.S.R. Did not even go to San Francisco (where I was invited to
lecture). Travelled through Mexico, U.S.A. and bits of France and Spain.' And
about 1926: 'I continue the traditions of the troubadours and minstrels. Travel
from city to city, reciting my verses.'[1]

Between his propaganda poem, *Very Good (Khoroshó*, 1927), commemorat-
ing the tenth anniversary of the Revolution, and his impressive personal confession, *At the Top of My Voice (Vo ves' gólos)*, written in 1930, Mayakovsky
finished two satirical comedies, *The Bedbug (Klop)* and *The Bathhouse (Bánya)*.
The first is a fantastic satire—in nine pictures—on the eternal Philistine who
emerged in many a Soviet citizen during the NEP period. We see a drunken NEP

1. Translated by Herbert Marshall. *Op. cit.*

wedding, in the course of which a fire breaks out and burns all the revellers to death. Fifty years later one of them is resurrected (exactly as he was) by a special scientific method and he proves to be such a mean and vulgar bug in human form as to cause general panic. *The Bathhouse*, in six acts—'with a circus and a display of fire-works'—is grotesque satire of bureaucratic careerists in the new Soviet State. In this case the fantastic element is provided by a time-machine which can transfer one into the future. During one of such journeys the principal character (a cut-and-dried Soviet bureaucrat is left behind together with all his piled-up luggage, since the future has no room for such opportunists. None of these highly amusing works contains as much as a hint to the poet's personal secret. But in *At the Top of My Voice*,[1] the social and the personal motifs are mingled, once again, as one can see in this brief extract taken from its beginning:

> I was a sanitary man
> > and a watercarrier,
> I was mobilised,
> > called up by the Revolution,
> I went to the Front
> > from the lordly estate
> Of Poetry—
> > a capricious old lady.
> . . . .
> Yet I'm
> > utterly fed up
> > > with propaganda:
> Yes, I'd have liked
> > to strum
> > > love songs to you,
> They bring in good money
> > and they're delightful.
> But I
> > conquered myself
> > and stamped
> On the throat of my own song.
> So listen here,
> > comrade posterity,
> Listen to an agitator,
> > a wild bawling ranter.[2]

These anti-propagandist lines often were interpreted as proof of Mayakovsky's disappointment with the Revolution. They prove, however, only one thing: that even his work for the Revolution was not enough to save him from the complications of an intimate personal dilemma. Moreover, if he deliberately

1. This was to be the prologue to a long poem about The Five-Year Plan which he intended to write shortly before his suicide in 1930.
2. Translated by V. de Sola Pinto.

chose to flee from it, to 'stamp on the throat' of his own love song, then his revolutionary activities may often have been escapism from himself. To make things worse, during his stay in Paris in 1928 he fell violently in love with Tatyana Yakovleva—a beautiful refugee girl to whom he proposed. But his Parisian charmer evidently did not respond to his love and would not hear of returning with him to Russia. This was another painful frustration. Back in Moscow again, Mayakovsky became more and more involved in the squabbles of the literary cliques. He also had some misunderstandings with the Soviet authorities. In addition to all this he was suffering from a chronic throat complaint and general exhaustion, not to mention those inner complications which were now coming to a head. These were due above all to the paradox that Mayakovsky the fighter for the future of mankind was yet too much of an egotist ever to merge entirely with those masses whose poetic and ideological leader he was supposed to be. His very exhibitionism and self-dramatisation at the top of his voice were a proof that he was not only conscious of the gap but also desperately anxious to close it. His frustration in love made his predicament all the more painful. So much so that when, on 14 April 1930, he put an end to his life, he gave away his secret (in his last farewell letter) by these two simple statements: 'My love-boat has been smashed against the rock of everyday trivialities,' and 'For me there is no outlet'.

7

It is not yet easy to entirely assess Mayakovsky's place in Russian literature. Nor was the appreciation of his work unanimous as one can judge by this rather venomous remark of Ivan Bunin:

> We have lived through Decadence and Symbolism; through Neo-naturalism and pornography calling itself the solution of the sex-problem; through the struggle with God, myth-making, mystical Anarchism, Dionysus and Apollo; through the 'break into eternity', sadism, snobism, the 'acceptance of the world', the 'non-acceptance of the world'; through primitive fakes of the Russian style, Adamism, Acmeism—and now we have arrived at the shallowest kind of hooliganism bearing the unsuitable label of Futurism. Is this not the Valpurgis night?

Such condemnation on the part of Bunin (enumerating all the fashionable though mostly ephemeral literary cliques and currents of the modernist period) is of course a voice of extreme opposition. This does not detract from Mayakovsky's importance in modern Russian poetry, since he did his best to revolutionise, not only the poetic technique, but the very role of poetry by insisting, in his later phases, on its social function almost at the expense of everything else. No wonder that Stalin himself canonised him (in 1935) as the greatest poet of the Revolution; and in those days any pronouncement which came from Stalin was sacrosanct. Among the poets who joined Mayakovsky largely on account of his new poetic technique were some of the Constructivists (Ilya Selvinsky,

Edward Bagritsky, Vera Inber, K. Zelinsky and V. Lugovskoy). They were connected with Mayakovsky's periodical *LEF* (Left Front in Art, 1923–24), with its equally short-lived successor, *New LEF* (1928), and they regarded Mayakovsky's technique as the most suitable for an age of industry in which the competent artisan of poetry was presumably going to replace the artist.

‾ One of the prominent poetic works of that period was Bagritsky's *Lay about Opanas* (*Dúma pro Opanása*, 1926). This is a well-told poetic narrative about an Ukrainian Red soldier captured during the Civil War by the Whites and compelled by them to shoot his own Red commander who was also one of their prisoners. Later on Opanas is recaptured by the Reds, confesses whom he has shot, and quietly accepts death as a just punishment for what he has done. During those years propaganda poetry, as devised by Mayakovsky, found its most popular exponents in Damyan Bedny (E. Pridvorov, 1883–1945) and Alexander Bezymensky (b. 1898). Both were topical in their civic poetry—to the extent of being journalists in verse and mouthpieces of the Party. Among the well-known early followers of Mayakovsky were also Nikolai Aseyev (b. 1889), Vasily Kamensky (b. 1884) and Nikolai Tikhonov (b. 1896).

Nikolai Aseyev, a talented Siberian poet, joined Mayakovsky in 1913 and achieved fame by his collection of anti-NEP poems, *Lyrical Digression* (*Lirícheskoe otstuplénie*, 1924). His *Twenty-Six* (1925), a ballad about the twenty-six Red Commissars, executed by the British two years earlier in Baku, was one of the popular poems of the time. Vasily Kamensky, one of the Formalist group,[1] became widely known after he had switched over to Mayakovsky's team. Broader in his range was Nikolai Tikhonov. Soon after 1921 he made a mark by a number of ballads, satires and lyrics, as well as by some good prose. As a lover of life, travel and adventure he always found plenty of material on which to exercise his talent. Finally, a certain affiliation with Mayakovsky was claimed even by such an accomplished poet as Boris Pasternak (1890–1960) whose literary culture was definitely more solid than that of Mayakovsky.

Pasternak's autobiographic *Safe Conduct* (*Okhránnaya grámota*), written in fine impressionistic prose and dedicated to Rainer Maria Rilke—surely the greatest contrast to Mayakovsky—contains an account of his own early contacts and meetings with the leader of Russian Futurism. And while reading those pages one cannot help being startled by Pasternak's shrewd remark that the mainspring of Mayakovsky's aggressive aplomb or lack of shyness was a 'wild shyness, and beneath his pretended freedom his phenomenally apprehensive lack of freedom, inclined towards a purposeless moroseness'. But in the beginning Pasternak was a sincere admirer of Mayakovsky's work, talent and vitality. It was only later that he adopted a more critical attitude towards him and his work. When referring to Mayakovsky's reading of 150,000,000 to a circle of friends, Pasternak tells that 'for the first time I had nothing to say to him. We met in Russia and abroad, we tried to work together and I found myself understanding him less and less.'[2]

1. The Formalists paid particular attention to a good structure and a fine pattern of words.
2. *Boris Pasternak—Prose and Poems*, edited by S. Schimansky (Benn).

This was the beginning of a rift between the two important representatives of post-Symbolist poetry in Russia. While Mayakovsky, with his deafening voice, remained a poet for the platform and the masses, Pasternak became a poet's poet, intimately subjective, discreet and in his early phase accessible to the few. In contrast to Mayakovsky, who was all of this world, Pasternak never forgot the realities of man's spirit, no matter whether the Party approved of it or not. The difference between himself and such thundering 'loudspeakers' of Bolshevism as Mayakovsky, Bedny or Bezymensky was stressed openly in one of Pasternak's late poems, a few stanzas of which are worth quoting also as an indication of his own poetic creed.

> To give your all—this is creation,
> And not—to deafen and eclipse.
> How shameful, when you have no meaning,
> To be on everybody's lips.
>
> Into obscurity retiring,
> Try your development to hide;
> As autumn mist on early mornings
> Conceals the dreamy countryside.
>
> Another, step by step, will follow
> The living imprint of your feet;
> But you yourself must not distinguish
> Your victory from your defeat.
>
> And never for a single moment
> Betray your *credo* or pretend,
> But be alive—this only matters—
> Alive and burning to the end.[1]

8

Yet Pasternak himself had taken over from Mayakovsky some of those technical devices which he needed for his own poetic creations. His first real success in this respect was his third collection of poems, *My Sister Life* (*Sestrá moyá zhizn'*), written in 1917 and published in 1922. This booklet was inevitably considered difficult poetry, since it demanded a considerable effort on the part of the reader to assimilate it at all. Pasternak, like Mayakovsky, gave up the old melodious flow of the Russian verse as well as the exclusive use of a 'poetic' vocabulary, but not to the same extent as Mayakovsky. In the majority of his poems he preserved the traditional versification. On the other hand he filled them with assonances, unexpected metaphors and associations—all this in addition to the peculiar texture of his verses and to his art of *ostranénie*, that is of making obvious things look strange. He certainly knew how to approach familiar objects and phenomena from a new and unfamiliar angle.

1.   *Poems by Boris Pasternak*. Translated by E. Slater (Peter Russell).

Only one year after *My Sister Life* Pasternak published his *Themes and Variations* (*Témy i variyátsii*) which further enhanced his reputation. His next booklet, *Spektórsky* (1926), consisting of nine narrative poems in five-footed iambics, was obviously autobiographical with a complex love story during the NEP period. Technically it was more accessible than his previous verses. And so were his *The Year 1905* and *Lieutenant Schmidt*, both of them written about the same time and showing the poet's wish to abandon his apolitical attitude. He tackled here the first Russian Revolution on the one hand, and the tragic fate of the leader of the rebellious marines on the cruiser *Potyomkin* on the other. In *The Second Birth* (*Vtoróe rozhdénie*, 1932), he became again predominantly a poet's poet and a romantic concerned with the task of man's inner growth and rebirth. A number of those poems reflect his stay in the Caucasus with the motifs and landscapes reminiscent at times of Lermontov, with whom Pasternak had certain affinities and to whom he had dedicated *My Sister Life*.

During Stalin's blood-stained purges in the 1930s Pasternak was busy mainly as translator. He was responsible for excellent Russian versions of Shakespeare's *Hamlet*, *Othello*, *Romeo and Juliet*, and *Anthony and Cleopatra*. His translations of Goethe's *Faust*, of Petöfi's lyrics, as well as of verses from several Georgian poets further increased his prestige. They also strengthened his decision to achieve a greater amount of lucidity and significance in everything he wrote. What this meant to him was proved by his subsequent controversial novel, *Doctor Zhivago*. An appreciation of this work can, however, best be made in conjunction with the character and evolution of the Soviet novel as a whole.

CHAPTER TWENTY-SIX

Towards a pattern of the Soviet novel

I

The cataclysm of 1917 brought chaos not only to Russia's political, economic and social life, but also to her culture, beginning with her proudest heritage—literature. Moreover, during the Civil War printing became so disorganised that practically no books could be published. Lack of paper was a further reason for such a lull. Unpublished poetry, though, found an outlet, or rather a shelter, during those harrowing months in certain bohemian cafés where it was recited by the poets to any customers willing (or even unwilling) to listen. It was only from 1921–22 onwards that printing, as well as publishing, began to be restored, but in conditions entirely different from those before the Revolution and the Civil War.

The ferment caused by the Revolution inevitably made most of the established writers feel displaced and bewildered. Quite a few of the well-known literary men preferred to leave the country and settle as *émigrés* abroad—in Paris, Berlin, and other places where they felt safe. Among those who left Russia were Ivan Bunin, Alexey Remizov, Ivan Shmelyov, Konstantin Balmont, Dmitry Merezhkovsky, Vladislav Khodasevich, Boris Zaitsev and Zinaida Hippius. One of the early émigrés was the gifted young woman poet Marina Tsvetayeva (Marina Efron) whose intensely rhythmical and very 'Russian' narrative poem, *The King Maiden* (*Tsar' Devítsa*) made quite a stir when it appeared in 1922. Later she returned to the Soviet Union, but evidently unable to fit into the conditions she found there, she committed suicide in 1941.

Some of those authors who had remained in Russia were forced to become 'internal émigrés': Fyodor Sologub, for example, and the modernist poets Maximilian Voloshin (1877–1932) and Osip Mandelshtam. As for the writers who had settled abroad the majority were only too eager to fume against the Soviet government and the Soviet system—Merezhkovsky being at the head of them all. But while Merezhkovsky himself failed to create any significant works after he left Russia, such authors as Ivan Bunin and Alexey Remizov (1877–1957) showed undiminished creative activity in exile. In this way they were helping to increase the bulk of Russian émigré literature with its centres in Paris, Berlin and partly in Prague.[1] Remizov even managed to remain as 'Russian' as ever. This prolific follower of Leskov's *skaz* and master of the

1. For further particulars consult Professor Gleb Struve's *Russian Literature in Exile* (in Russian, N.Y. 1956).

racy folk speech continued to live in the same fairyland of Russian folklore as he had indulged in before he left Russia.

Such was, however, only one aspect of Remizov's stylised prose. Its other aspect consisted of gloomy and tragic themes. His early Moscow novel, *The Pond* (*Prud*, 1907) and his Petersburg narrative, *The Sisters of the Cross* (*Krestóvye syóstry*, 1910) are in this category. And so are such stories of provincial life as *Iván Semyónovich Stratilátov* (1909) and *The Fifth Pestilence* (*Pyátaya yázva*, 1912). But he was able to present his readers also with such an idyllic picture of a country girl's mind and growth as his *On a Field of Azure* (*V póle blakítnom*, 1910, 1922). Moreover, both the Revolution and the Civil War were amply recorded by him in his *Chronicle of 1917* and a crop of other documentary accounts. Remizov will best be remembered, however, for his renderings and paraphrases of the people's tales. His voluminous collection *Tales of the Russian People* (*Skázki rússkogo naróda*, Berlin 1923) is always a delight to open. In a similar manner he composed his own *Tales of the Monkey King Asyka* (*Skázki obezyányego tsaryá Asýki*, Berlin 1922). He was equally keen on compiling old apocrypha and legends. In all this Remizov proved to be a great connoisseur and stylist of his native tongue. In fact, together with Bely he exercised a considerable influence upon several young Soviet authors.

Among the most prolific émigré writers was Mark Aldanov (1886–1957) whose numerous historical novels, dealing mainly with Russia's past, are well documented and written with a true narrative verve. A notable contribution to émigré literature was Shmelyov's *The Sun of the Dead* (*Sólntse myórtvykh*, 1923), a nightmarish novel about the Crimea during the famine and chaos after the Revolution. Ivan Shmelyov (1879–1956) had begun his literary activity in Gorky's *Znánie* group, and one of his early successes was *The Man from the Restaurant* (*Chelovék iz restoróna*, 1911)—a narrative describing the fate of a pathetic old-world waiter. Of Shmelyov's other narratives and novels published abroad his *Inexhaustible Cup* (*Neupiváyemaya chásha*, Paris 1922), *Love Story* (*Istóriya lyubóvnaya*, Paris 1929), and *Heavenly Paths* (*Putí nebésnye*, Paris 1937–38) can be mentioned.

2

There were several authors who stayed put, threw in their lot with the new regime, and carefully watched the shape of things to come. The towering figure among these was Maxim Gorky. Although opposing, even violently opposing, at first, the dictatorial Bolshevist methods, he welcomed the Revolution itself; and it was for its sake that he soon became not only a tireless organiser, but the very pivot of Soviet literary activities. He remained a great cultural and moral force of the nascent new era even during his prolonged stay abroad (1922–28), mainly in Italy. Nor did his literary output suffer any eclipse. On the contrary, he even increased it. His last novel, *Life of Klim Samgin*, for example, is also one of his biggest creative efforts. Whatever its single faults, it is indispensable for anyone anxious to get an idea of the cultural, social and political climate whose outcome was the Revolution of 1917.

Among the authors who refused to emigrate were the two leaders of Russian Symbolism—Alexander Blok and Andrey Bely, while their third partner, Vyacheslav Ivanov, eventually went abroad. Symbolist poetry as such was now a matter of the past. But whereas Blok died a tired and puzzled man soon after completing *The Twelve*, Andrey Bely continued writing as hectically as ever. It was after the Revolution that he published his autobiographic narrative, *Kitten Letayev* (*Kótik Letáyev*, 1922), which is likely to amaze and at times exasperate a careful reader. It begins with the author's pre-natal state, that is with his traumatic experiences while still in his mother's womb. The narration continues up to his fifth year through all sorts of impressions, mythological perceptions, images and symbols. Parents, his nurse, relatives, visitors, servants, the first views of Moscow—they all are arranged in such a way as to show the gradual formation of his early consciousness and self-consciousness. The narrative is of great psychological interest; but presented in Bely's ornate rhythmical prose, it is at times so full of neologisms and syntactic tricks as to demand considerable strain on the part of the reader. Moreover, reminiscences of a child are mixed up with comments of a man of thirty-five, which add some further difficulties to its structure. Less effort is required in its unfinished sequel, *The Baptized Chinaman* (*Kreshchóny kitáyets*, 1920–28), its curious title being the nickname of his own unprepossessing-looking father, who now becomes the central figure of the narrative.

In 1921 Bely was allowed by the Soviet government to go to Berlin. In the German capital he completed his somewhat chaotic—in a way pathologically chaotic—*Memoirs of a Queer Fellow* (*Zapíski chudaká*, 1922) and issued a revised edition of his *Petersburg*, as well as a revised but questionable collective edition of all his poems, with comments interpreting them as a kind of spiritual and esoteric autobiography. It was in Berlin, too, that he had a last interview with his wife, Asya, who came for this purpose from Dornach and then parted from him for ever, regardless of his despair. On his return to Russia, in 1923, Bely wrote his Moscow novel in two volumes: *A Moscow Eccentric* (*Moskóvsky chudák*, 1925) and *Moscow Under the Blow* (*Moskvá pod udárom*, 1925), to which he added, later on, *The Masks* (*Máski*, 1932). Actually the characters presented in this novel are more like grotesque masks than people made of flesh and blood. Bely's parents and Bely himself are parodied. The plot hinges on Professor Korobkin's mathematical formula or calculation which is capable of leading to an invention powerful enough to reduce the world to ruin. The German secret service gets wind of it and its agents are anxious to obtain the formula whatever the cost. What follows is a number of confusing scenes, including sadistic tortures inflicted upon the Professor in order to extract his secret from him. And the background of it all is Moscow drifting towards chaos and 'dancing over an abyss' on the very eve of the Revolution.

These novels were a sign that Bely's creative power was on the wane. Written in more extravagant rhythmic prose than even his previous narratives, they are far below the excellence of *Petersburg* and *The Silver Dove*. On the other hand, those very years were responsible for a series of Bely's important memoirs, the most fascinating of which are his *Reminiscences of Blok* (begun in 1922). His *On the Border of two Centuries* (*Na rubezhé dvukh stolétiy*) was published in 1930, *The Turn of the Century* (*Nachálo véka*) in 1933, and *Between the Two Revolutions* (*Mézhdu dvukh revolyútsiy*) in 1935. With all their caprices and subjectivity, these works are of great interest to readers studying the history of Russian symbolism on the one hand, and the mental and cultural ferment of the period concerned on the other. Towards the end of his life Bely had, moreover, summoned enough energy to finish a solid investigation of the peculiarities of Gogol's prose under the title, *The Craft of Gogol* (*Masterstvó Gógolya*, 1934).

Bely remained in Russia probably because he hoped to see the Russian Revolution imbued with some of those spiritual values which he regarded as being of utmost importance. In this he failed. Yet he did not quarrel with the Soviets and did his best to be on good terms with them ideologically. Considering his many changes, as well as the contradictions of his split personality, such adaptability was not surprising. During the last few years of his erratic existence his mind often seemed to grow clouded. He died in a state of mental disturbance on 8 January, 1934.

3

The younger writers, those born after 1890, came into their own as soon as the brunt of the revolutionary turmoil was over. They were divided into 'fellow travellers' (as Trotsky labelled them) on the one hand, and open supporters of Bolshevism on the other. Whereas the 'fellow travellers' accepted the Revolution without necessarily accepting the Communist creed, a number of newly-fledged proletarian writers, dogmatically adhering to that creed, demanded a literature and indeed a culture representing the proletarian class mentality to the exclusion of everthing else. The Proletcult,[1] supported by some other cliques (the Futurists included), advocated a proletarian literature in the name of which they were ready to throw overboard the classical literary heritage and destroy the continuity between past and present. Lenin, Trotsky, Gorky and Lunacharsky (the Commissar for Education) were however among the first to point out the fallacy of this attitude. According to them there was no such thing as a purely proletarian culture. And as for a true Socialist culture or literature, it should be above class and at the same time absorb all that was best and truly valuable in past cultures. Nevertheless, there were plenty of dogmatic Proletcult champions clamouring for a proletarian literature as such. But since they were only too often concerned with ideological orthodoxy rather than with the artistic quality of their literary products, they could hardly compete with the team of able 'fellow travellers', or else with the small but creatively agile group of the so-called 'Serapion Brothers'.

1. Out of it sprang during the first Five-Year Plan the intolerant RAPP (Russian Association of Proletarian Writers), under the chairmanship of the critic Leopold Averbakh.

This group, which lasted as a more or less compact body from 1921 until 1924, included some of the brightest lights of the younger generation.[1] It is significant that its very name was taken from one of the romantic tales by E. T. A. Hoffmann. This was proof of their wish to be independent of any didactic or utilitarian purposes as far as literature was concerned. Nor did they see a work of art as a passive copy of reality, but as a creation with a life of its own. As the prematurely deceased playwright Lev Lunts had put it (in 1922): 'Art is as real as life itself, and like life itself it exists because it is unable not to exist.' During the Civil War, and immediately after, it was, however, above all 'engaged' poetry that mattered.

In his periodical *LEF* Mayakovsky was joined by experimenting Constructivists and Formalists—at least for a while. The Formalists, led by V. Shklovsky, were keen on the 'return to craft' (*masterstvó*). They did not reject the ideological contents in art, but regarded the so-called contents as one of the aspects of the form itself. In architecture they adhered to Le Corbusier's formula that a 'house is a machine to live in'. Literature they conceived as a result of a rationalistic technical process, but concerned with contemporary themes and facts.[2] After 1930 this group practically ceased to exist. Whereas the 'Serapion Brothers', as well as the 'fellow travellers', were apolitical, the Proletcult writers, especially those of the *On the Guard* (*Na postú*) group, led by A. A. Bogdanov, continued to stick to their idea of a proletarian class literature as a panacea for all ills.

4

In spite of the chaotic conditions between 1917 and 1922, the literary results, even immediately after that period, were not without interest. There was an abundance of material to draw upon from happenings during the Revolution and the Civil War. Such elderly authors as Alexander Serafimovich, Vikenty Veresayev (V. Smidovich) and especially Alexey N. Tolstoy[3] were so much carried away by what they had witnessed that they recorded their experiences in narratives and novels of great documentary value. Veresayev's *Deadlock* (*V tupiké*) appeared as early as 1922 and gave a fair diagnosis of that difficult transition from the old to the new which to some intellectuals must have seemed almost insuperable. A Marxist of the Gorky group, he treated the

1. Among its members were Konstantin Fedin, Evgeny Zamyatin, Vsevolod Ivanov, Venyamin Kaverin, Mikhail Zoshenko, Victor Shklovsky, Lev Lunts, Nikolai Nikitin, Nikolai Tikhonov and Vladimir Pozner.
2. It sounds strange that some of the Formalists (V. Shklovsky, B. Tomashevsky), who were connected with Mayakovsky's *LEF*, advocated the theory that the novel as a literary genre was doomed and had no future. It was to be replaced by the newspaper and literature of facts. This idea was voiced in the 1920s, when the Soviet novel itself celebrated some of its early triumphs.
3. Alexey N. Tolstoy was among the first to go abroad, but he soon returned to Russia, made peace with the Soviets and became one of the most prominent Soviet authors. It was while abroad, that he had written his autobiographic *Nikita's Childhood* (*Détstvo Nikity*, 1921)—one of the great pictures of a child's life in the Russian language.

situation from the standpoint of the bankrupt intelligentsia. Serafimovich, on the other hand, who already had an anti-capitalist novel, *A Town in the Steppe* (*Górod v stepí*), to his credit, was more interested in the reactions of the masses and the mass mentality. In his *Iron Flood* (*Zhelézny potók*, 1924) he gave an agitated account of the fighting between the Reds and the Whites in the northern Caucasus. This is how he describes the predicament of a village crowd escaping from tsarist Cossack attacks :

> In a frenzied congestion at the approach to the bridge people were hacking with axes at the wheels of one another's carts, falling upon each other with poles and whips; roars, imprecations, shrieks, the dirge-like wailing of women, the whimpering of infants; the bridge itself was blocked with carts locked together, snorting horses, trapped people and children moaning and crying in anguish . . . unable to go either back or forwards . . . and from behind the orchards came the menacing rat-tat-tat.[1]

His picture of mass movements is one of heroic nightmares made all the more grim by starvation, torrents of rain, as well as by continuous Georgian and Cossack invasions. Yet the author of this novel was concerned not only with the turmoil, but also with the deeper meaning of the happenings described.

Broader in its scope and canvas was Alexey Tolstoy's voluminous *The Road to Calvary*.[2] Begun in 1919 at Berlin, it was finished in Moscow as late as 1941. It is a panorama of Russia on the eve of World War I, of the war years, and of the Revolution as it affected four sensitive and seeking members of the intelligentsia who in the end accept the change and all it stands for. In this important Soviet novel the facts of history are closely intertwined with personal fates, while history itself is treated in a manner transcending the peripeties of a mere class struggle. The dramatic character of this novel is not devoid of optimism either.

The same period of the struggle between the old and the new was tackled by S. Sergeyev-Tsensky in a series of novels which he started in 1923 under the general symbolic title 'Transfiguration'. In contrast to Alexey Tolstoy's broad epic vein, Sergeyev-Tsensky adheres more to the chronicle type of narration, but with a skill and zest of his own. Another older author, Panteleimon Romanov, made a hit with his *Comrade Kislyakóv* (1930)[3]—a novel depicting the moral decay among the intellectuals and the intelligentsia women during the years of the cataclysm. To the names of the established authors who continued to work in the Soviet Union Mikhail Prishvin and Ivan Novikov should be added. Prishvin (1873–1954) came into prominence in 1907 as a splendid observer and admirer of nature. After the Revolution he presented Soviet literature with the largely autobiographic narratives, *Kurýmushka* and *Kashchéy's Chain* (*Kashchéyeva tsep'*, 1924). But in his much later work, *The Forest Thaw* (*Lesnáya Kapél'*, 1945) he gave vent, once more, to his exceptionally intimate feeling for nature. As for Ivan Novikov (b. 1879), he distinguished him-

1.   *The Iron Flood* (Lawrence).
2.   Such is the title of the English translation (1945). The original title is *The Path of Suffering* (*Khozhdénie po múkam*).
3.   *Three Pairs of Stockings* in the English translation.

self mainly by his biographical novels about Pushkin in connection with the centenary of the great poet's death. Another older writer, Vyacheslav Shishkov (1873–1945) gave in his *The Gang* (*Vatága*, 1923) a lively description of a quaint community of Siberian Old Believers who joined the partisans during the Civil War. He dealt with life in Siberia also in such fine narratives as *Taigá* and *The Ugryum River* (*Ugryúm-reká*). His long and much later historical novel *Pugachóv* (about the same leader of the rebellious Cossacks as in Pushkin's *The Captain's Daughter*) remained unfinished. One of the writers who stayed in Russia, P. P. Bazhov (1879–1950), published in 1939 a remarkable collection of tales about the Russian people with an intense folkloristic flavour in his *Malachite Box* (*Malakhítovaya shkatúlka*). His *Stone Flower* (*Kámenny tsvetók*) was the origin of an opera by Prokofyev.

In addition to these elderly authors there was a profusion of young new-comers, some of whom succeeded in raising the Soviet novel to quite a high level. The exciting experiences they had gone through during the Civil War were presented by them in a lively and agitated style which was not devoid of technical devices taken over from Remizov and Bely, or from such 'Sera-pions' as Victor Shklovsky and Evgeny Zamyatin. Symbolically coloured 'dynamic' prose, mixed up with naturalism, was one of their frequent methods. Some of these young writers were quick to establish a link with the classical prose of Russian literature—the prose of Tolstoy, Dostoevsky, Turgenev and Chekhov, thus keeping, as far as possible, the continuity in Russian *belles lettres* alive. The majority of the early Soviet novelists also wrote short stories and *nouvelles*, often of no mean artistic quality.

The literary leadership during that stage of the Soviet prose was in the hands of 'fellow travellers' and the allied 'Serapion Brothers'. They were anxious to assert their creative independence, however much the Proletcult writers (entrenched in such organisations as 'The Smithy', 'October', 'On the Guard', 'On the Literary Guard') demanded a literature subservient to the Party line. In his defence of artistic freedom Evgeny Zamyatin [1] maintained that literature should be concerned only with truth and not with any Party dictates or dogmas. As a kind of warning of what might happen under a bureaucratic totalitarian system, whether from the left or from the right, he wrote in suggestively abbreviated or even unfinished sentences a vitriolic skit under the title *We* (*My*). It is about the Single State in some distant future, when instead of individuals there will be only human numbers preferring—in the spirit of Dostoevsky's Grand Inquisitor—happiness without freedom to freedom without happiness. In such a system 'all days are of the same colour—yellow, like dried up parched sand'. The great dangers are, of course, man's soul and imagination. But the citizens of the Single State are relieved of burdens of this kind by a special surgical operation from which no one is exempt. Such a protest against de-

---

1. Zamyatin, who was one of the Formalist innovators, had made a name as a writer even before 1914 by his volume of *Parochial Sketches* (*Uyézdnoe*) with its ruthless pictures of provincial existence—not unlike Sologub's *Petty Demon*—in its process of disintegration. He was also one of the masters of the *skaz*. After his stay in England during the war he wrote two satirical narratives about the English of which *The Islanders* (*Ostrovityáne*) in particular is hardly complimentary.

personalisation of individuals and de-humanisation of humanity could obviously not be published in the Soviet Union. Some portions of it appeared in a Russian periodical at Prague (in 1929). The hue and cry aroused against its author in the Soviet Union was so great that he preferred to leave—in 1931—for France where he died in 1937.

Zamyatin wrote in his laconic style a number of remarkable short stories, as well as four plays, in all of which he fought the static and stagnant forms of life. Like Andrey Bely and such active young Formalists as Victor Shklovsky, Yury Tynyanov, Boris Eikhenbaum and Leonid Grossman, Zamyatin, too, was a good critic and literary theoretician. The Formalists were anxious to keep the level of literary criticism above any official ideological dogmas during the 1920s, while the Marxists claimed their infallibility not only in politics and economics, but also in art and literature. One of the broader critics of the Marxian type was Leon Trotsky whose book *Revolution and Literature* (1925) proved to be a brilliant work of its kind.

It should be stated in fairness that in the 1920s there was a certain amount of freedom left not only with regard to numerous formal experiments (most of which came to an end in the 1930s), but also with regard to contents. Moreover, the critic and editor Alexander Voronsky (1884–1943) had the good sense to invite several non-proletarian writers to contribute to his important monthly, *The Red Virgin Soil* (*Krásnaya nov'*), as a result of which its quality greatly improved. In 1923 the central committee of the Party proclaimed its own tolerance in this respect, while preserving a violently anti-bourgeois attitude towards life. It even admitted a certain amount of free competition between all sorts of literary currents, provided they were not hostile to the regime.

Being an enlightened Marxist, Voronsky was associated with the *Perevál* ('The Pass') group of young writers who demanded that a Socialist system should not be inimical either to individualistic or to humanist principles in the best sense of the word. However, the promulgation of the First Five-Year Plan by Stalin in 1928 curtailed a number of the still existing freedoms, and things became worse in the later 1930s. Voronsky himself was accused of Trotskyite sympathies. In 1935 he was arrested and probably died in a labour camp.

In the 1920s the variety of literary works was surprisingly great. It ranged from V. Zazubrin's tendentiously pamphleteering novel *The Two Worlds* (*Dva míra*, 1921) about the struggles with Kolchak, to Alexey N. Tolstoy's Wellsian romance *Aelita* (1922) with its action taking place on Mars; from Zamyatin's cruel *Cave* (*Peshchéra*, 1922), identifying the ordeals in a cultured couple's flat in 1919 with those of a prehistoric ice-age cave, to Ilya Ehrenburg's violently satirical and cynical *Adventures of Julio Hurenito* (1922);[1] and from the sophisticatedly naturalistic *Naked Year* (*Góly god*, 1922) by Boris Pilnyak to the romantic yarns removed from past and present by A. Grin (Alexander Grinevetsky, 1890–1932). In Mikhail Bulgakov's novel, *The White Guard* (*Bélaya gvárdiya*, 1925) there is even a eulogy of some patriotic White officers for

---

1. Ehrenburg, like Alexey Tolstoy, was among the first to return from his voluntary exile abroad, after which he soon became an outspoken pamphleteering novelist and fighter for world peace.

showing both courage and self-sacrifice during the Ukrainian nationalist terror at Kiev in 1918, although Bulgakov himself was not openly hostile to the Soviets. This novel, which ends with the victorious arrival of the Reds, was subsequently very ably dramatised under the title of *The Days of the Turbins* (*Dni Túrbinykh*) and performed by the Moscow Art Theatre. Incidentally, Bulgakov asserted himself not only as a writer of grotesque satirical stories (in his collection called *Diavoliáda*), but also as a playwright. Apart from *The Days of the Turbins* he earned further laurels with his *The Flight* (*Beg*)—a play about the ordeals of certain White generals who, after their defeat in the Crimea, had settled abroad, in Constantinople and Paris. His play *The Last Days* (*Poslédnie dni*), deals with the tragic death of Pushkin (but without Pushkin appearing on the stage), while his *Intrigue of the Hypocrites* (*Kabála svyatósh*) is about the last phase and death of Molière. His comedy, *The Crimson Island* (*Bagróvy Óstrov*, written in 1927, performed and finally banned in 1928) is a rollicking satire on Soviet theatre censorship. It has never been published in the Soviet Union. Nor has his *Adam and Eve* (*Adam i Eva*, written in 1931), a science fiction comedy about a few survivors after a suicidal universal war. Both have recently been issued for the first time in Russian by the Ardis Publishers in Michigan. A similar fate was shared by his bewilderingly fantastic novel *The Master and Margarita* (written in 1938), the manuscript of which was smuggled abroad and published in English by Collins Harvill in 1967. This satirical novel, with the background of Soviet Moscow, is full of macabre humour and incredible absurdities, with Satan (duly disguised) and his mad or semi-mad henchmen and witches helping him in his exploits. Yet there is 'method' and meaning in this madness, not to mention the author's implied digs at the Soviet realities of his time. When, in 1940, Bulgakov died blind at the age of forty-nine, he left an unfinished 'theatrical' novel—*Black Snow* (*Chórny sneg*): an account of his own experiences with the Moscow Art Theatre. In his excellent taut prose he described here not only the general atmosphere of the theatre, its actors and actresses, but also gave a scarcely flattering portrait of its director Stanislavsky.[1] As for the further efforts of the early Soviet novelists, they were connected above all with the names of Boris Pilnyak, Vsevolod Ivanov, Konstantin Fedin, Leonid Leonov and Mikhail Sholokhov—writers whose reputation was to become international.

5

The events that followed the Revolution of 1917 became the all-absorbing theme of these authors. The sudden break with the old, the awakening of the working masses and their struggle against the conservative or reactionary forces of history was regarded by them as a fact whose magnitude and significance were beyond questioning. This influenced the very style of their prose which was

1. An English translation of *Chórny sneg* was published by Hodder and Stoughton in 1965.

inclined to be emotional and 'dynamic'. Thus one of the first major novels of the Soviet era, *The Naked Year* (*Góly god*, 1922), by Boris Pilnyak (Boris Wogau, 1894–1937), presenting a thoroughly subjective vision of events, is written in a jerky, nervous and agitated language. Its structure, too, is fragmentary, disjointed, but somehow consistent with the chaotic state during the Civil War, with all the muddle, destruction, and hosts of starving town people invading the countryside in search of food. Devoid of any traditional plots or rules, this novel yet provides absorbing reading. Concentrating above all on the fate of the distant steppe town of Ordynin and its one-time lordly but now expropriated family of the same name, the author often indulges in such naturalism as could hardly be translated into foreign languages.[1] Yet his descriptions, even in their fragmentary shape, are always intensely vivid and concrete. This is how he depicts the desperate crowds fleeing the famine area in search of food.

> Mixed train No. 58 slides across the inky plains. People, human legs, arms, heads, bellies, backs, and human droppings; people as thick in lice as the wagons are in people. People herded here maintained their right to travel by force of their fists, because out there, in the famine districts, at every station, scores of famine refugees have rushed the train, struggling over heads and backs and necks and legs over other people inside—and these struck out, tearing off and throwing those already aboard, the scrimmage going on till the train started and bore off those that happened at the moment to be stuck on—and then those that had got in the last time get ready for another fight at the next station.[2]

Still, this unusual book about Russia in travail ends with a hopeful note. Like the poet Esenin, Pilnyak distrusts the advent of the machine and of the new industrial era. One often feels in him the spirit of patriarchal Pre-Petrine Russia; but the elemental sweep of the Revolution, with its interplay of irrational forces and destruction of all former standards, appealed to him sufficiently not to make him despair or bring him into open conflict with the watchful Soviets.

Hardly less impressive in its colourful idiomatic ruggedness was the prose of Vsevolod Ivanov (1895–1963): a Siberian who had started his literary career under the auspices of Maxim Gorky. He was fond of brutally primitive characters whose ferocity had been released by the anarchy of the Civil War. His early narratives are about the Red guerillas' exploits in Siberia. In his *Coloured Winds* (*Tsvetnýe vetrá*, 1922) he deals with the partisans in a region where Russian peasants live in the vicinity of the even more primitive Kirghises with their herds and shamans. Kolchak's Whites are eventually beaten by the peasant bands, after which something resembling a new life begins, but no one knows for how long. Ivanov's next narrative *Blue Sands* (*Golubýe peskí*, 1922–23), often rewritten, takes us to a small town on the river Irtysh, where we watch the gruesome struggle between the Reds and the Whites. And when the fortunes

1. Several passages in its English version have actually been omitted.
2. Translation by Alec Brown (Payson and Clarke, N.Y.).

have turned against the Whites, the victors contact by chance a community of conservative 'Old Believers' with some rather queer results. All this is told in racy Siberian Russian, passing at times into the *skaz* manner. The action of his *Armoured Train 1469* (*Bronepóyezd 1469, 1923*), too, takes place in Siberia, this time in a maritime town where the climax of the struggle between the two factions is around an armoured train the seizure of which enables the Reds to occupy the town (Vladivostok) and the surrounding region. Even when the structure of Ivanov's narratives is not faultless, his prose vibrates with the verve of a man who is in love with the adventurous and dramatic side of life, although he himself may not have much respect for the human material at his disposal.

About the same time there appeared Dmitry Furmanov's documentary novel *Chapáyev*, Lydia Seyfullina's *Lawbreakers* (*Pravonarushíteli*), Marietta Shaginyan's *Change* (*Pereména*) and Alexander Neverov's *Tashkent the City of Bread* (*Tashként górod khlébny*). The first is a brilliant documentary account of the deeds of a guerilla leader—one of the born leaders—from among the peasants in the Urals during the worst period of the Civil War. *The Lawbreakers* by Lydia Seyfullina, a teacher of half-Tartar origin, raises the problem of homeless waifs and strays with a refreshing faith in the betterment of human nature. We witness how a crowd of such 'lawbreakers', brought into a children's colony amidst rural surroundings, improve, through their active contact with nature, and adopt a happy and purposeful attitude towards life. Seyfullina's two novels, *Mulch* (*Peregnóy*, 1922) and *Virinéya* (1925), give a picture of poverty and degradation of Siberian villagers awakening to a new and better life after the great upheaval.

Narratives and novels about the transition to a new Russia (or Soviet Union) poured out of the press, although their literary quality was bound to vary from mere reportage to serious literary presentation of what was taking or had taken place. A nightmare picture of the famine in Petrograd (Leningrad) is recorded in Sergey Semyonov's *Hunger* (*Gólod*): a day-to-day diary of how a whole family starved during 1919 and drifted to death without any hope of getting enough food in time to end their ordeal. The appalling conditions of the famine-stricken Volga area in 1921 form the background of Alexander Neverov's *Tashkent—the City of Bread*, but with a cheerful note of hope provided by a twelve-year-old peasant boy (Mishka Dodonov) who bravely undertakes, together with a young friend, a long journey right down to Tashkent in order to get some corn and bring it home. The adventures of the boy and his gradual maturing through all the trials involved are the substance of this narrative which is full of faith in man and life. The same optimism permeates some of Neverov's plays and village stories, especially his *Andrón Neputyóvy* portraying a Red ex-soldier who returns to his village and stubbornly fights for that new pattern of life in which he believes. His motto, 'It is impossible to pity and impossible not to pity', is typical of the complex conditions and the struggle he has to sustain. Neverov's longish novel *Geese-Swans* (*Gúsi-lébedi*), depicting the fierce class-struggle in a Volga village during the Civil War in 1918, remained unfinished. The already-mentioned novel *Change* by Marietta Shaginyan (b.

1888) has for its subject the Civil War in the Don region with certain beneficial prospects for the victors, once the reactionary forces are beaten. This authoress, a talented experimenter with romantic leanings, also made some attempts at creating the Soviet detective novel.

Narratives and novels about the Civil War in various regions were so numerous and so different in their artistic value that only the best can be mentioned. A striking specimen of these is Alexander Malyshkin's *The Fall of Dair* (*Padénie Daíra*, 1924). It deals with the Bolshevist victory over the Whites at Perekop (key to the Crimea), with the proletarian mass of the soldiers as the actual hero of this struggle. Quite a different region is introduced to the reader by Alexander Fadeyev's *Rout* (*Razgróm*, 1926)—a bracing narrative which takes us to the Russian Far East near the border of Korea. Here a partisan detachment of local miners, fighting against Kolchak and his Cossacks, was trapped in a village by a much larger enemy force. While trying to escape through a marsh, the partisans came up against the enemy and were routed by them. Only nineteen fighters escaped at the end of that struggle. The peculiar feature of this narrative is the absence of any idealisation of the partisans. The author—a proletarian by conviction—shows them with all their human weaknesses, their roughness, their carousals, and their cynical attitude towards women. Yet a true communal and comradely spirit binds them all in adversities, especially when they have to share their final catastrophe. During those very years Fadeyev was writing his long chronicle-novel, *The Last of the Udeghés* (*Poslédniy iz Udegé*), which he worked on for some thirty years and died (in 1957) before he could finish. Of the planned six parts only four were completed, with a fragment of the fifth. But even as it is, this work is of great interest, since the author here tackles the same remote region as in *Rout* : that part of Siberia where Russian settlers are mixed up with Koreans, Tunghouses, Chinese and the decayed or even moribund semi-nomadic tribe of the Udeghé. The impact the Revolution and the Civil War have had upon this multi-racial community, and above all upon the primitive Udeghés, is further complicated by the American and Japanese interventionists helping Kolchak. All the events are cunningly interwoven, describing the ordeals of a number of individual characters, in the treatment of which the author shows his understanding of human nature, especially its weaker aspects.

A region much nearer home was taken up by another talented author, Isaac Babel, in his cruelly realistic collection of sketches written in stylised prose under the title of *Red Cavalry* (*Konármiya*, 1926). This is a record of what he had seen and endured while fighting in Budyonny's army against the Poles in 1920. The book is a masterpiece of condensed and detached realism which yet verges at times on the incredible. One night he had to sleep on the floor of a dingy Jewish hut beside someone who already seemed fast asleep upon a mattress. As the author shouted rather loudly in his nightmares, the hostess woke him up and said : 'I'll arrange a bed for you in another corner, because you are pushing my father.' When she removed the blanket from his sleeping neighbour, there was a dead old man, 'his glottis torn out and his face split in two; his beard clotted with blood resembling a piece of lead.'

'Sir,' says the Jewess, shaking the mattress, 'the Poles killed him, and he begged them, "Kill me in the back yard so that my daughter doesn't see how I died." But they did it as it was most convenient to them. And now I'd like to know,' cried the woman with sudden terrible violence, 'I'd like to know whether you'd find in the whole world another father like my father.'[1]

Among Babel's other writings are some highly amusing stories about the Odessa Jews and Jewish smugglers. Independent not only in his art, but also in his opinions, the author became a victim of Stalin's 'purges' and died in prison in 1941.

A retrospective record and evaluation of the happenings between 1917 and 1921 was not the only theme of the young Soviet writers. Their other important themes were the tasks of rebuilding and reconstructing the whole of Russia upon a basis demanded by the first Socialist State in history. The problem of the gradual remoulding of life in town and country, with the prospect of collectivism, went hand in hand with efforts to create much needed industries and to foster a new mentality, a new set of values, in a country where the traditional old attitudes were dying hard. Individual and society, education, family, marriage, laws concerning property and human relations in general had now to be approached by literature in a spirit that was likely to shape the hoped-for Soviet man and the Soviet way of life. Thus the proletarian author Yury Libedinsky (1898-1959) gave in his narrative, *A Week* (*Nedélya*, 1922), a chronicle of what happened to a group of dedicated Communists in one single week during a peasant rising in a little town in the Urals when the worst of the Civil War was more or less over—the year is 1921. And in his later novel, *The Commissars* (*Komisáry*, 1925) we follow the setting up of a special course in which a group of young Commissars and Civil War heroes (some of them hardly literate) are trained for further tasks in the service of Socialism. There was one literary work of the 'engaged' kind which made a particular mark at that very period, namely *Cement* (1925) whose elderly author, Fyodor Gladkov (1883-1958), was a proletarian writer of peasant origin.

Cement is an 'industrial' novel about the new types of Soviet workers, imbued with the group-consciousness of Socialist ideals and fanatically determined to build up their country after the wreckage caused by the Civil War. 'We've got to start things going! Coal and oil! Warmth and bread for the workman. The industrial revival of the Republic.' The practical effort of such a process is shown in the rebuilding of a huge but derelict cement factory in one of the southern ports of Russia, while the Civil War in the environs (with attacks and counter-attacks, rapes and executions on the part of the Cossacks) is still going on. Parallel with this, transvaluations of the former ways of life are taking place, since 'the old life has perished and will not return'. This is a thoroughly optimistic propaganda novel, but it is written with great force and conviction in spite of its frequent declamatory passages. Gladkov's next novel, *Energy*, about the building of a hydro-station on the Dnieper is weaker. The economic turmoil caused by the Civil War was, however, so great all over the

1. Translated by J. Harland (Knopf).

country that a temporary compromise with the old capitalist methods had to be adopted during the so-called NEP (New Economic Policy) period. It was under these conditions, that such authors as Fedin, Leonov and Sholokhov—the distinguished trio of Soviet fiction—rose to fame.

6

Konstantin Fedin, a former 'Serapion Brother', scored a success with his *Cities and Years* (*Gorodá i gódy*, 1924). This novel (his first) is about the Revolution, but with a difference. His quiet and lucid prose has more in common with the prose of Tolstoy, Turgenev and Bunin than with the 'explosive' manner of Pilnyak or of some other early chroniclers of the cataclysm. A seeker and questioner by nature, Fedin is familiar not only with Russia, but also with the West (this time with Germany) both of which he tackles with competence. The problem of the Revolution is viewed from the angle of life and civilisation, but with the integrity of an artist who knows how to combine the facts of history with personal destinies in the spirit of humanism, however 'engaged' or involved his plot. *Cities and Years* may still be experimental and at times even somewhat confusing in its disregard of the sequence of events in time; yet it is fresh and bold in its psychological realism as well as in the author's acute observations of a world breaking down both in the Eastern and Western parts of Europe. His main character, the student Startsov, is a typical Hamlet-like intellectual, faced by complexities of the Civil War which he is unable to master. He was first a civic internee in Germany where he saw the war from a German angle. Repatriated after the peace of Brest-Litovsk, he is anxious to take part in the Revolution, but is unable to merge wholeheartedly with any cause. His wayward and wavering soul of a Russian intellectual muddles him up even where love is concerned. After numerous adventures he (not unlike Nezhdanov in Turgenev's *Virgin Soil*) comes to the conclusion that he is 'superfluous' even as a revolutionary. In the end he is shot as a traitor by his German artist-friend Kurt Wahn who, during his captivity in Russia, had become a fanatical Communist. Fedin's next narrative, *Transvaal* (1926), is remarkable by the portraiture of its principal character—a shrewd, unscrupulous and dominant village *kulák* (in the Smolénsk province) at a time when it was still possible to fish in troubled waters. In his second large novel, *The Brothers* (*Brátya*, 1928), Fedin depicts three brothers, all of them intellectuals, who are doing what they can to adapt themselves (each in his own way) to the realities of the Soviet era. Incidentally, the problem of art, notably of music, is prominent in this work, since one of the brothers happens to be a dedicated musician.

Fedin's younger contemporary, Leonid Leonov (b. 1899), is also in the wake of the classical tradition. His master was above all Dostoevsky; yet he became a seeker in his own right and one of the main representatives of the philosophic novel in Soviet literature. He is profoundly concerned with ethical and spiritual dilemmas. These are not hitched on to his characters but treated as authentic experiences of their inner lives. He started modestly with short stories and fairy tales. But already in his first longer tale, *The End of an Insignificant Man* (*Konéts mélkogo chelovéka*, 1924), Dostoevsky's impact is unmistakable. The hero of this narrative is a scientist who becomes a helpless victim of cold and famine during the *sauve-qui-peut* period in the ravaged Russian capital. Leonov's undisputed success was his stylised Civil-War novel, *The Badgers* (*Barsukí*, 1925) in which he showed, with great insight, the eternal antagonism between town and village. The 'badgers' are the counter-revolutionary peasants who rise against the Soviets. The protagonists are two brothers; one on the side of the Revolution while the other supports the 'badgers' who are eventually beaten. But the conflict is not solved by their defeat.

Leonov's next work, *The Thief* (*Vor*, 1927), is a novel set against the NEP background, but permeated throughout with acute psychological insight. Its hero is a former Commissar who had distinguished himself during the Civil-War years and is now unable to adapt himself to the routine of a quieter existence. As a leader of a criminal gang he drifts morally and socially from bad to worse. Unable to mix with others, he becomes spiritually poorer the more he steals from life. However, after a number of shocks he seems to awaken to his better self and leaves for the countryside with something like a promise of moral rebirth. Several characters presented in this work are reminiscent of Dostoevsky's heroes and even find themselves in occasional Dostoevskian situations. Leonov's interest in the irrational forces of life comes out here in quite a conspicuous manner.

The youngest of the above-mentioned trio, Mikhail Sholokhov, was born in 1905 and is now a well known Soviet author, his novel-epic, *Quiet Flows the Don* (*Tíkhy Don*), having earned him due appreciation all over the world. Bulky though it is (its first three volumes were published in 1928-31 and an additional volume in 1940), this vast panorama of Cossack life is often referred to as a Soviet counterpart of *War and Peace*, whatever the differences. And the differences are not small. *War and Peace* is an epic of complete national unity in the face of great danger from outside, whereas in Sholokhov's novel we see the drama of a nation divided by Civil War, by social-economic class interests and conflicts. The leading characters in *War and Peace* (the seekers Andrey Bolkonsky and Pierre Bezoukhov) are cultured aristocrats looking for spiritual values which might enable them to accept life outside and above any class barriers or prejudices. Sholokhov's principal hero, Grigory Melekhov, on the other hand, is a primitive elemental character whose inner chaos and self-contradictions are in a way symbolic of the divided Russian nation desperately struggling for (or against) a new pattern of existence, of contradictions symbolic of the tragic division of aims and purposes inherent in the Revolution itself. But in other respects *Quiet Flows the Don* is a magnificent presentation of a Cossack community with its reactions to the first World War, the Revolution and the Civil War, roughly from 1912 until 1921. With a sure artistic touch the author makes us follow the various individual, social and family destinies of that community, the passionate love between Grigory and his sweetheart Aksinya being at the centre of it all. This, in fact, is the strongest part of the novel: the kind of love which holds an impetuous, irrational sway over any other considerations. The anarchic Grigory Melekhov is contrasted with his subsequent brother-in-law Misha Koshevoy—a sober, conscientious Red whose values and behaviour are determined by the Party catechism, according to which every individual is important only as a working cog of the community.

Throughout the novel there are some wonderful passages about the Cossacks' work and way of life, about the seasonal changes of nature; but the Melekhov-Aksinya passion provides the intensely human *leitmotif* in this kaleidoscope of happenings. As a Party man Sholokhov is bound to be on the side of Koshevoy; yet secretly he admires the full-blooded Melekhov who is eventually banned from the community. Aksinya herself dies of a wound while escaping with her lover from the sovietised village. There is an amazing abundance of characters in this work, in which truth to art and truth to life are convincingly blended. What is more, Sholokhov himself is doing his best to be objective and to abstain from any blatant propaganda at the expense of art, although in later editions he had to make certain changes in the text. It is quite surprising that the bulk of this novel must have been written during the aftermath of the disturbed NEP era.

7

Although the NEP period lasted only a few years, from 1921 until the First Five-Year plan which was launched in 1928, it marked a temporary retreat from too rapid a transition to Socialism. In the prevailing economic chaos concessions had to be made to the free market and private enterprise. But once this had been done, capitalist speculation came back with a vengeance, as depicted by Ilya Ehrenburg in his novel *The Grabber* (*Rvach*, 1925), and in his other writings attacking the same period. In short, private trade was unleashed and, together with it, some of the most objectionable types of the old regime made their reappearance. So much so that even a poet as phlegmatic as Velemir Khlebnikov, with his philological and archaic interests, could not help expressing his indignation in one of his poems (*It's no Joke—Ne shalít'*) which begins with these two stanzas:

> It was not for this that we expressed
> Our high desire for truth,
> That you should ride in sable furs
> Mocking us as you prance along.
>
> It was not for this that the enemy's blood
> Was spilt so recklessly,
> That every shopkeeper's wife
> Should flaunt her pearls.[1]

Mayakovsky, Aseyev, Bezymensky, Demyan Bedny and many other poets reacted in a belligerent way. Nor were prose writers slow in taking up the

1. Translated by Bella Costello.

cudgels and describing in a satirical manner the *byt* of those years. Libedinsky's narrative, *Tomorrow* (*Závtra*, 1923), for instance, deals with Moscow in the heat of the NEP period, the ideas of which were now so discredited, and the features so disgusting, that the only salvation the author (being a Socialist) could envisage was universal revolution. A hope of this kind was raised by the sudden Communist upheaval in Germany. The German revolt was quickly suppressed, however, and the eternal bourgeois was out to celebrate his victory even in Soviet Russia. One of the weapons of Soviet literature became laughter and satire. The immensely popular Mikhail Zoshchenko (1895-1958), who always knew how to write with his tongue in his cheek, kept pouring out amusing sketches and stories the 'between-the-lines' of which made him famous all over the Soviet Union and also abroad. There were plenty of other authors who disagreed with what they saw and did not mind saying it. As a result, there emerged a profusion of satirical narratives and novels, while reminiscences of the Revolution and especially of the Civil War were still quite conspicuous in Soviet fiction.

Thus Mikhail Slonimsky (one of the 'Serapions', trained by Zamyatin) looked upon War and Revolution with evident perplexity as shown by his two novels, *The Lavrovs* (*Lavróvy*, 1926) and *The Middle Prospect* (*Srédniy prospékt*, 1927). In the first we watch the impact of the Revolution upon an intelligentsia family, but with at least one of its members—the young Boris—intent on finding something tenable in life, for the sake of which he joins the Revolution. *The Middle Prospect*, on the other hand, is a NEP-novel pure and simple, with Leningrad as its background. Among its puzzling characters is a disillusioned and degraded one-time Commissar and, of course, a successful opportunist. Another ex-'Serapion', Nikolai Nikitin (b. 1897), revealed his own perplexed attitude in some of his early stories which bear the influence of several authors: from Leskov to Bely, and from Pilnyak to Zamyatin. His negative view of the NEP period came out in his narrative *The Crime of Kiril Rudenko* (*Prestuplénie Kiríla Rudénko*, 1922)—with far from attractive scenes of demoralised factory workers in the provinces.

Among the growing output of realistic fiction the book of stories under the title, *A Parrot's Luck* (*Popugáyevo schástie*, 1924), by Mikhail Kozakov (b. 1897) stands out. Kozakov, in whose work one feels the influences of Dostoevsky, Andreyev and Remizov, presents here a medley of curious types—stunned as it were by the Revolution. Two years later appeared his *Tale about Max the Dwarf* (*Póvest' o kárlike Mákse*), with a Jewish innkeeper as a sinister product of the NEP period. Rather Dostoevskian is Kozakov's psychological novel, *Adameyko the Philistine* (*Meshchanín Adaméyko*, 1927) with its new variety of the Raskolnikov dilemma in the conditions created by the Revolution. His next novel, *Nine Points* (*Dévyat' tóchek*, 1929) remained unfinished. But even as it is, it gives a reliable picture of the crumbling tsarist empire before and during the first World War, with Rasputinism and other nefarious happenings preceding the February Revolution of 1917.

During the second half of the 1920s psychological narratives and novels, whether dealing with the NEP situation or with the Civil War in retrospect, were much in vogue. One of the writers who secured for himself a distinguished position was Boris Lavrenyov (b. 1892). His literary apprenticeship had been that of a poet with acmeist leanings; but he achieved success as a good story-teller with a preference for involved plots and characters. The title of one of his collections, *Crazy Tales* (*Shálye póvesti*, 1926) is typical of his grotesquely whimsical vein. His satirical mood permeates the whole of his *Downfall of the Republic of Itl* (*Krushénie repúbliki Itl'*, 1926)—a skit on the English and their collaboration with the reactionaries trying to back up a 'democratic' republic in the south of Russia in order to appropriate, by hook or by crook, its rich oil deposits. One of Lavrenyov's most popular narratives was his lively tale, *The Forty-First* (*Sórok pérvy*, 1924). It is about a White officer and a Red girl-sniper. Both are stranded, during the Civil War, on a bleak island in the Aral Sea and become lovers. Yet when, later on, a party of White officers approaches the island the girl—true to her convictions—shoots her lover (who becomes the forty-first reactionary victim of her sniping activities) in spite of realising the kind of penalty she would have to pay.[1] Lavrenyov's skill also comes out in his other Civil War narratives, especially in the *Seventh Satellite* (*Sed'móy spútnik*, 1927) which describes the chaos in Petrograd in 1918 and the fate of a White one-time professor of jurisprudence who is arrested and then released by the Reds only to be arrested again and shot by the Whites. His romantically complex novel, *Wood Engraving* (*Gravyúra na déreve*, 1928), tackles art as an important problem of the new society.

Another lover of exciting plots was Venyamin Kaverin (Venyamin Zilber, b. 1902). In his early narrative, *The End of Khaza* (*Konéts Khazý*, 1926) he made an excursion into the criminal underworld of Leningrad. In his *Nine Tenths of Fate* (*Dévyat' desyátykh sud'bý*, 1926) he went back to the October Revolution, describing its effects on certain members of the intelligentsia. His *Troublemaker* (*Skandalíst*, 1928), on the other hand, is largely a facetious chronicle of literary cliques and quarrels in Leningrad, with the problem of freedom cropping up time and again.

Soviet education, too, was one of the literary themes during that period. Certain aspects of current student life can be gleaned from Vladimir Lidin's novel, *The Renegade* (*Otstúpnik*, 1927). Its hero is a destitute provincial boy who comes to Moscow and succeeds in becoming a student. Demoralised by one of his NEP friends, he goes morally bankrupt, gets involved in a murder and—as a consequence—passes through painful inner reactions. But under the influence of positive ethical and social values he undergoes a change and evidently finds a way back to life. Of quite absorbing interest was *The Diary of Kostya Ryábtsev* (1927) by N. Ognyov (Mikhail G. Rozanov, 1888-1938). This is a vivid document of a Soviet grammar-school boy during the NEP period, in the days of educational chaos and confusion. To complete it the author added a year later the diary of a Soviet undergraduate, which is less exciting.

One of the most human and humane documentary books in those years was Anton Makarenko's *Educational Epic* (*Pedagogícheskaya poéma*).[2] It ap-

---

1. This narrative was made into a successful film.
2. Its English translation bears the title *The Road to Life.*

peared in 1932, when the NEP era was already over, but the book itself is still connected with it. It is a moving account of how a group of young delinquents gradually became decent citizens as well as responsible human beings owing to the sympathetic and warm-hearted educational treatment which was applied to them.

Entirely different aspects of those years are recorded in some satirical novels of the NEP period, such as *The Embezzlers* (*Rastrátchiki*, 1927) by Valentin Katayev and even more so by the writings of the joint authors Ilya Ilf and Evgeny Petrov. The heroes of Katayev's novel are two Soviet clerks in Moscow. Having embezzled a considerable sum of money, they keep hiding all over the country until they are caught and brought to justice. This motif is worked out with freshness, while the wanderings of the two vagabonds introduce the reader to some phony aspects of Soviet existence in the provinces, and these are often described with an almost Gogolian touch. The vagaries of provincial life are also wittily tackled in Katayev's collection of short stories under the title *The Father* (*Otéts*, 1928).

Humour, satire and adventure, but on a larger scale, fill the pages of the novels *Twelve Chairs* (*Dvenádtsat' stúlyev*, 1928) and *The Little Golden Calf* (*Zolotóy telyónok*, 1931), written by Ilf and Petrov. The unscrupulous adventurer Ostáp Bender, the principal hero in both novels, is a born NEP cheat and speculator. He is devoid of any norms which even distantly resemble straight or honest dealings, yet he always gets away with it. Whether in search for diamonds hidden by their former owner in one of the twelve chairs (sold at an auction and scattered all over Russia), or else engaged in some fantastic transactions in honour of the Golden Calf, he never loses his presence of mind or his capacity for blackmail. Although killed at the end of the first novel, he is brought back to life in the second in order to provide some further illustrations of how cheating could and did flourish during the NEP era.[1]

While industrialisation of Soviet Russia was making big strides in the late 1920s, a marked interest in the psychological novel and in the inner man was on the increase—partly as an instinctive reaction against a possible dictatorship of technology. This was actually a continuation of the nineteenth century psychological novel. Yury Olesha's *Envy* (*Závist'*, 1927), was a true 'conspiracy of feeling' against a mechanistic or any other ready-made straitjacket imposed upon man's inner life. As one of their victims acknowledges, such basic though irrational human feelings as love, devotion, loyalty and tenderness have not perished, yet they may no longer exist for people like himself. Hence the only feeling he still knows is envy—the main disposition of his old age. The two characters who want to organise a kind of conspiracy of old feelings against the threatening mechanical age, do not succeed; but this does not mean

---

1. Among their other writings the two authors gave, in 1936, a witty account of a visit to the U.S. in their *One-storeyed America* (*Odnoetázhnaya Amérika*, 1937). Their fanciful story about Columbus landing in present-day New York is also full of irrepressible amusement, culminating in the reply Columbus receives from (contemporary) American natives: 'The important thing is not that you should discover America, but that America should discover you. . . .' Unfortunately, both authors died young: Ilf in 1937, and Petrov was killed (as a war correspondent) in 1942.

that they are wrong or that the conspiracy itself is bound to be a failure.

Another psychological novel was *The Imaginary Interlocutor* (*Voobrazháyemy sobesédnik*, 1928) by Ovady Savich, which bears traces of the influences of Tolstoy's *The Death of Ivan Ilyich*, as well as of Dostoevsky. The hero of this novel is a minor Soviet official whose provincial existence is mere senseless monotony and humdrum. In a fit of mental aberration he appropriates some government money : a transgression for which he is pardoned. He is granted leave of absence during which his physical and mental state grows worse. He also suffers from hallucinations and sees his double with whom he converses. Feeling more and more alienated from everybody and everything, he finally dies—all this in a setting of provincial officialdom with its pettiness, drabness and dull efficiency.

A notable psychological novel, with the problem of death in the centre, is *The Tale of a Suffering Mind* (*Póvest' o stradániyakh umá*, 1929) by Sergey Budantsev. Born in 1896, Budantsev had had some success with a well written Civil War narrative, *A Revolt* (*Myatyézh*, 1923). In this work we are taken, however, to a respectable Swiss pension of the 1860s. One of its inmates is a gifted Russian Darwinist who is going blind. While musing about his fate, his own early life and unhappy marriage, he tries twice to escape from his predicament through suicide, but in vain. And the philosophy of life which torments his suffering mind, is far from being in favour of any official optimism. In V. Kaverin's experimental novel *The Artist Unknown* (*Khudózhnik neizvésten*, 1931), one of the characters states, however, that 'history gives us only one choice—to win or to lose, and every day we choose the first'. As a former Serapion, Kaverin is fond of a rich plot which he evolves here with plenty of psychological complications. The background is that of the first Five-Year Plan, showing, together with brave collective efforts, also a complex personal tragedy : in this case it is the marriage tragedy of a gifted anonymous artist whose wife lives with another man (the actual father of his baby son) and eventually commits suicide. Her death is commemorated by a magnificent portrait—painted by her legitimate husband who yet prefers to remain, also this time, unknown. The contrast between the uprooted artist Arkhimedov and the energetic Shpektorov is the hackneyed old contrast between a romantic and a purposeful realist, only this time they are both shown in the conditions of the Five-Year Plan.

8

A great deal of psychological probing was done during the same period by the authors of biographic-historical novels, beginning with Yury Tynyanov's *Kyúkhlya* (1925). Tynyanov, who died in 1944 at the age of fifty, was a cultured literary historian and theoretician of the 'formalist' school. Yet in this work he proved himself to be also a novelist with a fine psychological vein. Kyukhlya was the nickname of Pushkin's friend, the poet Kuechelbecker—a queer but lovable fellow of German origin who had been connected with the Decembrists and died in Siberia. The personality of the man, as well as the entire historical and social-political background of the age, is rendered by Tynyanov with lucidity, skill and knowledge. The same applies to his *Death of Vazir Mukhtar* (*Smert' Vazír Mukhtára*, 1929), which is a novel about the playwright and diplomat Alexander Griboyedov. The author describes here the last phase of Griboyedov's diplomatic career right up to his death in 1829, when he was murdered at Teheran by a Persian mob. This work is imbued, however, with a more sceptical and pessimistic attitude towards life than his previous masterpiece. Somewhat apart stands the social-historical novel, *The Golden Beak* (*Zolotóy klyuv*, 1925) by Anna Karavayeva—an authoress with a strongly proletarian class consciousness and a hater of privileges. The action takes place in the distant Siberian town of Barnaul at the end of the eighteenth century, when twenty-four rebellious miners and a house-serf escaped from the local mines and settled down to a contented existence on a hidden plateau in the Altai region. Because of an abortive attempt to kidnap the house-serf's former sweetheart, their secret settlement is found out. They are all brought back to Barnaul and publicly executed. The authoress, who had made use of local archives, also displays in this work her knowledge of the Siberian speech used by the characters concerned.

Pushkin proved to be a particularly attractive subject for *biographies romancées*, or biographic-historical novels. In the 1930s Tynyanov himself was preparing a meticulous novel about Pushkin (for the hundredth anniversary of his death), and its principal fault is that it has remained unfinished.[1] The already mentioned author Ivan Novikov wrote two novels for that occasion : *Pushkin at Mikhailovskoe* (*Pushkin v Mikháilovskom*) and *Pushkin in the South* (*Púshkin na yúge*). Both are about the poet's early creative years and were published in 1937. Considerable interest was aroused by the fictitious *Memoirs of d'Archiaque* (*Dnevník d'Archiáque-a*, 1937) whose author was Leonid Grossman (b. 1888). Vicomte d'Archiaque was d'Anthès's second during the duel in which Pushkin was mortally wounded by the Frenchman. Grossman's book gives a good account of all the circumstances and intrigues which had led to the duel and the poet's death. Previous to this work the same author had published *Rulettenburg* (1932)—a narrative about Dostoevsky's gambling mania in Germany. Another biographical novel by him was *The Velvet Dictator* (*Bárkhatny diktátor*, 1933), about the last years of Alexander II.

Among the novels of the variety mentioned above those written by Olga Forsh (1873–1961) are of particular interest. They are well documented, and full of social, philosophic and cultural dilemmas typical of the period or periods concerned. Although belonging to an older generation, the authoress, who began life as a painter, started writing rather late and made a name with her historical novel, *Clad in Stone* (*Odéty kámnem*, 1925). This is a narrative about Mikhail Beideman—a supporter of A. Herzen's free press in London and a rebel who went back to Russia during the years of the revolutionary ferment, when an attempt on the Tsar's life was made by Karakozov in 1866. Being a terrorist

1. Its two volumes (about Pushkin's childhood and boyhood) appeared in 1936.

himself, Beideman was sentenced to life imprisonment in the notorious Peter-Paul dungeons which the authoress makes us inspect in all their gruesome reality. The novel is written in the form of reminiscences of one of Beideman's old contemporaries who has survived the cataclysm of 1917 and keeps watching (with some dismay) the incredible changes brought about during the span of his life. Memoirs of old days are thus alternating with what is taking place in Soviet Russia.

Olga Forsh's second novel, *The Contemporaries* (*Sovreménniki*, 1926), is about Gogol and the religious painter Alexander Ivanov during their stay at Rome in the 1840s, when several talented Russians lived and worked in the 'Eternal City'. In her approach to the inner drama of Gogol and Ivanov the authoress tackles those deeper aspects of the problem of art and life which the two 'contemporaries' had failed to solve. As a result neither of them could come to terms either with art or with life. That was why Gogol died in religious semi-madness, in the grip of which he burned the manuscript of the second volume of his *Dead Souls*. The events are narrated with psychological insight as well as with due attention to the spirit of the age, although the chronological sequence of events is not always reliable. A year after *The Contemporaries* Olga Forsh finished her narrative about the revolution of 1905, *A Hot Corporation* (*Goryáchiy tsekh*), and during 1932–39 she worked upon *Radishchev*—dealing, in three volumes, with the life and the times of that radical who had had the courage to make a vigorous protest (in his *Journey from Petersburg to Moscow*) against autocracy and serfdom under Catherine II. The cultural, political and social background of both Russia and the West of the period, with all the currents and cross-currents, is well displayed in this work. And so is a whole gallery of portraits: from Catherine II to a number of other significant figures both Russian and foreign.

Less accomplished is her novel, *The Mikhailovsky Castle* (*Mikháilovsky zámok*, 1946). Its hero is the crazy Tsar Paul I during the last two years before his assassination in the palace which he himself had built. Here, too, the problems of art in the service of the community, notably architecture, are implied and discussed by such architects as Voronikhin, Bazhenov and Rossi. Among other personalities of the novel, that of Suvorov, with his exploits against the French in the Swiss Alps, is particularly memorable.

A few years before embarking upon this novel the authoress published (in 1931) an amusing narrative under the provocative title *The Mad Ship* (*Sumasshédshiy korábl'*). Such was the nickname of the 'House of Arts' organised by Gorky at Petrograd in 1920 (during the worst sufferings brought about by the Civil War) in order to save writers from cold and starvation regardless of their political allegiance. Among its inmates and visitors were such prominent men of letters as Gorky, Blok, Sologub, Gumilyov, Mandelshtam and Klyuyev. They all figure under different names in the novel, but they can easily be identified. Olga Forsh really aimed at depicting 'the last phase of Russian literature before it was put into the archives of history'. The whole work is a fragmented chronicle and an ironical pastiche. In addition to muddle, uncertainty, professional discussions, gossip and official imbecility there are also pathetic passages in this book: Blok's (he is called Gaetan) last public reading of his own poems, the suicide of Sologub's wife through drowning, and finally the description of Blok's funeral. There are plenty of reflections concerning *belles lettres*, Russia and the intelligentsia throughout the pages of this work whose concluding remark is thoroughly humanistic and humanitarian: 'The path of man's evolution is to broaden his uncomplicated private rhythm into the rhythm of universal life; but only by preserving his loving relationship with the world and all the suffering creatures.' [1]

Without touching upon a number of other biographic-historical novels, Anatoly Vinogradov's *The Two Colours of Time* (*Dva tsvéta vrémeni*, 1930) can be mentioned, since it deals with Stendhal, or rather with Napoleon's retreat from Moscow in which Stendhal had taken part. One of Vinogradov's novels is about the life of Paganini, another about the Masonic brothers Turgenev at the beginning of the nineteenth century, and a third about the famous scientist Mendeleyev. Furthermore, his 'cinema-narrative', *Black Consul* (*Chórny kónzul*, 1930), has for its theme Toussaint l'Ouverture, the leader of the Haiti rebels against the French. The much older author, Alexey Chapygin (1870–1937) gives in his long *Rázin Stepán* (1927) a powerful portrait of a seventeenth-century Russian Robin Hood and rebel leader.

Another work, in which personal biography and the facts of history were unusually well blended was *Peter I* by Alexey N. Tolstoy. The three volumes of this novel appeared in 1929, 1933 and 1945 respectively, while the unfinished fourth volume was published after the author's death in 1945. Chronologically as well as technically this masterpiece is linked up with the biographic-historical novels of the period. Peter himself is shown in his process of development as a rebel from above, but against the Russian setting of that epoch. We see Russia mainly in terms of dramatically agitated contrasts and conflicts in which the author glories. Yet underneath it all one feels the *arrière-pensée* that everything ought to be subordinated to the building up of a strong centralised State—an idea with which the dictator Stalin must have been rather pleased. A Soviet critic defined this work as 'an approach to our present epoch from its distant rear'. The unpleasantly flattering idea 'between the lines' was, of course, that Peter the Great was a predecessor of Stalin. [2]

9

After Stalin's victory over Trotsky the slogan of 'Socialism in one country' triumphed over Trotsky's dream of a universal revolution. At the same time great and rapid changes were taking place when the first Five-Year Plan—

1. The House of Arts came to an end in 1922, after Gorky had left for abroad. It might be interesting to note that this novel was not reprinted among Olga Forsh's *Collective Works* published in 8 vols. at Moscow and Leningrad in 1962–1964. A new Russian edition appeared, however, in Washington (1964).
2. A. Tolstoy's novel, *Bread* (*Khleb*, 1937) presented a falsification of historical facts in order to show Stalin as the great hero of Tsaritsyn during the Civil War, which—to put it mildly—was a bit exaggerated.

aiming at collectivisation of land and complete industrialisation of the Soviet Union—was launched by Stalin in 1928. The Five-Year Plan itself, however ruthless its method, called for a great national endeavour, to which everything, literature included, should be subservient. B. Romashov's play, *The Fiery Bridge* (*Ógnenny most*, 1929) sounded like a kind of prelude to concentrated new efforts, in spite of sabotage and other obstacles. The name of the play itself meant that a bridge of fire was separating those who worked for the future and those who had remained behind—stuck on the other bank. There followed a number of 'special commands' obligatory for writers. Most of the eccentric literary experiments were from now on gradually abandoned, while the acceptance of the good old classical tradition in verse and prose met with approval. What really mattered during those years was the stress on collective interests as distinct from things individual. Constructive activism at the expense of any subjective or personal dispositions was the battle-cry. Thus Boris L. Gorbatov's novel about working-class youths, *My Generation* (*Moyó pokolénie*, 1933) rejected the introspective type and affirmed the collective man of will and action instead. That apotheosis and cult of work, an example of which had been given in Gladkov's *Cement*, became the ideal. Ehrenburg's novel, *The Second Day* (*Den' vtoróy*, 1932–33) belongs to the same category. And so does Marietta Shaginyan's *Hydro-central* (1931). The novels of industrial production, as well as the *kolkhóz* (collective farm) novels, were on the increase. The more so because the Communist Party felt by now strong enough to be a law unto itself and to punish anyone who deviated from the *idéynost'* or Party-mindedness. Men of dogmatic Marxian persuasion, such as the critic Averbakh, had their say. And so had the other spokesmen advocating a narrow utilitarian art and literature. The gifted 'fellow travellers' and former 'Serapion Brothers', some of whom had already gone quite a long way towards being on good terms with the regime and 'travelling' in comfort, were expected to hitch their wagon to the Five-Year Plan with its practical aims and purposes.

Among the numerous 'new village' novels Fyodor Panfyorov's *Bruskí* (1930) aroused much attention. Written in a naturalistic style it is about the collectivisation of a village community on the Volga, with the obvious note of propaganda. The author's knowledge of the peasants, of their mentality, conditions and ways of life, cannot be denied. Yet this bulky narrative is rather drawn out and not well constructed. Its author was eventually reproached on account of his bad craftsmanship. In the same year appeared Pilnyak's 'industrial' novel, *Volga Flows into the Caspian* (*Vólga vpadáet v Kaspíyskoe móre*).[1] Pilnyak, who had already had some scrapes with the authorities, evidently came to the conclusion that 'safety first' was not such a bad thing, after all. And so he conformed to prescribed injunctions even at the risk of occasionally lowering the artistic level of his work. His subject is the building of a dam at Kolomna in the Moscow region. The workers and technicians are, of course, full of enthusiasm. In addition a number of mental and emotional crises take place among

1. This was a new, enlarged and more 'loyal' version of his previous narrative called *Mahogany* (*Krásnoe dérevo*), which had been published at Berlin in 1929: presumably without the author's consent.

the engineers in charge. Still, Socialist virtue is bound to triumph, and triumph it does in the end. Pilnyak's manner is more sober this time, but he indulges in scientific digressions and technical details which slow the narrative down and make it even somewhat boring at times.

Encumbered with technical details are the two otherwise powerful Five-Year Plan novels, *Sot'* (1931) and *Skutarévsky* (1932), by Leonid Leonov, who, by this time, seemed to be quite in sympathy with the Soviet efforts. *Sot'* is a regular epic about the foundation of a huge paper mill in a remote and very primitive forest village of northern Russia. We follow all the phases of the work in progress: its difficulties and its success (in spite of sabotage) which is shared by the entire village population. As one of the characters puts it: 'Until the Revolution our present was determined by the past, now it is determined by the future'. The hero of the second novel, Professor Skutarevsky, on the other hand, is a fine character-study of a bourgeois scientist in the process of changing from an isolated individual to a sincere member of a collective, intent on working for the benefit of the nation. He is experimenting in the wireless transmission of energy and is trusted by the authorities even after his initial failure. The somewhat angular, grudgingly pedantic yet solid old savant stands out as a memorable figure amidst the difficulties inseparable from the tasks involved.

Another Five-Year Plan novel, Katayev's *Forward O Time* (*Vrémya, vperyód,* 1932) is striking not only for its cleverly applied film technique similar to that of Dos Passos, but also for its optimistic view about Russia's industrial future—the action takes place in a huge combine at Magnitogorsk. Those years (1932–34) were also responsible for a different but in its own way remarkable book: *How the Steel was Tempered* (*Kak zakalyálas' stal'*). Its author, Nikolai Ostrovsky (1904–1936), was of proletarian origin. After a hard boyhood he took part, from the age of sixteen, in the fighting against the Ukrainian and Polish reactionaries, was severely wounded and, in addition, contracted typhus and pneumonia. Having passed the barrier of death, he became an ardent worker on behalf of the Young Communist League. He was eventually promoted to the rank of a military commissioner in a battalion of territorials and proved a tireless organiser in the activities of the Party whose tenets he accepted with youthful enthusiasm. Yet the hardships he had undergone ruined his health. He became a hopeless invalid. After a futile treatment in a Crimean sanatorium he not only lost the use of his left arm and both legs, but went totally blind. By dint of sheer will-power he faced his ordeal bravely and even decided to record his struggle and experiences of those years in a novel written in such a way as to make its chief hero, Pavel Korchagin, a paragon of courage for the entire younger generation. Because of its authenticity, as well as its simple natural prose, the book aroused the enthusiasm of young Soviet readers and sold in millions of copies. A special frame (cut out of pasteboard) was provided for its author in order to enable him to write in spite of his blindness. He started another novel, *Born of the Storm* (*Rozhdyónnye búrey*), which was to be a narrative of his experiences in the Red Cavalry fighting the Poles in Western Ukraine during 1920. But of the three planned parts only the first part was finished when, in 1936, death put an end to its author's painful but courageous existence.

Fedin's novel, *The Rape of Europe* (*Pokhishchénie, Evrópy*, 1930–35), is painted on a large and crowded canvas which makes its structure look at times somewhat disjointed. Its characters, too, may strike one as being less firmly outlined than those of some of his previous works. On the other hand, the author displays here to advantage his knowledge of Western business methods and of the Western world in general. He takes one first to Norway, then to Germany, and finally to Holland, the description of which (especially of life in Amsterdam) provides a proper background for the financial magnates, the brothers van Rossum, who have secured for their firm huge timber concessions in Soviet Russia. A Soviet journalist, Rogov by name, travels abroad, becomes emotionally involved with Claudia, the Russian wife of one of the magnates, while carefully watching the economic and political crisis of the West during the early 1930s. He found a contrast to that crisis in the dynamic activities of Soviet Russia who, at that very time, was engaged in her first Five-Year Plan and was conscious of having 'discovered and begun to write a new volume of human history'.

The second part of the novel takes place in Leningrad, Moscow, and above all in the wooded regions of northern Russia where, despite the tricky schemes of the two van Rossum brothers, the concessions granted to them are eventually annulled. Frans (Claudia's husband) commits suicide, and his body is conveyed by his surviving brother and Claudia back to Holland where it all started. The completion of *The Rape of Europe* coincided with the rise of Socialist Realism which, in its own way, was a continuation of the activist Five-Year Plan fiction—modified by rules and tenets affecting Soviet literature as a whole.

CHAPTER TWENTY-SEVEN

Under the sign of socialist realism

I

A significant step with regard to Soviet literature was taken in 1932. While the first Five-Year Plan was still at its height, the purely proletarian RAPP was abolished by the central authority and had to merge with the general Soviet Writers Union. This meant stiffer control over all literary products since, from now on, injunctions given by the Party were obligatory for all Soviet writers without exception. Official pressure upon art and literature became automatic. Two years later the first Congress of Soviet Writers took place. It was there that Socialist Realism was proclaimed the basic (or rather the only) accepted trend in Soviet *belles lettres*. Its motto was that to improve life is more important than only to describe it—a point of view which had already been inherent in several Five-Year Plan novels. Yet the stress was now on the desideratum that reality should be interpreted as an evolution of life towards the Marxist Utopia as understood by the Party. Henceforth Soviet writers were expected to give a 'truthful, historically concrete representation of reality in its revolutionary development' in this particular direction at the expense of any subjectivism on the one hand, or art for art's sake on the other. Maxim Gorky (whose novel, *Mother*, was regarded as an example of Socialist Realism *avant le mot*) formulated this kind of engaged literature as an 'accurate description of reality in so far as this is necessary for a deeper and closer understanding of all that we must abolish and of that which we must build up.' According to him, literature should be written in the service of Socialist humanism. Much of the best Soviet writing during the 1920s was actually created in this spirit which was also the spirit of *true* Socialist Realism, as distinct from Stalinism with its narrow demands that literary portrayals of life ought to go hand in hand with the ideological remoulding of the toiling masses—a process in which a writer's role would amount to the function of an 'engineer of the human soul' helping to pave the way towards the dogmatic Marxist pattern of existence as envisaged by the Party. Stalin's 'engineers of the human soul' were expected to be thoroughly busy, and so they were. Positive heroes, full of prefabricated public virtues, became a literary formula, an obligation, a command.

Otherwise there was nothing new in the idea that literature should serve life. About a century earlier the critic Belinsky had expected from literature a 'poetic analysis of social life', but with a view to fostering active aspirations towards a better and worthier existence, in which the individual would be integrated with society instead of being exploited, oppressed or repressed by it. The same idea was sponsored later—in a narrower utilitarian sense—by Dobrolyubov and Chernyshevsky. A socially engaged theme can, of course, always be sublimated to an aesthetic level into art, provided it is done organically : in terms of true art and not mechanically—by means of pamphleteering sermons or indoctrination. The trouble begins, however, when instead of transmuting social ideas into creative art, art itself (in the form of plays, novels and stories) is turned into blatant propaganda. This danger became quite a common reality among a number of minor Soviet authors after the official introduction of Socialist Realism—with the cult of Stalin as a 'super-genius of all times' thrown in. Hence the growing number of dull narratives and novels which were more 'engaged' than convincing or artistically competent.

As has already been pointed out, formalist experiments and ornate rhythmic prose, with some other extravagances, were receding into the past. And so was the explosive manner of Pilnyak's *Naked Year* or Artyom Vesyoly's ecstatic *My Native Country* (*Straná rodnáya*) and *Russia Washed in Blood* (*Rossíya króvyu omýtaya*). What mattered now, even apart from direct propaganda, was a literature of facts arranged in such a way as to work at least by implication in the direction mapped out by the Party. And the Party itself was beginning to mean more and more the will of Stalin who was determined to turn the country into a police-state controlled by him and his yes-men. Instead of serving the cause of true Socialism, Stalin wanted Socialism to serve his own self-will. Fortunately, true talents were able to assert their creative power in spite of the pressure from above. And so amidst a vast number of mediocre writings, with their facile optimism, there was also a crop of good ones—even though not necessarily opposed to the Party line.

A notable literary product of those days was Leonid Leonov's *The Road to the Ocean* (*Doróga na okeán*, 1935). This longish novel was something of a *tour de force* in style and structure. The title itself suggests the road to the socialist city of Utopia in the realisation of which Kurilov, the principal character of the novel, firmly believes. He holds a responsible post in a railway system, but suffers from an incurable disease to which he eventually succumbs. Yet being on the side of life, he retains his faith in the possibility of a united mankind and a better existence here on earth in spite of all. Kurilov's Socialism is, of course, not a matter of imposed or pasted recipes, but of his own passionate conviction. It is part and parcel of his consciousness, and this makes all the difference. The novel is written at Leonov's high literary level, which was also the best guarantee for its influence and success.

Among the numerous other books during those early years of Socialist Realism Venyamin Kaverin's novel, *Fulfilment of Wishes* (*Ispolnénie Zhelániy*, 1936, 1939), combines this time, too, an exciting plot with certain well-worked out moral and psychological problems—Kaverin's usual method. The principal characters of this novel are several Leningrad students and a famous professor of history who is in possession of most valuable historical letters and documents, including some of Pushkin's manuscipts. A number of these are being gradually stolen by the professor's son who, through an associate, sells them to greedy speculators. The professor's able young assistant is wrongly accused of these thefts, but after the professor's death the actual culprits are found out and punished. The striking personality of Professor Bauer and the sure outline of his assistant Trubachevsky are examples of Kaverin's fine character-drawing. About the same time Vsevolod Ivanov published his *Adventures of a Fakir* (*Pokhozhdénia fakíra*, 1935). This amazing autobiographical record of life in Siberia during the period leading up to the first World War and the birthpangs of a new Russia is written with a humorous and ironic inflection which makes the book all the more readable. Such a work as Fedin's concentrated short novel, *Sanatorium Arcturus* (1940), however, takes one away from the Soviet Union altogether: to Davos, the Swiss spa for tubercular patients—a place which had been made use of also by Thomas Mann in his *Zauberberg* (*The Magic Mountain*).[1] Like Mann, Fedin is concerned with human characters of various nations temporarily placed together in entirely new conditions and surroundings. In the centre of his plot there are the Soviet intellectual Levshin, a German girl-patient (Inga), and a German woman-doctor who is in love with Levshin. But after Inga's death and the proprietor's suicide (because of financial difficulties) the bankrupt Sanatorium comes to an end.

It is significant that in the second half of the 1930s quite a few authors turned again to the Revolution and the Civil War: this time not necessarily in terms of personal experience but as important historical material which had to be further explored and elucidated. Valentin Katayev gives us in his lively narrative *The Lone White Sail* (*Beléyet párus odinókiy*, 1936) a flashback to the Revolution of 1905 as experienced by two enterprising little boys in Odessa during the mutiny of the battleship *Potyomkin* and other exciting happenings —all of them a distant prelude to 1917. Vassily Grossman (1905–49) wrote a lengthy novel recording the revolutionary moods and underground activities between 1905 and 1917 entitled *Stepan Kol'chúgin*, the three volumes of which appeared between 1937 and 1940. Alexander Malyshkin's 'engaged' novel, *People from the Backwoods* (*Lyúdi iz zakholústya*, 1938) depicts the workers' feverish efforts during their building of the huge industrial centre of Krasnogorsk in the Urals as their particular task of Socialist reconstruction. The novel brims over with a cheerful and active faith in life, as well as with that 'poetisation of work' which became a frequent note in Soviet fiction. The same spirit prevailed also in a number of plays written during those years.

2

It is strange to say that the most dramatic happenings in Russian history have not yet produced a dramatist great enough to do full justice to them. This is all the more surprising because the cult of the theatre has been and still is one of the national characteristics of Russia, where such men as Stanislavsky, Meierhold, Tairov and Vakhtangov enjoyed great popularity and even contributed what they could to the development of the theatre abroad. Stanis-

1. In his *Sanatorium Arcturus* Fedin makes allusions to Mann's novel.

lavsky's meticulous psychological realism, so typical of the Moscow Art Theatre, may have differed from Meierhold's intensely stylised constructivist method, but it was equally stimulating for theatrical productions. Tairov's 'pure' theatre evolved its own peculiar style; and so did Vakhtangov's more eclectic approach to the matter. The only feature these men had in common was the supremacy of the producer over the author. But while the Russian theatre, with its daring experiments, was at its height, the Soviet era failed to give rise to playwrights of the same stature as Ostrovsky or Chekhov, although it had quite a few single good plays to its credit. This may partly explain why so many Soviet narratives and novels have been dramatised: Bulgakov's *The White Guard*, Vsevolod Ivanov's *Armoured Train 1469*, Leonov's *Badgers* and *Skutarevsky*, and scores of others.

The bulk of the Soviet plays after the great cataclysm were mainly of the 'engaged' and pamphleteering kind, often rather schematic, not to say lifeless. Like the Soviet novel, the early plays treated the Revolution and the Civil War, as well as the entire transition from the old to the new, with a strong ideological colouring. The first real Soviet play was Mayakovsky's grotesquely propagandist *Mystery-Bouffe*—'a heroic, epic and satirical presentation' of a conquest of the world by the proletariat. This piece, and even more so Mayakovsky's two subsequent dramatic satires—*The Bedbug* and *The Bathhouse*, stand by themselves. In contrast to them the majority of early 'engaged' plays which kept invading Soviet theatres and literature were of little artistic interest and are now justly forgotten.

Exceptions in the 1920s were *The Storm* (*Shtorm*, 1925) by V. 'Bill'-Belotserkovsky, *Lybóv' Yarováya* (1926) by K. Trenyov, and *The Breaking Up* (*Razlóm*, 1927) by B. Lavrenyov. They are about the Civil War. In the largely documentary *Storm* we see a provincial town in the grip of typhus, of saboteurs, and finally of the attacking Whites who are victoriously beaten off. The *Breaking Up* shows what was happening on the cruiser Aurora in 1917 at Kronstadt (as well as in the house of its commander) during the critical days when she sailed to Petrograd in order to help Lenin. *Lyubóv' Yarováya*, too, presents an agitated picture of those days when fortunes in the Civil War were still fluctuating. The central figure, Lyubov', a schoolmistress and a sincere Communist, thinks that her husband has been killed in the War. In spite of her love for him she remains cold and quiet when her husband returns as a White officer and having been caught as a saboteur, is led away to be shot. *The First Cavalry Force* (*Pérvaya kónnaya*, 1929), by Vsevolod Vishnevsky (1910–51), on the other hand, is an ingeniously dramatised historical chronicle—with a narrator commenting upon each important scene of the struggle—from the disruption of the imperial Russian army during the Revolution until the formation of Budyonny's cavalry force and its victories over the Whites. In this documentary chronicle mass movements play a conspicuous part.

The practices of the NEP during the 1920s gave rise to a number of plays of indictment. Thus Mikhail Bulgakov's *Zoyka's Apartment* (*Zóikina kvartíra*), staged by Vakhtangov in 1926, shows a disreputable brothel disguised as a Soviet workshop, with criminals and drug addicts as its customers. The play was in fact so frank that in 1928 it had to be banned. Among the satirical plays inspired by the NEP Nikolai Erdman's comedy, *The Mandate* (*Mandát*), stands out, and so does the biting *Aereal Cake* (*Vozdúshny piróg*) by B. Romashov, which shows the orgy of cheating and speculating in Moscow. As one of the characters put it : 'Of one thousand eyes, which look at you in the streets, nine hundred and ninety-nine are blackguards' eyes'. Yet all the expert cheats are cheated by an equally unscrupulous but more astute American speculator. The comedy ends rather like Gogol's *Inspector General*—with catastrophe at the time of an expected triumph. Such a piece as *Tempo* (*Temp*) by Nikolai Pogodin (pseudonym of Nikolai F. Stukalov, b. 1900) was again typical of the first Five-Year Plan. It is a dramatised picture of a large tractor plant being constructed at Stalingrad—a process in which the Russian workers (encouraged by a U.S.A. engineer) outstrip even the pace of their American equivalents. Another of Pogodin's plays, *An Epic about the Axe* (*Poéma o toporé*), which is on a similar theme, is documentary in its realism. In his comedy, *Aristocrats* (*Aristokráty*), however, Pogodin gave a bizarre collection of criminal types—male and female —brought together by forced labour to build the White-Sea Baltic Canal. Accustomed to live without working, like aristocrats, they gradually became not only good workers, but even decent human beings through the right kind of approach on the part of their leaders to both work and human nature. Another Five-Year-Plan piece was Vladimir Kirshon's *Bread* (*Khleb*). Produced in 1930, it contained good propaganda for the collectivisation of the village. As purely comic relief amidst Civil War pieces Katayev's farcical comedy, *Squaring of the Circle* (*Kvadratúra krúga*, 1925) can be mentioned. It deals in a deliberately lighthearted way with the marriage muddle of two young Soviet friends living in the same room, who get married unknown to each other on the same day. But as in overcrowded Moscow the two newly married couples are compelled to share the same room (now divided by a flimsy partition), each married youth falls in love with his friend's wife and an analogous change takes place also in the two young wives. A number of comic situations follow, ironically interspersed with the usual Party jargon.

The period of Socialist Realism in the theatre during the 1930s was anticipated by Maxim Gorky's *Bulichov and Others* (1932) and *Dostigayev and Others* (first published as *Vássa Zheléznova*). Both were an expression of the triumph of revolutionary forces over the decayed bourgeoisie. There were, in addition to the problems of industrialisation and collectivisation, all sorts of moral or ethical dilemmas connected with the transition period. These were tackled by A. Korneychuk (an Ukrainian playwright), by N. Virta, and particularly by A. Afinogenov (1904-41). Afinogenov has written, during his brief span of life, about twenty-five plays, some of which have withstood the passage of time. His *Fear* (*Strakh*, 1930), for instance, transfers the class struggle even to the realm of science. The aged director of a scientific institute investigating the root-causes of human behaviour makes the 'discovery' that fear is at the bottom of most of our actions. He is refuted, however, when in the ensuing controversy the element of fearlessness and courage (on the part of those who have been held down by fear) proves to be a more convincing factor. Life-affirming in its optimism is Afinogenov's *The Distant Point* (*Dalyókoe*, 1936) in which Chekhov's dramatic technique has been used to advantage. The play is about a Red Army Commander on his way from the Far East to Moscow. Because of some repairs his special railway carriage remains stuck at a tiny Siberian station some seven thousand kilometres away from the Soviet capital. The Commander, his wife and a few simple inhabitants of that distant spot develop the friendliest mutual contacts, the warm atmosphere of which is disturbed by the rumour of the Commander's fatal illness. Yet he bears the prospect of impending death with such fortitude as to leave no room for despondence or resignation.

The twentieth anniversary of the Revolution was celebrated in a number of propaganda plays written by such established playwrights as Virta, Korney-chuk, Trenyov, and Pogodin. Pogodin in his *Man With a Rifle* (*Chelovék s ruzhyóm*, 1937) put Lenin himself on the stage, stressing his human simplicity as well as his intensely active and practical nature. Another play with Lenin appearing (in the last act) was K. Trenyov's *On the Bank of the Neva* (*Na beregú Nevý*, 1937), celebrating Lenin's decisive victory in the autumn of 1917, over Kerensky and the provisional bourgeois government. V. Vishnevsky, in *The Unforgettable 1919* (*Nezabyváyemy 1919-Y*), however, shows Stalin as one of the dramatis personae. These plays may be more 'engaged' than artistically perfect, yet their documentary value cannot be denied. Even so their authors were not allowed to mention the truth about Stalin's rival Trotsky, who was the principal organiser of the Soviet army in its early triumphs over the White forces.

3

As the first Socialist State in history, the Soviet Union could not help pointing out the universal or international character of its revolution; the more so because Russian nationalism as such had always been closely connected with the tsarist governments of the past. Yet when in 1933 Hitler had risen to power in Germany, the lingering internationalism of the Soviets was replaced by a patriotic disposition. The long, factual novel, *Tsusima* (1934), by I. Novikov-Priboy, describing the disaster of the Russian fleet during the war with Japan in 1904-05, was full of wounded patriotic feeling. The value of this book was increased by the fact that its author had taken part in the fighting. Intensely patriotic was the novel *In the East* (*Na vostóke*, 1937) by Peter Pavlenko (1899–1951). After his exotic stories about Asia and his novel *The Barricades* (*Barikády*, 1932)—about the Paris Commune—Pavlenko now combined his militant Communism with the patriotic zeal of the younger generation active in the Soviet Far East. He even included an imaginary war with Japan, whose happy ending for the USSR amounted to a promise of the brotherhood of all nations in a not too distant future.

Another weapon that emerged on the 'literary front' was the historical novel as well as the historical play. In 1939, the year of Hitler's invasion of Europe, V. Solovyov's play, *Field-Marshal Kutúzov*, appeared. Another play,

The Army-Leader Suvorov (Polkovódets Suvórov), by L. Bakhterev and A. Razumovsky came out in the same year. The importance of such plays and novels was all the greater after Hitler's invasion of Russia in the summer of 1941. Everything that glorified the Russian past, whether distant or recent, was welcomed. Even such a sadistic 'gatherer of the Russian lands' as Ivan the Terrible had to be shown in the light of a great patriot and statesman. This was done competently enough by Valentin Kostylyov in his trilogy of novels, *Ivan the Terrible (Iván Grózny*, 1941–45). Sergey Borodin (Amir Sergidjan, b. 1902), on the other hand, tackled a much earlier period in his *Dmitry Donskóy* (1942), a vigorous narrative about the first Russian victory over the Tartars on the Kúlikovo Field in 1380 under the leadership of Prince Dmitry. Borodin's description of historical conditions, as well as of the cautious preparations for war, are incisive and convincing. V. Yan takes us even further back in his trilogy about the Mongolian invasion: *Genghis Khan* (1939), *Batu Khan* (1941) and *To the Last Sea (K poslédnemu móryu*, 1955). The author seems to be familiar not only with the historical facts of the period described, but also with oriental sources and documents upon which he must have drawn to advantage. The cunning *arrière-pensée* behind this trilogy was the parallel between the Mongolian savagery and that of Hitler's Nazis.

One of the most popular books during the German invasion was, quite naturally, Leo Tolstoy's *War and Peace*. Historical narratives about the Crimean Campaign and World War I were also in demand. Both were tackled in S. Sergeyev-Tsensky's series of novels. His *Ordeal of Sebastopol (Sevastópol'skaya stradá*, 1937-38) had conjured up the old drama of that city and the Crimean débâcle of the corrupt autocratic system under Nicholas I. His *Brusilov's Break Through (Brusílovsky prorýv*, 1943), *Guns Forward (Púshki výdvigáyut*, 1944) and *Guns Have Spoken (Púshki zagovoríli*, 1945) were, however, encouraging records of World War I. Up to his death in 1958 Sergeyev-Tsensky wrote fifteen chronicle-novels and narratives in his 'Transfiguration' (*Pererozhdénie*) series, the aim of which was to show the inner and external changes undergone, during that time, by Russia. Popular in those days was also A. Stepanov's novel *Port Arthur* (1940-41), describing the heroic defence of that city against the Japanese.

While Hitler's hordes were being fought on Soviet soil, anti-German propaganda was the order of the day. Journalistic reportage, fiery articles, sketches from the front, patriotic plays, poems, stories and novels—they all had to serve one purpose only: liberation of the Country. Writings without such a purpose were looked at askance. In 1943, Zoshchenko began to print in the periodical *October (Oktyábr')* a series of personal reminiscences under the title *Before the Sunrise (Péred voskhódom sólntsa)*—a delightful series of autobiographical sketches interspersed with his personal impressions of Mayakovsky, Remizov, Esenin, etc. But he was promptly reminded that this kind of 'subjective' literature should not be indulged in when the very existence of the country was at stake. His transgression was not forgiven even when the war was over: in 1946 he was 'excommunicated' from the Soviet Writers Union.

There were numerous war-time narratives, ranging from descriptions of the inhuman atrocities of the German invaders, recorded in *The Rainbow*

(*Ráduga*, 1942) by the Polish-born Vanda Vasilevskaya, to *The People Immortal* (*Naród bessmérten*, 1942) by Vasily Grossman who dwells on the ordeal of the Russian retreat during the early weeks of Hitler's invasion, when the Russian armaments were inferior to those of the enemy. Yet the retreat itself was of such a nature as to make one of the observers exclaim that a people who can fight like this even during its retreat will never be conquered. The narrative ends with the first Soviet victory over the Germans. In contrast to the agitated accounts by Vasilevskaya and Grossman, Alexander Bek's *Volokolamsk Road* is a quiet yet absorbing tale of how Moscow was saved during the German offensive in October-November, 1941. A small Soviet force, composed of Russian, Ukrainian and Kazakh detachments, stationed near Volokolamsk, only some thirty kilometers from Moscow resisted the German onslaught until the auxiliary forces from the Far East arrived just in time to bar the way to the Soviet capital.

Considerable attention was aroused by Fadeyev's novel *The Young Guard* (*Molodáya gvárdiya*, 1943-45): a chronicle of the sabotaging activities on the part of the Komsomol (Communist Soviet Youth) members during the German occupation of one of the mining regions in the South. There is a stirring account of the arrival of Hitler's army in Krasnodon. Most of the young saboteurs were caught, tortured and executed even while Hitler's troops were already retreating after the Russian victory at Stalingrad. The narrative seems to have been hastily written; yet it should be pointed out that all the facts described in this novel had been checked and investigated by the author on the spot. The workers' resistance to the Germans in the Ukraine is recorded in Boris Gorbatov's novel, *The Unconquered Ones, or The Taras Family* (*Nepokoryónnye, ili Semyá Tarása*, 1943) whereas the gruesome fight for Stalingrad is dealt with by Konstantin Simonov (who had distinguished himself also as a war poet and dramatist) in his *Days and Nights* (*Dni i nóchi*, 1944). Captain Saburov, the chief character of this novel, is in the tradition of such unassuming Russian heroes as are depicted in *War and Peace*. Another highly documentary account of how that city was defended is Victor P. Nekrasov's *In Stalingrad Trenches* (*V okópakh Stalingráda*, 1946) which, like M. Bubyonnov's long novel, *The White Birch* (*Bélaya berióza*), deals also with the painful early phase of the war when the badly equipped Soviet armies were in retreat.

The ordeals during the stubborn defence of Leningrad are described above all in *Almost Three Years* (*Pochtí tri góda*, 1945)—a personal diary of the woman-poet Vera Inber. The feats and exploits of Soviet soldiers in other parts of the country were not neglected either. *The Taking of Velikoshúmsk*, (1944) by Leonov depicts the self-sacrificing crew of a repaired tank during the retaking of a Ukrainian town from the Germans. The soldier-types (from the commander downwards) are portrayed with Leonov's usual skill. The battle scene, in which the tank with its crew runs right into the struggling German division, is breathtaking in its intensity. The tank itself is destroyed, but only after having helped to liberate the town. In the same year there appeared (serially) Sholokhov's narrative, *They Fought for Their Country* (*Oní srázhális' za ródinu*)—a description of the Cossack resistance to the Germans in the Don region. This was but a portion of a more substantial work expected to follow. Among the countless novels about World War II there was Konstantin Paustovsky's *Smoke of the Fatherland* (*Dym otéchestva*). Paustovsky already had to his credit some excellent adventure stories, but here he gave an unpretentious account of the wanderings of a few intellectuals (two painters, a writer, an actress, and a Spanish woman refugee) who, after all their troubles during the war, find a refuge in Siberia. The novel was written in 1944, but—for various reasons—came out only twenty years later.

4

As long as the War lasted, the 'literary front' was active also in poetry and drama. Intimate subjective lyrics were more or less replaced by social and war lyrics full of patriotism as well as of moral indignation against the enemy whom Ilya Ehrenburg was among the first to lampoon in his poem *The German*:

> From childhood he's been melancholy and methodical,
> loved order, never got bad marks at school,
> earned his small pittance, worked long hours.
> They said to him: 'Henceforth the whole world's yours.'
> He learned to kill blindly, systematically,
> and went from corpse to corpse—relentlessly.
> Land, precious land, they promised him,
> and corn and gold and sables fine.
> Now he lies here. There's blood upon his chin:
> and his white hand a scrap of earth is clutching,
> as if even in death he would retain
> the foreign earth that had deluded him.[1]

Of the many poets who were active during the War years Alexander Tvardovsky (1910)—deserves to be referred to in the first place. He had distinguished himself earlier by his narrative poem, *The Land of Muraviya* (*Straná Murdviya*, 1934–36). Written in the tradition of Nekrasov's *Who can be Happy and Free in Russia?*, it deals with the phase of collectivisation. The hero of the poem is a dissatisfied peasant, Morgunok by name, who sets out on an adventurous journey in order to find a country where there are no collective farms. After a number of incidents, encounters and mishaps he comes to the conclusion that his quest is futile and gets reconciled to the unavoidable change. A master of colloquial poetic language and diction, Tvardovsky (who is of peasant extraction) applied the same tone and manner to his next work, *Vasíly Tyórkin*—a 'warrior's book', as its subtitle would have it. This long series of episodes in verse, written between 1941 and 1945, portrays a typical Russian peasant soldier with all the endurance, shrewd commonsense, humour and good temper without which it would have been impossible for him to cope with the trials and

1.   Translated by Alan Moray Williams in *The Road to the West* (Muller).

P.R.L.—11

vicissitudes of Hitler's warfare. No wonder such an amusingly 'engaged' book became a companion and a source of good cheer with officers and privates alike. *Verses about the War* (*Stikhí o voyné*, 1942) and *Verses about Smolensk* (*Stikhí o Smolénske*, 1943) by the same poet were also in great demand.

As a contrast the pathetic yet courageous booklet of poems, *The Son* (*Syn*, 1943), by Pavel Antokolsky (b. 1896) can be mentioned. Combining a strongly aesthetic sense with simplicity and severity, Antokolsky gives here a poetic biography of his only son who had died the death of a hero at the front. In the same year appeared Aseyev's collection of poems with the programmatic title *To the West* (*Na západ*). The defence of Leningrad found its echoes in the verses of such talented poets as Nikolai Tikhonov, Olga Bergholts and Vera Inber. Further war poetry was written by Konstantin Simonov, Alexey Surkov, Evgeny Dolmatovsky, and many others. Even such 'subjective' poets as Boris Pasternak and Anna Akhmatova made their contribution to the war effort. During the war with Hitler, Pasternak published two slender volumes of simple lyrics, a number of which included war themes: *On Early Trains* (*No ránnikh poyezdákh*, 1941) and *Terrestrial Expanse* (*Zemnóy prostór*, 1945). Anna Akhmatova, who had been evacuated from Leningrad to Tashkent, also wrote some war lyrics which, however, are not among her best.

Patriotic enthusiasm was kept alive by many a poet also when the War was over, notably by Semyon Kirsanov in his epic poems, *The Sky over the Fatherland* (*Nébo nad ródinoy*, 1947) and Mikhail Isakovsky's *Songs about the Fatherland* (*Pésni o ródine*, 1948). A similar spirit prevailed in the plays written and performed during those strenuous years. Among the first dramatists to spur on the nation's resistance was Afinogenov whose play, *On the Eve* (*Nakanúne*, 1941), was full of encouraging notes during the early weeks when the Russian armies were retreating under pressure of the better equipped Germans. The title of the play should actually be *On the Eve of Victory*. A cruelly romantic war play was Leonov's *Invasion* (*Nashéstvie*, 1942), full of the most daring exploits by guerrillas operating in a German-occupied town which in the last act is liberated by the Red Army. The belligerent patriotic note was particularly strong in Konstantin Simonov's *The Russians* (*Rússkie Iyúdi*, 1942), while A. Korneychuk's controversial play *The Front* (*Front*, 1942) advocated the idea that after the initial Russian reverses the old generals and army leaders (however distinguished) should be replaced by young ones who are familiar with such new methods of warfare as would be likely to defeat the Germans. Highly patriotic were Lavrenyov's two pieces, *The Song about the Black-Sea Sailors* (*Pesn' o chernomórtsakh*, 1944) and *For Those at Sea* (*Za tekh, kto v móre*, 1945). Alexey N. Tolstoy, on the other hand, was responsible for two plays about Ivan the Terrible: *The Eagle and His Mate* (*Oryól i Orlítsa*, 1942) and *Hard Years* (*Trúdnye gódy*, 1943), both of them eulogising that ruler. These and other patriotic plays had been performed all over the Soviet Union, thus helping to keep up the morale of the people during the critical war years. And the historical miracle that happened was even greater than that of 1812 for the very reason that Hitler's threat was infinitely more brutal and formidable than the threat of Napoleon. Yet no sooner had the German hordes been driven out of the USSR than the entire Soviet population had to face the task of rebuilding all that had been demolished.

The 'literary front' was again helpful with plenty of 'engaged' plays and narratives. The majority of these were about the various aspects of reconstruction all over post-war Russia, with the obvious voice of propaganda. But after 1945 propaganda was directed also against the Western allies as a prelude to the subsequent Cold War. The anti-Western note became almost obligatory. Such plays as K. Simonov's *The Russian Problem* (*Rússky voprós*) or B. Lavrenyov's *America Speaking* (*Gólos Amériki*) are turned above all against the reactionary forces in the U.S.A. Alexey Arbuzov's *European Chronicle* (*Evropéiskaya khrónika*, 1953) even gave a dramatised picture of European affairs in four acts as seen by some Danes and a French painter at Copenhagen. The first act is about the Spanish Civil War in 1936, the second about the betrayal of Czechoslovakia at Munich in 1938; the third act takes us to Paris of 1940, and the fourth once more to Copenhagen, this time in 1952, when the West was enforcing its measures against the Soviet Union. Needless to say, such a chronicle can hardly give an objective picture of Russia's former allies.

It was during those years, too, that Nikolai Pogodin, who is regarded as one of the leading Soviet dramatists, continued his trilogy by adding in 1956 its second play, *The Kremlin Chimes* (*Kremlyóvskie kuránty*), with Lenin as the principal hero. The theme is the electrification of the whole of Russia and the simultaneous conversion of a bourgeois specialist to Lenin's creed at the very time when the damaged Kremlin carillion has been repaired in order to chime —no longer the tsarist anthem, but the Internationale. The play includes Lenin's prediction that those chimes will now resound over a country reborn by its own deeds and dreams. The last part of the trilogy, *Third Pathetique* (*Trétya patetícheskaya*), is about Lenin's death.

Among the more recent plays Alexey Arbuzov's *The Years of Wanderings* (*Gódy stránstviy*, 1954) gives an interesting account of what happened to several medical students of both sexes between 1937 and 1945, that is between the Spanish Civil War and the end of World War II. The play is without a conventional plot, and without any rhetorical passages. It is written instead with that deliberate understatement of tone and situation which makes the fortunes of the characters concerned all the more poignant. Another play by Arbuzov is called *It Happened in Irkutsk* (*Irkútskaya istóriya*, 1959). It deals with love and marriage among the somewhat idealised Soviet workers in Siberia, but is remarkable for its technique. It has a chorus interpreting certain aspects of the action and conversing with the actors. The rapid changes in the play are in the style of an up-to-date film. The effect of such innovations depends, of course, on the producer; and since this play was produced by Vakhtangov, its success was assured.

The same theatre accepted (in 1956) the play *Alone* (*Odná*) by Samuil Alyoshin, one of the 'engaged' post-war dramatists. *Alone* may not be a great play, but it aroused much attention by reason of its theme, which is closely connected with sex, love and married life. It deals, and quite subtly at times, with illicit love between a married man and a married woman. The man abandons his wife and daughter in order to join the woman with whom he has fallen in love. Yet the deserted wife—a teacher who sincerely loves and admires her run-away husband, refuses to be broken by what has happened. 'Not a single day shall be spoiled! They all belong to me. And that is that!' In addition to Alyoshin, Arbuzov, and Konstantin Simonov there are a number of young Soviet dramatists, mostly of the 'engaged' kind: A. Surov, A. Sofronov, V. Minko, A. Stein, L. Zorin and others.

5

As far as post-war Soviet fiction is concerned, novels and stories about the War continued to pour out for years after hostilities were over. One of the unusual narratives, which stands somewhat apart, was Boris Polevoy's *The Tale of a Real Man* (*Póvest' o nastoyáshchem chelovéke*, 1947). This is an account of the ordeals undergone by a Soviet airman who had been shot down by the Germans and then crawled—in Russian midwinter—for more than a fortnight through an endless forest until, half dead, he reached an improvised refugee settlement. From here he was flown, a complete wreck, to a military hospital where both his frost-bitten legs had to be amputated. Yet by sheer will-power he trained himself so that he was able to walk with artificial legs. Persistent as he was, he succeeded in being employed again by the air force, and during the fierce air battles on the Kursk in 1943 he distinguished himself as a pilot. A work of this kind, with its infectious courage and optimism, was read and admired all over the country. It also served as a reminder that the hoped for new Soviet man as a positive hero was not a mere myth.

Heroic collective efforts were narrated in countless routine writings, beginning with Vasily N. Azhayev's *Far from Moscow* (*Dalekó ot Moskvý*, 1948). This documentary novel describes the exertions of a group of ordinary people building in record time a long and important pipe-line far away in the Siberian *taigá* as their contribution to the general war effort. Significant both for its theme and its artistic level is the novel *Travel Companions* (*Spútniki*, 1947) by Vera Panova (b. 1905). In a placid objective manner the authoress describes a war-time ambulance train and its personnel. She is concerned not only about their dedicated work but also the emotional attitudes and relations between the various members of both sexes; nor does she overlook some of their negative features. All this is done with the psychological tact of an acute and sensitive observer. Her subsequent novels, such as *Kruzhílikha* (the name of a factory, 1948) and *The Bright Shore* (*Yásny béreg*, 1949), deal with the problems and efforts, whether in factories or *kolkhózes*, during the transition period from war to peace. One of the successful authors writing about the return of the victorious Russian soldiers to their post-war villages and collective farms was Semyon Babayevsky. His novel, *The Knight of the Golden Star* (*Kavalér zolotóy zvezdý*, 1947), combining such a theme with a Kuban' settlement, won him the Stalin prize. And so did his subsequent novel, *The Light over the Land* (*Svet nad zemlyóy*, 1949). A deeper and psychologically more complex treatment of the theme is to be found in *Happiness* (*Schástie*, 1947)—a novel by P. Pavlenko. Among the newcomers who described the last phases of the war Emanuil Kazakevich deserves a mention. He was born in the Ukraine in 1913 and took part in the 'mopping-up' of the retreating Germans, the storming of Berlin included. His narratives *The Star* (*Zvezdá*, 1947) and *A Spring on the Oder* (*Vesná na Ódere*, 1949) give a good account of his impressions and adventures during the final period of the great struggle.

An indefatigable chronicler of what the war was like from within and from without was the usually well-informed Ilya Ehrenburg. A high-class journalist (with an eye for the dramatic and sensational side of things) by his very nature, he wrote novels which were topical, pamphleteeringly 'engaged' and yet well told. As he himself confessed : 'for me the penetration of the newspaper into the novel was bound up with the search for a modern form of narration.' Ehrenburg certainly kept to such a role in the majority of his novels. A notable and rather caustic achievement of this nature was his *Fall of Paris* (*Padénie Parízha*, 1941-42) : a novel laying bare all the intrigues and treacherous activities of those right-wing politicians who were responsible for the surrender of Paris to Hitler and for the plight of the refugees in occupied France. Ehrenburg's anti-Nazi articles, too, were among the most outspoken utterances of moral disgust during Hitler's invasion of Russia. And soon after the German defeat he wrote his documentary novel, *The Storm* (*Búrya*, 1948), in which the resistance of the Soviet people and the defence of Stalingrad in particular formed the greatest possible contrast to what had happened in France in 1940. Less than four years later his novel, *The Ninth Wave* (*Devyáty val*), formed a bulky account of the early phase of the Cold War.

It is worth recalling that, while the World War lasted, there was a certain latitude in quite a few realms of Soviet life. Even the Russian suspicions of everything that came from the capitalist West were, temporarily, at least, in abeyance. But once the War was over and Roosevelt was followed by Truman and Truman's anti-Soviet policy, the old Soviet mistrust and misgivings came back with a vengeance. The Party line in literature began to assert itself. When, in 1946, Andrey Zhdanov became a virtual dictator in the Republic of Letters, he also behaved like a dictator. The bureaucratic red tape in the name of Stalin's police-state grew stronger than ever. In August 1946 both Zoshchenko and Anna Akhmatova were expelled from the Soviet Writers Union. Socialist Realism was insisted upon in a narrow dogmatic sense, which did not, however, prevent some good narratives and novels from coming out. Among these were Fedin's *Early Joys* (*Pérvye rádosti*, 1946) and *An Unusual Summer* (*Neobyknovénnoe léto*, 1948), both being parts of a trilogy. The first is a record of the author's boyhood at Saratov before World War I, while the second gives a picture of the same town in 1919, when the Communists were doing their best to clear away the remnants of the old bourgeois-capitalist order.

Now that the War was over, the traditional Western misgivings with regard to Communism were revived—partly because nobody in the West had expected that the Soviet Union would have come out of the War as triumphantly as she did. Churchill's Fulton Speech, the formation of the North-Atlantic Pact

in 1949, the Korean Campaign (unleashed in the following year) only strengthened that Cold-War atmosphere which in the Soviet Union was also engineered
in literature by Stalin and Zhdanov almost since the day of Hitler's defeat.
Fortunately Zhdanov died in 1948, and Stalin in 1953, after which things began
to look easier. There certainly was a sigh of relief when Zhdanov was gone.
Only one year after his death Valentin Katayev's belated but cheerful war-
novel, *For the Power of the Soviets* (*Za vlast' Sovétov*) came out. It deals with
the underground activities in Odessa during the Second World War. We meet
in it again the same two characters as in *The Lone White Sail*, now as mature
grown-up men. Fyodor Gladkov's *Story of My Childhood* (*Póvest' o détstve*,
1949) was a touching literary achievement. The literary standard of this book
compares favourably even with Gorky's autobiographic trilogy. It is a
chronicle of Gladkov's early years and of his peasant family living in a village
towards the end of the last century. It abounds in rural types, with that curious
mixture of brutality and goodness, of coarseness and tenderness, which was
one of the characteristics of Russian peasants before the Revolution. Here one
breathes the authentic village air, its language, its manners and folklore, in
fact the atmosphere of Gladkov's own boyhood, redolent of his love for the
soil and particularly for the people, whatever their virtues or defects.

Another memorable literary event, some four years later was (after a long
silence on the part of its author) Leonov's *Russian Forest* (*Rússkiy les*, 1953).
This is a novel pregnant with Leonov's own belief in the possibility of an integrated kind of life in which the individual and society, man and nature, man
and his work, would no longer be antagonistic but harmoniously balanced
with each other. Ivan Vikhrov, the hero of Leonov's novel, is a poor peasant
boy born in a remote forest region. Yet, being one of those who make good
and rise through hard work, he is eventually appointed professor of forestry
at Moscow—a post which he holds even after 1917, i.e. during the 'volcanic
eruption of all values'. The beauty of the Russian forest is one of his passions.
His main problem is how to save all those forests from systematic destruction.
In one of his would-be lectures he emphasises that the 'forest was our home, and
perhaps no other element of Nature has set so strong a stamp upon the morals
and manners of our ancestors.' This *leitmotif* is enriched by a broad picture of
the Russian people, while the personal life of the professor (he is separated from
his wife and daughter) becomes somewhat hectic, especially during Hitler's
savage exploits in Russia. Vikhrov's native countryside is swamped by the
Nazis, and in the ensuing partisan activities both his wife and daughter are
extremely active. But after Russia's military victories all ends well. Vikhrov
becomes reconciled to his wife, and despite the intrigues of envious careerists,
his pioneering work meets with well-earned awards. This novel abounds in a
variety of problems, yet the conservation of the Russian forests and their
beauty is in the centre of them all. The triumph of their beauty is also the
triumph of work and science serving life in such a way as to make it more
worthwhile.

Together with the enormous effort of reconstruction, the 1950s were also a
decade of faith in work and in the active Soviet man dedicated to his vision of

a better future, after the havoc caused by the Second World War. A mood of optimism and faith permeates *The Open Book* (*Otkrýtaya kníga*, 1949–56) by V. Kaverin and *Donbass* (1951–54) by B. Gorbatov, not to mention dozens of other novels. Some of these, *The Zhúrbins* (*Zhúrbiny*) by V. Kochetov, *The Seekers* (*Iskáteli*) by D. Granin, *The Harvest* (*Zhátva*) and *The Struggle on the Way* (*Bítva v putí*) by Galina Nikolayeva, were much discussed at the time. Enthusiasm was the slogan of the day. The prolific Yury Gherman (b. 1910), who in 1936 had made a hit with *Our Acquaintances* (*Náshi znakómyie*)—a novel about ordinary Soviet people, with the fate of an average Soviet girl in the centre—now published an historical novel, *Russia the Young One* (*Rossíya molodáya*, 1952) with the aim of keeping the enthusiasm alive. This narrative, about the creation of the Russian fleet in the North Sea under Peter the Great, is told in such a way as to intensify not only the Soviet people's attitude to life, but also their awakened patriotic zeal and pride after the Germans, with all their military might, had been beaten and driven out of Russia. Notable historical figures and events of the past were again singled out for such a purpose.

Thus V. Yan in his novel *To the Last Sea* (1955), with which he concluded his trilogy, implied that the Mongols, led by Batu Khan, were stopped from invading Europe because of Alexander Nevsky's smashing victories over the Swedes on the Neva in 1240 and over the German Knights on lake Peipus two years later. A favourite with Soviet readers became Yermak, the conqueror of Siberia under Ivan the Terrible, as was proved by the sales of V. Safonov's novel, *The Road into the Expanse* (*Doróga na prostór*, 1945, 1960), dedicated to his exploits. Another great favourite was Stepan Razin, the leader of the Don Cossacks uprising in 1670–71. After A. Chapygin it was S. Zlobin who took him up as the hero for his novel. Whereas Chapygin had concentrated on Razin's personality, Zlobin made a broader and more comprehensive approach. In his *Stepán Rázin* (1951) he covered much of the historical background with the stress on the social conditions and mass-movements in seventeenth century Russia. The range of the historical novels even included one about the Russians in Alaska—*The Raven of Yukon* (*Yúkonsky vóron*, 1958) by S. Markov.

Another literary genre which flourished during the 1950s and 1960s was science fiction, with such a lively ancestor as Alexey Tolstoy's *Aelita* to its credit. Whatever the foreign influences, from Jules Verne to H. G. Wells and Rider Haggard, they had a rich progeny in Soviet Russia, ranging from fantastic and exotic narratives to utopian novels predicting even an era of cosmic Communism. Among the best-known authors of this kind of fiction are K. Tsiolkovsky, A. Belyayev and I. Efremov. Such a space-age novel as *The Mistiness of Andromeda* (*Tumánnost' Andrómedy*) by I. Efremov had quite a vogue when it appeared in 1957. It presents a picture of that distant future when the many races and nations on earth 'united into one friendly and wise family', will be able to afford interstellar flights to new planets and even colonise them. This optimistic narrative ends with the send-off of a space-ship and its crew on an exploratory flight designed to last several years at a speed of millions of kilometres per hour. Last but not least, good stories and poems for children have always been welcomed in Russia, and so they are in the Soviet Union. Among the authors of books for children Korney Chukovsky and Lev Kassil stand out. S. Marshak, the translator of Shakespeare's Sonnets and of Burns' poems, wrote some excellent verses for children. Special plays for children's theatres are to the credit of such playwrights as S. Mikhalkov, V. Rozov and A. Stein.

6

All this proves that the creative spirit could not be stifled even by the strait-jacket imposed upon literature by Stalin and Zhdanov. Socialist Realism may have descended time and again to the level of mere propaganda, or to distortions of historical facts in order to flatter Stalin. Stalin's death, though, eased the mind of many a writer who knew only too well what was behind the Asiatic methods and the baffling 'purges' indulged in by that dictator. This time, too, it was Ilya Ehrenburg whose novel, *The Thaw* (*Óttepel'*, 1954), and its continuation, *The Spring* (*Vesná*, 1955), were portents of better times to come. In both narratives we follow up the lives and destinies of some Soviet intellectuals connected with a large factory in a provincial town, when the arrival of the political spring (after the stifling bureaucratic and autocratic winter) seemed to look like a real promise.[1] Vera Panova's novel, *The Four Seasons* (*Vreméná góda*, 1953), which is full of a refreshing love of life, was another early proof of de-Stalinisation. And so was Leonid Zorin's play *The Guests* (*Gósti*, 1954), with its virulent indictment of highly placed Soviet bureaucrats, who are shown up as bourgeois careerists and traitors to the ideals of the Revolution.

Only a few months after Stalin's death the second Soviet Writers Congress took place. Although held under the sign of Socialist Realism and 'collective guidance', it was on the whole moderate in tone and quite liberal in its attitude towards the republic of letters. Whereas the right wing of the writers still contained some old ideological diehards, the left wing counted (among others) Ehrenburg, the poets Tvardovsky, Rozhdestvensky and Evtushenko, with Fedin, Sholokhov, Katayev, and Simonov somewhere in the middle. It seemed that literature was no longer willing to be the Party's monopoly.[2] Stalin's labour camps for 'heretical' intellectuals were in the process of liquidation and several authors who had been silenced or executed during his rule were now rehabilitated. One of these was Babel whose rehabilitation took place in 1954. Even the works of some émigrés—Bunin's, for example—were allowed to be published in the Soviet Union. There were also quite a few satirical works which came out towards the middle of that decade. Noticeable among these was L. Solovyov's picaresque *Story about Hodja Nasreddin* (*Póvest' o Khódje Nasreddíne*, 1954), a satire upon the Eastern type of autocracy—presumably in old Bokhara, where the panegyrics showered upon its shrewd tyrant were not unlike those showered

1. Here it might be fair to draw the attention also to Ehrenburg's voluminous memoirs, *People, Years, Life* (*Lyúdi, gódy, zhizn'*, 1966–67), recording his wanderings, adventures, his relentless fight for peace, as well as his encounters with a number of prominent people in art, literature and politics both in the Soviet Union and abroad.
2. In 1953 even the Stalin prize for literature was abolished. It was replaced by the Lenin prize. And Stalingrad was renamed Volgograd.

upon Stalin in Moscow. Otherwise the late 1950s and the early 1960s were marked by a frequent return to narratives about the Great War and even to earlier periods.

Superior to the countless topical narratives and novels which appeared during those years was Sholokhov's *Virgin Soil Upturned* (*Pódnyataya tselína*, 1955 and 1956), representing in a way a pendant to *Quiet Flows the Don*. It deals with what had been happening in 1930, i.e., more than twenty years earlier, during the process of compulsory collectivisation of a Cossack community in the same Don region. The process had not been a smooth one, since the instinct of private property could not be eradicated by decrees. 'I've built up my farm, and got a hump on my back and calluses on my hands into the bargain, and now have I to give everything into the common stock: my cattle, and grain, and fowls, and my home too?'[1] Most of the chapters of this novel are factual, whether describing meetings, speeches, arguments in the village Soviet or else acts of sabotage. The poorer Cossacks favour collectivism at the expense of the *kuláks* who are ready to undermine any venture of this kind. A number of households prefer to slaughter their livestock rather than see it collectivised. For a time everything seems to be turning topsy-turvy, but collectivisation succeeds in the end and together with it the apotheosis of work and Socialism.

An encyclopaedic knowledge of the *kolkhose* problems and difficulties as they existed after the devastating Second World War was shown by Valentin Ovechkin (1904-68). His long narrative *A Difficult Spring* (*Trúdnaya vesná*, 1956), written in the style of documentary naturalism, is an account of the chaos that had to be overcome in a certain area by a large number of people whose endeavours were inseparable from all sorts of petty conflicts, quarrels and jealousies. The book is overladen with discussions, with technical and didactic passages, which reflect the situation as the author saw it between 1952 and 1956. It also abounds in criticism and self-criticism which does not, however, damp the author's final optimistic conclusions.

There were also other voices of violent criticism which gradually had their say, at least for a while, once Stalin was dead. Quite a stir in this respect was caused in 1956 by Vladimir Dudintsev (b. 1918). His outspoken novel, *Not by Bread Alone* (*Ne khlébom edínym*), was a definite symptom of what was in the air. Dudintsev's hero is a technical expert who came from Siberia to Moscow in order to put an important invention at the disposal of the nation. But he has to fight, and fight hard, against bureaucratic opportunists and their intrigues. All sorts of difficulties (imprisonment included) are mobilised by the Soviet mandarins in order to frustrate him. Yet he goes on fighting and in the end wins the battle in spite of all. This novel is permeated not only with strong civic indignation but also with an equally strong moral sense. Hardly less critical of certain negative features prevailing in Soviet life was the unexpectedly frank second volume of *Literary Moscow* (*Literatúrnaya Moskvá*, 1956). In the same year appeared another outspoken almanac, *The Day of Poetry* (*Den' poézii*). The fear of a renewed clamp-down on freedom and the systematic stress on collectivism at the expense of the individual could not but foster tendencies of

1. *Virgin Soil Upturned*, translated by S. Garry (Putnam).

the opposite kind. Among the young poets there were admirers of Pasternak and Pasternak's individualism: Ivan Kharabarov, for example. One of his later poems, 'Untrodden Paths', ends with these anti-bureaucratic lines in the name of independence:

> Often, perhaps,
>   I shall lose my way,
> My tracks will be lost
>   in far-off places;
> This is better than to tread
>   the beaten paths,
> Where the puddles collect
>   rotten with mould,
> Where so many feet
>   have passed before,
> Where they travel who like
>   the easy road,
> Where the dirt is trampled and pounded down
> By so many feet—
>   ahead of mine.[1]

After the merciless indictments of Stalin by Khrushchov at the twentieth Party Congress the situation would have continued to improve but for the Hungarian Revolt in 1956. Its consequences inevitably interfered with the 'thaw', which was not in the interests of some 'high-ups' either. As the young Evtushenko put it in one of his poems, the dead and embalmed Stalin had in his very tomb a telephone beside him in order to dictate his secret commands. As far as literature was concerned Pasternak's novel *Doctor Zhivago* was something of a test case. Boris Pasternak, who was a master of prose, finished this work in 1956 and sent it to the Editor of the 'New World' (*Nóvy Mir*), by whom it was rejected. The manuscript was however smuggled abroad and published —in Russian—by an Italian firm at Milan in 1957. A year later its author was awarded the Nobel Prize, and this unleashed the official fury against him. It was not so much the Prize (the receiving of which he was compelled to reject) that was resented by the Party pundits. What infuriated them was the independence with which in his novel Pasternak evaluated the happenings of 1917 and after. Those he looked upon not from the angle of ready-made clichés and bombastic phrases, but in the spirit of the best aspects of humanism as well as of true Christian ethics.

Doctor Zhivago is written in this sense, but with an involved plot. Having learned about the hero's boyhood and adolescence, we see him active at the front during the disintegration of the Russian army in 1917. Here he meets the nurse Lara—a woman with a complex and sensitive character. After that he stays for a while in revolutionary Moscow from which he escapes with his

---

1. Translated by W. N. Vickery in *Dissonant Voices in Soviet Literature*, edited by Patricia Blake and Max Hayward (Unwin).

wife Tonia and their little son Sasha to Yuriatin—a small town in the Urals where he comes across Lara again. But he is kidnapped by Siberian partisans and compelled to work as a doctor in a unit fighting the reactionary forces of Kolchak. He thus witnesses both 'White and Red atrocities rivalling each other in savagery, outrage breeding outrage'. While Kolchak is being defeated, Zhivago manages to return to Yuriatin where he learns that his wife and son had gone to Moscow whence they escaped to Paris. His passionate love affair with Lara brings other difficulties in its train. During the growing turmoil both of them find shelter in an isolated building in the snow-covered and wolf-infested region outside Yuriatin. Here they are visited by Lara's one-time seducer who, by a trick, persuades her to leave with him for Vladivostok, while Zhivago, instead of following her as expected, remains behind and soon undertakes a long journey to Moscow. He arrives in the Soviet capital, practically in rags and destitute, during the appalling NEP period. In Moscow he falls prey to another love, but does his best to pull himself together. He even finds work in a hospital. One morning, however, while on his way to the hospital, he has a stroke and dies. Among the many strange coincidences Lara who, during her separation from him had passed through years of horror, is now in Moscow and, standing by his bier, takes pathetic leave of him—a scene which, even with Pasternak's tact, verges on melodrama.

Around this plot a rich web of human destinies is woven under the shadow of one of the most crucial epochs of human history. Pasternak attached to the novel twenty-five poems, evidently as a kind of symbolic commentary to the book as a whole. Needless to say, the Western world was only too eager to welcome a novel which was a subtle attack (whether overt or by implication) on so many things the sectarian Soviet pundits stood for. A great deal has been written for and against this masterpiece both in Europe and America. But the plain truth is that Doctor Zhivago is unusual enough to occupy a niche of its own. Its structure may not be faultless, but this is redeemed by magnificent single passages, as well as by the author's attitude towards the happenings described, which can be interpreted on several planes. A chronicle of the Russian cataclysm as it was lived through by such a judge as the principal character of the novel certainly could not have been printed in the Soviet Union, where its author died (in his retreat near Moscow) in 1960 at the age of seventy.

7

While the hullabaloo caused by Pasternak's novel was not yet over, the third Congress of the Soviet Writers took place in May 1959, with Fedin as its Secretary. Khrushchov himself put in an appearance and even delivered a speech. It transpired that Party pressure was again almost as strong as ever; but on the surface at least the 'thaw' had not yet reverted to the freezing blight of the Stalin era. Thus the hero of Victor Nekrasov's, Kira Georgievna (1961), for example, is actually a released innocent victim of Stalin's labour camps who, after twenty years, meets again the sweetheart of his youth. As each of them is married, they both have to struggle with all sorts of dilemmas in order to renew their love and forget their hardships. It did not take long before a catalogue of hardships concerning the labour camps was made public in a brilliant narrative, *One Day in the Life of Ivan Denisovich* (*Odín den' v zhízni Ivána Denísovicha*) by Alexander Solzhenitsyn (b. 1918). Solzhenitsyn's book, which is entirely documentary, appeared in 1963. Based on his personal experiences, it records one single winter day in a labour camp, but this is enough to reveal its abominations —intensified as they were by subhuman treatment, inedible food and excessive cold. This work was not proscribed because the 'thaw' was still on. Solzhenitsyn's two subsequent novels, *The First Circle* (*V krúge pérvom*) and *Cancer Ward* (*Rákovy kórpus*) were, however, not only rejected but also condemned.

They are both written with a surprising sureness of touch in the tradition of Classical Realism. *The First Circle*, too, is about one of Stalin's labour camps, but this time we are taken to a special prison at Mavrino, a Moscow suburb. Here some two hundred and eighty prisoners, all of them qualified scientists (helped by low-grade free workers) live in better conditions than those in ordinary labour camps, since they have to do important research work, supervised by professional bureaucrats. A group of these exceptional prisoners are busy on a device for making 'voice prints' from telephone conversations—as a means of identifying citizens and indicting anyone who works or grumbles against the regime. This novel of some six hundred pages is not only a show of unusual characters and situations, but also one long diatribe against the practices of an autocratic pseudo-Socialist government. The author does not spare either his decriptive power or his ironic sallies which become particularly biting in his references to Stalin (the action takes place in 1949). There is also a description of the Lubianka prison where—after incredible tortures and humiliations—the victims would confess anything Stalin and his stooges wanted them to confess. But the 'special prison' of Mavrino too had its own secret informers who were ready to ruin anyone as long as they themselves derived some benefit from it. 'You were trapped and held in a deathly grip. The system crushed you, driving you harder and faster all the time, demanding more and more, setting inhuman time limits.'[1] The novel ends with some twenty prisoners being transferred for punishment to ordinary slave-labour camps in the arctic which, compared with Mavrino, are like the lower circles of Dante's *Inferno* differing from its somewhat milder first circle. Hence the title of the novel.

Cancer Ward records another set of experiences on the part of their irrepressible writer. As a political exile in Soviet Asia, Solzhenitsyn was sent (1956) for treatment to a cancer hospital in a large town, Tashkent, of the same region. Endowed with an uncanny gift of observation, he conjured up in this book the authentic atmosphere of those wards where there were sufferers from all corners of the Soviet Union gathered under the shadow of death and disease. What mattered to him this time, was the purely human element as it came out in the relations between the multi-racial patients themselves on the one hand, and between the patients and the personnel (doctors, women-doctors, nurses) on the other. And what a contrast between the dedicated woman-doctor Don-

1.   *The First Circle*. Translated by Michael Guybon (Collins, 1970).

sova and such an obtuse Party-snob and bureaucrat as Rusanov, who actually resents the fact that he is being treated on the same level as the rest of the patients!

Although devoid of any striking outbursts against the powers-that-be, this novel contains plenty of that common-sense wisdom the very nature of which is critical of abuses which cripple, whatever the name of the regime or the system. Being an outstanding realist himself, Solzhenitsyn does not repudiate those tenets of Socialist Realism which affirm the freedom of both art and literature on humane and humanistic lines. But he rejects all restrictions and distortions practised in the name of that realism. He shares his frankness with all those representatives of the younger generation who are anxious to see their country really worthy of the great role with which history has entrusted it. Oleg Kostoglotov, the principal character of *Cancer Ward*, is evidently the author himself who, after some improvement, returns—enriched but hardly made happy by his impressions—to his place of exile.

8

Like Pasternak's *Doctor Zhivago*, these two novels were smuggled abroad. Published first in Russian (1968), they were soon translated into a number of languages. In 1970, that is only twelve years after Pasternak, Solzhenitsyn, too, was awarded the Nobel Prize for literature—to the great indignation of the bosses behind the Kremlin walls. As a result, this powerful Soviet author can now be read and enjoyed all the world over except in his own native country. In the Soviet Union his novels are banned under severe penalties. At this juncture it might be worth recalling that in May 1967 Solzhenitsyn sent to the Soviet Writers Union a letter in which he bitterly complained that he was boycotted by its members whose tendency to fawn on the high-ups was by no means a thing of the past. Moreover, in the autumn of 1969 he was excommunicated by the same Union. The 'thaw', which after Stalin's death looked promising at first, gave way to a renewed bureaucratic control over literature as soon as Khrushchov had been tricked out of power. But since even the stiffest official repression cannot smother man's spirit, recent Soviet writers, with all their ordeals, have yet, amidst the welter of topical and tendentious novels, managed to produce some fine works.

The Bonfire (*Kostyór*, 1961) by Fedin, and Paustovsky's *Story of a Life* (*Póvest' o zhízni*, 1955) are among them. *The Bonfire* is the first book of the final part of Fedin's trilogy. It deals with the early days of the German attack on the Soviet Union, with Fedin's usual integrity and skill. The German air raid on Brest in particular, as described by him, is unforgettable in its horror. Of an entirely different kind is Paustovsky's autobiography. While Fedin is concerned with the fate and formation of the new Soviet man and society, Konstantin Paustovsky's book dwells upon the meaning of life derived not from any doctrines or dogmas, but from life itself. Hence his serene outlook which he reveals at the very outset of that work. 'I was thinking that I would never believe anyone who told me that life, with all it contained of love, of longing for truth and happiness; with its summer lightning and its distant sound of water in the night —that it could be without reason or meaning. I would assert its meaning always and everywhere as long as I lived.'[1] Among his best passages are the ones about his Ukrainian boyhood and his student years in Kiev before 1914. Very amusing were his experiences at Odessa when the Civil War and the interventions were not yet over. Here he contacted several other young writers and journalists (Ilf, Babel, Olesha, etc.) whose portraits are rendered with tolerance and kindness. After his Caucasian ventures at Sukhum, Batum and Tiflis we follow him once more to Kiev and then to Moscow where he secured for himself a living as a writer. Paustovsky, a romantic realist by nature, wrote a number of narratives, some of which he constructed in such a way as to make the theme combine several generations. He may take us back to the Decembrists of 1825 and then deal with one or two of their descendants in the Leningrad of 1930.

Another personal work was *The Day Stars* (*Dnevnýe zvyózdy*, 1959) by the woman-poet Olga Bergholts. While the 'thaw' was not yet entirely banned, such a lyrical novel and confession in one, the subjective character of which could hardly be missed, was not only tolerated by many a Soviet reader but rather welcomed. Now that Zhdanov was dead, a number of authors who had passed through the horrors of the second World War were outspoken not only about their war experiences, but also about the conditions they saw around them. Dudintsev's novel *Not by Bread Alone* was not an isolated case. And as for Solzhenitsyn's *One Day in the Life of Ivan Denisovich*, it was greeted by its readers as a milestone in the struggle for literary freedom. A frank, individual approach to realities might have been discouraged but it certainly was not silenced.

9

There still are Party diehards among the Soviet authors: the poets Nikolai Gribachov and Alexey Surkov, for example; or the prose-writers Vsevolod Kochetov, Alexander Chakovsky, as well as Anna Karavayeva whose trilogy, *Motherland* (*Ródina*), about the Soviet working class [2] had been much discussed in the Soviet press. In contrast to any ideological 'conservatives' the case of J. Daniel and A. Sinyavsky (Abram Terts), or that of Alexander Ginsburg and Yury Galanskov, may be pointed out as a symptom of the rift between the new Soviet intelligentsia and the government. An ominous hint at the nightmare of a possible return to Stalinism can be read between the lines of Daniel's political satire, *This is Moscow Speaking* (*Gólos Moskvý*), which was smuggled out and published abroad. Its author was sentenced to five years imprisonment, but this does not prove that he was wrong. It only proves that opposition on the

1. *Story of a Life*, translated by Manya Harari (Harvill Press).
2. The first two books of this bulky trilogy, written between 1941 and 1950, are about the dedicated workers in a tank factory in the Urals during the worst period of the war with Hitler. The third book describes some of these workers after their return to their entirely ruined home-town which they rebuild.

part of the young intellectuals to autocratic methods is growing, whatever the price.

A more recent victim of the system is Andrey Amalrik, the author of *An Involuntary Journey to Siberia* (*Ne zhelánnoe puteshéstvie v Sibír*).[1] This is a well presented picture of Soviet existence as experienced by a young intellectual who, for a trifling reason, has been condemned to be sent to Siberia to do compulsory work on a collective farm. Amalrik produced a book which is not only conscientious reportage but also something of a documentary epic illustrating the conditions of work among people who could hardly have been regarded as human. Mixing his contempt with irony and humour, the author unfolds certain aspects of Soviet life which often seem to be as far from true Socialism as was life under the tsars. The author has been sentenced to jail for it—a fairly mild punishment under the Soviets.

Tense reading, especially because of its documentary value, is *A Harsh Itinerary* (*Krutóy marshroút*) by Evgenya Ginzburg,[2] an account of cruelties inflicted upon a sincere and cultured communist by the sadistic fanatics of the regime. Arrested on trumped-up charges, she had to pass through all the horrors and humiliations of Soviet prisons and labour camps. In this book the authoress describes the early stages of her tribulations which lasted altogether eighteen years. Most of the facts, recorded with simple directness, are almost unbelievable in their brutality. One cannot escape the impression that Stalin's regime favoured a system of torment for torment's sake—a system dehumanising ordinary human relations in order to enhance the power of an inflated tyrant.

No wonder many young Soviet authors are intensely critical of certain Soviet methods even if they happen to be more cautious in their indictments than Amalrik or Evgenya Ginzburg. Having discarded all highfalutin' clichés, they show their non-conformity by exploring man's individual self in terms of psychological and moral problems without paying much attention to the official injunctions, or else they still continue to dwell on some particular phases of the giant war against Hitler.

Among the more recent literary achievements Konstantin Simonov's Stalingrad novel, *One is not Born a Soldier* (*Soldátami ne rozhdáyutsya*, 1966) stands out. What the author claims to say is that true warriors, intrepid in their fight for a just cause, are made by he struggtle itself, which can be a kind of university for such a purpose. And this he tries to show in his long novel (over seven hundred pages) dealing with the last phase of the struggle for Stalingrad in January 1943, when General Paulus and his army surrendered to the Russians. We meet here several officers from Simonov's previous war novels. But instead of dwelling on any striking heroics, the author describes for the most part routine life in the trenches: the ordeals bravely shared by all while resisting, attacking and harrowing the enemy as a matter of their daily duty. We watch the behaviour of commanders, ordinary officers, privates, doctors and nurses,

1. An English translation by Manya Harari and Max Hayward was published in 1970 (Collins Harvill).
2. The Russian original of this book appeared in Milan in 1967. An English version (by Paul Stevenson and Manya Harari) is available in Penguin.

regardless of the difficulties involved by each change of situation. After the German surrender the commander of the Russian army at Stalingrad is summoned to Moscow for a talk with Stalin—an illuminating interview in which the Soviet dictator is portrayed not without ironical emphasis upon his coldly shrewd and cruel nature.

Another recent Stalingrad novel bears the curious title of *The Snow Afire* (*Goryáchiy sneg*, 1970) by Bondaryov. Born in 1924, Yury Vasilyevich Bondaryov, like Simonov, was one of the Stalingrad defenders and has since made his reputation as author of short narratives and novels, usually with a solid psychological lining. This novel also tackles the period of the battle for Stalingrad, with its effect upon the soldiers as well as the nurses who, for all their spirit of self-sacrifice, are yet unable to stifle their human need of love. In a previous novel, *Silence* (*Tishiná*, 1963), Bondaryov describes the adventures of two young Soviet intellectuals, both of them with excellent war records, who are trying to start a new life in Moscow immediately after the end of the war in 1945. Their prospects do not look bad until Stalinism, with its careerists and bureaucratic time-servers, steps in. In some three years the hopes of one of the two young men are ruined, while his father—an old Socialist of integrity—is arrested by the secret police in consequence of a deliberate calumny. What happened to him after the arrest is anybody's guess. The author is silent about it but for the secret letter the victim sends to his own son from prison. 'It is impossible to believe that all the monstrous things I have seen here can survive under cover of love for Stalin,'[1] he wrote in it. Anyhow, this novel became an indictment of the shape of things under Stalin even after all the sacrifices the Soviet nations had had to bear in order to win their victory over Hitler and Hitlerism.

Yury Bondaryov too is one of those prose-writers who cultivate the short story in preference to novels dealing with Soviet conditions on a level comparable to the novels of the 1920s and early 1930s. This is why the Soviet critic M. Kuznetsov complains in his book, *The Soviet Novel*: 'We have not, alas, novels about our after-war reality which could stand in line with *The Life of Klim Samgin*, *Quiet Flows the Don*, *The Road to Calvary*.'[2] He further substantiates such a judgement by pointing out that the serious danger of the latter-day Soviet novels is 'the prevalence of descriptiveness over the creative design, a kind of new-fangled naturalism expressed by the invariable passion to register everything that falls within the compass of the novelist's eyes. Hence the unhealthy 'fullness' in a number of our novels, a lack of control over the form'.

The critic wrote these lines before the two now famous works by Solzhenitsyn aroused the admiration of the world and the wrath of the Soviet authorities for the very reason that they tackled the post-war realities in that spirit which should be welcomed by any Soviet citizen eager to build up Socialism 'with a human face'. The latest of Solzhenitsyn's works, *August 1914* (*Ávgust chetýrnadtsatogo*), is the first part of a war novel, though with a difference:[3] it

---

1. *Silence*, translated by Elisaveta Fen (Chapman Hall, 1965).
2. *Sovétsky román* (Soviet Academy of Sciences, 1963).
3. Written in 1969–70, it represents only about one half of a large and important work. It was published in Paris (by the Y.M.C.A.) in 1971, and in London (by Bodley Head) in 1972.

takes us back to the first month of the First World War as seen by a frank observer of the tsarist Russian army during its initial invasion of East Prussia. Written in Solzhenitsyn's vigorous and lucid prose, this novel too proves to be conceived by a great observer of human beings under any circumstances, including those of a complex war situation. The author certainly knows how to make history come alive. This part of the planned work deals with the Russian advance in East Prussia (the Allenstein region) during the first half of August 1914 (O.S.) up to the complete rout of the Second Russian Army at Tannenberg under General Samsonov. Without mincing words he plunges us into the whirl of men and events. We are shown the unpreparedness, the muddle and chaos of the Russian army whose incompetent generals and the majority of officers were devoid of any real war experience. And as for the soldiers, 'nineteen out of twenty' did not even understand such a word as fatherland. We are afforded also some glimpses into immediate reactions to the war by the civilian population (in Rostov on Don and the nearby region). Those chapters are not devoid of ideas about history and the spiritual aspects of life which could by no means appeal to hardened bureaucratic minds. The novel ends with a heated debate in the army headquarters where the mood of depression after the defeat in Germany is mitigated by the announcement that on the Austrian front the town of Lvov has been occupied by the Russians.

Although only one half of it is published, *August 1914* is bulky enough (about six hundred pages) to make a reader who has not much time to spare think twice before tackling it, however lively and interesting its contents. Among the Soviet authors of the present generation there seem to be quite a few preferring short narratives to bulky novels, whether 'engaged' or not. On the other hand, it has already been said that short narratives and especially short stories have always been a genre which Russian readers enjoyed and still enjoy for its own sake. No matter whether the younger Soviet authors write about people working on collective farms, or about teenagers in their process of ferment, they are fond of stressing, time and again, the value of individual experience and freedom. Among the talented realists or neo-realists, born after 1920, Yury Nagibin, Yury Kazakov and Vladimir Tendryakov have achieved a wide popularity with their narratives or stories. And so have Vasily Aksyonov, Yulian Semyonov and the Siberian author Sergey Zalygin.

10

Several features of Soviet drama have already been mentioned. However uneven its artistic value, its range and abundant crop can by no means be ignored, since the Russians are still as keen on the theatre as ever. Surprisingly enough, the interest in poetry too is very much alive among Soviet readers, and this at a time when the West cannot boast of any strong propensity of the sort. Also public recitals of poetry (before large audiences) by the poets themselves are an established Russian tradition—now fostered by the fact that the stunning prosodic experiments (typical of some modernists) are no longer indulged in.

Of the early Soviet poets Mayakovsky and Esenin are widely read. Pasternak's poetry is enjoyed by cultured 'highbrow' readers. And so are the intensely subjective lyrics of Anna Akhmatova. Some of the older poets—Aseyev, Tvardovsky, Isakovsky, Margarita Aliger, Vera Inber, Olga Bergholts—have their constant admirers. A blow to Soviet poetry was the death (in 1957) of Vladimir Lugovskoy who knew how to combine in an adequate form civic themes with philosophic meditations. As for the younger ones, they seem to be less and less afraid of saying what they want to say, in spite of the watchful bureaucratic 'engineers of the soul'. Whatever the impact of poetic innovations bequeathed by the preceding generation of poets, the Pushkinian cult of simplicity and clarity has yet had a beneficent influence upon the recent Soviet Parnassus as a whole, Nekrasov's civic tradition, too, is strong—notably in the poetry of Robert Rozhdestvensky, Mikhail Lukonin, Evgeny Vinokurov, Semyon Kirsanov, and Andrey Voznesensky, to mention only a few.

Both the realistic-lyrical and the civic vein are conspicuous in Evgeny Evtushenko (b. 1933).[1] Not so long ago he was widely, even too widely, advertised as a kind of international 'star' of contemporary Soviet poetry. But he does not seem to have become a victim of his own popularity and has remained a poet in his own right in spite of it. Nor does he shut his eyes to the shady side of official or dogmatic Communism. And like a born seeker he prefers to look for an answer to the life-problems within himself. In his longish autobiographic poem, *Zima Junction* (*Stántsiya Zimá*), he combines a series of pictures of his Siberian background with meditative and symbolic passages. This is how his revisited native soil speaks to him at the moment of his departure:

> Abandon not the search, seek night and day;
> and if you do not find, seek nonetheless;
> truth's good, but happiness is better—so they say;
> but without truth there is no happiness!
> March forward with your head held high and proud,
> with the good earth beneath, the sky above,
> through all the world, my son, fearless, uncowed,
> through good and bad go on. And people love.
> And you will understand then, you will see.
> Remember too, I have an eye on you,
> and if the going's hard, come back to me.[2]

One of Evtushenko's best known poems is called *Bábiy Yar*. It is about more than seventy thousand Jews massacred in cold blood by the Nazis during the second World War and buried in a ravine of the same name outside Kiev.[3]

One of Evtushenko's rivals in popularity is Andrey Voznesensky (b. 1933). An architect by training and a poet by vocation, he is something of a disciplined architect also in his poetry. Having passed through the influence of Pasternak

1. His name is often spelt Yevtushenko in English transliteration.
2. From *The Year of Protest*, translated and edited by McLean and W. N. Vickery (Knopf).
3. There is a documentary novel about it under the same title by Anatoly Kuznetsov, who has defected from the USSR and now lives in England.

and Mayakovsky, he has preserved a high standard of poetic craft and knows how to be eliptic in his sentences without impairing his original and often extravagant metaphors. His emphasis is on the value of life and on all that is best in man's nature. Because of his economy and frequent intellectual detachment he is not always easy to read. Yet his collections of poems, like Evtushenko's, are published and sold in fabulous numbers.

There is no lack of other talents. Several of these are still too young to be properly assessed. Yet in conclusion one is not wrong in saying that what is really good in Soviet literature is far from being indifferent, whatever obstacles the Soviet writers had, and still have, to cope with for the sake of their creative independence. Fortunately, many a talent has had the wit and the courage to go beyond the imposed straitjacket at the risk of open conflict with dogmatic bureaucrats on top. Nor can it be denied that the achievements of the best Soviet authors are expressive not only of the realities of Soviet life in its various phases, but also of what is valuable in the deeper recesses of the Russian mind and spirit in general.

Russian literature at its most typical has always been a literature of seekers accustomed to facing the problems of existence without flinching. But this is only one of its facets. Another is that universal sympathy which has been voiced by so many of its representatives. And Socialism itself in its true aspect i.e. 'Socialism with a human face' is actually but another name for the kind of universality which implies the idea and the ideal of a united mankind. Whatever the difficulties and complexities of the costly historical experiment on the part of the Soviet people, its literature at its best undoubtedly harbours also that faith in man and life without which no work for a truly constructive future is possible.

We all know the colossal external achievements of the Soviet Union. One of these is the abolition of illiteracy which, under the tsars, amounted to about 80 per cent of the population. Things are now different. As a result, in no other part of the world are books printed and spread about in such astronomic numbers as in the USSR. Yet the obstacles which still impede the growth of Soviet literature and culture as a whole will be removed only when bureaucratic pressure from above is finally replaced by that genuine political and personal liberty which alone is worthy of a great nation.

Bibliography

General Works

Vogüé, M. de, *Le roman russe* (1885)
Pypin, A. N., *Istoriya russkoy literatury*, 4 vols. (1898-99)
Brückner, A., *Geschichte der russischen Literatur* (1908)
Phelps, W. L., *Essays on Russian Novelists* (N.Y., 1911)
Baring, M., *An Outline of Russian Literature* (1914)
Vengerov, S. A. (ed.), *Russkaya literatura XX veka*, 3 vols. (1914-16)
Hapgood, I. F., *The Epic Songs of Russia* (1916)
Masaryk Th. G., *The Spirit of Russia* (1919, repr. 1955)
Magnus, L. A., *The Heroic Ballads of Russia* (1921)
Eliasberg, A., *Russische Literaturgeschichte* (1922)
Wiener, L., *The Contemporary Drama of Russia* (1924)
Luther, A., *Geschichte der russischen Literatur* (1924)
Trotsky, L., *Literature and Revolution* (1925)
Sakulin, P. N., *Russkaya literatura*, 2 vols. (1926-28)
Sakulin, P. N., *Die russische Literatur* (1927)
Mirsky, D. S., *A History of Russian Literature from the Earliest Times to the death of Dostoevsky* (1927)
Pozner, V., *Panorama de la litterature russe contemporaine* (1929)
Lo Gatto, E., *La Letteratura Sovietica* (1929)
Milioukov, P., *Le mouvement intellectual russe* (1931-32)
Markov, P. A., *The Soviet Theatre* (1934)
Neumann, F. W., *Geschichte der russischen Ballade* (1937)
Dana, H. W. I., *Handbook on Soviet Drama* (N.Y., 1938)
Kaun, A., *Soviet Poets and Poetry* (Berkeley, 1943)
Hare, R., *Russian Literature from Pushkin to Present Day* (1947)
Muchnic, H., *Introduction to Russian Literature* (1947)
Orlov, A. S., Adrianova, Perets (eds.), *Istoriya russkoy literatury*, 10 vols. (1941-48)
Byalik, B. (ed.), *Problemy sotsialisticheskogo realizma* (1948)
Lukacs, G., *Der russische Realismus in der Weltliteratur* (1949)
Jakobson, R and Simmons, E. J., *Russian Epic Studies* (1949)
Struve, Gleb, *Russian Literature in Exile* (in Russian; N.Y., 1956)
Borland, H., *Soviet Literary Theory and Practice during the First Five-Year Plan* (1950)
Struve, G., *Soviet Russian Literature 1917-50* (1950)
Blagoi, D. D., *Istoriya russkoy literatury XVIII veka* (1951)
Brown, E. J. *The Proletarian Episode in Russian Literature 1928-32* (1953)
Aragon, L., *Littératures sovietiques* (1955)
Erlich, V., *Russian Formalism* (1955)

Phelps, G., *The Russian Novel in English Fiction* (1956)

Besharov, J., *Imagery of the Igor Tale in the Light of the Byzantine-Slavic Poetic Theory* (1956)

Poggioli, R., *The Poets of Russia 1890-1930* (1957)

Blagoi, D. D., *Istoriya russkoy literatury*, 3 vols. (1958)

Lo Gatto, E., *Storia della letteratura russa contemporanea* (1958)

Matheson, R. W., Jr., *The Positive Hero in Russian Literature* (1958)

Donchin, G., *The Influence of French Symbolism on Russian Poetry* (1958)

Simmons, E. J., *Russian Fiction and Soviet Ideology* (1958)

Gibian, G., *Interval of Freedom, Soviet Literature during the Thaw 1953–57* (1960)

Venturi, F., *Roots of Revolution* (1960)

Yarmolinsky, A., *Literature under Communism* (Bloomington, 1960)

Muchnic, H., *From Gorky to Pasternak* (1961)

Swayze, H., *Political Control of Literature in the U.S.S.R.* (1962)

Čiževsky, D., *History of Russian Literature from the Eleventh Century to the End of the Baroque* (1962)

Eng-Liedmeier, A., *Soviet Literary Characters* (1962)

Brown, E. J., *Russian Literature since the Revolution* (1963)

Slonim, M., *From Chekhov to the Revolution* (1963)

Spector, I., *The Golden Age of Russian Literature* (1963)

Vickery, W. N., *The Cult of Optimism. Political and Ideological Problems of Recent Soviet Literature* (1963)

Eikhenbaum, B., and Tynyanov, Y. (eds.), *Russkaya Proza—Sbornik Statey* (1963)

Oulanoff, H., *The Serapion Brothers: Theory and Practice* (1963)

Passage, Ch., E., *The Russian Hoffmanists* (1963)

Slonim, M., *Russian Theater* (1963)

Slonim, M., *Soviet Russian Literature* (1964)

Clifford, H., *The Novel in Russia* (1964)

Alexandrova, V., *A History of Soviet Literature* (1964)

Mirsky, D. S., *A History of Russian Literature*. Edited and abridged by F. J. W. Whitfield (new ed. 1968)

Anthologies

Bowring, John, *Specimens of Russian Poets*, 2 vols. (1821, 1823)

Wiener, Leo, *Anthology of Russian Literature from the Earliest Period to the Present Time* (N.Y., 1902-03)

Friedland, L. S., Piroshnikov, J. R., *Flying Osip*. Stories of New Russia (1925)

Robbins, J. J., *Azure Cities*. Stories of New Russia (NY., 1929)

Graham, S., *Great Russian Stories* (1929)

Coxwell, C. F., *Russian Poems* (1929)

Cournos, J., *Short Stories of Soviet Russia* (1929)

Deutsch, B. and Yarmolinsky, A., *Russian Poetry* (N.Y., 1930)

Konovalov, S., *Bonfire*. Stories of Soviet Russia (1932)

Noyes, G. R., *Masterpieces of the Russian Drama* (N.Y., 1933)

Reavey, G. and Slonim, M., *Soviet Literature* (1934)

Lyons, E., *Six Soviet Plays* (Boston, 1934)

Blake, B., *Four Soviet Plays* (N.Y., 1937)

Flores, A., *Literature and Marxism*. A Controversy of Soviet Critics (N.Y., 1938)

Grindea, M., *Soviet Literature, Art, Music* (1942)

Shelley, G., *Modern Poems from Russia* (1942)

Montague, I. and Marshall, H., *Soviet Short Stories* (1942)

Guerney, B. G., *A Treasury of Russian Literature* (N.Y., 1943)

Rodker, J. (ed.), *Soviet Anthology* (1943)

Cournos, J., *A Treasury of Russian Life and Humour* (N.Y., 1943)

Bowra, C. M., *A Book of Russian Verse* (1943)

Fen, E., *Modern Russian Stories* (1943)

Doren, M. van, *The Night of the Summer Solstice and Other Stories of the Russian War* (N.Y., 1943)

Lavrin, J., *Representative Russian Stories*, 2 vols. (1946)

Bakshy, A., *Soviet Scene.* Seven Soviet Plays (New Haven, 1946)

Dana, H. W. L., *Seven Soviet Plays* (N.Y., 1946)

Guerney, B. G., *The Portable Russian Reader* (N.Y., 1947)

Bowra, C. M., *A Second Book of Russian Verse* (1948)

Yarmolinsky, A., *A Treasury of Russian Verse* (N.Y., 1949)

Kunitz, J., *Russian Literature since the Revolution* (1948)

Guerney, B. G. (ed. and trs.), *New Russian Stories* (N.Y., 1952)

Lindsey, J. (ed.), *Russian Poetry* (1957)

Reavey, G. (ed.), *Fourteen Great Short Stories by Soviet Authors* (N.Y., 1959)

Kapp, Y. (ed.), *Short Stories of Russia Today*, tr, by Tatiana Shebanina (Boston, 1959)

Guerney, B. G. (ed.), *An Anthology of Russian Literature from Gorky to Pasternak* (1960)

Noyes, C. R. (ed.), *Masterpieces of the Russian Drama.* Vol. II (1960)

Reeve, F. (ed. and tr.), *An Anthology of Russian Plays.* Vol. II (1961)

Reavey, G. (ed. and tr.), *Modern Soviet Short Stories* (1961)

McLean, H. and Vickery, W., *Year of Protest 1956* (N.Y., 1961)

Obolensky, D. (ed.), *The Penguin Book of Russian Verse* (1962)

Snow, C. P. and Johnson, P. H., *Stories from Modern Russia* (N.Y., 1962)

Hayward, M. and Labedz, L. (eds.), *Literature and Revolution in Soviet Russia 1917-62* (1963)

Blake, P. and Hayward, M. (eds.), *Dissonant Voices in Soviet Literature* (1964)

Blake, P. and Hayward, M. (eds.), *Half-way to the Moon.* New Writings from Russia (1964)

Costello, B. and Foote (eds.), *Russian Folk Literature* (1967)

Werth, Alexander, *Russia: The Post-War Years* (1971)

Glenny. M. (ed.), *Novy mir 1925–1967* (1972)

Index of Names